THE BIG
INSTANT
POT COOKBOOK
500 RECIPES

ROCKRIDGE
PRESS

For general information on our other products and services, please contact our Customer Care Department within the United States at (866) 744-2665, or outside the United States at (510) 253-0500.

All the recipes originally appeared, in different form, in *Instant Pot Vegetarian Cookbook, Gluten-Free Instant Pot Cookbook, The Complete Vegan Instant Pot Cookbook, Everyday Mexican Instant Pot Cookbook, The Healthy Meal Prep Instant Pot Cookbook, Plant-Based Instant Pot Cookbook, Instant Pot Obsession, Clean Eating Instant Pot Cookbook, Vegetarian Indian Instant Pot Cookbook,* and *Instant Pot Cookbook for Beginners.*

Paperback ISBN: 978-1-68539-044-0
eBook ISBN: 978-1-68539-666-4

Manufactured in the United States of America

Interior and Cover Designer: Jennifer Hsu
Art Producer: Melissa Malinowsky
Editor: Amy Deputato
Production Editor: Emily Sheehan
Production Manager: David Zapanta

Cover photography: © Darren Muir, © Nadine Greeff, © Elysa Weitala

10 9 8 7 6 5 4 3 2 1 0

CONTENTS

Grains and Beans

Pasta and Noodles

Soups and Stews

Vegetable Sides and Mains

Fish and Seafood

Poultry

Beef, Pork, and Lamb

INSTANT POT 101

At its core, the Instant Pot is a smart, programmable multi-cooker. It includes the functionality of many cooking modes and methods: It can sauté, pressure cook, slow cook, steam, and sterilize—all in the same vessel. It also acts as a warmer. You can make yogurt, rice, soup, or stews. The list goes on and on.

Unlike the pressure cookers of yore, the Instant Pot doesn't require you to babysit it. While it works its cooking magic, you can hang out in the kitchen or catch up on some reading or whatever you have to do. The timer lets you know when cooking has finished. Even then, it automatically moves into Keep Warm mode. It's stress-free cooking at its finest.

Most people turn to the Instant Pot because of its pressure-cooking capabilities. The term "pressure cooking" refers to using liquid in a sealed vessel to cook food. When heated, the liquid inside begins to boil. The sealed pot traps all the steam from the boiling process. This environment causes the internal pressure and temperature to rise at a very fast rate, cooking the ingredients very quickly.

MODELS AND SIZES

There are currently no fewer than thirteen Instant Pot models available in stores. Some have additional bells and whistles like built-in Wi-Fi, air fryer lids, or sous vide functions, but they all have basic pressure-cooking abilities.

Each model also comes in several different size options. The most common size is the 6-quart version. This is considered standard, and most Instant Pot recipes are written for this size. It's perfect for families of four or five people or couples who love leftovers.

If you have a larger family or like to cook for a crowd, the 8-quart model might be more your speed. If you like to host parties or are big on cooking ahead and stocking the freezer, the Duo Nova is available in a massive 10-quart option.

A 3-quart model is available if you're cooking for one or have minimal space, but note that it has fewer features than the larger models.

KNOW YOUR PARTS

In addition to the base unit and lid, the Instant Pot comes with several other important components. These include the inner pot, the condensation collector, and a metal trivet. Depending on your model, the power cord might arrive detached, and there might be some other accessories included, like a measuring cup or spoons.

As outlined in the following paragraphs, a few components need special care that might not be obvious right away.

Inner Pot

For most recipes, food will cook directly inside the inner pot. This stainless steel pot is removable and can be washed in the dishwasher for easy cleanup. Always double-check to ensure the pot has been returned to the base unit before adding your recipe ingredients; you should never place food directly into the base.

Sealing Ring

The silicone sealing ring is a very important part of the Instant Pot. Without it, steam will escape, and the pot won't come to pressure. To remove the ring after cooking, gently pull it until it slips out from behind the wire holding it in place. You can wash the sealing ring in the top rack of your dishwasher or by hand. When replacing the ring, push it in firmly and make sure no pieces are sticking out from behind the wire. The sealing ring can stretch out and dry out over time, preventing your pot from getting a tight seal. Replacements are very affordable, and it's not a bad idea to have an extra on hand. Some people also like to use one ring for savory foods and another for sweets since the silicone can absorb some flavors.

Steam Valve

This valve, located on the pot's lid, regulates the pressure inside the pot. It should be cleaned periodically, especially after cooking starchy or highly fragrant foods. To remove the valve, take off the small silicone cap on the underside of the pot lid. Once the cap is removed, the valve should slip freely through the hole on the top of the lid. Wash the valve and cap with a soft brush, then replace both pieces.

Condensation Collector

This is a small, clear cup that attaches to the back of the Instant Pot and collects any moisture buildup on the pot rim. This can happen during the cooking process or if the lid is propped open. Remove this cup by sliding it straight out and empty it before putting the Instant Pot away. It can be washed by hand or on the top rack of your dishwasher and should easily slide back into place.

BUTTONS AND FUNCTIONS

The first step to getting confident with the Instant Pot is to familiarize yourself with its buttons and functions. Before making your first recipe in the Instant Pot, it can be helpful to start with a water test (basically just "cooking" 3 cups of water under high pressure for 3 minutes) so that you can get a feel for how everything works and how much time each step takes.

Here is a general overview of the basics to get you started, but your pot's exact buttons will depend on its size and model.

Start

If you have an Instant Pot Ultra, Duo Evo Plus, or Max, your pot will have a Start button. In this case, you'll need to press this button to turn on the Instant Pot. If your model doesn't have a start button, don't worry! The pot will turn on automatically when you press a function button or set the timer.

Keep Warm

If you don't plan to eat your meal right away, pressing the Keep Warm button will keep your cooked food at a safe temperature for up to 10 hours. You can enable this feature at the beginning of the cooking process or after the process has started. If this button is pressed before the cooking process starts, it will begin counting up once the cooking cycle is complete and will not turn off until you hit Cancel or after 10 hours. This feature helps keep track of how long pressure has been naturally releasing. If the Keep Warm button is pressed after the cooking cycle has completed, it will default to 10 hours. You can increase or reduce this time by pressing the +/- buttons.

Cancel

You can stop any function by hitting the Cancel button. Note that this button is combined with the Keep Warm button on older models. To completely cut off power to the device, you should unplug it.

Sauté

One of the most exciting features of the Instant Pot is that you can also use it to sauté or brown food right in the same pot before cooking it under pressure. Press the Sauté button and give the pot about a minute to heat up before adding your food. Depending on your model, press Sauté again to increase or reduce the heat level as necessary. When you're done, press Cancel. It is not necessary to use a lid when using the sauté function.

Pressure Cook

For pressure cooking, you'll need to decide if you want to use one of the preset buttons or manually adjust the pressure and time. The recipes in this book all use manual settings to give you the most control over the cooking process, but the preset buttons can be very convenient, too. Do note that there are some differences here between older and newer models.

Manual

Start by pressing the Manual button (this is the Pressure Cook button on some models, but the term *Manual* is used throughout the book). If the pressure level needs to be adjusted, hit the Pressure Level button to toggle between the high and low options. Most recipes use high pressure, but low pressure is useful for cooking delicate vegetables or rice. Finally, press the +/- buttons to adjust the timer. Press the Start button if your pot has one. If not, the pot will turn on automatically after about 10 seconds. The pot will beep several times to indicate that the cooking process has started.

Presets

Depending on the Instant Pot model, there will also be several preset buttons programmed with appropriate pressure and time settings for common recipes. Remember that the Instant Pot doesn't know what you put in it, so these presets are based on average cook times. You'll need to test your food when the time is up to ensure it's done. You can also use the +/- buttons to increase or decrease the preset cooking time, as appropriate.

Commonly used preset buttons include these:

Soup/Broth: For making brothy soups. For meatless soups, use the - button to reduce the cooking time.

Meat/Stew: For bigger pieces of meat or thick stews. The default setting is high pressure for 20 minutes.

Bean/Chili: For dried beans. The default setting is high pressure for 30 minutes, which will result in medium-soft beans.

Poultry: For cooking small, bite-size pieces of boneless chicken. The default setting is high pressure for 12 minutes.

Rice: For cooking white or jasmine rice. The default setting is low pressure for 12 minutes.

Multigrain: For brown rice and tougher whole grains. This setting has a built-in soaking time before the cooking process starts to help grains soften. The default setting is 45 minutes of soaking time followed by 40 minutes of cooking under high pressure.

Porridge: For making rice porridge. The default setting is high pressure for 20 minutes. For oatmeal, use the - button to reduce the cooking time.

Steam: For steaming fish or vegetables. Be sure to insert the steam rack to elevate the food over the cooking liquid and away from the heating element when using this setting. The default setting is high pressure for 10 minutes.

Slow Cook

The Instant Pot can double as a slow cooker when you aren't in a hurry. Hit Slow Cook and then press Slow Cook again to toggle through heat level options. Normal is equivalent to low heat, More is equivalent to high heat, and Less is equivalent to the Keep Warm setting. Once the appropriate heat level is selected, use the +/- buttons to set the timer manually. Place the lid on the pot, but do not lock or seal it. Alternatively, you can purchase a see-through glass lid.

Yogurt

The Yogurt button can be used to make yogurt by heating milk and then holding it at a steady temperature while it ferments.

Delay Start

The Delay Start button can be used if you don't want to start the pressure-cooking process right away. To use this function, choose your pressure cook settings and then press the Delay Start button. Use the +/- buttons to set the timer. Pressure will begin to build once the time has expired. This is useful for soaking dried beans, but keep in mind that it does not keep uncooked meat at a safe temperature.

SAFETY

Electric pressure cookers are very safe, but there are some standard precautions that you should take.

Set the pot on a sturdy surface. Be sure to place the Instant Pot on a sturdy, flat surface and keep it away from the edge of the counter. Don't overstretch the power cord or put it where someone might trip over it. A falling Instant Pot is a recipe for a major mess! Also, avoid placing the Instant Pot on the stove. I've heard so many stories about people who accidentally turned the burner on and melted the bottom of their pot.

Maintain your sealing ring. If the sealing ring is not in the proper condition or not positioned properly, steam can escape from under the lid, and the pot will not come to pressure. Check your ring before cooking and be sure it doesn't have any cracks, which can occur as it dries out. Rings should be replaced every year or two.

Do not overfill. Be sure to pay attention to the Max Fill line indicated on the inside of the inner pot, especially when doubling a recipe. Don't fill the pot more than halfway when cooking starchy ingredients like beans, grains, or pasta. Remember, food expands when it cooks. If the pot is overfilled, hot ingredients could spill out when the lid is removed. Additionally, starchy ingredients can create hot foam inside the pot that, when overfull, can shoot through the steam valve when releasing pressure.

Stay away from the steam. When switching the valve to Venting, always use an oven mitt and keep your face away from the pot. Similarly, always open the lid facing away from you so that you don't end up with a face full of hot steam.

Instant Pots have a built-in feature that prevents them from overheating and will automatically turn the appliance off if it detects a risk of food burning. If the Instant Pot shuts itself off before coming to pressure, this is likely what happened. Unplug it, and check to make sure there isn't any food stuck to the bottom of the inner pot, that there's enough liquid, and that the pot was inserted properly. If everything looks okay, you can plug the Instant Pot back in and reprogram the cooking cycle.

USEFUL ACCESSORIES

You'll be able to prepare tons of delicious recipes with the Instant Pot straight from the box, but a few extra accessories will help you take things to the next level and improve the versatility of your pot.

Trivet

Many recipes use a trivet to keep ingredients out of the cooking liquid. The Instant Pot will come with a metal trivet, but replacing it with a sturdier one can be useful. Look for trivets with long handles, making it much easier to remove large cuts of meat or baking pans from the pot.

Baking Pans

Speaking of baking pans, these can be used for pot-in-pot cooking and allow you to make baked goods in the Instant Pot! You'll need pans that are small enough to fit inside the inner pot easily. Round pans, 6 or 7 inches wide, are perfect for 6-quart Instant Pots. Pans that are 6 inches wide will also fit inside 3-quart models. A selection of cake pans, Bundt pans, and springform pans can be handy.

Steamer Basket

Steamer baskets are similar to trivets but have higher sides and are made from mesh, so small items won't fall through. They make it easy to remove loose items like baked potatoes and hard-boiled eggs from the pot.

Silicone Egg Bite Molds

These silicone molds are available in 7-cup and 4-cup models, designed to fit inside 6-quart and 3-quart Instant Pot models, respectively. They're great for making egg bites but can also be used to make muffins, pancakes, and even brownies!

Nonstick Insert

If you make a lot of creamy recipes or use the Sauté function often, it can be worth picking up a ceramic-coated insert. This helps prevent food from sticking to the bottom of the inner pot, helping you avoid a burn warning and making cleanup even easier.

Glass Lid

If you like to use the Instant Pot as a slow cooker or to simmer recipes or keep them warm, you may want to consider purchasing a clear glass lid with a steam vent.

Note that these lids cannot be used while pressure cooking.

Air Fryer Lid

If you're ready to go all out, you might want to invest in an air fryer lid. This will allow you to brown and crisp food right in the pot, so you can skip transferring recipes like ribs to the broiler.

5 COMMON INSTANT POT MISTAKES AND HOW TO AVOID THEM

Once you get the hang of it, using an Instant Pot will be second nature. But there are several common mistakes that even seasoned pressure cooker enthusiasts can make.

Keeping these five mistakes in mind will help set you up for success. They can also prevent you from thinking the Instant Pot is broken when you really just need a new sealing ring, a costly mistake that I'll never make again.

Not adding enough liquid. Instant Pots work because steam builds up inside them, creating a high-pressure environment. If you don't add enough water or broth, there won't be enough steam produced, and the pot won't pressurize. A good rule of thumb is to add at least 1 cup of liquid to 6-quart models.

Using too much liquid. The sealed nature of pressure cookers means that, unlike stovetop cooking, the liquid won't evaporate during the cooking process. Adding too much liquid can result in dishes coming out soggy and bland. Keep in mind that many ingredients, such as vegetables and meat, release additional liquid as they cook. Others, like rice and grains, absorb liquid. If your recipe comes out soggy, hit the Sauté button and simmer it uncovered for a few minutes to help the liquid reduce.

Using a damaged sealing ring. If your sealing ring is cracked or otherwise damaged, your pot will not come to pressure. Always be sure to check the sealing ring before starting to cook.

Not adding ingredients in the correct order. If the recipe instructs you to add things in a specific order, it's for a reason. Some ingredients, like dairy and tomato sauce, tend to stick to the bottom of the pot and trigger a burn warning. It's important to layer ingredients in the correct order—and don't stir unless the recipe tells you to!

Not planning enough time. Yes, the Instant Pot can dramatically reduce traditional cooking times. But it will take time for the pot to come to pressure as well as for that pressure to release. The recipes in this book indicate how much time you should allow for each step, so be sure to read through each recipe carefully and plan ahead.

SCALING UP OR DOWN

The recipes in this book were designed for a 6-quart Instant Pot. If you have a 3-quart Instant Pot, cut the amount of each ingredient in half. Be sure to use the minimum amount of liquid (½ cup).

Many of the recipes in this book can be made in an 8-quart Instant Pot without any adjustments. As long as the original recipe includes at least 2 cups of liquid, you're good to go. If the recipe has less liquid than that, scale it up; most recipes can be doubled without any issues.

If a recipe uses the pot-in-pot cooking technique or the liquid is used only to make steam and doesn't come into contact with the ingredients, you can keep the recipe as is and simply increase the amount of water to 2 cups.

No matter what size Instant Pot you have, be sure to keep an eye on the Max Fill line and remember that you only need to adjust the ingredient amounts; the cooking time will stay the same.

USING AT HIGH ALTITUDES

Air pressure is lower at high elevations. This reduces the boiling point of water, meaning that food will be cooking at a lower temperature. To account for this, increase the cooking time by 5 percent for every 1,000 feet above 2,000 feet in elevation.

For example, Denver is a little over 5,200 feet in elevation, so you'll need to increase cooking time by 15 percent if you live there. That means a recipe that typically needs 20 minutes of cooking time would need to cook for 23 minutes.

Some newer Instant Pot models, like the Ultra and Max, can be programmed to make these time adjustments automatically. Press the center dial to change the system-level settings, and then rotate the dial to "Alt." Enter your altitude and hit Start to save. Once this adjustment has been made, you can follow the recipe instructions as written without making manual adjustments.

BREAKFAST AND BRUNCH

Mexican-Style Coffee

SERVES 8 | PREP TIME: 5 minutes | MANUAL: 15 minutes high pressure | RELEASE: Natural | TOTAL TIME: 40 minutes

8 cups water	8 whole cloves
¼ cup ground Mexican coffee	1 piloncillo cone
2 (3-inch) cinnamon sticks, plus more for garnish	1 tablespoon finely grated orange zest (optional)
2 whole star anise	¼ to ½ cup sugar (optional)

In the Instant Pot, combine the water, coffee, and cinnamon sticks. Stir in the star anise, cloves, piloncillo cone, and orange zest (if using). Lock the lid. Select Manual and cook at high pressure for 15 minutes. When the cook time is complete, allow the pressure to release naturally. Remove the lid. Discard the cinnamon sticks and stir the coffee gently to combine. Sweeten with the sugar (if using). Strain the coffee into mugs. Garnish with cinnamon sticks.

Lemon Yogurt

MAKES 8 (8-ounce) servings | PREP TIME: 15 minutes | YOGURT SETTING: about 25 minutes, plus 8 to 10 hours | TOTAL TIME: 9 to 11 hours, plus 4 hours cooling time

2 quarts whole milk	2 tablespoons lemon curd per 1 cup yogurt
1 tablespoon plain whole-milk yogurt with live cultures, at room temperature	

Pour the milk into the Instant Pot to heat. Select Yogurt and press Adjust so that BOIL shows in the display. Lock the lid. When the beeper sounds, unlock and remove the lid. Use a meat or candy thermometer to check the temperature of the milk in the center of the pot. It should read between 179°F and 182°F. Fill a large bowl with ice water or fill the sink with a few inches of ice water and nestle the inner pot in the ice water to cool the milk. Stir the milk occasionally, without scraping the bottom of the pot, for about 5 minutes, then take the temperature in the center of the milk. It should read between 110°F and 115°F. Remove the pot from the ice bath and dry off the outside of the pot. In a small bowl, stir together the yogurt and about ½ cup of the warm milk. Add this to the pot and stir thoroughly but gently. Again, don't scrape the bottom of the pot (if there is any coagulated milk on the bottom, stirring it in can make your yogurt less smooth). Lock the lid (or use a glass lid). Select Yogurt. The display should read 8:00, which indicates 8 hours of incubation time. If you prefer a longer incubation, press the + button to increase the time by increments of 30 minutes. When the yogurt cycle is complete, remove the lid. Remove the inner pot and cover it with a glass or silicone lid or place a plate on top. Refrigerate until cool, about 4 hours. To serve, measure out 1 cup of yogurt into a bowl and stir in the lemon curd.

Strawberry Yogurt "Romanoff"

MAKES 8 (8-ounce) servings | PREP TIME: 15 minutes | YOGURT SETTING: about 25 minutes, plus 8 to 10 hours | TOTAL TIME: 9 to 11 hours, plus 4 hours cooling time

2 quarts whole milk	¼ cup sliced fresh or frozen strawberries, thawed, per 1 cup yogurt
1 tablespoon plain whole-milk yogurt with live cultures, at room temperature	1 tablespoon brown sugar per 1 cup yogurt

Pour the milk into the Instant Pot. Select Yogurt and press Adjust so that BOIL shows in the display. Lock the lid. When the beeper sounds, unlock and remove the lid. Use a meat or candy thermometer to check the temperature of the milk in the center of the pot. It should read between 179°F and 182°F. Fill a large bowl with ice water or fill the sink with a few inches of ice water and nestle the inner pot in the ice water to cool the milk. Stir the milk occasionally, without scraping the bottom of the pot, for about 5 minutes, then take the temperature in the center of the milk. It should read between 110°F and 115°F. Remove the pot from the ice bath and dry off the outside of the pot. In a small bowl, stir together the yogurt and about ½ cup of the warm milk. Add this to the pot and stir thoroughly but gently. Again, don't scrape the bottom of the pot (if there is any coagulated milk on the bottom, stirring it in can make your yogurt less smooth). Lock the lid (or use a glass lid). Select Yogurt. The display should read 8:00, which indicates 8 hours of incubation time. If you prefer a longer incubation, press the + button to increase the time by increments of 30 minutes. When the yogurt cycle is complete, unlock and remove the lid. Remove the inner pot and cover it with a glass or silicone lid or place a plate on top. Refrigerate until cool, about 4 hours. To serve, measure out 1 cup of yogurt into a bowl. Toss the strawberries with the brown sugar to coat them. Gently fold the strawberries into the yogurt.

Raspberry-Peach Yogurt

MAKES 8 (8-ounce) servings | PREP TIME: 15 minutes | YOGURT SETTING: about 25 minutes, plus 8 to 10 hours | TOTAL TIME: 9 to 11 hours, plus 4 hours cooling time

2 quarts whole milk	1 tablespoon seedless raspberry jam per 1 cup yogurt
1 tablespoon plain whole-milk yogurt with live cultures, at room temperature	¼ cup chopped fresh or frozen peaches, thawed, per 1 cup yogurt

Pour the milk into the Instant Pot. Select Yogurt and press Adjust so that BOIL shows in the display. Lock the lid. When the beeper sounds, unlock and remove the lid. Use a meat or candy thermometer to check the temperature of the milk in the center of the pot. It should read between 179°F and 182°F. Fill a large bowl with ice water or fill the sink with a few inches of ice water and nestle the inner pot in the ice water to cool the milk. Stir the milk occasionally, without scraping the bottom of the pot, for about 5 minutes, then take the temperature in the center of the milk. It should read between 110°F and 115°F. Remove the pot from the ice bath and dry off the outside of the pot. In a small bowl, stir together the yogurt and about ½ cup of the warm milk. Add this to the pot and stir thoroughly but gently. Again, don't scrape the bottom of the pot (if there is any coagulated milk on the bottom, stirring it in can make your yogurt less smooth). Lock the lid (or use a glass lid). Select Yogurt. The display should read 8:00, which indicates 8 hours of incubation time. If you prefer a longer incubation, press the + button to increase the time by increments of 30 minutes. When the yogurt cycle is complete, unlock and remove the lid. Remove the inner pot and cover it with a glass or silicone lid or place a plate on top. Refrigerate until cool, about 4 hours. To serve, measure out 1 cup of yogurt into a bowl. Fold the raspberry jam and peaches into the yogurt.

Vanilla-Almond Yogurt

MAKES 8 (8-ounce) servings | PREP TIME: 15 minutes | YOGURT SETTING: about 25 minutes, plus 8 to 10 hours | TOTAL TIME: 9 to 11 hours, plus 4 hours cooling time

2 quarts whole milk
1 tablespoon plain whole-milk yogurt with live cultures, at room temperature
1 tablespoon honey per 1 cup yogurt

¼ teaspoon vanilla extract per 1 cup yogurt
2 drops almond extract per 1 cup yogurt
1 tablespoon toasted slivered almonds per 1 cup yogurt

Pour the milk into the Instant Pot. Select Yogurt and press Adjust so that BOIL shows in the display. Lock the lid. When the beeper sounds, unlock and remove the lid. Use a meat or candy thermometer to check the temperature of the milk in the center of the pot. It should read between 179°F and 182°F. Fill a large bowl with ice water or fill the sink with a few inches of ice water and nestle the inner pot in the ice water to cool the milk. Stir the milk occasionally, without scraping the bottom of the pot, for about 5 minutes, then take the temperature in the center of the milk. It should read between 110°F and 115°F. Remove the pot from the ice bath and dry off the outside of the pot. In a small bowl, stir together the yogurt and about ½ cup of the warm milk. Add this to the pot and stir thoroughly but gently. Again, don't scrape the bottom of the pot (if there is any coagulated

milk on the bottom, stirring it in can make your yogurt less smooth). Lock the lid (or use a glass lid). Select Yogurt. The display should read 8:00, which indicates 8 hours of incubation time. If you prefer a longer incubation, press the + button to increase the time by increments of 30 minutes. When the yogurt cycle is complete, unlock and remove the lid. Remove the inner pot and cover it with a glass or silicone lid or place a plate on top. Refrigerate until cool, about 4 hours. To serve, measure out 1 cup of yogurt into a bowl. Stir in the honey, vanilla, and almond extract. Top with the toasted almonds.

Blueberry-Lemon Bliss Bowls

SERVES 4 to 6 | PREP TIME: 2 minutes | MANUAL: 10 minutes high pressure | RELEASE: Natural for 10 minutes, then Quick | TOTAL TIME: 22 minutes

2¼ cups water
1 cup millet, rinsed
2 tablespoons maple syrup
1 tablespoon freshly squeezed lemon juice
¼ teaspoon ground nutmeg
¼ teaspoon ground cinnamon

¼ to ½ teaspoon salt
1 cup nondairy milk, plus more as needed
1 cup fresh blueberries
½ cup sliced toasted almonds
Zest of ½ lemon

In the Instant Pot, stir together the water, millet, maple syrup, lemon juice, nutmeg, cinnamon, and salt. Lock the lid. Select Manual and cook at high pressure for 10 minutes. When the cook time is complete, let the pressure release naturally for 10 minutes, then quick-release any remaining pressure. Remove the lid and stir in the milk, adding more if you like a creamier texture. Top with the blueberries, almonds, and lemon zest before serving.

Coconut-Blueberry Chia Pudding

SERVES 8 | PREP AND FINISHING: 10 minutes | MANUAL: 3 minutes high pressure | RELEASE: Natural for 5 minutes, then Quick | TOTAL TIME: 28 minutes, plus 1 hour to chill

1 (14-ounce) can full-fat coconut milk
2½ cups water
1 (12-ounce) bag frozen blueberries
1 cup chia seeds

1 cup rolled oats
½ cup maple syrup
½ teaspoon vanilla extract
Fresh berries, for garnish (optional)

In the Instant Pot, combine the coconut milk, water, blueberries, chia seeds, oats, maple syrup, and vanilla. Lock the lid. Select Manual and cook at high pressure for 3 minutes. When the cook time is complete, naturally release the pressure for 5 minutes, then quick-release any remaining pressure. Remove the lid. Pour the pudding into individual serving cups and refrigerate until it sets, about 1 hour. Serve cold, garnished with berries.

Steel-Cut Oatmeal

SERVES 4 | PREP TIME: 5 minutes | MANUAL: 2 minutes high pressure | RELEASE: Natural for 20 minutes | TOTAL TIME: 40 minutes

3 cups water	½ teaspoon ground
1 cup steel-cut oats	cinnamon
2 teaspoons vanilla extract	½ teaspoon salt
	2 tablespoons maple syrup

In the Instant Pot, combine the water, oats, vanilla, cinnamon, and salt. Lock the lid. Select Manual and cook at high pressure for 2 minutes. When the time is up, allow for full natural release of pressure, 15 to 20 minutes. Stir in the maple syrup and serve with any other toppings you like.

Healthy-Yet-Tasty Oatmeal

SERVES 4 to 6 | PREP TIME: 2 minutes | MANUAL: 12 minutes high pressure | RELEASE: Natural for 10 minutes, then Quick | TOTAL TIME: 24 minutes

4½ cups water	¼ teaspoon salt (optional)
2 cups steel-cut oats	¼ to ½ cup chia seeds
½ to 1 cup nondairy milk	1 cup chopped walnuts
2 tablespoons agave or	1 cup fresh blueberries
maple syrup (optional)	

In the Instant Pot, stir together the water and oats. Lock the lid. Select Manual and cook at high pressure for 12 minutes. When the cook time is complete, let the pressure release naturally for 10 minutes, then quick-release any remaining pressure. Remove the lid and add the milk. Stir in the agave (if using) and salt (if using) and top with the chia seeds, walnuts, and blueberries.

Strawberry Oatmeal with Maple-Toasted Walnuts

SERVES 4 to 6 | PREP TIME: 15 minutes | STOVE: 5 minutes | MANUAL: 12 minutes high pressure | RELEASE: Natural for 10 minutes, then Quick | TOTAL TIME: 42 minutes

FOR THE MAPLE-TOASTED WALNUTS

3 cups walnut halves	½ teaspoon salt
½ cup maple syrup	

FOR THE OATS

2½ cups water	¼ teaspoon salt
2½ cups unsweetened	2 cups strawberries,
nondairy milk, divided	chopped or sliced
2 cups steel-cut oats	½ cup packed light
2 teaspoons vanilla extract	brown sugar

TO MAKE THE MAPLE-TOASTED WALNUTS

Cover a heat-resistant flat surface with parchment paper. In a large skillet over medium-high heat, heat the walnuts, maple syrup, and salt. Cook for 3 to 4 minutes, stirring frequently, or until the maple syrup has caramelized and the walnuts are toasted. Pour the mixture onto the parchment-covered surface, spreading it out so it doesn't clump into one large piece. Let it cool, then break into bite-size pieces.

TO MAKE THE OATS

In the Instant Pot, combine the water, 2 cups of milk, the oats, vanilla, and salt. Stir well. Lock the lid. Select Manual and cook at high pressure for 12 minutes. When the cook time is complete, let the pressure release naturally for 10 minutes, then quick-release any remaining pressure. Remove the lid and stir in the remaining ½ cup of milk, the strawberries, and brown sugar. Top individual servings with the toasted walnuts.

Mexican-Style Oatmeal

SERVES 6 to 8 | PREP TIME: 5 minutes | MANUAL: 20 minutes high pressure | RELEASE: Natural | TOTAL TIME: 50 minutes

4 cups whole milk	1 cup old-fashioned oats
3 cups water	2 (3-inch) cinnamon sticks,
½ to ¾ cup sugar	plus more for garnish
⅛ teaspoon coarse salt	

In the Instant Pot, whisk together milk, water, sugar, and salt until the sugar has completely dissolved. Stir in the oats and cinnamon sticks. Lock the lid. Select Manual and cook at high pressure for 20 minutes. When the cook time is complete, allow the pressure to release naturally. Remove the lid. Discard the cinnamon sticks. Stir the oatmeal gently to combine. Ladle into mugs. Garnish with more cinnamon sticks.

Pumpkin Spice Oatmeal

SERVES 6 | PREP AND FINISHING: 10 minutes | MANUAL: 3 minutes high pressure | RELEASE: Quick | TOTAL TIME: 23 minutes

4 cups low-fat milk	⅛ teaspoon sea salt
2 cups rolled oats	¼ cup maple syrup
½ cup pumpkin puree	¼ cup chopped,
1 teaspoon vanilla extract	unsalted almonds
½ teaspoon ground	
cinnamon	

In the Instant Pot, combine the milk, oats, pumpkin, vanilla, cinnamon, and salt. Mix well. Lock the lid. Select Manual and cook at high pressure for 3 minutes. When the cook time is complete, quick-release the pressure. Remove the lid. Stir in the maple syrup and almonds.

Peanut Butter and Jelly Oatmeal

SERVES 4 to 6 | PREP TIME: 3 minutes | MANUAL: 3 minutes high pressure | RELEASE: Natural for 10 minutes, then Quick | TOTAL TIME: 25 minutes

3 cups water, divided
2 cups gluten-free rolled oats
2 cups unsweetened plant-based milk
1 tablespoon ground flaxseed
½ cup peanut butter
½ cup no-sugar-added fruit preserves

In a heatproof bowl, stir together 2 cups of water, the oats, milk, and flaxseed. Place the trivet in the Instant Pot and pour in the remaining 1 cup of water. Place the bowl with the oatmeal mixture on top of the trivet. Lock the lid. Select Manual and cook at high pressure for 3 minutes. When the cook time is complete, let the pressure release naturally for 10 minutes, then quick-release any remaining pressure. Remove the lid. There may be some liquid on top of the oatmeal. Add the peanut butter and stir well to incorporate. Top each serving with about 2 tablespoons of preserves and serve immediately.

Cinnamon-Raisin Steel-Cut Oatmeal

SERVES 4 | PREP AND FINISHING: 10 minutes | SAUTÉ: 3 minutes | MANUAL: 10 minutes high pressure | RELEASE: Natural for 10 minutes, then Quick | TOTAL TIME: 35 minutes

2 tablespoons unsalted butter
1 cup steel-cut oats
2 cups water
1 cup whole milk, plus more for serving
1 tablespoon granulated sugar, plus more for serving
¼ teaspoon salt
½ cup packed raisins
1 teaspoon ground cinnamon
1 tablespoon packed light brown sugar

Preheat the Instant Pot by selecting Sauté and adjust to More for high heat. Put the butter in the pot to melt. When the butter has stopped foaming, add the oats and stir them to coat with the butter. Continue cooking, stirring frequently, until the oats smell nutty, 2 to 3 minutes. Add the water, milk, granulated sugar, and salt and stir to combine, then stir in the raisins and cinnamon. Select Cancel. Lock the lid. Select Manual and cook at high pressure for 10 minutes. When the cook time is complete, let the pressure release naturally for 10 minutes, then quick-release any remaining pressure. Remove the lid. Stir the oatmeal and spoon it into four bowls. Stir in the brown sugar, add more milk or sugar to taste (if needed), and serve.

Almond-Date Steel-Cut Oatmeal

SERVES 4 | PREP AND FINISHING: 10 minutes | SAUTÉ: 3 minutes | MANUAL: 10 minutes high pressure | RELEASE: Natural for 10 minutes, then Quick | TOTAL TIME: 35 minutes

2 tablespoons unsalted butter
1 cup steel-cut oats
2 cups water
1 cup whole milk, plus more for serving
1 tablespoon sugar, plus more for serving
½ teaspoon vanilla extract
¼ teaspoon salt
½ cup toasted chopped almonds
½ cup chopped dates

Preheat the Instant Pot by selecting Sauté and adjust to More for high heat. Put the butter in the pot to melt. When the butter has stopped foaming, add the oats and stir them to coat with the butter. Continue cooking, stirring frequently, until the oats smell nutty, 2 to 3 minutes. Add the water, milk, sugar, vanilla, and salt and stir to combine. Select Cancel. Lock the lid. Select Manual and cook at high pressure for 10 minutes. When the cook time is complete, let the pressure release naturally for 10 minutes, then quick-release any remaining pressure. Remove the lid. Stir the oatmeal and spoon it into four bowls. Stir in the almonds and dates, add more milk or sugar to taste (if needed), and serve.

Creamy Banana Steel-Cut Oatmeal

SERVES 4 to 6 | PREP TIME: 5 minutes, plus 5 minutes to thicken | MANUAL: 4 minutes high pressure | RELEASE: Natural for 10 minutes, then Quick | TOTAL TIME: 35 minutes

3½ cups whole milk
1 cup gluten-free steel-cut oats
2 bananas, sliced
¼ cup packed light brown sugar
1 teaspoon salt
1 teaspoon vanilla extract
½ teaspoon ground cinnamon
¼ teaspoon ground nutmeg
2 tablespoons unsalted butter
½ cup chopped pecans

In the Instant Pot, combine the milk, oats, bananas, brown sugar, salt, vanilla, cinnamon, and nutmeg. Lock the lid. Select Manual and cook on high pressure for 4 minutes. When the cook time is complete, let the pressure naturally release for at least 10 minutes, then quick-release any remaining pressure. Remove the lid, stir in the butter, and let stand for 5 minutes to thicken. Stir in the pecans and serve.

Chocolate-Hazelnut and Banana Steel-Cut Oatmeal

SERVES 4 | PREP AND FINISHING: 10 minutes | SAUTÉ: 3 minutes | MANUAL: 10 minutes high pressure | RELEASE: Natural for 10 minutes, then Quick | TOTAL TIME: 35 minutes

2 tablespoons unsalted butter
1 cup steel-cut oats
2 cups water
1 cup whole milk, plus more for serving
1 tablespoon sugar, plus more for serving
¼ teaspoon salt
½ cup Nutella or another chocolate-hazelnut spread
2 ripe bananas, sliced

Preheat the Instant Pot by selecting Sauté and adjust to More for high heat. Put the butter in the pot to melt. When the butter has stopped foaming, add the oats and stir them to coat with the butter. Continue cooking, stirring frequently, until the oats smell nutty, 2 to 3 minutes. Add the water, milk, sugar, and salt and stir to combine. Select Cancel. Lock the lid. Select Manual and cook at high pressure for 10 minutes. When the cook time is complete, let the pressure release naturally for 10 minutes, then quick-release any remaining pressure. Remove the lid. Stir the oatmeal and spoon it into four bowls. Stir in the Nutella and banana slices, add more milk or sugar to taste (if needed), and serve.

Peanut Butter and Chocolate Steel-Cut Oatmeal

SERVES 4 to 6 | PREP TIME: 3 minutes | MANUAL: 12 minutes high pressure | RELEASE: Natural for 10 minutes, then Quick | TOTAL TIME: 25 minutes

2½ cups water
2½ cups nondairy milk, divided, plus more as needed
2 cups steel-cut oats
¼ cup chocolate chips
¼ teaspoon salt
¼ cup peanut butter
2 tablespoons agave or maple syrup

In the Instant Pot, combine the water, 2 cups of milk, the oats, chocolate chips, and salt. Stir to mix. Lock the lid. Select Manual and cook at high pressure for 12 minutes. When the cook time is complete, let the pressure release naturally for 10 minutes, then quick-release any remaining pressure. Remove the lid. Add the remaining ½ cup of milk (more if you want the oats thinner). Stir in the peanut butter and agave and enjoy.

Apple-Cinnamon Steel-Cut Oatmeal

SERVES 4 | PREP TIME: 5 minutes | MANUAL: 4 minutes high pressure | RELEASE: Natural for 15 minutes, then Quick | TOTAL TIME: 30 minutes

2 cups water
1 cup gluten-free steel-cut oats
2 apples, peeled, cored, and diced
1 teaspoon ground cinnamon
1 teaspoon vanilla extract
½ teaspoon salt
¼ cup maple syrup

In the Instant Pot, combine the water, oats, apples, cinnamon, vanilla, and salt. Lock the lid. Select Manual and cook at high pressure for 4 minutes. When the cook time is complete, let the pressure release naturally for about 15 minutes, then quick-release any remaining pressure. Remove the lid and stir in the maple syrup. Serve warm.

Triple-Berry Breakfast Quinoa

SERVES 4 to 6 | PREP TIME: 3 minutes | MANUAL: 2 minutes high pressure | RELEASE: Natural for 5 minutes, then Quick | TOTAL TIME: 25 minutes

1¾ cups unsweetened nondairy milk
1 cup white quinoa, rinsed
½ cup frozen blueberries
½ cup frozen strawberries
½ cup frozen raspberries
¼ cup maple syrup
2 teaspoons vanilla extract
1 cup water

In a heatproof bowl, stir together the milk, quinoa, blueberries, strawberries, raspberries, maple syrup, and vanilla. Place the trivet inside the Instant Pot and pour in the water. Place the bowl with the quinoa mixture on top of the trivet. Lock the lid. Select Manual and cook at high pressure for 2 minutes. When the cook time is complete, let the pressure release naturally for 5 minutes, then quick-release any remaining pressure. Remove the lid. Stir well to combine, then serve immediately.

Fruity Quinoa and Granola Bowls

SERVES 4 | PREP TIME: 2 minutes | MANUAL: 8 minutes high pressure | RELEASE: Natural for 10 minutes, then Quick | TOTAL TIME: 20 minutes

1½ cups water
1 cup quinoa, rinsed
2 tablespoons maple syrup, plus more for topping (optional)
1 teaspoon vanilla extract
½ teaspoon ground cinnamon
Pinch salt
½ to 1 cup nondairy milk
2 cups granola (any variety)
2 cups fruit compote
Sliced bananas, for topping (optional)
Toasted walnuts, for topping (optional)

In the Instant Pot, combine the quinoa, water, maple syrup, vanilla, cinnamon, and salt. Lock the lid. Select Manual and cook at high pressure for 8 minutes. When the cook time is complete, let the pressure release naturally for 10 minutes, then quick-release any remaining pressure. Remove the lid and stir the quinoa. Add enough milk to get the desired consistency. Spoon the quinoa mix into bowls and top with granola, compote, bananas (if using), and walnuts (if using).

Maple Morning Millet

SERVES 4 to 6 | PREP TIME: 2 minutes | MANUAL:
10 minutes high pressure | RELEASE: Natural for
10 minutes, then Quick | TOTAL TIME: 22 minutes

2 cups water
1 cup millet
½ teaspoon ground
  cinnamon

¼ to ½ teaspoon salt
¼ cup maple syrup
½ to 1 cup nondairy milk
Fresh berries, for topping

In the Instant Pot, stir together the water, millet, cinnamon, and salt. Lock the lid. Select Manual and cook
at high pressure for 10 minutes. When the cook time
is complete, let the pressure release naturally for
10 minutes, then quick-release any remaining pressure.
Remove the lid and stir in the maple syrup and as much
milk as you need to get the consistency you prefer (more
milk makes it creamier). Top with the berries and serve.

Nutty Maple Polenta

SERVES 4 to 6 | PREP TIME: 2 minutes | SAUTÉ:
5 minutes | MANUAL: 10 minutes high pressure |
RELEASE: Quick | TOTAL TIME: 20 minutes

3 cups water
2 cups unsweetened non-
  dairy milk
1 cup polenta

½ cup pecan or
  walnut pieces
¼ cup maple syrup

Select Sauté on the Instant Pot and whisk together the
water, milk, and polenta in the pot. Continue to whisk
frequently for 5 minutes, until the mixture reaches
a simmer, then cancel the Sauté. Lock the lid. Select
Manual and cook at high pressure for 10 minutes. When
the cook time is complete, quick-release the pressure.
Remove the lid. Add the nuts and maple syrup and stir
well to combine. Serve immediately.

Mexican-Style Hot Chocolate Porridge

SERVES 6 | PREP TIME: 5 minutes | MANUAL: 8 minutes
on high pressure | RELEASE: Natural | TOTAL TIME:
35 minutes

3 cups whole milk
½ cup masa harina
3 cups water
3 ounces Mexican choco-
  late, cut into eighths

1 (3-inch) cinnamon stick,
  plus more for garnish
¼ to ½ cup sugar

In a blender, puree the milk, masa harina, and water
until smooth. Pour into the Instant Pot. Add the Mexican
chocolate, cinnamon stick, and ¼ cup of sugar, stirring
until the sugar is completely dissolved. Lock the lid.
Select Manual and cook at high pressure for 8 minutes.
When the cook time is complete, allow the pressure to
release naturally. Remove the lid. Discard the cinnamon
stick. Stir the mixture gently to combine. Sweeten with

the remaining ¼ cup of sugar, if desired. Ladle into mugs.
Garnish with cinnamon sticks.

Savory Breakfast Porridge

SERVES 4 | PREP TIME: 5 minutes, plus 10 minutes to
simmer | MANUAL: 30 minutes high pressure |
RELEASE: Natural for 15 minutes | TOTAL TIME: 1 hour

2 cups chicken broth
2 cups water
½ cup long-grain white rice,
  rinsed and drained
1 tablespoon sugar
½ teaspoon salt, plus more
  for seasoning
1 tablespoon extra-virgin
  olive oil

4 large eggs
Freshly ground
  black pepper
4 scallions, white and green
  parts, chopped
2 teaspoons gluten-free
  soy sauce or tamari
Chili sauce (optional)

In the Instant Pot, combine the broth, water, rice, sugar,
and salt. Lock the lid, select Manual, and cook at high
pressure for 30 minutes. Meanwhile, heat the oil over
medium heat in a large skillet. Once hot, crack the eggs
into the skillet, next to each other but without touching.
Cook for 3 to 5 minutes, covering the skillet for half of
the time, until the whites are crispy and the yolks are
still runny. Season with salt and pepper. When the cook
time is complete, let the pressure release naturally for
15 minutes. If you want a thicker porridge, select Sauté
and simmer for up to 10 minutes. Serve topped with the
scallions, soy sauce, chili sauce (if using), and an egg.
Season with additional salt and pepper as desired.

Sweet Potato Hash

SERVES 4 | PREP TIME: 10 minutes | SAUTÉ: 10 minutes |
MANUAL: 3 minutes high pressure | RELEASE: Quick |
TOTAL TIME: 30 minutes

1 tablespoon extra-virgin
  olive oil
1½ pounds sweet potatoes,
  peeled and diced
1 yellow onion, chopped
1 red bell pepper, seeded
  and chopped
2 garlic cloves, minced
1 teaspoon dried oregano

½ teaspoon cay-
  enne pepper
½ teaspoon salt
¼ teaspoon freshly ground
  black pepper
½ cup low-sodium vegeta-
  ble broth
4 large eggs

Select Sauté on the Instant Pot and pour in the olive oil.
When the oil is hot, add the sweet potatoes and cook
for 10 minutes, stirring occasionally, until the potatoes
begin to brown and soften. Stir in the onion, bell pepper,
garlic, oregano, cayenne pepper, salt, and pepper until
well combined. Select Cancel. Stir in the broth, then
crack the eggs on top of the potato mixture. Lock the lid.
Select Manual and cook at high pressure for 3 minutes.
When the cook time is complete, quick-release the pressure. Remove the lid and serve.

Cheesy Grits

SERVES 4 | PREP TIME: 5 minutes | SAUTÉ: 2 minutes | MANUAL: 10 minutes high pressure | RELEASE: Natural for 15 minutes, then Quick | TOTAL TIME: 39 minutes

2 tablespoons unsalted butter	Freshly ground black pepper
1 cup stone-ground white grits	¾ cup whole milk
3 cups water	½ cup shredded sharp or mild Cheddar cheese
Salt	(or more to taste)

Select Sauté and melt the butter. When the butter is melted, add the grits and cook, stirring occasionally, for 2 minutes until fragrant. Add the water and season with salt and pepper. Select Cancel. Lock the lid. Select Manual and cook at high pressure for 10 minutes. When the cook time is complete, let the pressure release naturally for 15 minutes, then quick-release any remaining pressure. Stir the milk into the grits, followed by the cheese. You can serve as is or cover and cook for 2 minutes more for a creamier consistency. Season to taste and serve hot.

Breakfast Potatoes, Onions, and Peppers

SERVES 4 to 6 | PREP TIME: 10 minutes | MANUAL: 5 minutes high pressure | SAUTÉ: 3 minutes | RELEASE: Natural for 5 minutes, then Quick | TOTAL TIME: 30 minutes

1 cup water, plus more as needed	1 bell pepper, seeded and diced
2 pounds red or yellow potatoes, cut into 1½-inch cubes	1 teaspoon garlic powder
	¾ teaspoon paprika
	Salt
1 medium onion, diced	Freshly ground black pepper

Pour the water into the Instant Pot. Place the potatoes in a steamer basket inside the pot. Lock the lid. Select Manual and cook at high pressure for 5 minutes. When the cook time is complete, let the pressure release naturally for 5 minutes, then quick-release any remaining pressure. Remove the lid. Remove the steamer basket and the potatoes and drain the Instant Pot. Replace the inner pot and select Sauté. Allow the pot to preheat for 3 minutes, then combine the onion and peppers in the pot and sauté for about 3 minutes. If the veggies begin to stick, slowly add water, a tablespoon at a time. Add the potatoes, garlic powder, paprika, salt, and pepper and cook until the vegetables are done to your liking. Serve immediately.

Sausage-and-Potato Hash

SERVES 6 | PREP TIME: 10 minutes | MANUAL: 2 minutes for high pressure | SAUTÉ: 10 minutes | RELEASE: Quick | TOTAL TIME: 27 minutes

1 cup water	1 teaspoon onion powder
1½ pounds russet potatoes, peeled and cubed	½ teaspoon paprika
	½ teaspoon salt
2 tablespoons unsalted butter	½ teaspoon freshly ground black pepper
½ pound ground sausage	½ teaspoon dried thyme
½ teaspoon garlic powder	

Pour the water into the Instant Pot. Place the potatoes in a steamer basket and lower the basket into the pot. Lock the lid. Select Manual and cook at high pressure for 2 minutes. When the cook time is complete, quick-release the pressure. Remove the steamer basket and drain the liquid from the inner pot. Return the inner pot to the Instant Pot and select Sauté. When it is hot, melt the butter. Add the sausage and cook until browned, 5 to 7 minutes. Return the potatoes to the pot and stir in the remaining ingredients. Cook until browned, 2 to 3 minutes.

Biscuit Dumplings and Gravy

SERVES 4 | PREP TIME: 5 minutes | SAUTÉ: 15 minutes | MANUAL: 5 minutes high pressure | RELEASE: Natural for 5 minutes, then Quick | TOTAL TIME: 38 minutes

1 tablespoon unsalted butter	1½ teaspoons freshly ground black pepper, divided
1 pound pork sausage	
¼ cup all-purpose flour	1 teaspoon salt
2⅓ cups whole milk, divided	¾ cup baking mix (such as Bisquick)
2 teaspoons dried thyme	

Melt the butter using the Sauté function. When melted, add the sausage and cook until browned, about 8 minutes. Break up the sausage as it cooks, leaving some bigger pieces for better texture. Do not drain the pot. Add the flour and stir well. Continue to cook the flour and sausage mixture until brown, 2 to 3 minutes. Make sure to stir often. When the mixture starts to brown, slowly add 2 cups of milk and mix; then add the thyme, ½ teaspoon of pepper, and the salt. Scrape the bottom of the pot well to release any browned bits. Turn the pot off and allow it to cool for 3 to 4 minutes. In a medium bowl, mix the baking mix, remaining ⅓ cup of milk, and remaining 1 teaspoon of pepper. Stir until the dough just comes together. Drop dollops of the dough into the sausage gravy and lock the lid. Select Manual and cook at high pressure for 5 minutes. When the cook time is complete, let the pressure release naturally for 5 minutes, then quick-release any remaining pressure.

Banana Bread

SERVES 6 | PREP TIME: 10 minutes | MANUAL:
55 minutes high pressure | RELEASE: Natural for
15 minutes, then Quick | TOTAL TIME: 1 hour 25 minutes

Nonstick cooking spray	½ teaspoon vanilla extract
1 ripe banana, mashed	1 cup gluten-free oat flour
1 large egg, beaten	½ teaspoon baking powder
2 tablespoons honey	¼ teaspoon salt
1 tablespoon coconut oil, melted	1 cup water

Line a 6-inch cake pan with foil and grease it with non-stick cooking spray. In a large bowl, whisk the banana, egg, honey, coconut oil, and vanilla and mix until everything is incorporated. Stir in the flour, baking powder, and salt to form a smooth batter. Pour the batter into the prepared cake pan. Cover the top of the pan with foil. Pour the water into the Instant Pot and insert the trivet. Place the cake pan on top of the trivet. Lock the lid. Select Manual and cook at high pressure for 55 minutes. When the cook time is complete, let the pressure release naturally for 15 minutes, then quick-release any remaining pressure. Remove the lid and lift out the pan. Remove the foil cover and let the banana bread cool for 10 minutes on the trivet. Lift the bread from the pan and cut it into six wedges. Serve warm or at room temperature.

Banana Bread Mini Loaves

SERVES 4 to 6 | PREP TIME: 15 minutes | MANUAL:
50 minutes high pressure | RELEASE: Natural for
10 minutes, then Quick | TOTAL TIME: 1 hour 30 minutes

Nonstick cooking spray	½ teaspoon baking soda
1 cup plus 2½ tablespoons water	½ teaspoon ground cinnamon
1 tablespoon ground flaxseed	⅛ teaspoon salt
1¼ cups gluten-free oat flour	1 very ripe banana, mashed
1½ teaspoons baking powder	⅓ cup maple syrup
	3 tablespoons applesauce
	1 teaspoon vanilla extract

Spray two mini loaf pans with nonstick cooking spray and set them aside. In a small bowl, stir together 2½ tablespoons of water and the flaxseed. In a large bowl, whisk together the oat flour, baking powder, baking soda, cinnamon, and salt. In a medium bowl, whisk the banana, maple syrup, applesauce, vanilla, and flaxseed mixture. Pour the wet ingredients into the dry ingredients and stir well. Divide the batter evenly between the loaf pans. Cover them with a few layers of paper towels and wrap tightly with foil. Pour the remaining 1 cup of water into the Instant Pot and insert the trivet. Place the loaf pans side by side on the trivet. Lock the lid. Select Manual and cook at high pressure for 50 minutes. When

the cook time is complete, release the pressure naturally for 10 minutes, then quick-release any remaining pressure. Remove the lid. Remove the loaf pans, discard the paper towel and foil, and cool for 5 minutes before turning the breads out onto a cooling rack to cool for 10 minutes more before slicing.

Banana Pancake Bites

SERVES 3 | PREP TIME: 10 minutes | MANUAL: 7 minutes
high pressure | RELEASE: Natural for 7 minutes, then
Quick | TOTAL TIME: 29 minutes

Nonstick cooking spray	½ cup whole milk
¾ cup all-purpose flour	1 large egg
2 teaspoons sugar	1 tablespoon maple syrup
1½ teaspoons baking powder	½ banana, diced
¼ teaspoon salt	1 cup water

Spray a 7-cup silicone egg bite mold with cooking spray. In a medium bowl, whisk the flour, sugar, baking powder, and salt. In a measuring cup, whisk together the milk, egg, and syrup. Gently mix the wet ingredients into the dry ingredients. Stir in the banana. Divide the batter among the cups of the prepared egg mold, filling each cup about three-quarters full. Cover the mold with the lid or with foil. Set the trivet in the Instant Pot and pour in the water. Place the egg bite mold on the trivet and lock the lid. Select Manual and cook at high pressure for 7 minutes. When the cook time is complete, let the pressure release naturally for 7 minutes, then quick-release any remaining pressure. Remove the lid and let the pancake bites cool for a minute or two before inverting them onto a plate.

French Toast Cups

SERVES 4 | PREP AND FINISHING: 15 minutes | MANUAL:
Steam 8 minutes high pressure | RELEASE: Natural for
5 minutes, then Quick | TOTAL TIME: 30 minutes

3 tablespoons unsalted butter, divided	1 teaspoon orange juice concentrate
2 large eggs	Pinch salt
1 cup whole milk	4 cups (¾-inch) bread cubes (4 or 5 bread slices)
¼ cup heavy (whipping) cream	1 cup water
¼ teaspoon vanilla extract	

Using about 1 tablespoon of butter, coat the bottoms and sides of four small (1- to 1½-cup) ramekins or custard cups. In a large bowl, whisk the eggs, milk, cream, vanilla, orange juice concentrate, and salt to combine. Add the bread cubes and gently stir to coat with the egg mixture. Let it sit for 2 to 3 minutes to let the bread absorb some of the custard, then gently stir again. Spoon the bread mixture evenly into the cups. Cover each cup with foil. Pour the water into the pot. Place a trivet in the pot and place the ramekins on top, stacking them if necessary. Lock the lid. Select Manual and steam at high pressure for 8 minutes. When the cook time is complete, let the pressure release naturally for 5 minutes, then quick-release any remaining pressure. Remove the lid and use tongs to remove the French toast cups. Remove the foil and let the French toasts cool for a few minutes. While they cool, melt the remaining 2 tablespoons of butter in a large skillet. Unmold the French toasts. When the butter has just stopped foaming, place the French toasts in the skillet and cook until golden brown, about 2 minutes. Turn and brown the other side, 1 to 2 minutes more. Serve immediately.

Cinnamon-Apple Strata

SERVES 4 | PREP AND FINISHING: 10 minutes | MANUAL: 10 minutes high pressure | RELEASE: Natural For 10 minutes, then Quick | TOTAL TIME: 35 minutes

1 large apple, such as Gala, Braeburn, or Granny Smith, peeled, cored, and diced
½ cup packed light brown sugar, divided
2 teaspoons ground cinnamon, divided

3 large eggs
1 cup whole milk
½ teaspoon salt
3 cups (1-inch) stale bread cubes (3 or 4 bread slices)
1 teaspoon unsalted butter, at room temperature
1 cup water

In a small bowl, toss the apple with 2 tablespoons of brown sugar and ½ teaspoon of cinnamon. In a medium bowl, whisk the eggs, milk, salt, 2 tablespoons of brown sugar, and ½ teaspoon of cinnamon. Add the bread cubes and gently stir to coat with the egg mixture. Let it sit for 2 to 3 minutes to let the bread absorb some of the custard, then gently stir again. Coat the bottom and sides of a 1-quart baking dish with the butter. Spoon about a third of the custard and bread mixture into the dish. Spoon about a third of the apples over the bread. Repeat with a third of the bread mixture and a third of the apples, then finish with a final layer of both. Lay a square of foil over the top of the dish. Do not crimp the foil down because the strata will expand as it cooks; you just want to keep moisture off the top. Pour the water into the Instant Pot. Place a trivet with handles in the pot and place the baking dish on top. If your trivet doesn't have handles, use a foil sling to make removing the dish easier. Lock the lid. Select Manual and cook at high pressure for 10 minutes. When the cook time is complete, let the pressure release naturally for 10 minutes, then quick-release any remaining pressure. Remove the lid. While the strata cooks, mix the remaining ¼ cup of brown sugar and 1 teaspoon of cinnamon in a small bowl. Turn on the oven to broil. Carefully remove the baking dish from the pot. Remove the foil and sprinkle the cinnamon-sugar topping over the top of the strata. Place the baking dish under the broiler for several minutes until the top is bubbling. Let cool for a few minutes, then serve.

Holiday French Toast Casserole

SERVES 4 to 6 | PREP TIME: 5 minutes |
MANUAL: 25 minutes high pressure | RELEASE: Quick |
TOTAL TIME: 30 minutes

Nonstick cooking spray
1 cup water
1 large banana, plus more for topping (optional)
¼ cup maple syrup, plus more for serving
¼ cup Bailey's Almande Almond Milk Liqueur (or nondairy milk for alcohol-free)

1 teaspoon vanilla extract
¼ teaspoon kala namak or sea salt
6 cups cubed stale French bread
Vegan butter, for topping

Spray a 7-cup oven-safe glass bowl with nonstick spray and set it aside. Pour the water into the Instant Pot and place a trivet inside the inner pot. In a large bowl, mash the banana with a fork. Stir in the maple syrup, Bailey's, vanilla, and kala namak, making sure the banana is completely mixed in. Quickly toss the bread in the banana mixture. Transfer the soaked bread to the prepared bowl, cover tightly with foil, and place the bowl on top of the trivet in the Instant Pot. Lock the lid. Select Manual and cook at high pressure for 25 minutes. When the cook time is complete, quick-release the pressure. Remove the lid. Top with the butter and enjoy!

Berry Berry Cinnamon Toast Casserole

SERVES 4 to 6 | PREP TIME: 5 minutes | MANUAL: 25 minutes high pressure | RELEASE: Quick | TOTAL TIME: 30 minutes

Nonstick cooking spray
1 cup water
½ cup applesauce
¼ cup maple syrup, plus more for topping
1 teaspoon vanilla extract
1 teaspoon ground cinnamon

¼ teaspoon kala namak or sea salt
5 cups cubed, stale French bread
1½ cups fresh blueberries and strawberries (halve or quarter the strawberries)
Vegan butter, for topping

Spray a 7-cup oven-safe glass bowl with nonstick spray. Pour the water into the Instant Pot and place a trivet inside the inner pot. In a large bowl, whisk the applesauce, maple syrup, vanilla, cinnamon, and kala namak. Quickly toss the bread and berries in the apple mixture. Transfer the mixture to the prepared bowl and cover tightly with foil. Place the bowl on top of the trivet in the Instant Pot. Lock the lid. Select Manual and cook at high pressure for 25 minutes. When the cook time is complete, quick-release the pressure. Remove the lid and serve topped with butter.

Cinnamon-Sugar Monkey Bread

SERVES 4 | PREP TIME: 15 minutes | MANUAL: 10 minutes high pressure | RELEASE: Natural for 15 minutes, then Quick | TOTAL TIME: 45 minutes

Nonstick cooking spray
¼ cup (½ stick) salted butter, plus 2 tablespoons, melted, divided
½ cup packed light brown sugar
⅓ cup granulated sugar
2 tablespoons ground cinnamon
3 (7½-ounce) cans refrigerated biscuits, quartered
1 cup water

Grease a 7-inch Bundt pan with cooking spray. In a small bowl, combine ¼ cup of melted butter and the brown sugar. Pour the mixture into the bottom of the prepared pan. In a separate small bowl, combine the granulated sugar and cinnamon. Roll each biscuit piece in the cinnamon-sugar mixture until evenly coated, then place them in the pan. Once all the biscuit pieces are stacked evenly, pour the remaining 2 tablespoons of melted butter over the top. Cover with foil. Set the trivet in the Instant Pot and pour in the water. Place the covered pan on the trivet and lock the lid. Select Manual and cook at high pressure for 10 minutes. When the cook time is complete, let the pressure release naturally for 15 minutes, then quick-release any remaining pressure. Remove the foil from the pan and place a rimmed serving plate on top of the monkey bread. Flip it over in a swift motion to release the bread and enjoy at once.

Soft-Boiled Eggs

SERVES 4 | PREP AND FINISHING: 3 minutes | MANUAL: Steam 3 minutes low pressure (soft eggs) or 2 minutes high pressure (slightly firmer eggs) | RELEASE: Quick | TOTAL TIME: 10 minutes

4 large eggs, refrigerated
1 cup water
Toast, for serving (optional)

Fill a medium bowl about halfway with cold water. Add a handful of ice cubes. Set it aside. Place the eggs in the pot. Pour the water in and place a steamer trivet or basket inside. Place the eggs on the steamer. Lock the lid. For soft eggs: Select Manual and steam on low pressure for 3 minutes. For slightly firmer eggs: Select Steam and cook on high pressure for 2 minutes. When the cook time is complete, quick-release the pressure. Remove the lid and use tongs to transfer the eggs to the ice bath. Leave the eggs in the ice bath until just cool enough to handle, about 30 seconds. For soft eggs: Place the eggs in eggcups. Use a sharp knife or egg topper to cut the tops off the eggs. Serve immediately. For slightly firmer eggs: Working quickly, gently crack the shell and peel each egg. Serve immediately over toast.

Hard-Boiled Eggs

SERVES 4 | PREP AND FINISHING: 3 minutes | MANUAL: Steam 4 minutes high pressure | RELEASE: Quick | TOTAL TIME: 10 minutes

4 large eggs
1 cup water

Fill a medium bowl about halfway with cold water. Add several handfuls of ice cubes. Set it aside. Place the eggs in the pot. Pour the water into the Instant Pot and place a steamer trivet or basket inside. Place the eggs on the steamer. Lock the lid. Select Manual and steam at high pressure for 4 minutes. When the cook time is complete, quick-release the pressure. Remove the lid and use tongs to transfer the eggs to the ice bath. For warm eggs, remove from the ice bath as soon as they're cool enough to handle. Peel and serve. For cold eggs, leave them in the ice bath until thoroughly chilled, 10 to 15 minutes. Peel and serve.

Poached Eggs

SERVES 4 | PREP TIME: 10 minutes | MANUAL: 4 minutes high pressure | TOTAL TIME: 15 minutes

2 quarts water
2 tablespoons table salt
1 tablespoon white vinegar
4 large eggs
Buttered toast or English muffins, for serving (optional)

Pour the water into the Instant Pot and add the salt and vinegar. Select Sauté and adjust to More for high heat. As the water heats, stir to dissolve the salt. Heat the water to just below the boiling point—between 200°F and 205°F. Place a small strainer over a custard cup or ramekin. Crack an egg into the strainer and let it sit for a couple of minutes to drain off the thin egg whites. Gently tip the egg in the strainer into a new custard cup. Repeat with the remaining eggs, placing each egg in a separate cup. When the water has heated, tip the eggs, one at a time, from the cup into the water. Space the eggs evenly and keep track of the order you put them in the water so you can ensure that each egg cooks for 3 ½ to 4 minutes. Use a large, slotted spoon to remove the eggs. Drain briefly on paper towels. Place the eggs in cups or on buttered toast or English muffins (if using) to serve.

Sous Vide Egg Bites

SERVES 3 | PREP TIME: 5 minutes | MANUAL: 12 minutes high pressure | RELEASE: Natural for 10 minutes, then Quick | TOTAL TIME: 32 minutes

Nonstick cooking spray
4 large eggs
¼ cup cottage cheese
½ cup shredded Cheddar cheese
4 cooked bacon slices, crumbled
1 cup water

Spray a 7-cup silicone egg bite mold with cooking spray. In a medium bowl, whisk the eggs until they're fluffy. Beat in the cottage cheese until it is fully incorporated. Stir in the Cheddar cheese and bacon. Divide the egg mixture among the cups of the prepared egg mold, filling each cup about three-quarters full. Cover the mold with the lid or with foil. Set the trivet in the Instant Pot and pour in the water. Place the egg bite mold on the trivet and lock the lid. Select Manual and cook at high pressure for 12 minutes. When the cook time is complete, let the pressure release naturally for 10 minutes, then quick-release any remaining pressure. Remove the lid and let the egg bites cool for a minute or two before inverting them onto a plate.

Ham and Swiss Egg Bites

MAKES 12 bites | PREP TIME: 10 minutes | MANUAL: 12 minutes high pressure | RELEASE: Natural for 10 minutes, then Quick | TOTAL TIME: 40 minutes

Nonstick cooking spray
8 large eggs, beaten
½ cup milk of choice
½ cup shredded
   Swiss cheese
½ cup finely diced red
   bell pepper
¼ cup diced uncured ham
½ teaspoon salt
½ teaspoon freshly ground
   black pepper
1 cup water

Grease the outer 6 wells of two 7-well silicone egg bite molds with nonstick cooking spray. In a medium bowl, whisk the eggs and milk until frothy. Stir in the cheese, bell pepper, ham, salt, and pepper. Divide the egg mixture between the prepared egg bite wells, filling each well about three-quarters full. Cover the molds with their lids or foil. Pour the water into the Instant Pot and insert the trivet. Stack the egg bite molds on top of the trivet. Lock the lid. Select Manual and cook at high pressure for 12 minutes. When the cook time is complete, let the pressure release naturally for 10 minutes, then quick-release any remaining pressure. Remove the lid and let the eggs cool for a minute or two before releasing them from the molds. Serve warm.

Individual Spinach Quiches in Ham Cups

SERVES 4 | PREP TIME: 10 minutes | MANUAL: Steam 7 minutes high pressure | RELEASE: Quick | TOTAL TIME: 25 minutes

4 thin slices deli ham
¼ cup frozen spinach,
   thawed and well drained
½ cup shredded Cheddar
   cheese (about 2 ounces)
4 large eggs
¼ cup milk
¼ cup heavy
   (whipping) cream
½ teaspoon salt
1 cup water

Place a slice of ham in each of four small (1- to 1½-cup) ramekins or custard cups and press it into the bottom and up the sides to form a cup shape. Divide the spinach and cheese among the ramekins. In a medium bowl, whisk the eggs, milk, cream, and salt. Pour the custard evenly into the ramekins. Pour the water into the Instant Pot. Place a trivet in the pot and place the ramekins on top, stacking if necessary. Place a piece of foil over the ramekins to keep water out of the quiches. Lock the lid. Select Manual and steam at high pressure for 7 minutes. When the cook time is complete, quick-release the pressure. Remove the lid. Use tongs to carefully remove the ramekins from the pot. Let them cool for a few minutes, then serve.

Kale and Sweet Potato Mini Quiches

MAKES 7 quiches | PREP TIME: 7 minutes | SAUTÉ LOW: 2 minutes | MANUAL: 18 minutes high pressure | RELEASE: Natural for 10 minutes, then Quick | TOTAL TIME: 37 minutes

Nonstick cooking spray
1 (14-ounce) package firm
   tofu, lightly pressed
¼ cup nondairy milk
¼ cup nutritional yeast
1 tablespoon cornstarch
½ to 1 teaspoon kala
   namak or sea salt, plus
   more for seasoning
½ teaspoon garlic powder
½ teaspoon onion powder
½ teaspoon ground
   turmeric
½ cup shredded
   sweet potato
Handful kale
   leaves, chopped
1 cup plus
   1 tablespoon water
Vegan-buttered toast,
   for serving
Freshly ground
   black pepper

Lightly coat an 8¼-inch silicone egg bites mold with nonstick spray and set aside. In a food processor, combine the tofu, milk, yeast, cornstarch, kala namak, garlic powder, onion powder, and turmeric. Blend until smooth. Select Sauté Low. When the display reads HOT, add the sweet potato, kale, and 1 tablespoon of water. Sauté for 1 to 2 minutes (you may need to turn off the Instant Pot if the vegetables start to stick to the bottom). Select Cancel. Stir the veggies into the tofu mixture and spoon the mixture into the prepared mold. Cover the mold tightly with aluminum foil and place it on a trivet. Add the remaining 1 cup of water to the Instant Pot and use the trivet's handles to lower the trivet and mold into the pot. Lock the lid. Select Manual and cook at high pressure for 18 minutes. When the cook time is complete, let the pressure release naturally for 10 minutes, then quick-release any remaining pressure. Remove the lid. Remove the silicone mold from the Instant Pot and pull off the foil. Leave the mold on the trivet and let it cool for a few minutes. The bites will continue to firm as they cool. When ready to eat, smear the tofu bites onto vegan-buttered toast and season with salt and pepper.

Crustless Quiche Lorraine

SERVES 4 | PREP AND FINISHING: 15 minutes | SAUTÉ: 9 minutes | MANUAL: 10 minutes high pressure | RELEASE: Natural for 10 minutes, then Quick | TOTAL TIME: 40 minutes

3 bacon slices, chopped
1 small onion, thinly sliced
¾ teaspoon salt, divided
3 large eggs
½ cup whole milk
½ cup heavy (whipping) cream
⅛ teaspoon freshly ground black pepper
1 teaspoon unsalted butter, at room temperature
1¼ cups grated Swiss cheese (about 3 ounces)
1 cup water

Preheat the Instant Pot by selecting Sauté and adjust to Normal for medium heat. Cook the bacon until most of the fat has rendered and the bacon is crisp, about 6 minutes. Use a slotted spoon to remove the bacon, and drain on paper towels, leaving the rendered fat in the pot. Add the onion and sprinkle with ¼ teaspoon of salt. Cook, stirring frequently, until the onion pieces separate and soften, 2 to 3 minutes. Transfer the onion to the paper towels with the bacon. Select Cancel. Rinse out the inner pot, scraping off any browned bits. In a medium bowl, whisk the eggs, milk, cream, pepper, and remaining ½ teaspoon of salt. Coat the bottom and sides of a 1-quart baking dish with the butter. Sprinkle half of the cheese over the bottom of the dish. Top with the bacon and onion, then add the remaining cheese. Carefully pour the custard over the cheese. Lay a square of foil over the top of the baking dish. Do not crimp the foil down because the quiche will expand; you just want to keep moisture off the top. Pour the water into the Instant Pot. Place a trivet with handles in the pot and place the baking dish on top. If your trivet doesn't have handles, use a foil sling to make removing the dish easier. Lock the lid. Select Manual and cook at high pressure for 10 minutes. When the cook time is complete, let the pressure release naturally for 10 minutes, then quick-release any remaining pressure. Remove the lid. Carefully remove the quiche from the pot. Let the quiche cool and set for about 10 minutes before slicing and serving.

Broccoli and Cheddar Crustless Quiche

SERVES 6 | PREP AND FINISHING: 10 minutes | MANUAL: 30 minutes high pressure | RELEASE: Natural for 10 minutes, then Quick | TOTAL TIME: 60 minutes

Nonstick cooking spray
1 cup water
8 large eggs
1½ cups shredded Cheddar cheese, divided
1 cup chopped broccoli florets
½ cup low-fat milk
½ cup whole wheat flour
¼ teaspoon sea salt
¼ teaspoon freshly ground black pepper
Chopped fresh parsley, for garnish (optional)

Spray an 8-inch ceramic soufflé dish with the cooking spray. Place the trivet in the Instant Pot, then pour in the water. If needed, make a sling. In a large bowl, whisk together the eggs, 1 cup of cheese, the broccoli, milk, flour, salt, and pepper. Pour the mixture into the soufflé dish. Use the sling to lower the soufflé dish onto the trivet. Lock the lid. Select Manual and cook on high pressure for 30 minutes. When the cook time is complete, naturally release the pressure for 10 minutes, then quick-release any remaining pressure. Remove the lid. Use the sling to remove the soufflé dish. Sprinkle the remaining ½ cup of cheese on top of the quiche. Using a sharp knife, slice the quiche into 6 wedges. Serve immediately, garnished with parsley (if using).

Spinach and Mushroom Tofu Scramble

SERVES 4 to 6 | PREP TIME: 5 minutes | SAUTÉ: 10 to 12 minutes | RELEASE: None | TOTAL TIME: 17 minutes

1 medium onion, diced
1 medium red bell pepper, seeded and diced
2 tablespoons no-salt-added vegetable broth or water, divided
1 garlic clove, minced
1 (14-ounce) package firm tofu, drained and crumbled
2 teaspoons ground turmeric
½ teaspoon garlic powder
½ teaspoon paprika
3 ounces fresh baby spinach
Salt (optional)
Freshly ground black pepper

Select the Sauté on the Instant Pot and allow it to preheat for 3 minutes. Combine the onion and bell pepper in the pot with 1 tablespoon of broth and sauté until the onion begins to brown and the bell pepper is soft, about 5 minutes. Add the broth, 1 teaspoon at a time, to keep the veggies from sticking. Stir in the garlic. Add the tofu, turmeric, garlic powder, and paprika. Stir to combine and cook until the tofu has a yellowish color that resembles scrambled eggs. Add the spinach and stir. Cook about 5 minutes more, until the tofu is heated through and the spinach is just wilted. Season to taste with salt (if using) and pepper. Serve immediately.

Savory Tofu and Potato Casserole

SERVES 4 to 6 | PREP TIME: 30 to 60 minutes | MANUAL: 52 minutes high pressure | RELEASE: Quick | TOTAL TIME: 1 hour 30 minutes to 2 hours

Nonstick cooking spray
2 cups frozen hash browns, thawed
Salt
¼ teaspoon freshly ground black pepper, plus more for seasoning
1 (14-ounce) package firm tofu, pressed for 30 to 60 minutes
⅓ cup nutritional yeast
¼ cup nondairy milk
1 teaspoon kala namak or sea salt
1 teaspoon onion powder
1 teaspoon garlic powder

1 teaspoon ground cumin
½ teaspoon dried oregano
8 ounces tempeh (or other vegan) sausage
1 cup water
Hot sauce, for serving

Sliced scallion, green and light green parts, for serving
Salsa, for serving
Cashew sour cream (or another type of vegan sour cream), for serving

Lightly coat the bottom of a 7-inch springform pan with nonstick spray and set it aside. In a large bowl, toss the hash browns with salt to taste and pepper and set it aside. In a food processor, combine the tofu, yeast, milk, kala namak, onion powder, garlic powder, cumin, and oregano. Blend until smooth. Add the tempeh sausage to the hash browns along with one-fourth of the tofu mixture. Stir to combine. Layer this mixture on the bottom of the prepared pan. Top with the remaining tofu mixture. Cover the pan with a paper towel and wrap it tightly in foil. Pour the water into the Instant Pot and place a trivet inside the inner pot. Put the springform pan on the trivet. Lock the lid. Select Manual and cook at high pressure for 52 minutes. When the cook time is complete, quick-release the pressure. Remove the lid and remove the pan from the Instant Pot. Take off the foil and paper towel. Let cool before releasing the sides of the pan. Serve with hot sauce, scallions, salsa, and cashew sour cream.

Maple Sausage Breakfast Casserole

SERVES 4 | PREP AND FINISHING: 10 minutes | SAUTÉ: 5 minutes | MANUAL: 10 minutes high pressure | RELEASE: Natural for 10 minutes, then Quick | TOTAL TIME: 35 minutes

8 ounces breakfast sausage, removed from its casings
3 large eggs
1 cup whole milk
¼ cup plus 1 tablespoon maple syrup, divided

½ teaspoon kosher salt
3 cups (1-inch) stale bread cubes (3 or 4 bread slices)
1 teaspoon unsalted butter
1 cup water

Preheat the Instant Pot by selecting Sauté for medium heat. Put the sausage in the pot, breaking it up with a spatula into bite-size pieces. Cook, stirring frequently, until the sausage pieces are browned, about 5 minutes. Select Cancel. Remove the sausage and rinse out the inner pot, scraping off any browned bits. In a medium bowl, whisk the eggs, milk, 1 tablespoon of maple syrup, and salt. Add the bread cubes and gently stir to coat them with the egg mixture. Let them sit for 2 to 3 minutes to let the bread absorb some of the custard, then gently stir again. Add the sausage and gently stir to combine with the bread. Coat the bottom and sides of a 1-quart baking dish with the butter. Pour the bread and sausage mixture into the baking dish and lay a square of foil over the top of the dish. Do not crimp the foil down

because the casserole will expand as it cooks; you just want to keep moisture off the top. Pour the water into the Instant Pot. Place a trivet with handles in the pot and place the baking dish on top. If your trivet doesn't have handles, use a foil sling to make removing the dish easier. Lock the lid. Select Manual and cook at high pressure for 10 minutes. When the cook time is complete, let the pressure release naturally for 10 minutes, then quick-release any remaining pressure. Remove the lid. Carefully remove the baking dish from the pot. Remove the foil and drizzle the remaining ¼ cup of maple syrup over the top. Let the casserole cool for a few minutes, then serve.

Spicy Broccoli-Cheese Breakfast Casserole

SERVES 6 | PREP TIME: 10 minutes, plus 10 minutes to cool | MANUAL: 10 minutes high pressure | RELEASE: Natural for 10 minutes, then Quick | TOTAL TIME: 30 minutes

1 tablespoon unsalted butter, at room temperature
6 cups frozen hash browns, defrosted
4 cups diced broccoli
1 red bell pepper, seeded and diced

8 large eggs
2 cups shredded pepper Jack cheese
1 cup half-and-half
1½ teaspoons salt
1 cup water

Coat the bottom and sides of a 1-quart baking dish with butter. Layer the hash browns, broccoli, and bell pepper in the dish. In a large bowl, whisk the eggs, cheese, half-and-half, and salt. Pour the egg mixture into the baking dish. Pour the water into the Instant Pot. Place a trivet with handles in the pot and place the baking dish on top of the trivet. Lock the lid. Select Manual and cook at high pressure for 10 minutes. When the cook time is complete, let the pressure release naturally for 10 minutes, then quick-release any remaining pressure. Remove the lid. Allow to cool for at least 10 minutes before serving.

Ham, Egg, and Cheese Bake

SERVES 6 | PREP AND FINISHING: 10 minutes | MANUAL: 30 minutes high pressure | RELEASE: Natural for 10 minutes, then Quick | TOTAL TIME: 60 minutes

Nonstick cooking spray
1 cup water
8 large eggs
1 cup chopped ham (about ⅓ pound)
½ cup low-fat milk

1 cup shredded Cheddar cheese, divided
¼ teaspoon fine sea salt
¼ teaspoon freshly ground black pepper

Spray an 8-inch ceramic soufflé dish with the cooking spray. Place the trivet in the Instant Pot, then pour in the water. If needed, make a sling. In a large bowl, whisk together the eggs, ham, milk, ½ cup of cheese, the salt, and pepper. Pour the mixture into the soufflé dish. Use the sling to lower the soufflé dish onto the trivet. Lock the lid. Select Manual and cook on high pressure for 30 minutes. When the cook time is complete, naturally release the pressure for 10 minutes, then quick-release any remaining pressure. Remove the lid. Use the sling to remove the soufflé dish. Sprinkle the remaining ½ cup of cheese on top of the casserole. Using a sharp knife, slice the casserole into wedges.

Breakfast Enchiladas

SERVES 8 to 10 | PREP TIME: 45 minutes to 1 hour | SAUTÉ LOW: 8 to 10 minutes | MANUAL: 2 minutes high pressure | RELEASE: Quick | TOTAL TIME: 1 hour 12 minutes

FOR THE TOFU SCRAMBLE

1 (14-ounce) package firm tofu, pressed for 30 to 60 minutes
½ teaspoon kala namak or sea salt
½ teaspoon ground turmeric
1 to 2 tablespoons extra-virgin olive oil
1 small onion, cut into large dice
1 bell pepper, any color, seeded and cut into 1-inch chunks

1 jalapeño pepper, seeded and diced
2 garlic cloves, minced
1 medium or large tomato, diced
¼ cup nutritional yeast
1 teaspoon ground cumin
½ teaspoon dried oregano
Few pinches red pepper flakes
Salt
Freshly ground black pepper

FOR THE ENCHILADAS

Nonstick cooking spray
8 ounces tempeh (or other vegan) sausage
12 (6-inch) or 10 (8-inch) tortillas

1 (10-ounce) can red enchilada sauce
4 scallions, green and light green parts, sliced

TO MAKE THE TOFU SCRAMBLE

In a small bowl (or in your tofu press), use a fork to crumble the tofu. Stir in the kala namak and turmeric. Set it aside. On the Instant Pot, select Sauté Low. When the display reads HOT, heat the oil until it shimmers. Add the onion, bell pepper, and jalapeño. Cook for 2 to 3 minutes, stirring frequently. Turn off the Instant Pot and add the garlic. The inner pot will still be hot. Let the veggies cook for another minute or so. Stir in the tomatoes, tofu mixture, nutritional yeast, cumin, oregano, and red pepper flakes. Season to taste with salt and pepper. Lock the lid. Select Manual and cook at high pressure for 2 minutes. When the cook time is complete, quick-release the pressure. Remove the lid. Select Sauté Low again and cook off the remaining liquid, 3 to

5 minutes, stirring frequently. Taste and adjust the seasonings as desired.

TO MAKE THE ENCHILADAS

Preheat the oven to 375°F. Spray the bottom of a 9-by-13-inch glass baking dish with nonstick spray. To build your enchiladas, add 1 spoonful of tempeh sausage to a tortilla, followed by two or three spoonfuls of tofu scramble (depending on the size of the tortillas), and roll tightly. Place in the prepared baking dish, seam-side down. Repeat for the remaining tortillas. Spoon about two-thirds of the enchilada sauce over the top and sprinkle on the scallions. Cover the dish with foil and bake for 20 minutes. Top with the scallions before serving.

Ham-and-Cheese Omelet

SERVES 4 | PREP TIME: 10 minutes | MANUAL: 6 minutes high pressure | RELEASE: Quick | TOTAL TIME: 21 minutes

Nonstick cooking spray
5 large eggs
2 tablespoons whole milk
1 cup roughly chopped fresh baby spinach
½ cup chopped deli ham
½ cup shredded Cheddar cheese
¼ cup sliced or cubed red bell pepper

¼ cup chopped fresh flat-leaf parsley
¼ teaspoon garlic powder
¼ teaspoon red pepper flakes (optional)
Salt
Freshly ground black pepper
1 cup water

Grease a 7-inch Bundt pan with cooking spray. In a medium bowl, whisk together the eggs and milk. Add the spinach, ham, Cheddar, bell pepper, parsley, garlic powder, red pepper flakes (if using), salt, and pepper. Pour the mixture into the prepared pan. Do not cover the pan. Set the trivet in the Instant Pot and pour in the water. Place the Bundt pan on the trivet and lock the lid. Select Manual and cook for 6 minutes on high pressure. When the cook time is complete, quick-release the pressure.

Vegetable Tortilla Española

SERVES 6 | PREP TIME: 5 minutes | SAUTÉ: 6 minutes | MANUAL: 30 minutes high pressure | RELEASE: Natural for 10 minutes, then Quick | TOTAL TIME: 1 hour

Nonstick cooking spray
1 tablespoon extra-virgin olive oil
½ cup thinly sliced Yukon Gold potato
½ cup thinly sliced zucchini

½ cup thinly sliced yellow onion
6 large eggs, beaten
¼ teaspoon salt
¼ teaspoon freshly ground black pepper
1 cup water

Grease a 6-inch cake pan with nonstick cooking spray. Select Sauté on the Instant Pot and pour in the olive oil.

When the oil is hot, add the potato, zucchini, and onion. Cook, stirring occasionally, for about 6 minutes, until the onions begin to brown and the potatoes crisp. Select Cancel. Transfer the cooked vegetables to the prepared cake pan. In a large bowl, whisk together the eggs, salt, and pepper. Pour the egg mixture over the vegetables. Cover the top of the cake pan with foil. Pour the water into the Instant Pot and insert the trivet. Place the cake pan on top of the trivet. Lock the lid. Select Manual and cook at high pressure for 30 minutes. When the cook time is complete, let the pressure release naturally for 10 minutes, then quick-release any remaining pressure. Remove the lid and lift out the cake pan. Uncover the tortilla and let it cool for 10 minutes on the trivet, then cut it into six wedges. Serve warm.

Vegetable Frittata

SERVES 4 | PREP TIME: 10 minutes | SAUTÉ: 6 minutes | PRESSURE BUILD: 10 minutes | MANUAL: 20 minutes high pressure | RELEASE: Natural for 10 minutes, then Quick | TOTAL TIME: 56 minutes

6 large eggs
1 teaspoon salt, divided
¼ teaspoon freshly ground black pepper
Nonstick cooking spray
2 teaspoons canola or vegetable oil
1 small onion, finely chopped
1 small red or green bell pepper, seeded and finely chopped

1 small potato, peeled and finely chopped
2 garlic cloves, finely minced
1 small tomato, chopped
½ cup fresh or frozen green peas
½ teaspoon cayenne pepper
½ teaspoon garam masala
2 cups water

In a medium bowl, whisk the eggs with ½ teaspoon of salt and the black pepper. Set aside. Lightly grease a 7-inch round stainless steel or silicone baking pan with cooking spray. Select Sauté and pour in the oil once the Instant Pot is hot. Add the onion, bell pepper, potato, and garlic and cook, stirring occasionally, until the veggies are crisp-tender, 3 to 5 minutes. Add the tomato, peas, cayenne pepper, garam masala, and remaining ½ teaspoon of salt and cook until the tomato is soft, about 1 minute. Press Cancel. Use oven mitts to carefully remove the pot and transfer the veggie mixture to a bowl to cool, then return the pot to the base. Select Sauté and pour the water into the Instant Pot. The water will start to simmer in 2 to 3 minutes. Place the rack in the pot, add the slightly cooled veggies to the egg mixture, and mix well. Pour the veggie-egg mixture into the prepared baking pan and cover tightly with aluminum foil. Carefully place the baking pan on the rack in the Instant Pot. Lock the lid and close the steam valve. Cook on high pressure for 20 minutes. Release the steam naturally for 10 minutes, then quick-release any remaining pressure.

Open the lid and let the frittata sit for a couple of minutes, until it deflates and settles into the pan. Using oven mitts, carefully lift the baking pan out of the pot and remove the foil. Cut the frittata into wedges and serve warm.

SNACKS AND APPETIZERS

Chocolate Peanut Butter Popcorn

SERVES 4 | PREP TIME: 5 minutes | SAUTÉ: 5 minutes | TOTAL TIME: 10 minutes

1 tablespoon coconut oil
¼ cup popcorn kernels
1 tablespoon creamy peanut butter

2 tablespoons dairy-free dark chocolate chips

Select Sauté on the Instant Pot and heat the coconut oil. When the oil is hot, add the popcorn kernels. When the popcorn begins to sizzle, place the lid on the pot but do not lock it. Cook for 5 to 6 minutes or until the kernels stop popping on a regular basis. Select Cancel. Remove the lid and stir in the peanut butter, using the heat of the pot to help it melt and coat the popcorn. Stir in the chocolate chips. Serve warm or let the chocolate set at room temperature before eating.

Sweet and Salty Cereal Mix

SERVES 6 | PREP TIME: 5 minutes, plus 10 minutes to cool | MANUAL: 3 hours slow cook | TOTAL TIME: 3 hours 15 minutes

2 cups corn cereal
2 cups rice cereal
1 cup gluten-free pretzel sticks
1 cup gluten-free bagel chips
1 cup toasted cashews or peanuts
¼ cup melted unsalted butter

2 tablespoons gluten-free Worcestershire sauce
2 tablespoons packed light brown sugar
¼ teaspoon cayenne pepper
1 teaspoon garlic powder
1 teaspoon onion powder
1 teaspoon salt

In the Instant Pot, combine the corn cereal, rice cereal, pretzel sticks, bagel chips, and cashews. In a small bowl, whisk together the butter, Worcestershire sauce, brown sugar, cayenne pepper, garlic powder, onion powder, and salt. Pour it evenly over the cereal mixture. Stir to combine. Slow Cook on Normal for 3 hours, stirring a few times throughout. Pour the mix onto a baking sheet to cool and crisp up for 10 minutes before serving.

Spiced Pecans

SERVES 8 | PREP TIME: 5 minutes, plus 10 minutes to cool | MANUAL: 2 minutes high pressure | RELEASE: Quick | TOTAL TIME: 30 minutes

3 cups toasted pecans
¼ cup packed light brown sugar
¼ cup unsalted butter, melted
1 tablespoon smoked paprika
1 teaspoon salt
¼ teaspoon cayenne pepper

Line a baking sheet with parchment paper. In the Instant Pot, combine the pecans, brown sugar, butter, paprika, salt, and cayenne pepper. Lock the lid. Select Manual and cook at high pressure for 2 minutes. When the cook time is complete, quick-release the pressure. Pour the pecans onto the baking sheet and allow to rest for 10 minutes.

Nacho Cheese Sauce

MAKES 5 cups | PREP TIME: 5 minutes | SAUTÉ: 1 minute | MANUAL: 8 minutes high pressure | RELEASE: Quick | TOTAL TIME: 15 minutes

1 tablespoon butter
¾ cup Mexican crema or sour cream
1 (12-ounce) can pickled jalapeño pepper slices, plus more for garnish
2 pounds Cheddar cheese, cut into bite-size cubes

Set the Instant Pot to Sauté and adjust to More for high. Melt the butter in the pot. Stir in the crema and the jalapeño peppers with their juices. Add the cheese. Select Cancel. Lock the lid. Select Manual and cook at high pressure for 8 minutes. When the cook time is complete, quick-release the pressure. Remove the lid. Stir the sauce gently to combine. Ladle over tortilla chips or French fries. Garnish with the pickled jalapeño slices.

Boozy Queso Fundido

SERVES 8 | PREP TIME: 5 minutes | SAUTÉ: 10 minutes | MANUAL: 10 minutes high pressure | RELEASE: Natural | TOTAL TIME: 25 minutes

1 tablespoon canola oil
8 ounces Mexican pork chorizo, casings removed
¼ medium white onion, thinly sliced
6 ounces sliced mushrooms
2 garlic cloves, minced
2 serrano chiles, seeded and finely chopped
2 Anaheim chiles, seeded and thinly sliced
1 (12-ounce) bottle Mexican beer, light or dark
2 cups shredded Colby Jack cheese
2 cups shredded white Cheddar cheese
1 cup shredded Oaxaca or mozzarella cheese
⅓ cup Mexican crema or sour cream
Coarse salt
Freshly ground black pepper
Tortilla chips or warm corn or flour tortillas, for serving

Set the Instant Pot to Sauté and adjust to More for high. Heat the canola oil in the pot, add the chorizo, and fry for 5 to 7 minutes, or until cooked through. Add the onion, mushrooms, garlic, and chiles. Sauté for about 3 minutes, or until the onion is translucent. Stir in the beer, cheeses, and crema. Season lightly with salt and pepper. Select Cancel. Lock the lid. Select Manual and cook at high pressure for 10 minutes. When the cook time is complete, allow the pressure to release naturally. Stir gently to combine. Pour into a heatproof bowl. Serve with tortilla chips.

Queso Blanco Dip

MAKES 4 cups | PREP TIME: 5 minutes | SAUTÉ: 3 minutes | MANUAL: 10 minutes high pressure | RELEASE: Quick | TOTAL TIME: 20 minutes

2 tablespoons butter
2 Anaheim chiles, seeded and finely chopped
2 fresh serrano chiles, seeded and finely chopped
1 garlic clove, minced
¾ cup Mexican crema or sour cream
½ cup whole milk
16 ounces Monterey Jack cheese, cut into bite-size cubes
10 ounces queso fresco, cut into bite-size cubes
½ teaspoon coarse salt, plus more for seasoning (optional)
½ teaspoon ground cumin
Tortilla chips, for serving

Set the Instant Pot to Sauté and adjust to More for high. Heat the butter in the pot until completely melted. Add the chiles and garlic and sauté for 2 to 3 minutes. Stir in the Mexican crema and milk until well combined. Add the cheeses, salt, and cumin. Select Cancel. Lock the lid. Select Manual and cook at high pressure for 10 minutes. When the cook time is complete, quick-release the pressure. Remove the lid. Gently stir the dip to combine. Season with more salt, if necessary. Ladle into a heatproof bowl. Serve with tortilla chips.

Jalapeño Popper Dip

SERVES 4 to 6 | PREP TIME: 10 minutes | MANUAL: 30 minutes high pressure | RELEASE: Natural for 5 minutes, then Quick | TOTAL TIME: 1 hour

2 jalapeño peppers, divided
½ pound dried great northern beans, rinsed and sorted
½ medium onion, roughly chopped
4 cups water, divided
½ cup cashews
¼ cup unsweetened nondairy milk
2 garlic cloves, crushed
2 tablespoons nutritional yeast
1 tablespoon chickpea miso paste
1 tablespoon apple cider vinegar

Halve 1 jalapeño pepper lengthwise and remove the seeds. In the Instant Pot, combine the halved pepper, beans, onion, and 3 cups of water. Lock the lid. Select Manual and cook at high pressure for 30 minutes. Place the cashews in a medium bowl, boil the remaining 1 cup of water, and pour it over the cashews. Let the nuts soak for at least 30 minutes. Drain the cashews and discard the soaking liquid. When the cook time is complete, let the pressure release naturally for 10 minutes, then quick-release any remaining pressure. Remove the lid. Remove the jalapeño from the pot and finely chop it. Finely chop the remaining raw jalapeño, removing the seeds if you prefer a milder dish. Set both peppers aside. Drain the beans and onion, then combine them in a blender with the cashews, milk, garlic, nutritional yeast, miso, and vinegar. Blend until creamy. Spoon into a medium mixing bowl and stir in the jalapeños. Serve immediately.

Cauliflower Queso

MAKES 5 cups | PREP TIME: 5 minutes | MANUAL: 5 minutes high pressure | RELEASE: Quick | TOTAL TIME: 25 minutes

1 head cauliflower, cut into florets (about 4 cups)	½ cup nutritional yeast
2 cups water	1 tablespoon white miso paste
1½ cups carrots, chopped into ½-inch-thick round pieces	2 teaspoons gluten-free chili powder
½ cup raw cashews	1 red bell pepper, seeded and diced
1 (15-ounce) can no-salt-added diced tomatoes, divided	4 scallions, white and green parts, diced

In the Instant Pot, combine the cauliflower, water, carrots, and cashews. Lock the lid. Select Manual and cook at high pressure for 5 minutes. When the cook time is complete, quick-release the pressure. Remove the lid. Drain the water, then transfer the mixture to a blender or food processor. Pour in the liquid from the can of tomatoes and set the drained tomatoes aside. Add the nutritional yeast, miso, and chili powder and blend until very smooth. Transfer to a medium bowl and stir in the drained tomatoes, bell pepper, and scallions. Serve immediately.

Spinach-Artichoke Dip

SERVES 6 | PREP TIME: 10 minutes | SAUTÉ: 5 minutes | MANUAL: 7 minutes high pressure | RELEASE: Natural for 10 minutes, then Quick | TOTAL TIME: 37 minutes

3 tablespoons unsalted butter	1 (14-ounce) can artichoke hearts, drained and chopped
1 small onion, diced	
3 garlic cloves, minced	1 (10-ounce) package frozen spinach, thawed, drained, and squeezed
8 ounces cream cheese, at room temperature	
	½ cup shredded mozzarella cheese
½ cup finely grated Parmesan cheese	½ teaspoon Italian seasoning
	1 cup water

Select Sauté on the Instant Pot and melt the butter. Add the onion and garlic and cook until the onion starts to turn translucent, about 5 minutes. Select Cancel. In a medium bowl, mix the cream cheese, artichokes, spinach, mozzarella, Parmesan, and Italian seasoning. Add the cooked onions and garlic to the spinach mixture. Stir to combine. Transfer the mixture to a 7-inch round cake pan. Clean the inner pot and return it to the Instant Pot. Set the trivet in the Instant Pot and pour in the water. Place the pan on the trivet. Lock the lid. Select Manual and cook at high pressure for 7 minutes. When the cook time is complete, let the pressure release naturally for 10 minutes, then quick-release any remaining pressure. Stir the dip to make sure everything is incorporated before serving.

Classic Hummus

MAKES 1½ cups | PREP TIME: 5 minutes | MANUAL: 1 hour high pressure | RELEASE: Natural for 15 minutes, then Quick | TOTAL TIME: 1 hour 25 minutes

¾ cup dried chickpeas	1 tablespoon freshly squeezed lemon juice
1½ cups water	
4 garlic cloves	¼ teaspoon salt
½ teaspoon baking soda	¼ teaspoon ground cumin (optional)
2 tablespoons tahini	

In the Instant Pot, combine the chickpeas, water, garlic, and baking soda. Lock the lid. Select Manual and cook at high pressure for 1 hour. When the cook time is complete, let the pressure release naturally for 15 minutes, then quick-release any remaining pressure. Remove the lid and stir in the tahini and lemon juice. Use an immersion blender to puree the hummus into a smooth paste. Season with salt and cumin (if using). Serve warm or chilled.

Beet Hummus

SERVES 4 to 6 | PREP TIME: 5 minutes | MANUAL: 45 minutes high pressure | RELEASE: Natural for 10 minutes, then quick | TOTAL TIME: 1 hour 5 minutes

3 cups water	½ cup tahini
1 cup dried chickpeas, rinsed and sorted	2 tablespoons freshly squeezed lemon juice
1 medium beet, peeled and quartered	4 garlic cloves, crushed
	Salt (optional)

Combine the water, chickpeas, and beets in the Instant Pot. Lock the lid with the stem release knob in the sealing position. Select Manual and cook at high pressure for 45 minutes. When the cook time is complete, let the pressure release naturally for 10 minutes, then quick-release any remaining pressure. Remove the lid. In a blender or food processor, combine the tahini, lemon juice, garlic, and salt to taste (if using). Using a slotted spoon, remove the chickpeas and beets from the pot and add them to the other ingredients. Blend well to combine, adding a tablespoon at a time of the remaining liquid in the Instant Pot if necessary to thin the dip. Chill until cool.

Baba Ghanoush

MAKES 2 cups | PREP TIME: 5 minutes | SAUTÉ: 8 minutes | MANUAL: 5 minutes high pressure | RELEASE: Quick | TOTAL TIME: 25 minutes

¼ to ½ cup vegetable broth, divided	2 tablespoons freshly squeezed lemon juice
1 medium eggplant, peeled and cut into 1-inch-thick rounds	2 tablespoons tahini
	1 tablespoon white miso paste
1 cup water	½ teaspoon ground cumin, plus more for garnish
3 garlic cloves, unpeeled	

Select the Sauté on the Instant Pot and pour in 2 tablespoons of broth. Arrange as many slices of eggplant as possible in one layer on the bottom of the pot. Sauté for 2 minutes, then flip, adding more of the broth as needed. After another 2 minutes, pile the first batch of eggplant on one side of the Instant Pot and add the remaining eggplant. Sauté on each side for 2 minutes, adding broth as needed. Add the water and garlic. Select Cancel. Lock the lid. Select Manual and cook at high pressure for 3 minutes. When the cook time is complete, quick-release the pressure. Remove the lid. Using a pair of tongs, remove the garlic and take off the outer peel. In a blender, combine the garlic, eggplant, lemon juice, tahini, miso, and cumin. Blend until smooth. Garnish with cumin and serve warm or cover, refrigerate, and serve cold.

Lentil-Walnut Pâté

SERVES 4 to 6 | PREP TIME: 10 minutes | SAUTÉ: 3 to 5 minutes | MANUAL: 10 minutes high pressure | RELEASE: Natural for 10 minutes, then Quick | TOTAL TIME: 30 minutes

¾ cup walnuts	2 tablespoons freshly squeezed lemon juice
2 cups water	
1 cup green or brown lentils	1 tablespoon white miso paste
½ medium onion, roughly chopped	1 tablespoon apple cider vinegar
1 bay leaf	Freshly ground black pepper
2 garlic cloves, minced	

Select the Sauté on the Instant Pot and allow it to preheat for 2 minutes. Pour in the walnuts and sauté for 3 to 5 minutes, stirring occasionally, until slightly darker in color and the oils begin to release. Remove from the Instant Pot and set aside. In the Instant Pot, combine the water, lentils, onion, and bay leaf. Select Cancel. Lock the lid. Select Manual and cook at high pressure for 10 minutes. When the cook time is complete, let the pressure release naturally for 10 minutes, then quick-release any remaining pressure. Remove the lid. Remove and discard the bay leaf. In a blender or food processor, combine the lentils, onion, garlic, lemon juice, miso, vinegar, and pepper to taste. Blend until creamy. Serve either immediately as a warm dip or chill.

Cowboy Caviar

SERVES 4 to 6 | PREP TIME: 10 minutes | MANUAL: 17 minutes high pressure | RELEASE: Natural for 10 minutes, then Quick | TOTAL TIME: 50 minutes

1 pound dried black-eyed peas, rinsed and sorted	1 jalapeño pepper, seeded and diced (optional)
6½ cups water, plus 2 tablespoons	5 scallions, white and green parts, diced
Zest and juice of 2 limes	3 tomatoes, diced
2 tablespoons maple syrup	1 avocado, peeled, pitted, and diced
2 teaspoons gluten-free chili powder	½ bunch fresh cilantro, chopped
1 cup frozen corn	Freshly ground black pepper
2 bell peppers (any color), seeded and diced	Salt (optional)

In the Instant Pot, combine the peas and 6½ cups of water. Lock the lid. Select Manual and cook at high pressure for 17 minutes. In a large bowl, whisk together the lime zest and juice, maple syrup, chili powder, and the remaining 2 tablespoons of water. Add the corn, bell peppers, jalapeño (if using), scallions, tomatoes, avocado, and cilantro and toss. When the cook time is complete, let the pressure release naturally for 10 minutes, then quick-release any remaining pressure. Remove the lid. Using a slotted spoon, remove the peas to a baking sheet and spread in a single layer to cool. Add the cooled peas to the dressing and vegetables and gently toss. Season to taste with pepper and salt (if using). Serve immediately.

Deviled Potatoes

SERVES 6 | PREP AND FINISHING: 10 minutes | MANUAL: 10 minutes high pressure | RELEASE: Quick | TOTAL TIME: 45 minutes

6 medium Yukon Gold potatoes (about 1½ pounds), halved	½ teaspoon freshly squeezed lemon juice
1 cup water	½ teaspoon salt
5 tablespoons mayonnaise	½ teaspoon freshly ground black pepper
1 teaspoon Dijon mustard	1 tablespoon finely chopped fresh cilantro
1 tablespoon sweet pickle relish	1 teaspoon paprika
1 teaspoon sugar	

Place the halved potatoes in the steamer rack. Pour the water into the Instant Pot and place the trivet inside. Place the steamer rack on the trivet. Lock the lid. Select Manual and cook at high pressure for 10 minutes. When the cook time is complete, quick-release the pressure. Remove the lid. Using tongs, carefully transfer the potatoes to a platter. Set them aside to cool for 15 minutes. In a medium bowl, mix the mayonnaise, mustard, relish, sugar, lemon juice, salt, and pepper. Using a melon scooper or spoon, remove the middle part of the potatoes, creating a well. Spoon 1 to 1½ teaspoons of filling into each potato. Garnish each deviled potato with the cilantro and paprika before serving.

Vegetable Momos

SERVES 4 to 6 | PREP TIME: 20 minutes | SAUTÉ: 3 minutes | MANUAL: Steam 12 minutes high pressure | RELEASE: Natural for 5 minutes, then Quick | TOTAL TIME: 40 minutes

2 cups roughly chopped green cabbage
1 medium carrot, peeled and roughly chopped
2 scallions, white and green parts, roughly chopped
1 teaspoon grated fresh ginger
2 garlic cloves, peeled
½ teaspoon salt
¼ teaspoon freshly ground black pepper
20 wonton wrappers
2 cups water
Chili sauce, for serving

In a food processor, combine the cabbage, carrot, scallions, ginger, and garlic and process until finely chopped. Transfer the vegetable mixture to a medium bowl and season with the salt and pepper. Work with 1 wonton wrapper at a time; keep the rest under a damp towel. Rub water along the edge of the wrapper with your finger, then place about 2 teaspoons of filling in the center. Fold the dough over, then press the edges well to seal properly. Place the filled dumpling on a plate and keep it covered. Repeat with the remaining wrappers and filling. Select Sauté and pour the water into the Instant Pot. When the water starts to simmer, after 2 to 3 minutes, place the dumplings in a steamer basket and place the basket in the pot. Lock the lid with the steam release knob in the venting position. Select Manual and set a separate timer for 12 minutes. When the cook time is complete, release naturally for 5 minutes, then quick-release any remaining pressure. Remove the lid and use oven mitts to carefully remove the steamer basket. Serve the momos hot with chili sauce on the side.

Kathi Rolls with Steamed Egg Filling

SERVES 4 | PREP TIME: 10 minutes | SAUTÉ: 9 minutes | PRESSURE BUILD: 8 minutes | MANUAL: Steam for 12 minutes | RELEASE: Natural for 5 minutes, then Quick | TOTAL TIME: 44 minutes

2 cups water
Nonstick cooking spray
4 large eggs
¾ teaspoon salt, divided
½ teaspoon cayenne pepper, divided
⅛ teaspoon freshly ground black pepper
2 teaspoons canola or vegetable oil
1 small onion, finely chopped
1 small red or green bell pepper, seeded and chopped
2 garlic cloves, finely minced
1 medium tomato, chopped
½ teaspoon ground coriander
⅛ teaspoon chaat masala
4 whole wheat tortillas, warmed
¼ cup chutney of choice, for serving

Select Sauté and pour the water into the Instant Pot. When the water starts to simmer, after 2 to 3 minutes, place the rack in the pot. Lightly grease a 6- or 7-inch round stainless steel or silicone baking pan with cooking spray. Crack the eggs into a small bowl and add ¼ teaspoon of salt, ⅛ teaspoon of cayenne pepper, and the black pepper and whisk until well combined. Pour the mixture into the prepared pan, then cover tightly with aluminum foil. Carefully place the pan on the rack in the pot. Lock the lid with the steam knob in the venting position. Select Manual and steam for 12 minutes. When the cook time is complete, turn off the Instant Pot and release the pressure naturally for 5 minutes, then quick release any remaining pressure. Use oven mitts to remove the pan from the Instant Pot and invert it onto a cutting board. Cool for a couple of minutes, then cut the steamed egg into bite-size pieces. Empty and dry the Instant Pot. Select Sauté and pour in the oil when the pot is hot. Add the onion, bell pepper, and garlic and cook until the veggies are tender, 3 to 5 minutes. Stir in the tomato, coriander, chaat masala, remaining ½ teaspoon of salt, and remaining ⅜ teaspoon of cayenne pepper, and cook until the tomato is soft, about 2 minutes. Add the steamed egg and cook for 1 to 2 minutes until heated through. Assemble the roll by spreading some chutney on a tortilla, adding one-quarter of the steamed egg mixture on the bottom half, and folding the bottom and sides over the filling and rolling it to make a wrap. Repeat with the remaining tortillas and egg mixture. Serve immediately with more chutney on the side.

Sweet Potato and Peanut Salad

SERVES 4 | PREP TIME: 10 minutes | PRESSURE BUILD: 10 minutes | MANUAL: High for 2 minutes | RELEASE: Natural for 5 minutes, then Quick | TOTAL TIME: 27 minutes

2 medium sweet potatoes, peeled and cut into ½-inch pieces
¾ cup water
½ teaspoon salt
1 small red onion, finely chopped
1 medium tomato, seeded and chopped

2 tablespoons chopped, roasted, salted peanuts
2 tablespoons finely chopped fresh cilantro
1 tablespoon freshly squeezed lemon or lime juice
¼ teaspoon cayenne pepper
¼ teaspoon chaat masala

Put the sweet potatoes in the Instant Pot, add the water and salt, and stir. Lock the lid and close the steam valve. Cook on high pressure for 2 minutes. Naturally release the steam for 5 minutes, then quick-release any remaining pressure. Remove the lid and use oven mitts to carefully remove the pot and drain any excess water. Return the pot to the base and add the onion, tomato, peanuts, cilantro, lemon juice, cayenne pepper, and chaat masala. Gently toss to evenly coat the sweet potatoes with the spices. Serve immediately.

Creamy Beet and Corn Salad

SERVES 6 | PREP AND FINISHING: 30 minutes, plus 1 hour to chill | MANUAL: 8 minutes high pressure, divided | RELEASE: Quick | TOTAL TIME: 1 hour 50 minutes

2 medium red beets, peeled (about 1 pound)
1 corncob, husk removed, washed
1½ cups water
¼ cup finely chopped onion
¼ cup finely chopped fresh cilantro
3 tablespoons mayonnaise

1 tablespoon extra-virgin olive oil
2 teaspoons freshly squeezed lemon juice
1 teaspoon grated lemon zest
1 teaspoon sugar
1 teaspoon salt
1 teaspoon freshly ground black pepper

Place the whole beets and corn in the steamer rack. Pour the water into the Instant Pot and place the trivet inside. Place the steamer rack on the trivet. Lock the lid. Select Manual and cook at high pressure for 4 minutes. When the cook time is complete, quick-release the pressure. Remove the lid. Using tongs, transfer the corn to a plate and set aside to cool. Lock the lid. Select Manual and cook at high pressure for 4 minutes. When the cook time is complete, quick-release the pressure. Remove the lid. Using tongs, transfer the beets to the plate with the

corn and set them aside to cool. Using a knife, carefully remove the corn kernels from the cob. Cut the beets into ½-inch cubes. In a large bowl, combine the beets, corn, onion, cilantro, mayonnaise, olive oil, lemon juice, lemon zest, sugar, salt, and pepper. Mix thoroughly and chill in the refrigerator for 1 hour. Serve.

Chickpea Greek Salad

SERVES 6 | PREP AND FINISHING: 10 minutes, plus at least 6 hours to soak | MANUAL: 15 minutes high pressure | RELEASE: Natural | TOTAL TIME: 6 hours 35 minutes

1 cup dried chickpeas
3 cups water
2 tablespoons extra-virgin olive oil
1 tablespoon red wine vinegar
1 teaspoon salt
½ teaspoon freshly ground black pepper
½ cup finely chopped onion

10 cherry tomatoes, halved
10 pitted black olives, halved
1 cucumber, cut into ½-inch dice
¼ cup chopped green bell pepper
2 tablespoons finely chopped fresh cilantro
1 ounce feta cheese, crumbled

In a large bowl, cover the chickpeas with 2 to 3 inches of cold water. Soak at room temperature for 6 to 8 hours or overnight. Drain and rinse the chickpeas. Pour the water into the Instant Pot and add the chickpeas. Lock the lid. Select Manual and cook at high pressure for 15 minutes. When the cook time is complete, naturally release the pressure. Remove the lid. Drain the chickpeas and let them cool for about 5 minutes. In a small jar or bowl, combine the olive oil, vinegar, salt, and pepper. Seal and shake or whisk thoroughly. In a large bowl, combine the chickpeas, onion, tomatoes, olives, cucumber, bell pepper, and cilantro. Add the dressing and toss. Top with the feta and serve cold.

Cold Quinoa Salad with Fruit and Pecans

SERVES 4 to 6 | PREP TIME: 7 minutes | MANUAL: 8 minutes high pressure | RELEASE: Natural for 10 minutes, then Quick | TOTAL TIME: 25 minutes

1 cup quinoa, rinsed
1 cup water
¼ teaspoon salt, plus more as needed
2 apples, cored and cut into large dice
2 tablespoons freshly squeezed lemon juice
1 tablespoon white rice vinegar

½ bunch scallions, green and light green parts, sliced
2 celery stalks, halved lengthwise and chopped
¾ to 1 cup mixture of dried cranberries, white raisins, and regular raisins
2 tablespoons avocado oil or walnut oil

½ to 1 teaspoon chili powder, plus more as needed

Pinch freshly ground black pepper

½ cup chopped fresh cilantro

½ to 1 cup chopped pecans

In the Instant Pot, combine the quinoa, water, and salt and stir. Lock the lid. Select Manual and cook at high pressure for 8 minutes. When the cook time is complete, let the pressure release naturally for 10 minutes, then quick-release any remaining pressure. Remove the lid and transfer the quinoa to a large bowl. Refrigerate for 5 minutes to cool. In a small resealable container, combine the apples, lemon juice, and vinegar. Cover and shake lightly to coat the apples, then refrigerate. Remove the cooled quinoa from the refrigerator and stir in the scallions, celery, cranberry-raisin mix, avocado oil, and chili powder. Taste and season with more salt and pepper, as needed. Stir in the apples and liquid in the container. Add the cilantro and pecans right before serving.

Quinoa and Black Bean Salad

SERVES 8 | PREP AND FINISHING: 15 minutes, plus at least 6 hours to soak | MANUAL: 8 minutes high pressure | RELEASE: Natural | TOTAL TIME: 6 hours 35 minutes

1 cup dried black beans

1 cup quinoa, rinsed and drained

5 cups water, divided

3 tablespoons extra-virgin olive oil

2 tablespoons freshly squeezed lemon juice

1 tablespoon red wine vinegar

2 teaspoons freshly ground black pepper

1½ teaspoons salt

1 teaspoon ground cumin

1 green bell pepper, seeded and cut into ½-inch dice

2 serrano chiles, seeded and finely chopped

¼ cup frozen corn kernels, thawed to room temperature

¼ cup finely chopped fresh cilantro

2 shallots, finely chopped

In a large bowl, cover the black beans with 2 to 3 inches of cold water. Soak at room temperature for 6 to 8 hours or overnight. Drain and rinse the beans. Put the quinoa in a stackable pan and add 1½ cups of water. In another stackable pan, put the beans and 2 cups of water. Place the pan with the quinoa on top of the pan with the beans. Close the pan lids and place them on the interlocking handle. Pour the remaining 1½ cups of water in the Instant Pot and place the trivet inside. Place the stackable pans on the trivet. Lock the lid. Select Manual and cook at high pressure for 8 minutes. When the cook time is complete, naturally release the pressure. Remove the lid. Drain the beans and fluff the quinoa with a fork. Set both aside to cool for 5 minutes. In a small jar or bowl, combine the olive oil, lemon juice, vinegar, pepper, salt, and cumin. Seal and shake or whisk thoroughly. In a large bowl, combine the quinoa, black beans, bell pepper, chiles, corn, cilantro, and shallots. Pour the dressing over the salad, toss to combine, and serve.

Quinoa Salad with Beets and Sweet Potatoes

SERVES 6 | PREP AND FINISHING: 10 minutes | MANUAL: 5 minutes high pressure, divided | RELEASE: Natural for 17 minutes, divided, then Quick | TOTAL TIME: 35 minutes

1 cup quinoa, rinsed

1½ cups vegetable broth or water

¼ teaspoon salt (if using water), plus more as needed

1 cup water

1 large beet, peeled and cut into ¾-inch cubes

1 medium sweet potato, peeled and cut into ¾-inch cubes

1 medium shallot, thinly sliced

¼ cup extra-virgin olive oil

2 tablespoons freshly squeezed lemon juice

1 tablespoon chopped fresh mint

1 tablespoon chopped fresh parsley

Pour the quinoa into the Instant Pot. Add the broth and salt. Lock the lid. Select Manual and cook at high pressure for 1 minute. When the cook time is complete, naturally release the pressure for 12 minutes, then quick-release any remaining pressure. Remove the lid. Spoon the quinoa into a large bowl and fluff it with a fork. Set it aside. Wipe out the pot and pour in the water for steaming. Place the beet and sweet potato cubes in a steamer basket, keeping them separated (or use two small separate steamer baskets). Place the basket(s) in the pot. Lock the lid. Select Manual and cook at high pressure for 4 minutes. When the cook time is complete, naturally release the pressure for 5 minutes, then quick-release any remaining pressure. Remove the lid. Carefully remove the steamer basket(s). Let the beets and sweet potatoes cool. Add the cooled beets and sweet potatoes and the sliced shallot to the quinoa. Drizzle with the olive oil and lemon juice. Toss gently to coat. Taste and add more salt if desired. Top with the mint and parsley and serve.

Couscous Salad with Cucumbers, Olives, and Carrots

SERVES 6 | PREP AND FINISHING: 20 minutes | MANUAL: 2 minutes high pressure | RELEASE: Natural for 5 minutes, then Quick | TOTAL TIME: 35 minutes

FOR THE COUSCOUS

1 cup couscous

2¾ cups water, divided

FOR THE SALAD

½ cup salad greens (spinach, arugula, green lettuce leaves)

¼ cup finely chopped carrot

¼ cup finely chopped black olives

¼ cup finely chopped cucumber

½ cup thinly sliced red onion, marinated in 2 tablespoons each of lemon juice and water for 20 minutes, then drained

½ cup shredded red cabbage, marinated in 2 tablespoons each of lemon juice and water for 20 minutes, then drained

1 teaspoon salt

1 teaspoon freshly ground black pepper

2 tablespoons extra-virgin olive oil

TO MAKE THE COUSCOUS

Put the couscous and 1¼ cups of water in a heatproof bowl that fits inside the Instant Pot. Add the remaining 1½ cups of water to the Instant Pot and place the trivet inside. Place the bowl on the trivet. Lock the lid. Select Manual and cook at high pressure for 2 minutes. When the cook time is complete, naturally release the pressure for 5 minutes, then quick-release any remaining pressure. Remove the lid. Let the couscous cool for 15 minutes before fluffing it with a fork.

TO MAKE THE SALAD

Add the salad greens, carrot, olives, cucumber, onion, cabbage, olive oil, salt, and pepper to the couscous. Mix gently and serve.

Tabouleh Salad

SERVES 4 to 6 | PREP TIME: 5 minutes | MANUAL: 0 minutes high pressure | RELEASE: Natural for 2 minutes, then Quick | TOTAL TIME: 20 minutes

1 cup water

¾ cup red bulgur wheat

½ teaspoon garlic powder

1 cup chopped fresh flat-leaf parsley

¼ cup chopped fresh mint leaves

4 scallions, white and green parts, diced

2 tomatoes, diced

1 cucumber, peeled and diced

Zest and juice 1 lemon

2 tablespoons to ¼ cup extra-virgin olive oil (optional)

Freshly ground black pepper

Salt (optional)

In the Instant Pot, combine the water, bulgur, and garlic powder. Lock the lid. Select Manual and cook at high pressure for 0 minutes. (The food will cook as the pot comes up to pressure.) When the cook time is complete, let the pressure release naturally for 2 minutes, then quick-release any remaining pressure. Remove the lid. Transfer the bulgur to a large bowl and let it cool over an ice bath. In a large bowl, combine the parsley, mint, scallions, tomatoes, cucumber, lemon zest, lemon juice, and cooled bulgur. Drizzle with olive oil (if using) and season to taste with pepper and salt (if using). Stir well to combine. Serve immediately.

Mediterranean-Style Millet Salad

SERVES 4 to 6 | PREP TIME: 10 minutes | MANUAL: 10 minutes high pressure | RELEASE: Natural for 2 minutes, then Quick | TOTAL TIME: 45 minutes, plus 2 hours for chilling

1 cup millet

2 cups water, divided

2 medium tomatoes, diced

1 (14-ounce) can quartered artichoke hearts, drained

1 (6-ounce) jar pitted kalamata olives, drained

1 garlic clove, smashed

Zest and juice of 1 lemon

3 tablespoons tahini

2 teaspoons maple syrup

1 teaspoon no-salt-added Italian seasoning

Freshly ground black pepper

Salt (optional)

In the Instant Pot, combine the millet with 1¾ cups of the water. Lock the lid. Select Manual and cook at high pressure for 10 minutes. While the millet cooks, in a large bowl, stir together the tomatoes, artichokes, and olives and set it aside. In a blender or food processor, make the dressing by combining the garlic, lemon zest, lemon juice, tahini, maple syrup, and the remaining ¼ cup of water. Blend well. When the cook time is complete, let the pressure release naturally for 10 minutes, then quick-release any remaining pressure. Remove the lid. Fluff the millet with a fork and add it to the veggies. Add the dressing and Italian seasoning and season to taste with pepper and salt (if using). Toss to combine and chill for at least 2 hours before serving.

Warm Chickpea Salad

SERVES 4 | PREP TIME: 5 minutes, plus overnight to soak | SAUTÉ: 5 minutes | MANUAL: 15 minutes high pressure | RELEASE: Natural | TOTAL TIME: 40 minutes, plus 6 hours to soak

1 cup dried chickpeas

¼ cup plus 2 tablespoons extra-virgin olive oil, divided

1 red onion, diced

1 red bell pepper, seeded and diced

1 zucchini, diced

3 cups water

1 cup fresh baby spinach

3 tablespoons freshly squeezed lemon juice

¼ teaspoon salt

¼ teaspoon freshly ground black pepper

¼ cup crumbled feta cheese

1 teaspoon dried oregano

In a large bowl, cover the chickpeas with 2 to 3 inches of cold water. Soak at room temperature for 6 hours. Drain and rinse the chickpeas. Select Sauté on the Instant Pot and pour in 2 tablespoons of olive oil. When the oil is hot, add the onion, bell pepper, and zucchini. Cook, stirring frequently, for 4 to 5 minutes, or until softened. Select Cancel. Add the water and chickpeas. Lock the lid. Select Manual and cook at high pressure for 15 minutes. When the cook time is complete, let the pressure release naturally for 10 minutes, then quick-release any remaining pressure. Remove the lid and stir in the remaining ¼ cup of olive oil, the spinach, lemon juice, salt, and pepper. Top with the feta and oregano and serve.

Lemony Navy Bean Salad

SERVES 6 | PREP AND FINISHING: 5 minutes, plus 6 hours to soak, plus 1 hour to chill | MANUAL: 15 minutes high pressure | RELEASE: Natural | TOTAL TIME: 7 hours 30 minutes

1 cup dried navy beans
2 cups water
2 tablespoons freshly squeezed lemon juice
2 tablespoons grated lemon zest
1 tablespoon extra-virgin olive oil
1 teaspoon salt

1 teaspoon freshly ground black pepper
½ cup finely chopped onion
1 cucumber, cut into ½-inch cubes
½ cup grated carrot
2 tablespoons finely chopped fresh parsley

In a large bowl, cover the navy beans with 2 to 3 inches of cold water. Soak at room temperature for 6 hours. Drain and rinse the beans. Pour the water into the Instant Pot and add the beans. Lock the lid. Select Manual and cook at high pressure for 15 minutes. When the cook time is complete, naturally release the pressure. Remove the lid. Drain the beans and let cool for 5 minutes. In a small jar or bowl, combine the lemon juice, lemon zest, olive oil, salt, and pepper. Seal and shake or whisk thoroughly. In a medium bowl, combine the beans, onion, cucumber, carrot, and parsley. Add the dressing and toss to combine. Refrigerate for 1 hour and serve chilled.

Sweet Potato Slaw in Wonton Cups

MAKES 12 to 15 cups | PREP TIME: 15 minutes | MANUAL: Steam 2 minutes | RELEASE: None | TOTAL TIME: 23 minutes

Nonstick cooking spray
12 to 15 wonton or dumpling wrappers
1 cup water
2 cups sliced green cabbage (roughly 1 small head)
1 cup shredded sweet potato
½ sweet onion, sliced

2 tablespoons light soy sauce
1½ tablespoons freshly squeezed lime juice
1 tablespoon hoisin sauce
1½ teaspoons sesame oil
Zest of 1 lime
½ teaspoon ground ginger, plus more as needed
3 scallions, green and light green parts, sliced

Preheat the oven to 350°F. Lightly coat a muffin tin with the nonstick spray. Place 1 wonton wrapper in each well of the prepared tin, pressing down to create a cup shape. Bake for 5 to 6 minutes, or until the cups are crispy and lightly browned. Set aside to cool. Pour the water into the Instant Pot. Place the cabbage, sweet potato, and onion into a steamer basket and put the basket on a trivet. Lock the lid. Select Manual and steam for 2 minutes. While the veggies steam, in a medium bowl, stir together the soy sauce, lime juice, hoisin sauce, sesame oil, lime zest, and ginger. When the cook time is complete, carefully

remove the lid and stir in the veggies, making sure all are coated with the sauce. Taste and add more ginger, if desired. When ready to serve, fill the cups with the slaw and sprinkle with scallions. Enjoy warm or at room temperature.

German Vegetable Salad

SERVES 4 to 6 | PREP TIME: 8 minutes | SAUTÉ LOW: 7 minutes | MANUAL: 4 minutes high pressure | RELEASE: Quick | TOTAL TIME: 19 minutes

FOR THE DRESSING

½ cup apple cider vinegar
½ cup vegetable broth
2 teaspoons Dijon mustard

½ to 1 teaspoon salt
½ teaspoon garlic powder

FOR THE SALAD

1½ tablespoons extra-virgin olive oil
1 (8-ounce) package tempeh, chopped into bite-size pieces
1½ teaspoons smoked paprika
½ teaspoon salt, plus more as needed
¼ teaspoon garlic powder
1½ pounds red potatoes, chopped

2 cups Brussels sprouts, ends trimmed, outer leaves removed, rinsed with cold water, and halved
1 small red onion, sliced
2 bay leaves
¼ cup chopped fresh parsley
Freshly ground black pepper

TO MAKE THE DRESSING

In a medium bowl, whisk the vinegar, broth, mustard, salt, and garlic powder until well combined. Set it aside.

TO MAKE THE SALAD

Select Sauté Low. When the display reads HOT, heat the oil until it shimmers. Add the tempeh, paprika, salt, and garlic powder. Cook for 5 to 6 minutes, stirring occasionally. Transfer to a bowl and set aside. Select Cancel. Add the potatoes, Brussels sprouts, onion, and bay leaves. Pour the dressing over the vegetables. Lock the lid. Select Manual and cook at high pressure for 4 minutes. When the cook time is complete, quick-release the pressure. Remove the lid and remove and discard the bay leaves. Stir in the tempeh and parsley. Taste and season with more salt and pepper, as needed. There will be some liquid left in the bottom, which is perfect for spooning over the salad when it's served. If there's too much liquid for your taste, select Sauté Low again and cook for 2 to 3 minutes more.

Mexican-Style Street Corn Salad

SERVES 10 | PREP TIME: 5 minutes | SAUTÉ: 8 minutes | MANUAL: 2 minutes high pressure | RELEASE: Quick | TOTAL TIME: 20 minutes

2 tablespoons extra-virgin
   olive oil
1 cup frozen white and
   gold corn
1 cup frozen yellow corn
1 small onion, diced
1 jalapeño, seeded
   and diced
½ cup water
2 garlic cloves, minced
½ teaspoon paprika

½ teaspoon chili powder
½ teaspoon ground cumin
½ teaspoon salt
¼ teaspoon freshly ground
   black pepper
3 ounces cream cheese, at
   room temperature
Juice of 1 or 2 limes
½ cup cotija cheese or
   queso fresco

Select Sauté. When the Instant Pot is hot, pour in the oil. Add all the frozen corn and cook for 3 minutes while stirring. Add the onion and jalapeño and cook until the onion turns translucent, 3 to 5 minutes. Add the water, garlic, paprika, chili powder, cumin, salt, and black pepper. Select Cancel. Lock the lid. Select Manual and cook at high pressure for 2 minutes. When the cook time is complete, quick-release the pressure. Take off the lid and add the cream cheese, stirring until it's melted, then add the lime juice to taste. Spoon into bowls and top with the cotija cheese.

Barley Salad with Red Cabbage and Feta

SERVES 6 | PREP AND FINISHING: 20 minutes | MANUAL: 10 minutes high pressure | RELEASE: Natural for 15 minutes, then Quick | TOTAL TIME: 50 minutes

1 cup pearl barley
2½ cups vegetable broth
¼ cup plus 2 teaspoons
   extra-virgin olive
   oil, divided
2 teaspoons salt, divided,
   plus more as needed
2 cups shredded
   red cabbage

⅔ cup toasted walnut
   halves and pieces
2 tablespoons freshly
   squeezed lemon juice
½ cup crumbled
   feta cheese
1 tablespoon chopped
   fresh parsley

Pour the barley into the Instant Pot. Add the broth, 2 teaspoons of olive oil, and ½ teaspoon salt. Lock the lid. Select Manual and cook at high pressure for 10 minutes. When the cook time is complete, naturally release the pressure for 15 minutes, then quick-release any remaining pressure. Remove the lid. Taste the barley to make sure it's done; if not, place the lid back on, unlocked, and let the barley steam for a few more minutes. While the barley cooks, put the cabbage in a salad spinner or colander and sprinkle with the remaining 1½ teaspoons of salt. Toss to combine. Let the cabbage sit for 10 to 15 minutes, then rinse thoroughly and spin or pat dry. Combine the barley, cabbage, and walnuts in a large bowl. Drizzle with the remaining ¼ cup of olive oil and the lemon juice and toss gently to coat with the dressing. Taste and add more salt if necessary. Top with feta cheese and parsley and serve.

Potato and Snap Pea Salad

SERVES 6 | PREP TIME: 10 minutes | MANUAL: 4 minutes high pressure | RELEASE: Quick | TOTAL TIME: 25 minutes

1½ pounds (4 or 5) yellow
   potatoes, cut into
   1-inch chunks
2 cups water
¼ cup apple cider vinegar
¼ cup extra-virgin olive oil

1 shallot, finely chopped
1 teaspoon Dijon mustard
½ teaspoon salt
4 ounces sugar snap peas,
   halved lengthwise

Pour the water into the Instant Pot and insert the trivet or a steamer basket. Add the potatoes and lock the lid. Select Manual and cook at high pressure for 4 minutes. When the cook time is complete, quick-release the pressure. In a large bowl, whisk together the vinegar, oil, shallot, mustard, and salt. Remove the lid and transfer the cooked potatoes to the bowl of dressing. Stir in the peas. Serve this salad warm or chilled.

Potato Salad

SERVES 8 | PREP TIME: 10 minutes | MANUAL: 4 minutes high pressure | RELEASE: Quick | TOTAL TIME: 24 minutes, plus 1 hour to chill

8 medium russet potatoes,
   peeled and cut into
   1-inch cubes
4 cups water
2 tablespoons
   white vinegar
1 tablespoon salt
4 large eggs
1¼ cups mayonnaise

2 tablespoons sweet
   pickle relish
1 tablespoon
   prepared mustard
½ teaspoon freshly ground
   black pepper
1 small onion, diced
½ teaspoon paprika

Combine the potatoes, water, vinegar, and salt in the Instant Pot. Place the eggs on top of the potatoes. Fill a bowl with ice water. Lock the lid. Select Manual and cook at high pressure for 4 minutes. When the cook time is complete, quick-release the pressure. Remove the lid and place the eggs in the ice bath, then drain the potatoes. In a large bowl, mix the mayonnaise, relish, mustard, and pepper. Remove the eggs from the ice bath, peel, and chop them. Add the potatoes, eggs, and onion to the bowl with the dressing. Mix everything until well combined. Sprinkle with the paprika. Refrigerate the potato salad for at least 1 hour before serving.

GRAINS AND BEANS

White Rice

SERVES 6 to 8 | PREP TIME: 5 minutes | SAUTÉ:
3 minutes | MANUAL: 10 minutes high pressure |
RELEASE: Natural | TOTAL TIME: 28 minutes

2 cups chicken broth
½ medium white
  onion, peeled
2 garlic cloves, peeled

2 tablespoons butter
1 cup long-grain rice
Coarse salt
2 cilantro sprigs

In a blender, puree the broth, onion, and garlic until
smooth. Select Sauté and adjust to More for high. Heat
the butter in the pot until completely melted. Add the
rice and sauté for 2 to 3 minutes, or until just opaque.
Select Cancel. Pour in the onion puree. Season lightly
with salt and add the cilantro sprigs. Lock the lid. Select
Manual and cook at high pressure for 10 minutes. When
the cook time is complete, allow the pressure to release
naturally. Remove the lid. Remove the cilantro sprigs.
Fluff the rice with a fork. Serve.

Green Rice

SERVES 6 to 8 | PREP TIME: 5 minutes | SAUTÉ:
3 minutes | MANUAL: 10 minutes high pressure |
RELEASE: Natural | TOTAL TIME: 38 minutes

5 tomatillos,
  husks removed
6 to 8 cilantro sprigs
1 poblano pepper, seeded
  and stemmed
½ medium white onion, cut
  into large chunks

2 garlic cloves, peeled
2 cups chicken broth
2 tablespoons vegetable oil
1 cup long-grain rice
Coarse salt

In a blender, puree the tomatillos, cilantro, poblano,
onion, garlic, and chicken broth until smooth. Select
Sauté and adjust to More for high. Heat the vegetable
oil in the pot, add the rice, and sauté for 2 to 3 minutes,
or until just opaque. Select Cancel. Stir in the toma-
tillo puree. Season lightly with salt. Lock the lid. Select
Manual and cook at high pressure for 10 minutes.
When the cook time is complete, allow the pressure to
release naturally. Remove the lid. Fluff the rice with a
fork. Serve.

Garlic-Butter Rice

SERVES 4 to 6 | PREP TIME: 5 minutes | SAUTÉ LOW:
5 minutes | MANUAL: 27 minutes high pressure |
RELEASE: Natural for 10 minutes, then Quick | TOTAL
TIME: 47 minutes

2 tablespoons butter or
  extra-virgin olive oil
1 small sweet onion, diced

6 to 8 garlic cloves, minced
2½ cups vegetable broth

2 cups long-grain brown
  rice, rinsed and drained
1 teaspoon salt, plus more
  as needed
Pinch freshly ground
  black pepper, plus more
  as needed

1 teaspoon freshly
  squeezed lemon juice
1 tablespoon vegan butter
Fresh herbs, for garnish

Select Sauté Low. When the display reads HOT, heat
the oil until it shimmers. Add the onion. Sauté for 2 to
3 minutes, then turn off the Instant Pot. Add the garlic.
Cook for about 1 minute, stirring. Add the broth, rice,
salt, and pepper, stirring well. Lock the lid. Select
Manual and cook at high pressure for 27 minutes.
When the cook time is complete, let the pressure
release naturally for 10 minutes, then quick-release
any remaining pressure. Remove the lid and stir in
the lemon juice and butter. Taste and season with
more salt and pepper, as needed. Top with fresh herbs
and serve.

Coconut Rice

SERVES 6 | PREP TIME: 5 minutes | MANUAL: 5 minutes
high pressure | RELEASE: Natural for 10 minutes, then
Quick | TOTAL TIME: 27 minutes

1½ cups jasmine
  rice, rinsed
1 (14-ounce) can unsweet-
  ened coconut milk

½ cup chicken broth
¼ teaspoon salt

In the Instant Pot, combine the rice, coconut milk, broth,
and salt. Lock the lid. Select Manual and cook at high
pressure for 5 minutes. When the cook time is complete,
let the pressure release naturally for 15 minutes, then
quick-release any remaining pressure. Fluff the rice with
a fork and serve.

Mushroom Brown Rice

SERVES 4 | PREP TIME: 10 minutes | SAUTÉ: 10 minutes |
MANUAL: 25 minutes high pressure | RELEASE: Quick |
TOTAL TIME: 50 minutes

3 tablespoons unsalted
  butter, divided
1 small onion, diced
3 garlic cloves, minced
1 pound portobello mush-
  rooms, sliced
2 teaspoons Worcestershire
  sauce

½ teaspoon dried thyme
1¼ cups vegetable broth
1 cup long-grain brown rice
Salt
Freshly ground
  black pepper

Select Sauté. When the Instant Pot is hot, melt
1 tablespoon of butter. Stir in the onion and sauté until
it starts to soften, about 3 minutes. Add the garlic and
cook until fragrant, about 1 minute. Add the mushrooms, Worcestershire sauce, and thyme. Cook, stirring

occasionally, until the mushrooms reduce in size, 5 to 6 minutes. When the mushroom mixture is ready, stir in the broth and rice. Select Cancel. Lock the lid. Select Manual and cook at high pressure for 25 minutes. When the cook time is complete, quick-release any remaining pressure. Add the remaining 2 tablespoons of butter and stir to combine. Season with salt and pepper.

Turmeric Rice

SERVES 4 | PREP AND FINISHING: 5 minutes, plus 15 minutes to cool | SAUTÉ: 1 minute | RICE: 12 minutes low pressure | RELEASE: Natural | TOTAL TIME: 45 minutes

1 tablespoon butter
2 dried bay leaves
1 (½-inch) cinnamon stick
1 tablespoon cumin seeds
1 cup basmati rice, rinsed
1¼ cups water
½ teaspoon ground turmeric
½ teaspoon freshly ground black pepper
½ teaspoon salt

Select Sauté and melt the butter. Add the bay leaves, cinnamon stick, and cumin seeds and sauté for 45 to 60 seconds. Add the rice, water, turmeric, pepper, and salt and mix well. Select Cancel. Lock the lid. Select Rice and cook at low pressure for 12 minutes. When the cook time is complete, naturally release the pressure. Remove the lid. Let the rice cool for 15 minutes. Remove the bay leaves, fluff the rice with a fork, and serve hot.

Jollof Rice

SERVES 4 | PREP AND FINISHING: 10 minutes, plus 15 minutes to cool | SAUTÉ: 6 minutes | RICE: 12 minutes low pressure | RELEASE: Natural | TOTAL TIME: 50 minutes

1 tablespoon canola oil
2 dried bay leaves
1 onion, finely chopped
2 garlic cloves, finely chopped
1 teaspoon peeled and finely chopped fresh ginger
1 jalapeño pepper, seeded and finely chopped
2 tomatoes, coarsely chopped
2 tablespoons tomato paste
1½ teaspoons salt
1 teaspoon paprika
½ teaspoon curry powder
1 cup chopped carrots
1 cup cauliflower florets (7 or 8 florets)
1 cup short-grain white rice, rinsed
2 cups water

Select Sauté and pour in the oil. Once hot, add the bay leaves, onion, garlic, ginger, and jalapeños and sauté for 5 minutes or until the onion is translucent. Stir in the tomatoes, tomato paste, and salt. Loosely place the lid on top and cook for 3 minutes or until the tomatoes are soft. Mix in the paprika and curry powder, then stir in the carrots and cauliflower. Add the rice and water and mix well. Select Cancel. Lock the lid. Select Rice and cook at low pressure for 12 minutes. When the cook time is complete, naturally release the pressure. Remove the lid. Let the rice cool for 15 minutes. Remove the bay leaves. Using a fork, gently fluff the rice. Serve hot.

Classic Mexican-Style Rice

SERVES 6 to 8 | PREP TIME: 5 minutes | SAUTÉ: 7 minutes | MANUAL: 10 minutes high pressure | RELEASE: Quick | TOTAL TIME: 25 minutes

3 Roma tomatoes
2 cups chicken broth
½ medium white onion
2 garlic cloves
2 tablespoons vegetable oil
1 cup long-grain rice
2 cilantro sprigs

In a blender, puree the tomatoes, broth, onion, and garlic until smooth. Set it aside. Select Sauté and adjust to More for high. Heat the oil in the pot, add the rice, and cook for 5 to 7 minutes, or until golden brown. Select Cancel. Carefully pour in the tomato puree and stir gently to combine. Add the cilantro. Lock the lid. Select Manual and cook at high pressure for 10 minutes. When the cook time is complete, quick-release the pressure. Remove the lid. Remove the cilantro sprigs. Fluff the rice with a fork. Serve.

Yellow Rice with Peas and Corn

SERVES 6 | PREP AND FINISHING: 10 minutes | SAUTÉ: 5 minutes | MANUAL: 4 minutes high pressure | RELEASE: Natural for 10 minutes, then Quick | TOTAL TIME: 39 minutes

1 tablespoon extra-virgin olive oil
1 medium yellow onion, diced
2 garlic cloves, minced
½ teaspoon ground turmeric
½ teaspoon sea salt
½ teaspoon freshly ground black pepper
2¼ cups vegetable broth
2 cups basmati rice, rinsed
1 cup frozen peas
1 cup frozen corn kernels

Select Sauté and pour the olive oil into the Instant Pot. Once the oil is hot, add the onion, garlic, turmeric, salt, and pepper and sauté for 3 minutes, stirring occasionally. Select Cancel and pour the broth into the pot. Using a wooden spoon, scrape up any browned bits stuck to the bottom of the pot. Add the rice, peas, and corn and stir to combine. Lock the lid. Select Manual and cook at high pressure for 4 minutes. When the cook time is complete, naturally release the pressure for 10 minutes, then quick-release any remaining pressure. Remove the lid. Serve immediately.

Rice Pilaf

SERVES 4 | PREP TIME: 10 minutes | SAUTÉ: 7 minutes | MANUAL: 3 minutes | RELEASE: Natural for 15 minutes | TOTAL TIME: 40 minutes

¼ cup (½ stick) unsalted butter
⅓ cup vermicelli, broken into ½-inch pieces
1 cup long-grain white rice
1½ cups chicken broth
1 teaspoon garlic powder
1 teaspoon dried parsley
¾ teaspoon salt
½ teaspoon onion powder
¼ teaspoon paprika
¼ teaspoon freshly ground black pepper

Select Sauté. When the Instant Pot is hot, melt the butter. Stir in the vermicelli and cook until browned, 2 to 3 minutes, then add the rice. Cook until the rice starts to toast, another 3 to 4 minutes. Add the chicken broth, garlic powder, parsley, salt, onion powder, paprika, and pepper to the rice mixture. Stir well, scraping up any browned bits from the bottom of the pot. Lock the lid. Select Manual and cook at high pressure for 3 minutes. When the cook time is complete, let the pressure release naturally for 15 minutes, then quick-release any remaining pressure. Open the lid and give everything a good stir.

Spanish Rice

SERVES 4 | PREP TIME: 5 minutes | SAUTÉ: 4 minutes | MANUAL: 5 minutes high pressure | RELEASE: Natural for 10 minutes, then Quick | TOTAL TIME: 30 minutes

1 tablespoon unsalted butter
1 small red bell pepper, seeded and chopped
1 small onion, chopped
3 garlic cloves, minced
1½ cups water
1 cup long-grain white rice
2 tablespoons tomato paste
1 tablespoon ground cumin
1 teaspoon paprika
½ jalapeño pepper, seeded and diced
Salt
Freshly ground black pepper

Select Sauté. When the Instant Pot is hot, melt the butter. Stir in the bell pepper and onion and sauté until they start to soften, about 3 minutes. Add the garlic and cook until fragrant, about 1 minute. Turn off the Instant Pot and add the water, rice, tomato paste, cumin, paprika, and jalapeño. Stir to combine. Lock the lid. Select Manual and cook at high pressure for 5 minutes. When the cook time is complete, let the pressure release naturally for 10 minutes, then quick-release any remaining pressure. Fluff the rice with a fork, season with salt and pepper, and serve.

Cilantro-Lime Brown Rice

SERVES 4 | PREP TIME: 5 minutes | MANUAL: 15 minutes high pressure | RELEASE: Natural for 20 minutes, then quick | TOTAL TIME: 45 minutes

1¼ cups water
1 cup long-grain brown rice, rinsed
Zest and juice of 1 lime
¼ cup freshly chopped cilantro
1 teaspoon kosher salt

In the Instant Pot, combine the water and rice. Stir well. Lock the lid. Select Manual and cook at high pressure for 15 minutes. When the cook time is complete, let the pressure release naturally for 20 minutes, then quick-release any remaining pressure. Remove the lid and stir in the lime zest, lime juice, cilantro, and salt before serving.

"Dirty" Rice

SERVES 4 | PREP TIME: 10 minutes | SAUTÉ: 12 minutes | MANUAL: 6 minutes high pressure | RELEASE: Natural for 10 minutes, then Quick | TOTAL TIME: 43 minutes

1 pound 90 percent lean ground beef
½ cup chopped celery
1 small onion, chopped
½ cup chopped green bell pepper
1 cup beef broth
1 tablespoon Creole seasoning
1 teaspoon dried thyme
1 teaspoon dried oregano
Salt
Freshly ground black pepper
1 cup long-grain white rice

Select Sauté. When the Instant Pot is hot, cook the beef until browned, 5 to 7 minutes, breaking up the beef into smaller pieces as it cooks. Add the celery, onion, and bell pepper and cook until softened, 3 to 5 minutes. Select Cancel. Add the beef broth, Creole seasoning, thyme, and oregano and season with salt and pepper, stirring to scrape up all the browned bits from the bottom of the pot. Add the rice and press down with the back of a spoon to submerge, but do not stir. Lock the lid. Select Manual and cook at high pressure for 6 minutes. When the cook time is complete, let the pressure release naturally for 10 minutes, then quick-release any remaining pressure. Fluff the rice with a fork and serve.

Forbidden Black Rice with Black Beans

SERVES 4 to 6 | PREP TIME: 5 minutes | MANUAL: 30 minutes high pressure | RELEASE: Natural for 10 minutes, then Quick | TOTAL TIME: 50 minutes

4 cups water
1 cup black rice, rinsed
1 cup dried black beans, rinsed and sorted
½ cup diced onion
1 bay leaf
1 tablespoon maple syrup (optional)

In the Instant Pot, combine the water, rice, beans, onion, and bay leaf and stir well. Lock the lid. Select Manual and cook at high pressure for 30 minutes. When the cook time is complete, let the pressure release naturally for 10 minutes, then quick-release any remaining pressure.

Remove the lid. Remove and discard the bay leaf. Stir in the maple syrup (if using). Serve immediately.

Mango Sticky Brown Rice

SERVES 8 | PREP AND FINISHING: 10 minutes | MANUAL: 22 minutes high pressure | RELEASE: Natural for 10 minutes, then Quick | TOTAL TIME: 52 minutes

2 cups long-grain brown rice (not rinsed)
1 (13½-ounce) can light coconut milk
1 cup water
¼ teaspoon ground cardamom
½ teaspoon ground cinnamon
2 cups frozen mango chunks
2 tablespoons packed light brown sugar

In the Instant Pot, combine the rice, coconut milk, water, cardamom, cinnamon, and mango. Lock the lid. Select Manual and cook at high pressure for 22 minutes. When the cook time is complete, naturally release the pressure for 10 minutes, then quick-release any remaining pressure. Remove the lid. Stir in the brown sugar. Serve immediately.

Thai-Style Pineapple Fried Rice

SERVES 4 | PREP AND FINISHING: 10 minutes, plus 15 minutes to cool | SAUTÉ: 5 minutes | MANUAL: 3 minutes high pressure | RELEASE: Natural for 3 minutes, then Quick | TOTAL TIME: 45 minutes

1 tablespoon canola oil
3 tablespoons cashews
¼ cup finely chopped onion
¼ cup finely chopped scallions, white parts only
2 green Thai chiles, finely chopped
1 cup canned pineapple chunks
¼ cup roughly chopped fresh basil leaves, divided
½ teaspoon curry powder
¼ teaspoon ground turmeric
2 teaspoons soy sauce
1 teaspoon salt
1 cup steamed short-grain white rice, preferably a day old
1¼ cups water

Select Sauté and pour in the oil. Once hot, add the cashews and stir for 1 minute. Add the onion, scallions, and chiles and sauté for 3 to 4 minutes, until the onion is translucent. Mix in the pineapple, 2 tablespoons of basil, and the curry powder, turmeric, soy sauce, and salt. Add the rice and water and mix again. Select Cancel. Lock the lid. Select Manual and cook at high pressure for 3 minutes. When the cook time is complete, naturally release the pressure for 3 minutes, then quick-release any remaining pressure. Remove the lid. Let the rice cool for 15 minutes. Using a fork, fluff the rice. Serve hot.

Savory Rice Porridge

SERVES 8 | PREP AND FINISHING: 10 minutes | SAUTÉ: 4 minutes | PORRIDGE: 20 minutes high pressure | RELEASE: Natural | TOTAL TIME: 45 minutes

1 tablespoon sesame oil
½ cup finely chopped scallions, white and green parts, divided
1 cup halved white mushrooms
1 teaspoon salt
1 teaspoon freshly ground black pepper
3 tablespoons soy sauce, divided
1 cup sticky rice, rinsed
5 cups water

Select Sauté and pour in the oil. Once hot, add ¼ cup of scallions and the mushrooms, salt, and pepper. Sauté for 3 to 4 minutes or until the mushrooms start to brown. Stir in 1 teaspoon of soy sauce, then stir in the rice and water. Select Cancel. Lock the lid. Select Porridge and cook at high pressure for 20 minutes. When the cook time is complete, naturally release the pressure. Remove the lid. Using a potato masher or the back of a ladle, mash the rice until mushy. Stir in the remaining ¼ cup of scallions and 8 teaspoons of soy sauce. Serve hot.

Wild Rice with Chorizo

SERVES 4 to 6 | PREP TIME: 5 minutes | SAUTÉ: 10 minutes | MANUAL: 25 minutes high pressure | RELEASE: Natural for 10 minutes, then Quick | TOTAL TIME: 1 hour

1 pound pork chorizo
2 cups wild rice
½ red onion, diced
1 celery stalk, minced
1 tablespoon minced fresh rosemary
1 teaspoon minced garlic
1 teaspoon salt
4 cups chicken broth
½ cup dried cherries
¼ cup minced fresh parsley

Select Sauté. Put the chorizo in the Instant Pot and cook, breaking it up with a spoon. It will release some fat and begin to brown slightly. Sauté for 5 minutes. Add the wild rice, onion, celery, rosemary, garlic, and salt to the pot. Continue to sauté for 1 minute, until the rice smells toasted. Add the chicken broth and cherries. Stir to combine. Select Cancel. Lock the lid. Select Manual and cook at high pressure for 25 minutes. When the cook time is complete, let the pressure naturally release for 10 minutes, then quick-release any remaining pressure. Add the parsley and serve immediately.

Green Pea and Parmesan Risotto

SERVES 6 | PREP TIME: 10 minutes | MANUAL: 5 minutes high pressure | RELEASE: Natural for 5 minutes, then Quick | TOTAL TIME: 35 minutes

2 tablespoons extra-virgin olive oil
1 medium yellow onion, diced

2 garlic cloves, minced

4 cups vegetable broth

2 cups short-grain Arborio white rice, unrinsed

1 (16-ounce) bag frozen green peas

1 cup grated Parmesan cheese

Select Sauté. Heat the oil in the Instant Pot until it shimmers. Add the onion and garlic and cook for 3 minutes, or until they start to soften. Select Cancel and pour in the broth. Using a wooden spoon, scrape up any browned bits stuck to the bottom of the pot. Add the rice and peas and stir to combine. Lock the lid. Select Manual and cook at high pressure for 5 minutes. When the cook time is complete, allow the pressure to naturally release for 5 minutes, then quick-release any remaining pressure. Remove the lid and stir in the Parmesan. Serve immediately.

Butternut Squash Risotto

SERVES 4 | PREP TIME: 10 minutes | SAUTÉ: 3 minutes | MANUAL: 15 minutes high pressure | RELEASE: Natural for 10 minutes, then Quick | TOTAL TIME: 45 minutes

¼ cup extra-virgin olive oil

1 yellow onion, finely diced

2 garlic cloves, minced

½ ounce (about 10) whole fresh sage leaves

1½ cups short-grain brown rice

4 cups vegetable broth

1 small butternut squash, peeled and diced (about 2½ cups)

½ teaspoon salt

¼ teaspoon freshly ground black pepper

3 cups fresh arugula

Select Sauté on the Instant Pot and pour in the olive oil. When the oil is hot, add the onion, garlic, and sage. Cook for 3 minutes, stirring frequently, until softened. Select Cancel. Stir in the rice, then add the broth, squash, salt, and pepper. Lock the lid. Select Manual and cook at high pressure for 15 minutes. When the cook time is complete, let the pressure release naturally for 10 minutes, then quick-release any remaining pressure. Remove the lid and stir in the arugula before serving.

Mushroom and Leek Risotto

SERVES 4 to 6 | PREP TIME: 7 minutes | SAUTÉ LOW: 5 minutes | MANUAL: 8 minutes high pressure | RELEASE: Quick | TOTAL TIME: 20 minutes

¼ cup vegan butter, divided

1 leek, white and lightest green parts only, halved and sliced, rinsed well

12 ounces portobello mushrooms, sliced

2 garlic cloves, minced

1 cup Arborio rice, rinsed and drained

2¾ cups vegetable broth

1 teaspoon dried thyme

½ teaspoon salt, plus more as needed

Juice of ½ lemon

Freshly ground black pepper

Chopped fresh parsley, for garnish

Select Sauté Low. When the display reads HOT, melt 2 tablespoons of butter. Add the leek and mushrooms. Sauté for about 2 minutes, stirring frequently. Add the garlic. Cook for about 30 seconds, stirring—turn off the Instant Pot if it starts to burn. Add the rice and toast it for 1 minute. Turn off the Instant Pot. Stir in the broth, thyme, and salt. Lock the lid. Select Manual and cook at high pressure for 8 minutes. When the cook time is complete, quick-release the pressure. Remove the lid and stir in the lemon juice and remaining 2 tablespoons of vegan butter. Taste and season with more salt and pepper, as needed. Garnish with fresh parsley.

Creamy Veggie Risotto

SERVES 4 to 6 | PREP TIME: 4 minutes | SAUTÉ LOW: 4 minutes | MANUAL: 8 minutes high pressure | RELEASE: Quick | TOTAL TIME: 16 minutes

2 tablespoons extra-virgin olive oil

½ sweet onion, diced

1 garlic clove, minced

1 bunch asparagus tips, cut into 1-inch pieces

2¾ cups vegetable broth

1 cup Arborio rice, rinsed and drained

1 cup sugar snap peas, rinsed, tough ends removed

1 teaspoon dried thyme

½ teaspoon salt, plus more as needed

¼ teaspoon freshly ground black pepper

Pinch red pepper flakes

2 tablespoons vegan butter

Juice of ½ lemon

1½ to 2 cups fresh baby spinach, torn

Select Sauté Low. When the display reads HOT, pour in the oil and heat until it shimmers. Add the onion. Cook for about 2 minutes, stirring frequently. Turn off the Instant Pot and stir in the garlic and asparagus, cooking for 30 seconds. Add the broth, rice, peas, thyme, salt, black pepper, and red pepper flakes, stirring well. Lock the lid. Select Manual and cook at high pressure for 8 minutes. When the cook time is complete, quick-release the pressure. Remove the lid and stir in the butter, lemon juice, and spinach, being gentle so as not to tear the snap peas. Taste and season with more salt, as needed.

Farro Risotto

SERVES 4 to 6 | PREP TIME: 5 minutes | SAUTÉ: 3 to 5 minutes | MANUAL: 10 minutes high pressure | RELEASE: Natural for 10 minutes, then Quick | TOTAL TIME: 45 minutes

1 medium onion, diced

4 garlic cloves, minced

1½ cups no-salt-added vegetable broth

1 cup pearled farro

2 thyme sprigs or 1 teaspoon dried thyme

Freshly ground black pepper

Salt (optional)

Select Sauté. Sauté the onion for 3 to 5 minutes, until translucent, adding water as needed to prevent sticking. Add the garlic and stir for 30 seconds, until fragrant. Select Cancel. Add the broth, farro, and thyme. Stir well to combine, scraping any browned bits off the bottom of the pot. Lock the lid. Select Manual and cook at high pressure for 10 minutes. When the cook time is complete, let the pressure release naturally for 10 minutes, then quick-release any remaining pressure. Remove the lid. Remove the thyme stems. Season to taste with pepper and salt (if using). Serve immediately.

Farro and Spinach Salad

SERVES 4 | PREP AND FINISHING: 10 minutes | MANUAL: 3 minutes high pressure | RELEASE: Natural for 5 minutes, then Quick | SAUTÉ: 7 minutes | TOTAL TIME: 35 minutes

FOR THE FARRO

1 cup water	½ cup farro

FOR THE SPINACH

2 tablespoons butter	1 teaspoon red pepper flakes
4 garlic cloves, finely chopped	1 teaspoon kosher salt
4 cups baby spinach, roughly chopped	

Pour the water into the Instant Pot and add the farro. Lock the lid. Select Manual and cook at high pressure for 3 minutes. When the cook time is complete, naturally release the pressure for 5 minutes, then quick-release any remaining pressure. Remove the lid. Drain the farro. Select Sauté and melt the butter. Add the garlic and sauté for 30 seconds. Add the spinach, red pepper flakes, and salt. Cook until the spinach wilts, about 5 minutes. Add the farro and sauté for 1 minute. Serve hot.

Couscous Pilaf

SERVES 4 | PREP AND FINISHING: 5 minutes, plus 10 minutes to cool | SAUTÉ: 7 minutes | MANUAL: 3 minutes high pressure | RELEASE: Natural for 5 minutes, then Quick | TOTAL TIME: 35 minutes

1 tablespoon butter	¼ cup frozen peas, thawed to room temperature
1 dried bay leaf	
3 cardamom seeds	¼ cup frozen corn, thawed to room temperature
3 whole cloves	
1 (1-inch) cinnamon stick	1 cup pearl couscous, rinsed and drained
1 onion, thinly sliced	
1 green Thai chile, split lengthwise	1 cup full-fat coconut milk
	1 teaspoon salt

Select Sauté and melt the butter. Add the bay leaf, cardamom, cloves, and cinnamon stick and sauté for 30 seconds. Add the onions and chile and cook for 4 to

5 minutes or until the onion is translucent. Add the peas and corn and cook for another minute. Stir in the couscous, coconut milk, and salt until well combined. Select Cancel. Lock the lid. Select Manual and cook at high pressure for 3 minutes. When the cook time is complete, naturally release the pressure for 5 minutes, then quick-release any remaining pressure. Remove the lid. Let the couscous cool for 10 minutes, then remove the bay leaf. Fluff the couscous with a fork and serve hot.

Lemon Pepper Quinoa

SERVES 4 to 6 | PREP TIME: 2 minutes | MANUAL: 8 minutes high pressure | RELEASE: Natural release for 10 minutes, then Quick | TOTAL TIME: 20 minutes

1½ cups quinoa, rinsed	¼ teaspoon garlic powder
1½ cups water	¼ teaspoon dried basil
½ to 1 teaspoon salt, plus more as needed	1 tablespoon vegan butter
	Juice and zest of 1 lemon
½ teaspoon freshly ground black pepper, plus more as needed	

In the Instant Pot, combine the quinoa, water, salt, pepper, garlic powder, and basil. Lock the lid. Select Manual and cook at high pressure for 8 minutes. When the cook time is complete, let the pressure release naturally for 10 minutes, then quick-release any remaining pressure. Remove the lid and stir in the butter, lemon juice, and lemon zest. Taste and season with more salt and pepper, as needed.

Vegetable Quinoa Tabbouleh

SERVES 6 | PREP AND FINISHING: 10 minutes | MANUAL: 20 minutes high pressure | RELEASE: Quick | TOTAL TIME: 40 minutes

3½ cups water	4 scallions, white and light green parts only, chopped
2 cups quinoa, rinsed	
1 tablespoon extra-virgin olive oil	¼ cup chopped fresh flat-leaf parsley
Juice of 1 lemon	
1 English cucumber, peeled and diced	2 tablespoons chopped fresh mint
2 medium tomatoes, diced	⅓ cup pine nuts, toasted

In the Instant Pot, combine the water, quinoa, olive oil, and lemon juice. Lock the lid. Select Manual and cook at high pressure for 20 minutes. When the cook time is complete, quick-release the pressure. Remove the lid. Using a fork, fluff the quinoa, then stir in the cucumber, tomatoes, scallions, parsley, mint, and pine nuts. Serve immediately.

Enchilada Quinoa

SERVES 4 | PREP TIME: 5 minutes | MANUAL: 1 minute | RELEASE: Natural for 15 minutes, then Quick | TOTAL TIME: 29 minutes

2 cups water
1 cup uncooked quinoa, rinsed well
½ small onion, diced
1 (15-ounce) can black beans, drained and rinsed
1 (10-ounce) bag frozen corn

1 (4¼-ounce) can mild green chiles
1 cup chopped fresh tomatoes
1 teaspoon chili powder
½ teaspoon ground cumin
¼ teaspoon salt
1 cup enchilada sauce
1 cup shredded Monterey Jack cheese

In the Instant Pot, combine the water, quinoa, onion, beans, corn, chiles, tomatoes, chili powder, cumin, and salt and stir well. Lock the lid. Select Manual and cook at high pressure for 1 minute. When the cook time is complete, let the pressure release naturally for 15 minutes, then quick-release any remaining pressure. Stir in the enchilada sauce and cheese, then serve.

Polenta

SERVES 6 | PREP AND FINISHING: 5 minutes | MANUAL: 15 minutes high pressure | RELEASE: Natural for 10 minutes, then Quick | TOTAL TIME: 35 minutes

2 cups milk
2 cups chicken broth
1 cup polenta or grits (not instant or quick-cooking)
½ teaspoon kosher salt, plus more as needed

1 cup water
½ cup grated Parmesan or similar cheese
2 tablespoons unsalted butter

In a large bowl, combine the milk, broth, polenta, and salt. Pour the water into the Instant Pot. Place a trivet with handles in the pot and place the bowl on top. If your trivet doesn't have handles, use a foil sling to make removing the bowl easier. Lock the lid. Select Manual and cook at high pressure for 15 minutes. When the cook time is complete, naturally release the pressure for 10 minutes, then quick-release any remaining pressure. Remove the lid. Carefully remove the bowl from the Instant Pot. Add the Parmesan cheese and butter and stir to melt and incorporate. Taste and add more salt if necessary. Serve immediately.

Polenta and Kale

SERVES 4 to 6 | PREP TIME: 5 minutes | SAUTÉ LOW: 3 minutes | MANUAL: 20 minutes high pressure | RELEASE: Natural release for 15 minutes, then Quick | TOTAL TIME: 43 minutes

1 tablespoon extra-virgin olive oil
2 bunches kale, stemmed, leaves chopped
3 or 4 garlic cloves, minced
1 teaspoon salt, divided, plus more as needed
1 quart vegetable broth

1 cup polenta
2 tablespoons nutritional yeast
2 to 3 tablespoons vegan butter
Freshly ground black pepper

Select Sauté Low. When the display reads HOT, pour in the oil and heat until it shimmers. Add the kale, garlic, and ½ teaspoon of salt. Cook for about 2 minutes, stirring frequently so nothing burns, until the kale is soft and the garlic is fragrant. (You can always turn off the Instant Pot if it gets too hot.) Transfer the garlicky kale to a bowl and set aside. Select Cancel. In the Instant Pot, combine the broth, polenta, and remaining ½ teaspoon of salt. Lock the lid. Select Manual and cook at high pressure for 20 minutes. When the cook time is complete, let the pressure release naturally for 15 minutes, then quick-release any remaining pressure. Remove the lid and stir well (some liquid may have accumulated on top of the polenta). Add the nutritional yeast and butter along with salt and pepper, as needed. Serve in bowls topped with the kale.

Cheesy Herbed Polenta

SERVES 4 to 6 | PREP TIME: 5 minutes | MANUAL: 10 minutes high pressure | RELEASE: Natural for 5 minutes, then Quick | TOTAL TIME: 30 minutes

8 cups chicken broth or water
2 cups polenta
2 ounces grated Parmesan cheese (about 1 cup)

2 tablespoons melted unsalted butter
1 tablespoon Italian herb blend
1½ teaspoons salt

In the Instant Pot, combine the broth, polenta, Parmesan cheese, butter, Italian herb blend, and salt. Lock the lid. Select Manual and cook at high pressure for 10 minutes. When the cook time is complete, naturally release the pressure for 5 minutes, then quick-release any remaining pressure. Serve warm.

Basic Beans

MAKES 6 cups | PREP TIME: 5 minutes | MANUAL: 35 minutes high pressure | RELEASE: Natural | TOTAL TIME: 1 hour 10 minutes

4 cups low-sodium vegetable broth or water
1 pound dried beans
2 bay leaves

2 teaspoons extra-virgin olive oil
½ teaspoon kosher salt

In the Instant Pot, combine the beans, broth, bay leaves, olive oil, and salt. Lock the lid. Select Manual and cook at high pressure for 35 minutes. When the cook time is complete, let the pressure release naturally for 15 minutes, then quick-release any remaining pressure. Remove the lid and discard the bay leaves.

Baked Beans

SERVES 12 | PREP TIME: 10 minutes, plus overnight soaking time | SAUTÉ: 13 minutes | MANUAL: 60 minutes high pressure | RELEASE: Natural for 20 minutes, then Quick | TOTAL TIME: 1 hour 53 minutes, plus 9 to 10 hours soaking time

1 pound dried navy beans, rinsed and drained
1 pound thick-cut bacon, chopped
1 cup diced yellow onion
¼ cup apple cider vinegar
4 cups chicken broth
½ cup packed dark brown sugar
⅓ cup ketchup
1 tablespoon Worcestershire sauce
2 teaspoons mustard powder
¼ teaspoon freshly ground black pepper
½ cup water
3 tablespoons cornstarch
1 teaspoon sea salt

In a large bowl, cover the beans with 2 to 3 inches of cold water. Soak at room temperature for 9 to 10 hours or overnight. Drain and rinse the beans. Select Sauté and cook the bacon until crispy, about 5 minutes. Add the onion and vinegar. Cook until the onions are translucent and the vinegar is almost evaporated, 3 to 4 minutes. Scrape all the browned bits from the bottom of the pot. Select Cancel. Add the drained beans, chicken broth, brown sugar, ketchup, Worcestershire sauce, mustard powder, and pepper and mix well to combine. Lock the lid. Select Manual and cook at high pressure for 60 minutes. When the cook time is complete, let the pressure release naturally for 20 minutes. In a small bowl, combine the water and cornstarch to make a slurry, mixing until smooth. Select Sauté and add the cornstarch slurry and salt. Mix well and cook for 3 to 4 minutes, stirring frequently while the mixture thickens. Turn off the pressure cooker and let the beans sit for 10 minutes before serving.

Cowboy Pinto Beans

SERVES 4 | PREP AND FINISHING: 15 minutes, plus 9 to 10 hours soaking time | MANUAL: 15 minutes high pressure | RELEASE: Natural for 10 minutes, then Quick | TOTAL TIME: 45 minutes, plus 9 to 10 hours soaking time

1 quart water
1 tablespoon plus ½ teaspoon salt, divided
8 ounces dried pinto beans
2 or 3 bacon slices, chopped
1 large onion, chopped (about 1½ cups)
2 garlic cloves, minced
2 cups chicken broth
¼ cup ancho chile sauce
½ teaspoon pureed canned chipotle (optional)
1 small tomato, seeded and diced
1 tablespoon chopped fresh cilantro

In a large bowl, dissolve 1 tablespoon of salt in the water. Add the pinto beans and soak at room temperature for 8 to 24 hours. Drain and rinse the beans. Select Sauté and adjust to Normal for medium heat. Cook the bacon until most of the fat has rendered and the bacon is crisp, about 6 minutes. Use a slotted spoon to remove the bacon and drain on paper towels, leaving the rendered fat in the pot. Add the onion and garlic and sprinkle with ¼ teaspoon of salt. Cook, stirring, until the onion pieces separate and soften, 2 to 3 minutes. Select Cancel. Add the drained pinto beans, the remaining ¼ teaspoon of salt, the broth, ancho chile sauce, and chipotle puree (if using). Lock the lid. Select Manual and cook at high pressure for 15 minutes. When the cook time is complete, let the pressure release naturally for 10 minutes, then quick-release any remaining pressure. Remove the lid. Stir in the tomato and cilantro. Taste the beans and adjust the seasoning if needed. If the beans are too soupy, select Sauté and adjust to Normal for medium heat. Simmer until the beans thicken. Transfer to a serving bowl and serve.

Classic Black Beans

SERVES 4 | PREP TIME: 5 minutes | SAUTÉ: 5 minutes | MANUAL: 40 minutes high pressure | RELEASE: Natural for 15 minutes, then Quick | TOTAL TIME: 1 hour 15 minutes

2 tablespoons extra-virgin olive oil
1 yellow onion, diced
1 green bell pepper, seeded and diced
1 jalapeño pepper, seeded and minced
2 garlic cloves, minced
1 teaspoon dried oregano
1 teaspoon ground cumin
1½ cups water
1 cup dried black beans
1 tablespoon apple cider vinegar
½ teaspoon salt

Select Sauté on the Instant Pot and pour in the oil. When the oil is hot, add the onion, bell pepper, jalapeño, and garlic. Cook, stirring frequently, for 3 to 5 minutes, until softened. Select Cancel. Stir in the oregano and cumin, then add the water, beans, vinegar, and salt. Lock the lid. Select Manual and cook at high pressure for 40 minutes. When the cook time is complete, let the pressure release naturally for 15 minutes, then quick-release any remaining pressure. Remove the lid and serve.

Refried Black Beans

SERVES 4 | PREP AND FINISHING: 15 minutes | MANUAL: 30 minutes high pressure | SAUTÉ: 5 minutes | RELEASE: Natural for 15 minutes, then Quick | TOTAL TIME: 1 hour 5 minutes

8 ounces dried black beans
1 quart water
1 teaspoon kosher salt
1 bacon slice
1 medium onion, peeled and halved, divided
¼ cup lard, bacon fat, or extra-virgin olive oil
2 garlic cloves, lightly smashed
½ teaspoon pureed canned chipotle
¼ cup canned diced green chiles, drained

Put the beans in the Instant Pot and add the water, salt, bacon, and half of the onion. Lock the lid. Select Manual and cook at high pressure for 30 minutes. When the cook time is complete, let the pressure release naturally for 15 minutes, then quick-release any remaining pressure. Remove the lid. The beans should be starting to fall apart. Place a strainer or colander over a bowl and pour the beans into the strainer, reserving the cooking liquid in the bowl. Remove the onion and bacon (they may have partially dissolved) and discard. Wipe out the pot. Quarter the remaining onion half. Select Sauté and adjust to More for high heat. Heat the lard in the pot. When the fat just starts to smoke, add the onion quarters and garlic and cook, turning occasionally, until the vegetables are quite browned, 4 to 5 minutes. Remove and discard them, leaving the fat in the pot. Add the beans and ½ cup of the reserved bean liquid and mash the beans with a potato masher or the back of a fork. Add more liquid if necessary to make a smooth puree. Stir in the chipotle puree and green chiles. Transfer to a serving bowl and serve.

Drunken Beans

SERVES 8 | PREP TIME: 10 minutes | SAUTÉ: 12 minutes | MANUAL: 22 minutes high pressure | RELEASE: Natural for 20 minutes, then Quick | TOTAL TIME: 1 hour 19 minutes

¾ pound bacon, diced
1 large onion, diced
2 medium green bell peppers, seeded and diced
5 garlic cloves, minced
1 jalapeño pepper, seeded and diced
1 tablespoon chili powder
1 tablespoon ground cumin
1 teaspoon dried oregano
1 teaspoon salt
6 cups chicken broth
1 pound dried pinto beans
1 (12-ounce) Mexican lager beer
2 bay leaves
1 bunch cilantro, tied together for easy removal
1 (14-ounce) can diced tomatoes
6 cups fully cooked white rice or 6 servings cornbread (optional)

Select Sauté. When the Instant Pot is hot, cook the bacon, stirring occasionally, until crisp, 5 to 7 minutes. Remove the bacon and set it aside. Discard all but 2 tablespoons of the bacon grease. Add the onion and bell peppers and cook until the onion is translucent, 4 to 5 minutes. Then add the garlic and jalapeño and cook until fragrant, about 1 minute. Add the chili powder, cumin, oregano, and salt and stir well. Select

Cancel. Then stir in the broth, beans, beer, bay leaves, and cilantro. Return three-fourths of the cooked bacon to the pot. Add the tomatoes with their juices; do not stir. Lock the lid. Select Manual and cook at high pressure for 22 minutes. When the cook time is complete, let the pressure release naturally for 20 minutes, then quick-release any remaining pressure. Open the lid and discard the bay leaves and cilantro. Serve the beans over rice or cornbread.

Hoppin' John

SERVES 6 | PREP TIME: 10 minutes | SAUTÉ: 5 minutes | MANUAL: 12 minutes high pressure | RELEASE: Natural for 10 minutes, then Quick | TOTAL TIME: 44 minutes

2 tablespoons extra-virgin olive oil
1 medium yellow onion, diced
1 medium carrot, peeled and diced
2 celery stalks, diced
1 small jalapeño, seeded and diced
3 garlic cloves, minced
1 tablespoon apple cider vinegar
6 thyme sprigs
1 bay leaf
2½ cups chicken or vegetable broth
28 ounces frozen cooked black-eyed peas
1 cup long-grain white rice
2 teaspoons sea salt

Select Sauté. When hot, pour in the oil and stir in the onion, carrot, celery, and jalapeño. Cook for about 4 minutes, stirring frequently, until fragrant. Add the garlic, vinegar, thyme, and bay leaf and cook for 1 minute. Select Cancel. Add the broth, peas, rice, and salt. Stir well. Lock the lid. Select Manual and cook at high pressure for 12 minutes. When the cook time is complete, let the pressure release naturally for 10 minutes, then quick-release any remaining pressure. Fluff the rice. Remove the thyme sprigs and bay leaf before serving.

White Beans with Rosemary and Garlic

SERVES 4 to 6 | PREP TIME: 5 minutes | MANUAL: 32 minutes high pressure | RELEASE: Natural for 15 minutes, then Quick | TOTAL TIME: 60 minutes

2 cups water
1½ cups vegetable broth
1 cup dried great northern beans, rinsed and sorted
4 garlic cloves, minced, divided
2 rosemary sprigs or 2 teaspoons dried rosemary
Zest and juice of 1 lemon (optional)
Freshly ground black pepper
Salt (optional)

In the Instant Pot, combine the water, broth, beans, half the garlic, and the rosemary. Lock the lid. Select Manual and cook at high pressure for 32 minutes. When the cook time is complete, let the pressure release naturally for 15 minutes, then quick-release any remaining pressure. Remove the lid. Remove and discard the rosemary stems. Using a slotted spoon, transfer the beans to a medium bowl. Gently stir in the lemon zest (if using) and lemon juice (if using) and the remaining garlic and season to taste with pepper and salt (if using). Serve immediately.

Egyptian-Style Fava Bean Curry

SERVES 8 | PREP AND FINISHING: 10 minutes, plus at least 10 hours to soak | MANUAL: 40 minutes high pressure | RELEASE: Natural | SAUTÉ: 10 minutes | TOTAL TIME: 11 hours

2 cups dried fava beans	2 tomatoes, finely chopped
3 cups water	1 teaspoon ground cumin
2 teaspoons canola oil	2 teaspoons ground
1 yellow onion,	coriander
finely chopped	1 teaspoon dried oregano
6 garlic cloves,	2 tablespoons freshly
finely chopped	squeezed lemon juice
2 serrano chiles, seeded	2 tablespoons finely
and finely chopped	chopped fresh cilantro

In a large bowl, cover the beans with 2 to 3 inches of cold water. Soak at room temperature for 10 to 12 hours or overnight. Drain and rinse the beans. Pour the water into the Instant Pot and add the fava beans. Lock the lid. Select Manual and cook at high pressure for 40 minutes. When the cook time is complete, naturally release the pressure. Drain the beans and rinse them with cold water. Wipe the inner pot dry. Peel and discard the skins by squeezing the cooked beans between your thumb and forefinger. The skin should come off easily. Select Sauté and pour in the oil. Once hot, add the onion, garlic, and chiles and sauté until the onion is translucent, about 5 minutes. Add the tomatoes, cumin, coriander, and oregano and stir to combine. Cover and cook for 3 to 4 minutes or until the tomatoes are soft. Add the beans and cook for 2 minutes more. Select Cancel. Stir in the lemon juice and cilantro and serve hot.

Caribbean-Style Beans and Rice

SERVES 4 | PREP AND FINISHING: 15 minutes, plus 6 hours to soak | MANUAL: 13 minutes high pressure, divided | SAUTÉ: 7 minutes | RELEASE: Natural for 5 minutes, then Quick | TOTAL TIME: 6 hours 50 minutes

⅓ cup dried kidney beans	2 teaspoons seeded and
2 cups water	finely chopped jalapeño
1 teaspoon canola oil	1 tomato, finely chopped
1 yellow onion,	1 teaspoon dried thyme
finely chopped	1 teaspoon kosher salt
2 garlic cloves,	⅔ cup basmati rice, rinsed
finely chopped	and drained
	1 cup full-fat coconut milk

In a large bowl, cover the kidney beans with 2 to 3 inches of cold water. Soak them at room temperature for 6 hours. Drain and rinse the beans. Pour the water into the Instant

Pot and add the beans. Lock the lid. Select Manual and cook at high pressure for 10 minutes. When the cook time is complete, naturally release the pressure. Remove the lid. Drain the beans, reserving and setting aside ½ cup of bean water. Wipe the inner pot dry. Select Sauté and pour in the oil. Once hot, add the onion, garlic, and jalapeño and sauté until the onion is translucent, about 5 minutes. Stir in the tomato, thyme, and salt, and cook for 2 minutes. Select Cancel. Pour the reserved bean water into the inner pot. Stir in the rice and coconut milk. Lock the lid. Select Manual and cook at high pressure for 3 minutes. When the cook time is complete, naturally release the pressure for 5 minutes, then quick-release any remaining pressure. Remove the lid. Let the rice cool for 5 minutes, then fluff with a fork and serve hot with the beans.

Basic Lentils

SERVES 8 | PREP AND FINISHING: 5 minutes | MANUAL: 20 minutes high pressure | RELEASE: Natural for 10 minutes, then Quick | TOTAL TIME: 45 minutes

4 cups water	2 cups dried brown or green lentils, picked through and rinsed

In the Instant Pot, combine the water and lentils. Lock the lid. Select Manual and cook at high pressure for 20 minutes. When the cook time is complete, naturally release the pressure for 10 minutes, then quick-release any remaining pressure. Remove the lid. Stir the lentils. Serve immediately.

Mediterranean-Style Lentils

SERVES 2 to 4 | PREP TIME: 7 minutes | SAUTÉ LOW: 6 minutes | MANUAL: 18 minutes high pressure | RELEASE: Natural for 10 minutes, then Quick | TOTAL TIME: 41 minutes

1 tablespoon extra-virgin olive oil	½ teaspoon salt, plus more as needed
1 small sweet or yellow onion, diced	¼ teaspoon freshly ground black pepper, plus more
1 garlic clove, diced	as needed
1 teaspoon dried oregano	1 tomato, diced
½ teaspoon ground cumin	2½ cups vegetable broth
½ teaspoon dried parsley	1 cup brown or green lentils
	1 bay leaf

Select Sauté Low. When the display reads HOT, pour in the oil and heat until it shimmers. Add the onion and cook for 3 to 4 minutes until soft. Turn off the Instant Pot and add the garlic, oregano, cumin, parsley, salt, and pepper. Cook until fragrant, about 1 minute. Stir in the tomato, broth, lentils, and bay leaf. Lock the lid. Select Manual and cook at high pressure for 18 minutes. When the cook time is complete, let the pressure release naturally for 10 minutes, then quick-release any remaining pressure. Remove the lid and remove and discard the bay leaf. Taste and season with more salt and pepper, as needed. If there's too much liquid remaining, select Sauté medium or high and cook until it evaporates.

Spicy Southwestern Lentils

SERVES 4 to 6 | PREP TIME: 5 minutes | SAUTÉ LOW: 4 minutes | MANUAL: 15 minutes high pressure | RELEASE: Natural for 10 minutes, then Quick | TOTAL TIME: 34 minutes

1 tablespoon extra-virgin olive oil
1 small onion, diced
1 or 2 garlic cloves, finely diced
1 bell pepper, any color, seeded and diced
2 Roma tomatoes, diced
2 cups vegetable broth
1 cup green or brown lentils, rinsed and drained

½ to 1 teaspoon salt, plus more as needed
1 teaspoon ground cumin
1 teaspoon chili powder
1 teaspoon smoked paprika
1 cup chopped kale
Freshly ground black pepper

Select Sauté Low. When the display reads HOT, pour in the oil and heat until it shimmers. Add the onion. Sauté for 1 to 2 minutes and turn off the Instant Pot. Add the garlic. Cook for about 30 seconds, stirring (don't let it burn). Add the bell pepper, tomatoes, broth, lentils, salt, cumin, chili powder, and paprika. Lock the lid. Select Manual and cook at high pressure for 15 minutes. When the cook time is complete, let the Instant Pot go into Keep Warm mode and let the pressure release naturally for 10 minutes, then quick-release any remaining pressure. Remove the lid and stir in the kale, which will wilt after 1 to 2 minutes. Taste and season with salt and pepper, as needed.

Lentil Picadillo

SERVES 6 to 8 | PREP TIME: 5 minutes | MANUAL: 20 minutes high pressure | RELEASE: Natural | TOTAL TIME: 50 minutes

4 Roma tomatoes, quartered
2 or 3 serrano chiles, stemmed
2 garlic cloves
½ medium white onion, roughly chopped
3 cups water

1 pound dried lentils
4 medium carrots, diced
4 medium Yukon Gold potatoes, peeled and diced
6 cilantro sprigs (optional)
Coarse salt

In a blender, puree the tomatoes, chiles, garlic, onion, and water until smooth. Put the lentils in the Instant Pot. Pour in the tomato puree. Add the carrots, potatoes, and cilantro (if using). Lock the lid. Select Manual and cook at high pressure for 20 minutes. When the cook

time is complete, allow the pressure to release naturally. Remove the lid. Season with salt and serve immediately.

Ham-and-Barley Greens

SERVES 4 | PREP TIME: 5 minutes | SAUTÉ: 7 minutes, divided | MANUAL: 18 minutes | RELEASE: Quick | TOTAL TIME: 41 minutes

1 tablespoon unsalted butter
1 cup hulled barley
¼ cup finely chopped onion
4 cups water

½ teaspoon salt
½ cup diced cooked ham
½ cup mustard greens
4 large eggs, cooked to your preference

Select Sauté. When the Instant Pot is hot, melt the butter. Stir in the barley and onion and sauté until the barley starts to toast, 1 to 2 minutes. Select Cancel. Add the water and salt and give everything a stir. Lock the lid. Select Manual and cook at high pressure for 18 minutes. When the cook time is complete, quick-release the pressure. If there is liquid remaining, you can drain it if you wish. Select Sauté and add the ham and greens. Cook until the greens are just wilted, about 5 minutes. Scoop one-fourth of the barley into each bowl and top with an egg.

PASTA AND NOODLES

Pasta Primavera

SERVES 6 | PREP AND FINISHING: 10 minutes | MANUAL: 4 minutes high pressure | RELEASE: Quick | SAUTÉ: 7 minutes | TOTAL TIME: 30 minutes

FOR THE PASTA

5 cups water
1 pound penne pasta
2 teaspoons kosher salt

1 teaspoon extra-virgin olive oil

FOR THE VEGETABLES

2 tablespoons extra-virgin olive oil
1 tablespoon butter
1 cup (1-inch pieces) chopped asparagus
1 cup (1-inch pieces) chopped carrots
1 zucchini, cut into bite-size pieces
2 tablespoons finely chopped fresh basil leaves

1 teaspoon Italian seasoning
1 teaspoon kosher salt
1 teaspoon freshly ground black pepper
½ cup grated Parmesan cheese
1 teaspoon grated lemon zest

TO MAKE THE PASTA

Pour the water into the Instant Pot and add the pasta. Stir in the salt and oil. Lock the Lid. Select Manual and cook at high pressure for 4 minutes. When the cook time is complete, quick-release the pressure. Remove the lid. Drain the pasta, reserving about 2 tablespoons of the pasta water.

TO MAKE THE VEGETABLES
Select Sauté, pour in the olive oil, and add the butter. Once hot, add the asparagus, carrot, zucchini, basil, Italian seasoning, salt, and pepper. Add the reserved pasta water and mix well. Cook for 7 minutes or until the vegetables are tender. Stir in the pasta, Parmesan, and lemon zest and serve hot.

Vegetable Lo Mein

SERVES 4 | PREP AND FINISHING: 10 minutes | MANUAL: 2 minutes high pressure | SAUTÉ: 3 minutes | RELEASE: Quick | TOTAL TIME: 20 minutes

- 10 ounces (2 bundles) dried lo mein noodles
- 4 cups water
- 1 teaspoon kosher salt, divided
- 1 teaspoon corn oil
- 2 tablespoons peanut oil
- 5 scallions, white parts only, finely chopped
- 3 garlic cloves, finely chopped
- ¼ cup (1-inch pieces) chopped green beans
- ¼ cup thinly sliced red bell pepper
- ¼ cup shredded green cabbage
- ¼ cup (1-inch matchsticks) julienned carrots
- 1 teaspoon freshly ground black pepper
- 2 tablespoons soy sauce
- 1 tablespoon teriyaki sauce
- 1 tablespoon sriracha
- 1 tablespoon maple syrup

Soak the noodles in the water for 5 minutes in the Instant Pot. Add ½ teaspoon of salt and the corn oil, stirring gently. Lock the Lid. Select Manual and cook at high pressure for 2 minutes. When the cook time is complete, quick-release the pressure. Drain the noodles, then run them under cold water. Set them aside. Select Sauté, adjust the heat to More, and pour in the peanut oil. Once hot, add the scallions, garlic, green beans, bell pepper, cabbage, carrot, the remaining ½ teaspoon of salt, and the pepper. Cook for 3 minutes, stirring constantly. Stir in the soy sauce, teriyaki sauce, sriracha, and maple syrup. Add the noodles and gently mix. Serve hot.

Udon Noodles in Peanut Sauce

SERVES 4 | PREP AND FINISHING: 10 minutes | MANUAL: 3 minutes high pressure | RELEASE: Quick | SAUTÉ: 4 minutes | TOTAL TIME: 25 minutes

- 4 cups water
- 4 ounces or 2 individually wrapped bundles udon noodles
- 1 teaspoon corn oil
- ½ teaspoon kosher salt, divided
- 1 tablespoon peanut oil
- 6 scallions, white parts only, finely chopped
- 1 teaspoon finely chopped peeled fresh ginger
- 1 garlic clove, finely chopped

- 2 teaspoons soy sauce
- 1 teaspoon sriracha
- 1 tablespoon peanut butter
- 1 teaspoon white sesame seeds

Place the water and noodles in the Instant Pot and gently stir in the corn oil and ¼ teaspoon of salt. Lock the Lid. Select Manual and cook at high pressure for 3 minutes. When the cook time is complete, quick-release the pressure. Remove the lid. Drain the noodles and run them under cold water. Set them aside. Select Sauté and pour in the peanut oil. Once hot, add the scallions, ginger, and garlic and sauté for 2 minutes. Add the soy sauce, sriracha, peanut butter, and remaining ¼ teaspoon of salt. Mix until the peanut butter has thinned and combined with the other ingredients. Add the noodles and gently stir for 1 minute. Serve hot, sprinkled with the sesame seeds.

Sticky Noodles with Tofu

SERVES 8 | PREP AND FINISHING: 10 minutes | SAUTÉ: 5 minutes | MANUAL: 6 minutes high pressure | RELEASE: Quick | TOTAL TIME: 31 minutes

- 2 tablespoons extra-virgin olive oil
- 10 ounces extra-firm tofu, cubed
- 3 garlic cloves, minced
- 4 cups water
- ⅓ cup reduced-sodium soy sauce
- 3 tablespoons apple cider vinegar
- 2 tablespoons brown sugar
- 1 (16-ounce) package whole wheat spaghetti
- 2 red bell peppers, seeded and thinly sliced
- ¼ cup unsalted cashews, chopped

Select Sauté and pour the olive oil into the Instant Pot. Once the oil is hot, add the tofu and garlic and sauté for 2 minutes. Select Cancel. Using a wooden spoon, scrape up any browned bits stuck to the bottom of the pot. Add the water, soy sauce, vinegar, and brown sugar to the pot. Stir to combine. Break the spaghetti noodles in half and place them on top of the mixture; do not stir. Select Cancel. Lock the Lid. Select Manual and cook at high pressure for 6 minutes. When the cook time is complete, quick-release the pressure. Remove the lid. Stir in the bell peppers and cashews. Serve immediately.

Zucchini, Kale, and Mushroom Pasta Marinara

SERVES 4 to 6 | PREP TIME: 10 minutes | SAUTÉ: 8 minutes | MANUAL: 7 minutes high pressure | RELEASE: Quick | TOTAL TIME: 40 minutes

- 1 medium onion, diced
- 8 ounces white button or cremini mushrooms
- 4 garlic cloves, minced
- 3 tablespoons tomato paste
- 1 tablespoon Italian seasoning
- 3 cups water
- 2 (15-ounce) cans diced tomatoes
- 2 tablespoons balsamic vinegar

1 bunch kale, stemmed
and chopped

12 ounces whole wheat
penne or other
short pasta

1 medium zucchini, cut into
1-inch pieces

Freshly ground
black pepper

Salt (optional)

Select Sauté. Sauté the onion for 3 minutes, adding water as needed to prevent sticking. Add the mushrooms and sauté for 5 minutes. Add the garlic, tomato paste, and Italian seasoning and stir for 30 seconds, until fragrant. Select Cancel. Stir in the water, tomatoes with their juices, and vinegar. Layer the kale, pasta, and zucchini on top but do not stir. Lock the lid. Select Manual and cook at high pressure for 7 minutes. When the cook time is complete, quick-release the pressure. Remove the lid. Stir and season to taste with pepper and salt (if using). Serve immediately.

Sesame Peanut Soba Noodles

SERVES 4 | PREP TIME: 5 minutes | MANUAL: 2 minutes high pressure | RELEASE: Quick | TOTAL TIME: 15 minutes

4 cups water

¼ cup coconut aminos
or tamari

2 tablespoons sesame oil

1 (9½-ounce) package
soba noodles

12 ounces broccoli slaw mix

1 red bell pepper, seeded
and sliced

¼ cup creamy natural
peanut butter

½ teaspoon red
pepper flakes

½ teaspoon kosher salt
(optional)

In the Instant Pot, combine the water, coconut aminos, and sesame oil. Add the soba noodles, breaking them to fit in the pot if necessary. Press down on the noodles to submerge them. Top with the broccoli slaw and bell pepper. Lock the lid. Select Manual and cook at high pressure for 2 minutes. When the cook time is complete, quick-release the pressure. Remove the lid and stir in the peanut butter and red pepper flakes. Season to taste with salt (if using) and serve.

Broccoli-Basil Pasta

SERVES 4 | PREP TIME: 5 minutes | MANUAL: 2 minutes high pressure | RELEASE: Quick | TOTAL TIME: 20 minutes

2 cups water

8 ounces whole-grain or
gluten-free penne

½ teaspoon kosher salt

3 cups frozen
broccoli florets

1 cup fresh basil leaves,
finely chopped

½ cup shredded
Parmesan cheese

¼ cup extra-virgin olive oil

2 garlic cloves, minced

¼ teaspoon freshly ground
black pepper

In the Instant Pot, combine the water, penne, and salt. Top with the broccoli. Lock the lid. Select Manual and cook at high pressure for 2 minutes. When the cook time is complete, quick-release the pressure. Remove the lid and stir. Stir in the basil, Parmesan, olive oil, garlic, and pepper before serving.

Cheesy Shells with Artichokes and Spinach

SERVES 4 | PREP AND FINISHING: 20 minutes | MANUAL: 5 minutes low pressure | RELEASE: Quick | TOTAL TIME: 35 minutes

1½ cups water

1 (12-ounce) can evapo-
rated milk, divided

8 ounces shell pasta

12 ounces frozen artichoke
hearts, thawed and cut
into bite-size pieces

3 large garlic
cloves, minced

2 tablespoons
unsalted butter

1 teaspoon kosher salt

1 large egg

2 teaspoons freshly
squeezed lemon juice

1 teaspoon grated
lemon zest

¼ teaspoon freshly ground
black pepper

9 to 10 ounces
baby spinach

4 ounces Parmesan or sim-
ilar cheese, grated (about
1⅓ cups)

¼ cup heavy (whipping)
cream, plus more
as needed

Pour the water and ¾ cup of evaporated milk into the Instant Pot. Add the pasta, artichoke hearts, garlic, butter, and salt and stir to combine, submerging the pasta in the liquid. Lock the Lid. Select Manual and cook at low pressure for 5 minutes. When the cook time is complete, quick-release the pressure. Remove the lid. In a small bowl, whisk together the remaining ¾ cup of evaporated milk and the egg. Select Sauté and adjust to Less for low heat. Pour the milk mixture into the noodles and cook, stirring occasionally, until the sauce has thickened. Add the lemon juice, lemon zest, and pepper and stir to combine. Add the spinach and Parmesan cheese. Cook, stirring occasionally, until the spinach wilts and the cheese melts. Stir in the cream, adding more if the sauce is too thick. Serve immediately.

Creamy Mac and Cheese

SERVES 6 | PREP TIME: 5 minutes | MANUAL: 4 minutes high pressure | RELEASE: Quick | TOTAL TIME: 18 minutes

2½ cups elbow macaroni

2 cups water

1 cup chicken broth

3 tablespoons unsalted
butter, cubed

¼ teaspoon salt

¼ teaspoon freshly ground
black pepper

¼ teaspoon mus-
tard powder

¼ teaspoon garlic powder

2 cups shredded sharp
Cheddar cheese

⅓ cup whole or
2 percent milk

⅓ cup heavy (whip-
ping) cream

In the Instant Pot, combine the macaroni, water, broth, butter, salt, pepper, mustard powder, and garlic powder. Lock the lid. Select Manual and cook at high pressure for 4 minutes. When the cook time is complete, quick-release the pressure. Remove the lid and add the cheese, milk, and cream, stirring until it's smooth and creamy.

Vegan Butternut Mac and Cheese

SERVES 4 | PREP TIME: 10 minutes | MANUAL: 2 minutes low pressure | RELEASE: Natural for 8 minutes, then Quick | TOTAL TIME: 20 minutes

4½ cups water, divided

2 cups cooked cubed butternut squash

1 cup raw cashews, soaked in water for at least 3 to 4 hours or overnight, drained and rinsed well

⅓ cup nutritional yeast

2 tablespoons freshly squeezed lemon juice

2 to 2½ teaspoons salt

1 teaspoon Dijon mustard

⅛ teaspoon ground nutmeg

1 (16-ounce) box pasta of choice

1 cup nondairy milk, plus more as needed

Freshly ground black pepper

In a high-speed blender or food processor, combine 2 cups of water, the squash, cashews, nutritional yeast, lemon juice, salt, mustard, and nutmeg. Blend until smooth (the longer you soaked the cashews, the quicker this will be). Pour the cashew mixture into the Instant Pot. Pour the remaining 2½ cups of water into the blender and swish it around to capture any remaining cashew mixture. Add that to the Instant Pot as well, along with the pasta. Lock the lid. Select Manual and cook at low pressure for 2 minutes. When the cook time is complete, let the pressure release naturally for 8 minutes, then quick-release any remaining pressure. Remove the lid and stir in the milk, adding as much as needed to make it nice and creamy. Taste and season with more salt and pepper, as needed.

Indian-Style Mac and Cheese

SERVES 4 | PREP TIME: 5 minutes | SAUTÉ: 3 minutes | PRESSURE BUILD: 8 minutes | MANUAL: High for 2 minutes | RELEASE: 5 minutes Natural, then Quick | TOTAL TIME: 23 minutes

2 tablespoons unsalted butter

1 small onion, finely chopped

2 garlic cloves, finely minced

1 medium carrot, peeled and diced

½ cup fresh or frozen chopped green beans

1 cup canned tomato puree

1 cup cubed paneer

½ cup fresh or frozen corn

½ cup fresh or frozen green peas

1 teaspoon salt

1 teaspoon cayenne pepper

1 teaspoon garam masala

½ teaspoon ground cumin

2 cups water or vegetable broth

8 ounces macaroni pasta

½ cup heavy (whipping) cream

1 cup grated Cheddar or pepper Jack cheese

Select Sauté. Melt the butter in the Instant Pot, then add the onion, garlic, carrot, and green beans and cook until the onion turns translucent, 2 to 3 minutes, Add the tomato puree, paneer, corn, peas, salt, cayenne pepper, garam masala, cumin, and water. Mix well, scraping the bottom to loosen any browned bits. Add the pasta and submerge it with a wooden spoon, but do not stir. Lock the lid and close the steam valve. Cook at high pressure for 2 minutes. Release the steam naturally for 5 minutes, then quick-release any remaining pressure. Add the cream and cheese, stirring well to melt the cheese. Serve warm.

Penne Caponata

SERVES 4 | PREP AND FINISHING: 10 minutes | MANUAL: 5 minutes high pressure | RELEASE: Quick | TOTAL TIME: 20 minutes

2 tablespoons extra-virgin olive oil

1 medium onion, chopped

3 large garlic cloves, minced

1 teaspoon kosher salt, divided, plus more as needed

1 medium eggplant, chopped

1 large celery stalk, sliced

1 large red bell pepper, seeded and chopped

1 (14-ounce) can diced tomatoes

3 tablespoons red wine vinegar, divided

3 tablespoons drained capers, divided

2 tablespoons sliced green olives, divided

2 tablespoons sugar

6 ounces penne

1 cup water

1 tablespoon minced fresh basil

¼ cup grated Parmesan or similar cheese

Select Sauté and adjust to More for high heat. Heat the oil until it shimmers. Add the onion and garlic and ¼ teaspoon of salt. Cook, stirring frequently, until the onion pieces separate and begin to soften, 2 to 3 minutes. Add the eggplant, celery, and bell pepper and cook, stirring frequently, for 1 minute. Add the tomatoes with their juices, 2 tablespoons of vinegar, 1 tablespoon of capers, 1 tablespoon of green olives, and the sugar. Stir to combine. Select Cancel. Add the pasta, water, and remaining ¾ teaspoon of salt. Stir to combine. Lock the Lid. Select Manual, and cook at high pressure for 5 minutes. When the cook time is complete, quick-release the pressure. Remove the lid. Test the pasta; it should be tender with just a slightly firm center. If it's not done enough, simmer for 1 to 2 minutes until done to your liking. Add the remaining 1 tablespoon of vinegar, 2 tablespoons of capers, and 1 tablespoon of olives, and taste, adding more salt if necessary. Stir in the basil and Parmesan cheese and serve.

Kimchi Pasta

SERVES 4 to 6 | PREP TIME: 5 minutes | MANUAL: 1 minute high pressure | SAUTÉ LOW: 4 minutes | RELEASE: Quick | TOTAL TIME: 10 minutes

8 ounces dried small pasta
2⅓ cups vegetable broth
2 garlic cloves, minced
½ red onion, sliced
½ to 1 teaspoon salt
1¼ cups kimchi, with any larger pieces chopped
½ cup vegan sour cream

In the Instant Pot, combine the pasta, broth, garlic, red onion, and salt. Lock the lid. Select Manual and cook at high pressure for 1 minute. When the cook time is complete, quick-release the pressure. Remove the lid. Select Sauté Low. Stir in the kimchi. Simmer for 3 to 4 minutes. Stir in the sour cream and serve.

Hakka Noodles

SERVES 4 | PREP TIME: 15 minutes | SAUTÉ: 7 minutes | MANUAL: 1 minute high pressure | RELEASE: Natural for 3 minutes, then Quick | TOTAL TIME: 36 minutes

3¾ cups water, divided
3 garlic cloves, peeled
1 (2-inch) piece fresh ginger, peeled and roughly chopped
2 tablespoons tomato paste or ketchup
1 tablespoon sriracha
1 tablespoon canola or vegetable oil
4 scallions, both white and green parts, chopped
1 cup thinly sliced green cabbage
1 medium green or red bell pepper, seeded and thinly sliced
1 medium carrot, cut into thin matchsticks
1 teaspoon salt, divided
½ teaspoon red pepper flakes
1 cup broccoli florets
2 tablespoons low-sodium soy sauce
1 tablespoon rice wine or white wine vinegar
8 ounces hakka noodles or spaghetti, broken in half

In a blender or food processor, combine ¼ cup of water, the garlic, ginger, tomato paste, and sriracha. Blend to a smooth paste. Set it aside. Select Sauté, and once the pot is hot, pour in the oil. Add the scallions and cook for about 1 minute, until wilted. Stir in the paste and cook for 2 minutes, stirring constantly and scraping the bottom. Add the cabbage, bell pepper, carrot, ½ teaspoon of salt, and the red pepper flakes and cook for 2 minutes. Add the broccoli and cook for about 2 minutes, until crisp-tender. Select Cancel. Transfer the veggies to a medium bowl. Add the remaining 3½ cups of water, the soy sauce, vinegar, and remaining ½ teaspoon of salt to the pot and mix well. Add the noodles and push them down with a wooden spoon to make sure they are completely submerged, but do not stir. Lock the lid. Select Manual and cook at high pressure for 1 minute if using hakka noodles or 4 minutes if using spaghetti. When the cook time is complete, let the pressure release naturally for 3 minutes, then

quick-release any remaining pressure. Remove the lid, return the cooked veggies to the pot, and close the lid for 5 minutes. Stir the noodles and veggies together and serve hot.

Spicy Tomato Pasta

SERVES 4 | PREP TIME: 5 minutes | SAUTÉ: 3 minutes | MANUAL: 2 minutes high pressure | RELEASE: Natural for 5 minutes, then Quick | TOTAL TIME: 23 minutes

2 tablespoons canola or vegetable oil
1 large onion, chopped
1 large green or red bell pepper, seeded and chopped
8 ounces white button or cremini mushrooms, chopped
2 teaspoons peeled and grated fresh ginger
2 garlic cloves, finely minced
2 cups water
½ cup canned tomato puree
1 teaspoon salt
1 teaspoon cayenne pepper
1 teaspoon ground coriander
½ teaspoon garam masala
8 ounces short-cut pasta (such as penne or rotini)

Select Sauté, and once the pot is hot, pour in the oil. Add the onion, bell pepper, mushrooms, ginger, and garlic and cook for 2 to 3 minutes, until the onion turns translucent. Add the water, tomato puree, salt, cayenne pepper, coriander, and garam masala. Stir well, making sure to scrape the bottom to loosen any browned bits. Add the pasta and push down with a wooden spoon to make sure it is completely submerged, but do not stir. Select Cancel. Lock the lid. Select Manual and cook at high pressure for 2 minutes. When the cook time is complete, let the pressure release naturally for 5 minutes, then quick-release any remaining pressure. Remove the lid, gently mix the pasta, and serve warm.

Spaghetti "Not" Bolognese

SERVES 6 | PREP AND FINISHING: 10 minutes | MANUAL: 7 minutes high pressure, divided | SAUTÉ: 3 minutes | RELEASE: Natural for 5 minutes, then Quick | TOTAL TIME: 35 minutes

FOR THE PASTA
5 cups water
8 ounces spaghetti
1 teaspoon extra-virgin olive oil
1 teaspoon kosher salt

FOR THE SAUCE
1 tablespoon extra-virgin olive oil
1 onion, finely chopped
5 garlic cloves, finely chopped
2 cups canned crushed tomatoes
1 cup vegetable broth
½ cup dried green lentils
5 portobello mushrooms, roughly chopped

¼ cup finely chopped
   fresh basil
1 teaspoon kosher salt

2 teaspoons freshly ground
   black pepper
½ cup shredded
   Parmesan cheese

TO MAKE THE PASTA

Pour the water into the Instant Pot and add the spaghetti, olive oil, and salt. Stir gently. Lock the Lid. Select Manual and cook at high pressure for 2 minutes. When the cook time is complete, naturally release the pressure for 5 minutes, then quick-release any remaining pressure. Remove the lid. Drain the pasta and set it aside.

TO MAKE THE SAUCE

Select Sauté and pour in the oil. Once hot, add the onion and garlic and cook until the onion is translucent, about 3 minutes. Stir in the tomatoes with their juices, broth, lentils, mushrooms, basil, salt, and pepper. Mix thoroughly. Select Cancel. Lock the Lid. Select Manual and cook at high pressure for 5 minutes. When the cook time is complete, naturally release the pressure. Remove the lid. Use a potato masher to mash the lentils and tomatoes to get a chunky texture. Stir in the spaghetti, sprinkle with the cheese, and serve hot.

Vegetarian Lasagna

SERVES 4 | PREP AND FINISHING: 30 minutes | STOVE: 10 minutes | SAUTÉ: 5 minutes | MANUAL: 20 minutes high pressure | RELEASE: Natural for 10 minutes, then Quick | TOTAL TIME: 1 hour 10 minutes

FOR THE BALSAMELLA

¼ cup unsalted butter
¼ cup all-purpose flour
1½ cups whole milk

¼ teaspoon kosher salt
¼ teaspoon freshly ground
   white or black pepper

FOR THE LASAGNA

2 tablespoons extra-virgin
   olive oil
8 ounces white button
   or cremini mush-
   rooms, sliced
1 cup diced eggplant
   (about ½ medium
   eggplant)
½ teaspoon kosher salt
Unsalted butter, at room
   temperature, for greasing

2 cups arrabbiata sauce
1 (8-ounce) package egg
   roll wrappers
3 ounces Parmesan
   or similar cheese,
   coarsely grated
½ cup shredded
   whole-milk mozzarella or
   provolone cheese
1 cup water

TO MAKE THE BALSAMELLA

Heat the butter in a medium saucepan over medium heat until it melts. Once it stops foaming, whisk in the flour all at once, stirring until smooth. Add the milk, a little at a time, continuing to whisk. Once all the milk is added, bring the sauce to a low simmer. Stir in the salt and pepper. Simmer for 10 minutes until thickened, stirring often, then remove from the heat. Set it aside.

TO MAKE THE LASAGNA

Select Sauté and adjust to More for high heat. Heat the oil until it shimmers. Add the mushrooms and eggplant and salt. Cook, stirring frequently, until the vegetables release their liquid and begin to brown, about 5 minutes. Select Cancel. Transfer the vegetables to a bowl and rinse out the pot. Lightly coat the bottom of a 1-quart baking dish with butter and spread a spoonful of arrabbiata sauce over the bottom of the dish. Add a layer of egg roll wrappers, overlapping them as little as possible and trimming the edges so they fit. Spoon some arrabbiata sauce over the wrappers. Scatter some mushrooms and eggplant over the sauce, then dot them with dollops of balsamella (a small ice-cream scoop is useful here) and sprinkle with the Parmesan cheese. Repeat these layers (wrappers, sauce, vegetables, balsamella) as many more times as you have room for, ending with a layer of arrabbiata sauce. Press each layer of wrappers onto the fillings underneath it, which will even out the balsamella. Top with the mozzarella cheese. Place a sheet of aluminum foil over the top and crimp it lightly. Pour the water into the Instant Pot. Place a trivet with handles in the pot and place the baking dish on top. If your trivet doesn't have handles, use a foil sling to make removing the dish easier. Lock the Lid. Select Manual and cook at high pressure for 20 minutes. When the cook time is complete, naturally release the pressure for 10 minutes, then quick-release any remaining pressure. Remove the lid. If you like, place the lasagna under a preheated broiler until the cheese is browned on the top, 2 to 3 minutes. Regardless, let the lasagna rest for 10 to 15 minutes before serving, to allow it to set.

Basil-Butter Shrimp and Orzo

SERVES 4 | PREP TIME: 10 minutes | SAUTÉ: 4 minutes | MANUAL: 3 minutes high pressure | RELEASE: Quick | TOTAL TIME: 20 minutes

¼ cup unsalted butter
1½ cups gluten-free orzo
1 teaspoon minced garlic
¼ cup dry white wine
2¾ cups water

1 pound frozen peeled
   jumbo shrimp
1 cup roughly chopped
   fresh basil, plus more
   for garnish
½ teaspoon salt

Select Sauté. Put the butter and orzo in the Instant Pot and cook for about 2 minutes, until the butter is melted and the orzo smells toasted. Stir in the garlic and cook for another 30 seconds, until fragrant. Add the white wine, lock the lid, and cook for about 1 minute, until most of the liquid is evaporated. Select Cancel. Remove the lid. Stir in the water, shrimp, basil, and salt. Lock the lid. Select Manual and cook at high pressure for 3 minutes. When the cook time is complete, quick-release the pressure. Remove the lid. Let the shrimp and orzo rest for a few minutes before serving. Garnish with basil.

Penne Bolognese

SERVES 4 | PREP AND FINISHING: 15 minutes | MANUAL: 17 minutes high pressure, divided | RELEASE: Natural for 10 minutes, then Quick | TOTAL TIME: 50 minutes

2 tablespoons extra-virgin olive oil
½ medium onion, chopped (about ½ cup)
1 garlic clove, minced
1 medium carrot, chopped (about ⅔ cup)
1 medium celery stalk, chopped (about ½ cup)
1 pound lean (93 percent) ground beef (or half ground beef and half ground pork)

1¼ teaspoons kosher salt, divided, plus more as needed
¼ cup dry white wine
1½ cups strained tomatoes or tomato sauce
½ cup milk
8 ounces penne pasta
1 cup water
2 tablespoons chopped fresh parsley

Select Sauté and adjust to More for high heat. Heat the oil until it shimmers. Add the onion, garlic, carrot, and celery and cook, stirring occasionally, until the vegetables start to soften, 2 to 3 minutes. Add the ground beef and ½ teaspoon of salt. Stir to break the meat into small pieces and cook just until it starts to brown, about 3 minutes. Add the wine and stir, scraping the bottom of the pot to loosen the browned bits. Pour in the strained tomatoes, milk, and ¼ teaspoon of salt. Stir to combine. Select Cancel. Lock the Lid. Select Manual and cook at high pressure for 12 minutes. When the cook time is complete, naturally release the pressure for 10 minutes, then quick-release any remaining pressure. Remove the lid. Add the pasta, water, and remaining ½ teaspoon of salt. Stir to combine. Lock the Lid. Select Manual and cook at high pressure for 5 minutes. When the cook time is complete, quick-release the pressure. Remove the lid. Test the pasta; it should be tender with just a slightly firm center. If not, or if the sauce is too thin, simmer everything for a few minutes. Adjust the seasoning, adding more salt if necessary. Spoon into bowls, sprinkle with the parsley, and serve.

Spaghetti and Meatballs

SERVES 4 | PREP TIME: 20 minutes | SAUTÉ: 8 minutes | MANUAL: 3 minutes high pressure | RELEASE: Natural for 5 minutes, then Quick | TOTAL TIME: 50 minutes

1 pound lean (93 percent) ground beef
1 cup whole wheat breadcrumbs
1 large egg, beaten
1 yellow onion, finely chopped
2 garlic cloves, minced
1 tablespoon Italian seasoning
¼ teaspoon kosher salt

2 tablespoons extra-virgin olive oil
¾ cup water, divided
8 ounces whole wheat spaghetti, broken in half
3 cups marinara sauce
Fresh basil leaves, for garnish
Grated Parmesan, for garnish

In a medium bowl, combine the beef, breadcrumbs, egg, onion, garlic, Italian seasoning, and salt. Mix the ingredients together, being careful not to overwork the meat. Roll the mixture to form 16 meatballs. Select Sauté and pour in the olive oil. When the oil is hot, add the meatballs and cook for 8 minutes, turning occasionally, until browned. Remove the meatballs from the pot and set them aside. Into the pot, pour ¼ cup of water. Scrape up any browned bits from the bottom of the pot. Select Cancel. Return the meatballs to the pot and top with the spaghetti, marinara sauce, and remaining ½ cup of water. Do not stir. Lock the lid. Select Manual and cook at high pressure for 3 minutes. When the cook time is complete, let the pressure release naturally for 5 minutes, then quick-release any remaining pressure. Remove the lid and stir everything together. Garnish with fresh basil leaves and grated Parmesan, and serve.

Farfalle with Italian Sausage and Peppers

SERVES 4 | PREP AND FINISHING: 10 minutes | MANUAL: 16 minutes high pressure, divided | RELEASE: Natural for 10 minutes, then Quick | TOTAL TIME: 45 minutes

2 tablespoons extra-virgin olive oil
1 pound hot Italian sausage, casings removed, cut into 1-inch pieces
½ medium onion, sliced (about ½ cup)
¼ cup dry white wine

1½ cups strained tomatoes or tomato sauce
¾ teaspoon kosher salt, divided
8 ounces farfalle pasta
1 medium red or green bell pepper, seeded and chopped
1¼ cups water

Select Sauté and adjust to More for high heat. Heat the oil until it shimmers. Add the sausage in a single layer. Brown the sausage pieces on all sides, about 3 minutes, then push the meat to the sides of the pot. Add the onion and cook, stirring, until the onion pieces separate and begin to soften, 2 to 3 minutes. Add the wine and stir, scraping the bottom of the pot to loosen the browned bits. Pour in the tomatoes, add ¼ teaspoon of salt, and stir to combine. Select Cancel. Lock the Lid. Select Manual and cook at high pressure for 12 minutes. When the cook time is complete, naturally release the pressure for 10 minutes, then quick-release any remaining pressure. Remove the lid. Add the pasta, bell pepper, water, and remaining ½ teaspoon of salt. Stir to combine. Lock the Lid. Select Manual and cook at low pressure for 4 minutes. When the cook time is complete, quick-release the pressure. Remove the lid. Test the pasta; it should be tender with just a slightly firm center. If it's not done enough, simmer for 1 to 2 minutes until it is done to your liking. Stir and serve.

Mushroom Stroganoff

SERVES 4 | PREP TIME: 10 minutes | SAUTÉ: 4 minutes | MANUAL: High for 3 minutes | RELEASE: Quick | TOTAL TIME: 25 minutes

1 tablespoon extra-virgin olive oil
1 yellow onion, thinly sliced
3 garlic cloves, minced
1 pound portobello mushrooms, thinly sliced
1 tablespoon flour
1¾ cups low-sodium vegetable broth

8 ounces whole-grain rotini pasta
1 tablespoon vegan Worcestershire sauce
2 tablespoons Dijon mustard
¾ teaspoon kosher salt
½ teaspoon whole black peppercorns
½ cup full-fat sour cream

Select Sauté. Pour the olive oil into the Instant Pot. When the oil is hot, add the onion and garlic and cook until softened, 3 to 4 minutes. Add the mushrooms and flour and stir to combine. Press Cancel. Add the broth, pasta, Worcestershire sauce, mustard, salt, and peppercorns. Stir to combine. Lock the lid. Select Manual and cook on high pressure for 3 minutes. When the cook time is complete, quick-release the pressure. Remove the lid and stir in the sour cream before serving.

SOUPS AND STEWS

Beet Soup

SERVES 6 | PREP AND FINISHING: 10 minutes | SAUTÉ: 8 minutes, divided | MANUAL: 12 minutes high pressure | RELEASE: Natural | TOTAL TIME: 40 minutes

1 tablespoon corn oil
2 shallots, finely chopped
2 garlic cloves, finely chopped
1 pound red beets, peeled and quartered (about 4 medium beets)

1 medium carrot, cut into bite-size pieces
1 teaspoon kosher salt
1 teaspoon sugar
3 cups water, divided
¼ cup heavy (whipping) cream

Select Sauté and pour in the oil. Once hot, add the shallots and garlic and cook for 1 minute. Add the beets, carrot, salt, sugar, and 2½ cups of water. Stir to combine. Lock the Lid. Select Manual and cook at high pressure for 12 minutes. When the cook time is complete, naturally release the pressure. Remove the lid. Using a slotted spoon, transfer the beets and carrot to a blender. Pour the broth into a medium bowl. Pulse the beets and carrot, while little by little adding 1 cup of broth. Continue blending until you've reached a smooth and silky texture. It will still be thick at this point. Select Sauté. Pour the pureed beets and any remaining broth into the Instant Pot and stir to combine. Use the remaining ½ cup of water to rinse

out the blender; pour this into the Instant Pot. Simmer the soup for 5 minutes. Select Cancel, then stir in the cream. Serve warm.

Fresh Tomato Gazpacho

SERVES 4 | PREP AND FINISHING: 5 minutes, plus at least 1 hour to chill | MANUAL: 3 minutes high pressure | RELEASE: Quick | TOTAL TIME: 1 hour 20 minutes

1½ cups water
4 large tomatoes, slit on the top in a cross shape
4 fresh basil leaves, finely chopped
1 teaspoon kosher salt
1 teaspoon sugar

½ teaspoon ground cumin
½ teaspoon paprika
½ teaspoon freshly squeezed lemon juice
1 English cucumber, peeled, seeded, and cut into bite-size chunks

Pour the water into the Instant Pot, then add the tomatoes. Lock the Lid. Select Manual and cook at high pressure for 3 minutes. When the cook time is complete, quick-release the pressure. Remove the lid. Drain the tomatoes and let them cool for 5 minutes. Peel the tomato skin and discard. In a blender, combine the tomatoes, basil, salt, sugar, cumin, paprika, and lemon juice and puree until smooth (or your preferred consistency). Add the cucumber and pulse the mixture for a chunky gazpacho. Chill for at least for 1 hour before serving.

French Onion Soup

SERVES 8 | PREP AND FINISHING: 15 minutes | SAUTÉ: 25 minutes | MANUAL: 10 minutes high pressure | RELEASE: Quick | BAKE: 20 minutes | TOTAL TIME: 1 hour 20 minutes

3 tablespoons butter
2 pounds yellow onions, thinly sliced
¼ cup sugar
2 teaspoons kosher salt
2 tablespoons apple cider vinegar
4 cups vegetable broth

1 tablespoon dried thyme
2 bay leaves
1 tablespoon Worcestershire sauce
8 slices rustic bread
2 cups shredded Cheddar cheese

Select Sauté and adjust to More for high heat. Melt the butter and add the onions, sugar, and salt. Cook for about 25 minutes to caramelize, stirring every 3 minutes, until the onions are a deep brown. Add the vinegar and deglaze the pot, scraping up any browned bits from the bottom of the pot. Stir in the broth, thyme, bay leaves, and Worcestershire sauce. Preheat the oven to 375°F. Lock the Lid. Select Manual and cook at high pressure for 10 minutes. When the cook time is complete, quick-release the pressure. Remove the lid, mix, and discard the bay leaves. Ladle the soup into oven-safe ramekins or soup bowls. Top each with a bread slice and the cheese. Bake for 20 minutes or until the cheese melts. Serve hot.

Cream of Asparagus Soup

SERVES 6 | PREP AND FINISHING: 25 minutes | SAUTÉ: 12 minutes | MANUAL: 4 minutes high pressure | RELEASE: Natural | TOTAL TIME: 50 minutes

1 tablespoon salted butter	2 teaspoons kosher salt
½ cup finely chopped onion	1 teaspoon freshly ground black pepper
3 garlic cloves, finely chopped	1½ cups vegetable broth
1½ pounds asparagus (about 2 bunches or 25 single stalks), woody stems trimmed, cut into 1-inch pieces	1 cup heavy (whipping) cream

Select Sauté and melt the butter. Add the onion and garlic and cook until the onion is translucent, about 5 minutes. Add the asparagus, salt, pepper, and broth. Continue cooking, stirring frequently, for 6 to 7 minutes or until the asparagus is soft. Select Cancel. Lock the Lid. Select Manual and cook at high pressure for 4 minutes. When the cook time is complete, naturally release the pressure. Remove the lid. Using an immersion blender, puree the soup. Add the cream and mix thoroughly. Cover with the lid and leave the Instant Pot in Keep Warm mode for at least 15 minutes. Serve hot.

Tomato-Basil Soup

SERVES 6 | PREP AND FINISHING: 15 minutes | SAUTÉ: 3 minutes | MANUAL: 5 minutes high pressure | RELEASE: Natural | TOTAL TIME: 35 minutes

1 tablespoon butter	1 teaspoon freshly ground black pepper
¼ cup finely chopped onion	¼ teaspoon sugar
3 garlic cloves	2 cups water
6 medium tomatoes, roughly chopped (about 1¾ pounds)	¼ cup heavy (whipping) cream
1 cup fresh basil leaves, chopped, divided	½ cup store-bought croutons, for garnish (optional, omit for gluten-free)
1 teaspoon kosher salt	

Select Sauté and melt the butter. Add the onion and garlic and sauté for 1 minute. Add the tomatoes, half of the basil, the salt, pepper, and sugar. Add the water and stir to combine. Select Cancel. Lock the Lid. Select Manual and cook at high pressure for 5 minutes. When the cook time is complete, naturally release the pressure. Remove the lid. Stir the soup. Using an immersion blender, puree the soup. Stir in the cream and the remaining basil. Serve hot, garnished with the croutons (if using).

Curried Carrot and Ginger Soup

SERVES 4 | PREP AND FINISHING: 10 minutes | SAUTÉ: 3 minutes | MANUAL: 15 minutes high pressure | RELEASE: Natural | TOTAL TIME: 40 minutes

2 teaspoons corn oil	2½ cups water
2 teaspoons peeled and finely chopped fresh ginger	2 tablespoons red lentils, rinsed
5 large carrots, cut into bite-size pieces	2 teaspoons kosher salt
	1 teaspoon curry powder

Select Sauté and pour in the oil. Once hot, add the ginger and carrots and sauté for about 2 minutes, until the carrots start to soften. Stir in the water, lentils, salt, and curry powder. Select Cancel. Lock the Lid. Select Manual and cook at high pressure for 15 minutes. When the cook time is complete, naturally release the pressure. Remove the lid. Using an immersion blender, puree the soup. Mix thoroughly and serve hot.

Tibetan-Style Vegetable Noodle Soup

SERVES 6 | PREP AND FINISHING: 10 minutes | SAUTÉ: 6 minutes | MANUAL: 3 minutes high pressure | RELEASE: Natural for 5 minutes, then Quick | TOTAL TIME: 35 minutes

1 cup water	½ cup grated carrot
5 ounces wheat noodles	½ cup finely chopped mushrooms
2 tablespoons corn oil	2 teaspoons soy sauce
2 shallots, finely chopped	2 teaspoons sugar
2 garlic cloves, finely chopped	1 teaspoon sriracha sauce
1 bunch scallions, finely chopped, white and green parts separated	1 teaspoon curry powder
	1 teaspoon kosher salt
½ cup shredded green cabbage	4 cups vegetable broth

In a medium bowl, soak the noodles in the water for 5 minutes. Drain and set them aside. Select Sauté and pour in the oil. Once hot, add the shallots, garlic, and white parts of the scallions and cook for 2 minutes. Add the cabbage, carrot, mushrooms, soy sauce, sugar, sriracha, curry powder, and salt. Mix well and cook for 3 to 4 minutes. Add the noodles and the vegetable broth. Select Cancel. Lock the Lid. Select Manual and cook at high pressure for 3 minutes. When the cook time is complete, naturally release the pressure for 5 minutes, then quick-release any remaining pressure. Remove the lid. Stir the soup well and serve hot.

Potato Leek Soup

SERVES 4 | PREP TIME: 5 minutes | SAUTÉ LOW:
5 minutes | MANUAL: 5 minutes high pressure |
RELEASE: Natural for 15 minutes, then Quick | TOTAL
TIME: 30 minutes

3 tablespoons
　vegan butter
2 large leeks, white and
　very light green parts,
　cleaned well, chopped
2 garlic cloves, minced
4 cups vegetable broth
1 pound Yukon Gold pota-
　toes, peeled and cubed

1 bay leaf
½ teaspoon salt, plus more
　as needed
⅔ cup soy milk
⅓ cup extra-virgin olive oil
Freshly ground
　white pepper

Select Sauté Low. When the display reads HOT, melt the
butter. Add the leeks and cook for 2 to 3 minutes, until
soft, stirring occasionally. Add the garlic. Cook for 30 to
45 seconds, stirring frequently, until fragrant. Add the
broth, potatoes, bay leaf, and salt. Stir to combine. Select
Cancel. Lock the lid. Select Manual and cook at high
pressure for 5 minutes. When the cook time is complete,
let the pressure release naturally for 15 minutes, then
quick-release any remaining pressure. While waiting
for the pressure to release, in a blender, combine the soy
milk and olive oil. Blend until combined, about 1 minute.
Remove the lid. Discard the bay leaf and stir in the
soy milk mixture. Using an immersion blender, puree
the soup until smooth. Taste and season with salt and
pepper, as desired.

Curried Squash Soup

SERVES 4 to 6 | PREP TIME: 5 minutes | SAUTÉ LOW:
6 minutes | MANUAL: 30 minutes high pressure |
RELEASE: Quick | TOTAL TIME: 41 minutes

1 tablespoon extra-virgin
　olive oil
1 onion, chopped
2 garlic cloves, chopped
1 tablespoon curry powder

1 (2- to 3-pound) butternut
　squash, peeled, seeded,
　and cubed
4 cups vegetable broth
1 teaspoon salt
1 (14-ounce) can lite
　coconut milk

Select Sauté Low. When the display reads HOT, pour in
the oil and heat until it shimmers. Add the onion. Cook
for 3 to 4 minutes, stirring frequently. Select Cancel and
add the garlic and curry powder. Cook for 1 minute, stirring. Add the squash, broth, and salt. Lock the lid. Select
Manual and cook at high pressure for 30 minutes. When
the cook time is complete, quick-release the pressure.
Remove the lid. Using an immersion blender, blend the
soup until completely smooth. Stir in the coconut milk,
saving a little bit for topping when served.

Red Pepper and Tomato Bisque with Parmesan

SERVES 4 | PREP AND FINISHING: 20 minutes | SAUTÉ:
9 minutes | MANUAL: 12 minutes high pressure | BROIL:
2 minutes | RELEASE: Natural for 5 minutes, then Quick |
TOTAL TIME: 45 minutes

3 tablespoons extra-virgin
　olive oil
1 large onion, chopped
　(about 1½ cups)
3 large garlic
　cloves, minced
1 teaspoon kosher salt,
　divided, plus more
　as needed
⅓ cup dry sherry
2 (14-ounce) cans
　fire-roasted diced
　tomatoes

1 (16-ounce) jar roasted red
　peppers, drained, blotted
　dry, and cut into chunks
2 cups vegetable broth
½ cup strained tomatoes
　or tomato sauce
½ cup long-grain white rice
8 baguette slices
2 tablespoons unsalted
　butter, at room
　temperature
½ cup grated Parmesan or
　similar cheese

Select Sauté and adjust to More for high heat. Heat the
olive oil until it shimmers. Add the onion and garlic and
¼ teaspoon of salt. Cook, stirring frequently, until the
onion begins to brown, 3 to 4 minutes. Add the sherry
and cook, scraping up any browned bits from the bottom
of the pot, until the liquid has reduced by about half, 3 to
5 minutes. Add the tomatoes with their juices, roasted
red peppers, broth, strained tomatoes, rice, and remaining ¾ teaspoon of salt. Select Cancel. Lock the Lid.
Select Manual and cook at high pressure for 12 minutes.
When the cook time is complete, naturally release the
pressure for 5 minutes, then quick-release any remaining pressure. Remove the lid. Preheat the broiler.
Arrange the baguette slices on a baking sheet and butter
the top of each slice. Sprinkle with the Parmesan cheese.
When the soup has finished cooking and the pressure is
releasing, broil the baguette slices until golden brown
and bubbling, about 2 minutes. Puree the soup using an
immersion blender. Taste and add more salt if necessary.
Ladle the soup into four bowls and top with two croutons
each. Serve.

Baked Potato Soup

SERVES 4 | PREP AND FINISHING: 15 minutes | MANUAL:
8 minutes high pressure, divided | SAUTÉ: 8 minutes |
RELEASE: Quick, then Natural for 10 minutes | TOTAL
TIME: 40 minutes

3 russet potatoes (about
　2 pounds), peeled
2 cups very small broc-
　coli florets
1 cup water
3 tablespoons
　unsalted butter
½ medium onion, chopped
　(about ½ cup)

1 tablespoon
　all-purpose flour
1 teaspoon mus-
　tard powder
1 cup milk
2 cups vegetable broth
½ cup heavy (whip-
　ping) cream

1 teaspoon kosher salt,
  plus more as needed
¼ teaspoon freshly ground
  black pepper
¼ cup sour cream,
  for garnish

3 tablespoons minced
  fresh chives, for garnish
⅔ cup shredded sharp
  Cheddar cheese,
  for garnish

Chop one potato into ½-inch cubes and the other two into 1- to 2-inch chunks. Set aside the larger chunks. Put the small (½-inch) potato cubes and the broccoli in a steamer basket. Pour the water into the Instant Pot and place the steamer basket inside. Lock the Lid. Select Manual and cook at high pressure for 0 minutes. (The food will cook as the pot comes up to pressure.) After the cook time is complete, quick-release the pressure. Remove the lid. Use tongs or a potholder to remove the steamer basket. Set it aside. Pour the water out of the pot. Select Sauté and adjust to Normal for medium heat. Put the butter in the pot to melt. When it has stopped foaming, add the onion and cook, stirring frequently, until the onion pieces have separated and begun to soften, 2 to 3 minutes. Add the flour and mustard powder and stir to coat the onions. Cook, stirring frequently, until the flour has darkened slightly, about 2 minutes. Add the milk and stir. Bring the liquid to a simmer and cook until the milk is smooth and thickened, about 3 minutes. Add the broth, cream, large potato chunks, and salt. Stir to combine. Select Cancel. Lock the Lid. Select Manual and cook at high pressure for 8 minutes. When the cook time is complete, naturally release the pressure for 10 minutes, then quick-release any remaining pressure. Remove the lid. Use a potato masher to break up the potatoes and thicken the soup. Add the cooked potato and broccoli and let them simmer until warmed through. (Test a piece of potato first; if it's not quite done, add the potatoes to simmer for a couple of minutes before adding the broccoli.) Season with the pepper and additional salt if necessary. Ladle into bowls, garnish with the sour cream, chives, and cheese, and serve.

Mulligatawny Soup

SERVES 4 to 6 | PREP TIME: 10 minutes | SAUTÉ: 6 minutes | MANUAL: 6 minutes high pressure | RELEASE: Natural for 10 minutes, then Quick | TOTAL TIME: 42 minutes

2 teaspoons canola or vegetable oil
1 medium onion,
  finely chopped
2 garlic cloves,
  finely minced
2 teaspoons peeled and
  finely grated fresh ginger
1 medium potato, peeled
  and diced
2 medium carrots, diced
1 large tomato, chopped

1 teaspoon garam masala
½ teaspoon ground
  turmeric
2½ cups water
½ cup red lentils (masoor
  dal), rinsed and drained
1 teaspoon salt
¼ teaspoon freshly ground
  black pepper
½ cup full-fat coconut milk

1 tablespoon freshly
  squeezed lime or
  lemon juice

2 tablespoons finely
  chopped fresh cilantro

Select Sauté, and once the pot is hot, pour in the oil. Add the onion, garlic, and ginger and cook for 2 to 3 minutes, until the onion turns translucent. Add the potato, carrots, tomato, garam masala, and turmeric and cook for 2 to 3 minutes, until the tomato is soft. Stir in the water, red lentils, salt, and pepper. Stir to combine, making sure to scrape the bottom to loosen any browned bits. Select Cancel. Lock the lid. Select Manual and cook at high pressure for 6 minutes. When the cook time is complete, naturally release the pressure for 10 minutes, then quick-release the remaining pressure. Remove the lid. Use an immersion blender to blend the soup to a smooth mixture. Stir in the coconut milk, mix well, and replace and lock the lid for 5 minutes to heat through. Add the lime juice, mix well, and garnish with the cilantro. Serve warm.

Asparagus Ends Soup

SERVES 4 | PREP AND FINISHING: 15 minutes | SAUTÉ: 10 minutes, divided | MANUAL: 10 minutes high pressure | RELEASE: Natural for 10 minutes, the Quick | TOTAL TIME: 45 minutes

3 tablespoons
  unsalted butter
1 medium onion,
  thinly sliced
1½ teaspoons kosher salt,
  plus more as needed
⅔ cup dry white wine or
  vermouth

1½ pounds aspar-
  agus ends
3 cups chicken broth
½ cup heavy (whip-
  ping) cream
¼ teaspoon freshly ground
  white pepper (optional)

Select Sauté and adjust to More for high heat. Put the butter in the pot to melt. When it has stopped foaming, add the onion and sprinkle with the salt. Cook, stirring frequently, until the onion pieces separate and soften, 2 to 3 minutes. Add the wine and cook until it has reduced by about half and the raw alcohol smell is gone, 3 to 5 minutes. Add the asparagus and chicken broth. Select Cancel. Lock the Lid. Select Manual and cook at high pressure for 10 minutes. When the cook time is complete, let the pressure release naturally for 10 minutes, then quick-release any remaining pressure. Remove the lid. Pour about half of the soup into a blender, filling the jar only halfway. Remove the center of the blender lid and hold a dish towel tightly over the hole to allow steam to escape. Puree the soup thoroughly. Pour the soup through a medium-mesh strainer into a bowl, using a rubber spatula to push the soup through the strainer. Return the soup to the Instant Pot. Select Sauté and adjust to Normal for medium heat. Add the cream and bring the soup to a simmer, about 2 minutes. Adjust the seasoning, adding more salt and the white pepper (if using), if desired. Ladle into bowls and serve.

Chipotle Sweet Potato Chowder

SERVES 4 to 6 | PREP TIME: 3 minutes | MANUAL: 2 minutes high pressure | RELEASE: Natural for 5 minutes, then Quick | TOTAL TIME: 10 minutes

1¼ cups vegetable broth
1 (14-ounce) can lite coconut milk
2 large sweet potatoes, peeled and diced large
2 to 4 canned chipotle peppers in adobo sauce, diced

1 red bell pepper, seeded and diced
1 small onion, diced
1 teaspoon ground cumin
½ to 1 teaspoon salt
1½ cups frozen sweet corn
Adobo sauce from the canned peppers, for seasoning (optional)

In a medium bowl, whisk the broth and coconut milk, ensuring there are no solid bits of coconut milk left. Pour it into the Instant Pot and add the sweet potatoes, chipotles, bell pepper, onion, cumin, and salt. Lock the lid. Select Manual function and cook at high pressure for 2 minutes. When the cook time is complete, let the pressure release naturally for 5 minutes, then quick-release any remaining pressure. Remove the lid and add the frozen corn and adobo sauce (if you want more heat). Let it sit for 1 to 2 minutes while the corn warms and serve.

Vegetarian Pho

SERVES 6 | PREP AND FINISHING: 15 minutes | SAUTÉ: 10 minutes | MANUAL: 40 minutes high pressure | RELEASE: Natural | TOTAL TIME: 1 hour 15 minutes

1 tablespoon corn oil
1 bunch scallions, white parts only, coarsely chopped
2 garlic cloves, finely chopped
5 white mushrooms, halved
2 teaspoons peeled and finely chopped fresh ginger
1 tablespoon thinly sliced lemongrass
1 (1-inch) cinnamon stick
1 bay leaf
3 star anise pods
3 cardamom seeds
3 whole cloves

1 tablespoon coriander seeds
1 teaspoon fennel seeds
1 tablespoon sugar
2 teaspoons kosher salt
1 teaspoon soy sauce, plus more for drizzling
4 cups water
6 ounces rice noodles
4 ounces extra-firm tofu, cubed
Sprouts, for garnish
Fresh basil leaves, for garnish
Jalapeños, seeded and cut into rounds, for garnish
Sriracha sauce, for garnish

Select Sauté and pour in the oil. Once hot, add the scallions, garlic, mushrooms, and ginger and sauté for 2 minutes or until the mushrooms shrink. Add the lemongrass, cinnamon, bay leaf, star anise, cardamom, cloves, coriander seeds, fennel seeds, sugar, salt, and soy sauce and mix well. Add the water and mix again. Select Cancel. Lock the Lid. Select Manual and cook at high pressure for 40 minutes. About 10 minutes before the pho is done cooking, cook the rice noodles according to the package directions. When the cook time is complete, naturally release the pressure. Remove the lid. Using a fine-mesh strainer, strain the broth into a bowl, discarding the vegetables and spices. Divide the noodles among bowls. Add broth to each, and top each with tofu, sprouts, basil, and jalapeños. Drizzle with additional soy sauce and sriracha and serve hot.

Curried Cauliflower Soup

SERVES 4 to 6 | PREP TIME: 10 minutes | SAUTÉ: 3 to 5 minutes | MANUAL: 7 minutes high pressure | RELEASE: Natural for 10 minutes, then Quick | TOTAL TIME: 45 minutes

1 medium onion, chopped
3 garlic cloves, minced
1 tablespoon curry powder
3 cups vegetable broth
1 head cauliflower, roughly chopped

2 medium yellow potatoes, chopped
Freshly ground black pepper
Salt (optional)

Select Sauté. Sauté the onion for 3 to 5 minutes, until translucent, adding water as needed to prevent sticking. Add the garlic and curry powder and stir for 30 seconds, until fragrant. Select Cancel. Add the broth, scraping up any browned bits from the bottom of the pot. Stir in the cauliflower and potatoes and season to taste with pepper and salt (if using). Lock the lid. Select Manual and cook at high pressure for 7 minutes. When the cook time is complete, let the pressure release naturally for 10 minutes, then quick-release any remaining pressure. Remove the lid. Using an immersion blender, carefully puree the soup in the pot. Serve immediately.

Rich Mushroom Soup

SERVES 4 to 6 | PREP TIME: 10 minutes | SAUTÉ: 13 minutes, divided | MANUAL: 5 minutes high pressure | RELEASE: Natural for 5 minutes, then Quick | TOTAL TIME: 35 minutes

1 medium onion, diced
1 pound mushrooms, roughly chopped
4 garlic cloves, crushed
2 thyme sprigs or 1 teaspoon dried
3 cups vegetable broth
1 tablespoon chickpea miso paste

1 tablespoon vegan Worcestershire sauce
1 cup unsweetened plant-based milk
1 tablespoon arrowroot starch or gluten-free flour blend
Freshly ground black pepper
Salt (optional)

Select Sauté. Sauté the onion for 3 to 5 minutes until translucent, adding water as needed, a tablespoon at a time, to prevent sticking. Stir in the mushrooms, garlic, and thyme and sauté for 5 minutes. Select Cancel. Add the broth, miso, and Worcestershire sauce. Lock the lid.

Select Manual and cook at high pressure for 5 minutes. When the cook time is complete, let the pressure release naturally for 5 minutes, then quick-release any remaining pressure. Remove the lid. Discard the thyme stems. Set aside 2 cups of the soup. In a blender, puree the remaining soup. Select Sauté. Whisk the milk and arrowroot into the soup until boiling and slightly thickened, about 3 minutes. Add the reserved soup back into the pot and season to taste with pepper and salt (if using). Stir well to combine. Serve immediately.

Roasted Red Pepper Soup

SERVES 4 to 6 | PREP TIME: 10 minutes | SAUTÉ: 3 to 5 minutes | MANUAL: 6 minutes high pressure | RELEASE: Natural for 10 minutes, then Quick | TOTAL TIME: 45 minutes

1 medium onion, diced	1 tablespoon dried dill
4 garlic cloves, smashed	1 tablespoon maple syrup
¼ teaspoon red pepper flakes (optional)	2 teaspoons garlic powder
2½ cups water	1 teaspoon ground turmeric
2 (12-ounce) jars roasted red peppers, drained	1 (14-ounce) can full-fat coconut milk
1 (28-ounce) can crushed tomatoes	Freshly ground black pepper
1 (6-ounce) can tomato paste	Salt (optional)

Select Sauté. Sauté the onion for 3 to 5 minutes, adding water as needed, a tablespoon at a time, to prevent sticking. Add the garlic and red pepper flakes (if using) and sauté until fragrant, about 30 seconds. Select Cancel. Add the water, red peppers, tomatoes, tomato paste, dill, maple syrup, garlic powder, and turmeric. Stir well to combine. Lock the lid. Select Manual and cook at high pressure for 6 minutes. When the cook time is complete, let the pressure release naturally for 10 minutes, then quick-release any remaining pressure. Remove the lid. Stir in the coconut milk and season to taste with black pepper and salt (if using). Serve immediately.

Salsa Verde Soup

SERVES 4 to 6 | PREP TIME: 5 minutes | SAUTÉ: 3 minutes | MANUAL: 7 minutes high pressure | RELEASE: Natural | TOTAL TIME: 40 minutes

1 tablespoon butter	2 cups water, divided
1 tablespoon vegetable oil	Coarse salt
½ medium white onion, finely chopped	3 tablespoons masa harina
1 garlic clove, minced	Crumbled queso cotija, for garnish
3 cups fresh corn kernels	
2 cups spicy salsa verde or green enchilada sauce	
2 cups chicken broth	

Select Sauté and adjust to More for high. Heat the butter and vegetable oil in the pot until the butter is completely melted. Add the onion and garlic and sauté for 2 to 3 minutes, or until the onion is translucent. Stir in the corn kernels, salsa verde, chicken broth, and 1½ cups of water. Season lightly with salt. Select Cancel. Lock the lid. Select Manual and cook at high pressure for 7 minutes. When the cook time is complete, allow the pressure to release naturally. Remove the lid. In a small bowl, dissolve the masa harina in ½ cup of water. Immediately stir into the soup and stir for 1 to 2 minutes to thicken. Ladle into mugs. Sprinkle with crumbled queso cotija.

Mexican-Style Noodle Soup

SERVES 6 to 8 | PREP TIME: 5 minutes | SAUTÉ: 6 minutes | MANUAL: 6 minutes high pressure | RELEASE: Quick | TOTAL TIME: 20 minutes

3 cups water	8 ounces fideo pasta
3 Roma tomatoes	2 cups chicken broth
½ medium white onion	Coarse salt
2 tablespoons vegetable oil	3 cilantro sprigs

In a blender, puree the water, tomatoes, and onion until smooth. Select Sauté and adjust to More for high. Heat the vegetable oil in the pot, add the pasta, and sauté for 4 to 6 minutes, or until golden brown. Carefully pour in the tomato puree and chicken broth and season lightly with coarse salt. Add the cilantro. Lock the lid. Select Manual and cook at high pressure for 6 minutes. When the cook time is complete, allow the pressure to release naturally. Serve the soup immediately.

Chile Relleno Chowder

SERVES 6 | PREP TIME: 5 minutes | SAUTÉ: 3 minutes | MANUAL: 12 minutes high pressure | RELEASE: Quick | TOTAL TIME: 20 minutes

2 tablespoons butter	3 cups vegetable or chicken broth
½ medium white onion, roughly chopped	2½ cups milk, divided
2 garlic cloves, minced	1 cup Mexican crema or sour cream
8 roasted poblano peppers, peeled, seeded, and cut into thin strips	1 teaspoon coarse salt
	½ teaspoon freshly ground black pepper
4 medium Yukon Gold potatoes, peeled and chopped	3 tablespoons cornstarch
	10 ounces queso fresco, cut into bite-size cubes
1 (15½-ounce) can golden corn kernels, drained	1½ cups shredded Colby Jack cheese

Select Sauté and adjust to More for high. Heat the butter in the pot until completely melted, add the onion and garlic, and sauté for 2 to 3 minutes, or until the onion is translucent. Add the roasted poblano strips, potatoes, and corn. Pour in the broth, 2 cups of milk, and the Mexican crema. Season with the salt and pepper. Select Cancel. Lock the lid. Select Manual and cook at high pressure for 12 minutes. When the cook time is complete, allow the pressure to release naturally. Remove the lid. In a small bowl, stir the cornstarch into the remaining ½ cup of milk until completely dissolved. Stir into the hot soup immediately. Mash some of the potatoes lightly with a potato masher or the back of a spoon to help thicken the soup. Stir in the queso fresco. Ladle the soup into bowls. Top each bowl with ¼ cup of Colby Jack cheese.

Lentil Soup

SERVES 4 | PREP TIME: 10 minutes | SAUTÉ: 6 minutes | MANUAL: 5 minutes high pressure | RELEASE: Natural for 10 minutes, then Quick | TOTAL TIME: 41 minutes

½ tablespoon unsalted butter	1¼ cups dried lentils
1 medium onion, diced	½ teaspoon paprika
2 medium carrots, diced	1 teaspoon ground cumin
2 medium celery stalks, diced	4½ cups vegetable broth
4 garlic cloves, minced	Salt
2 large tomatoes, chopped	Freshly ground black pepper

Select Sauté, and when the Instant Pot is hot, melt the butter. Stir in the onion, carrot, and celery and sauté until they start to soften, about 3 minutes. Add the garlic and cook until fragrant, about 1 minute. Add the tomatoes, lentils, paprika, and cumin. Cook for 2 to 3 minutes, then add the broth. Mix well and season with salt and pepper. Select Cancel. Lock the lid. Select Manual and cook at high pressure for 5 minutes on manual high pressure. When the cook time is complete, let the pressure release naturally for 10 minutes, then quick-release any remaining pressure.

Red Lentil and Swiss Chard Soup

SERVES 4 | PREP TIME: 5 minutes | SAUTÉ: 4 minutes | MANUAL: 10 minutes high pressure | RELEASE: Quick | TOTAL TIME: 25 minutes

1 teaspoon extra-virgin olive oil	4 cups vegetable broth
1 yellow onion, diced	1 (14½-ounce) can diced tomatoes
2 carrots, cut into ½-inch slices	1 cup dried red lentils
1 bunch Swiss chard, stems and leaves separated, chopped	1 teaspoon ground cumin
	½ teaspoon ground turmeric
	¾ teaspoon kosher salt

Select Sauté and pour in the olive oil. When the oil is hot, add the onion, carrots, and chard stems. Sauté for 3 to 4 minutes, until softened. Select Cancel. Stir in the broth, tomatoes with their juices, lentils, cumin, and turmeric. Lock the lid. Select Manual and cook at high pressure for 10 minutes. When the cook time is complete,

quick-release the pressure. Remove the lid. Stir in the chard leaves and salt. Let sit for 3 to 4 minutes, or until the chard wilts, and serve.

15-Bean Soup

SERVES 8 | PREP TIME: 5 minutes | MANUAL: 40 minutes high pressure | RELEASE: Natural for 20 minutes, then Quick | TOTAL TIME: 1 hour 20 minutes

1 (20-ounce) package 15-bean soup mix, spice packet discarded, beans rinsed	1½ teaspoons dried thyme
	7 cups chicken broth
	1 teaspoon hot sauce
	1 pound diced ham
1 medium onion, diced	Salt
2 garlic cloves, minced	Freshly ground black pepper
2 bay leaves	

In the Instant Pot, combine the beans, onion, garlic, bay leaves, thyme, broth, hot sauce, and ham. Lock the lid. Select Manual and cook at high pressure for 40 minutes. When the cook time is complete, let the pressure release naturally for 20 minutes, then quick-release any remaining pressure. Remove the lid. Discard the bay leaves and season with salt and pepper to taste.

Minestrone Soup

SERVES 6 | PREP TIME: 10 minutes | SAUTÉ: 13 minutes, divided | MANUAL: 15 minutes high pressure | RELEASE: Quick | TOTAL TIME: 53 minutes

½ cup extra-virgin olive oil	1 (15-ounce) can dark red kidney beans, drained and rinsed
1 medium onion, diced	1 cup water
3 medium carrots, peeled and diced	1 tablespoon chopped fresh flat-leaf parsley
2 celery stalks, diced	1 teaspoon Italian seasoning
5 large garlic cloves, minced	Salt
4 cups chicken broth	Freshly ground black pepper
2 (14½-ounce) cans diced tomatoes	1 cup ditalini or other small pasta
2 medium russet potatoes, cut into ¼-inch chunks	
1 zucchini, diced	
2 (15-ounce) cans cannellini beans, drained and rinsed	

Select Sauté, and when the Instant Pot is hot, pour in the oil. Stir in the onion, carrot, celery, and garlic and sauté until soft, about 5 minutes. Add the broth, tomatoes with their juices, potatoes, zucchini, beans, water, parsley, and Italian seasoning, season with salt and pepper, and stir well. Select Cancel. Lock the lid. Select Manual and cook at high pressure for 15 minutes. When the cook time is complete, quick-release the pressure. Remove the lid. Select Sauté and add the pasta. Cook until al dente, about 8 minutes.

Cannellini Bean and Spinach Soup

SERVES 8 | PREP AND FINISHING: 15 minutes, plus 4 hours to soak | **MANUAL:** 18 minutes high pressure, divided | **RELEASE:** Natural for 5 minutes, then Quick | **SAUTÉ:** 5 minutes | **TOTAL TIME:** 4 hours 55 minutes

1 cup dried cannellini beans

3 cups water, divided

2 tablespoons corn oil

2 shallots, finely chopped

2 garlic cloves, finely chopped

1 medium carrot, grated

2 tomatoes, finely chopped

5 ounces fresh spinach leaves

2½ teaspoons kosher salt

1 teaspoon freshly ground black pepper

1 cup vegetable broth

2 tablespoons chopped fresh basil leaves, divided

In a large bowl, cover the cannellini beans with 2 to 3 inches of cold water. Soak at room temperature for 4 hours. Drain and rinse. Pour 2 cups of water into the Instant Pot and add the beans. Lock the Lid. Select Manual and cook at high pressure for 8 minutes. When the cook time is complete, naturally release the pressure. Remove the lid. Drain the beans and set them aside. Wipe out the inner pot. Select Sauté and pour in the oil. Once hot, add the shallots and garlic and sauté for 1 minute. Add the carrot, tomatoes, spinach, salt, and pepper. Cook until the spinach wilts, 4 to 5 minutes. Select Cancel. Add the beans, broth, remaining 1 cup of water, and 1 tablespoon of basil. Lock the Lid. Select Soup and cook at high pressure for 10 minutes. When the cook time is complete, naturally release the pressure for 5 minutes, then quick-release any remaining pressure. Remove the lid. Stir in the remaining tablespoon of basil and serve hot.

Chickpea Soup

SERVES 6 to 8 | PREP TIME: 10 minutes | **SAUTÉ:** 8 minutes | **MANUAL:** 40 minutes high pressure | **RELEASE:** Natural | **TOTAL TIME:** 1 hour 25 minutes

2 tablespoons vegetable oil

1 pound boneless smoked pork chops, cut into bite-size pieces

4 medium carrots, thinly sliced

½ medium white onion, thinly sliced

1 jalapeño pepper, seeded and finely chopped

2 garlic cloves, minced

3 Roma tomatoes, finely chopped

1 pound dried chickpeas

1 teaspoon freshly ground black pepper

1 teaspoon crushed dried Mexican oregano

1½ teaspoons coarse salt

2 cups roughly chopped baby spinach

Select Sauté and adjust to More for high. Heat the oil in the pot, add the pork chops, and sauté for about 5 minutes, or until lightly golden. Add the carrot, onion, jalapeño, and garlic. Sauté for an additional 3 minutes, or until the onion is translucent. Add the tomatoes, chickpeas, and enough water to reach the two-thirds mark inside the Instant Pot. Season with the black pepper and oregano. Lock the lid. Select Manual and cook at high pressure for 40 minutes. When the cook time is complete, allow the pressure to release naturally. Remove the lid. Season the soup with the salt. Stir in the spinach just before serving.

Quinoa and Corn Soup

SERVES 4 | PREP AND FINISHING: 10 minutes | **MANUAL:** 4 minutes high pressure, divided | **RELEASE:** Natural for 17 minutes, divided, then Quick | **TOTAL TIME:** 30 minutes

5½ cups vegetable broth or chicken broth, divided

1 cup quinoa, rinsed

1 small onion, diced

2 garlic cloves, minced

1 small red bell pepper, seeded and chopped

1 small green bell pepper, seeded and chopped

1 small russet potato, peeled and cut into ½-inch cubes

3 cups fresh or frozen corn

1 teaspoon ground cumin

1 teaspoon ground ancho chile

1 tablespoon freshly squeezed lime juice

¼ to ½ teaspoon kosher salt (optional)

Put 1½ cups broth and the quinoa in the Instant Pot. Lock the Lid. Select Manual and cook at high pressure for 1 minute. When the cook time is complete, let the pressure release naturally for 12 minutes, then quick-release any remaining pressure. Remove the lid. Spoon the quinoa into a small bowl and fluff it with a fork. Set it aside. Pour the remaining 4 cups of broth into the pot and add the onion, garlic, red and green bell peppers, potato, corn, cumin, and chile. Lock the Lid. Select Manual and cook at high pressure for 3 minutes. When the cook time is complete, let the pressure release naturally for 5 minutes, then quick-release any remaining pressure. Remove the lid. Add the quinoa to the soup. Stir in the lime juice and taste, adding salt if necessary. Ladle into soup bowls and serve.

White Bean Soup with Chard

SERVES 4 | PREP AND FINISHING: 15 minutes | **SAUTÉ:** 9 minutes, divided | **MANUAL:** 15 minutes high pressure | **RELEASE:** Natural for 10 minutes, then Quick | **TOTAL TIME:** 45 minutes, plus overnight to soak

1 tablespoon plus ½ teaspoon kosher salt, divided

1 quart water

12 ounces dried cannellini beans

2 tablespoons extra-virgin olive oil

1 medium onion, chopped (about 1 cup)

1 large carrot, chopped (about ⅔ cup)

2 garlic cloves, minced

1 cup diced cooked ham

2½ cups chicken broth

| 1 small bunch chard, stemmed and leaves cut into 1-inch ribbons | ¼ cup grated Parmesan or similar cheese |
| | 1 tablespoon chopped fresh parsley |

In a large bowl, dissolve 1 tablespoon of kosher salt in the water. Add the beans and soak at room temperature for 8 to 24 hours. Drain them and rinse. Select Sauté and adjust to Normal for medium heat. Heat the olive oil until it shimmers. Add the onion and carrot and ¼ teaspoon of salt. Cook, stirring frequently, until the onion pieces separate and soften, 2 to 3 minutes. Add the garlic and cook until fragrant, about another 1 minute. Select Cancel. Add the drained beans to the pot, along with the ham, broth, and remaining ¼ teaspoon of salt. Lock the Lid. Select Manual and cook at high pressure for 15 minutes. When the cook time is complete, naturally release the pressure for 10 minutes, then quick-release any remaining pressure. Remove the lid. Select Sauté and adjust to Normal for medium heat. Stir in the chard. Bring to a simmer and cook until the chard is tender, about 5 minutes. Taste the beans and season with more salt if needed. Ladle the beans into bowls, sprinkle with the cheese and parsley, and serve.

Spicy Chicken and Vegetable Soup

SERVES 6 | PREP TIME: 10 minutes | MANUAL: 20 minutes high pressure | RELEASE: Quick | TOTAL TIME: 30 minutes

2¼ pounds boneless chicken breasts or thighs, cut into large chunks	2 medium zucchini, cut into large chunks
2 ears corn, husks removed, and each ear cut into 3 pieces	1½ cups enchilada sauce
	2 teaspoons chicken bouillon
1 medium onion, quartered	1 teaspoon coarse salt, plus more for seasoning (optional)
2 whole garlic cloves, peeled	
5 cilantro sprigs	1 teaspoon crushed dried Mexican oregano
3 medium carrots, cut into bite-size pieces	½ teaspoon ground cumin
1 cup green beans, cut into bite-size pieces	½ teaspoon freshly ground black pepper
2 medium potatoes, peeled and cut into large chunks	Freshly squeezed lime juice, for garnish
¼ head cabbage, cut into large chunks	Warm corn tortillas, for serving (optional)

In the Instant Pot, combine the chicken, corn, onion, garlic, cilantro, carrots, green beans, potatoes, cabbage, and zucchini. Pour in the enchilada sauce and enough water to fill to the two-thirds mark into the Instant Pot. Add the chicken bouillon, salt, oregano, cumin, and pepper. Lock the lid. Select Manual and cook at high pressure for 20 minutes. When the cook time is complete, quick-release the pressure. Remove the lid. Season the soup with more salt, if necessary. Ladle the soup into

bowls. Top with a squeeze of fresh lime juice. Serve with warm corn tortillas (if using).

Mexican-Style Lime Soup

SERVES 6 to 8 | PREP TIME: 10 minutes | SAUTÉ: 3 minutes | MANUAL: 15 minutes high pressure | RELEASE: Natural | TOTAL TIME: 50 minutes

2 tablespoons vegetable oil	1½ teaspoons coarse salt
1 medium white onion, finely chopped	½ teaspoon freshly ground black pepper
3 Hungarian wax peppers, seeded and thinly sliced	Cubed avocado, for garnish
3 garlic cloves, minced	Chopped queso fresco, for garnish
3 Roma tomatoes, chopped	
2 pounds boneless, skinless chicken breasts, cut into 2-inch pieces	Mexican crema, for garnish
	Fried tortilla strips, for garnish
4 cilantro sprigs	Freshly squeezed lime juice, for garnish
4 cups water	
2 cups chicken broth	Warm corn or flour tortillas, for serving (optional)
Juice of 4 limes	
1 (3-inch) cinnamon stick	

Select Sauté and adjust to More for high. Heat the vegetable oil in the pot, add the onion, wax peppers, and garlic, and sauté for 2 to 3 minutes, or until the onion is just translucent. Stir in the tomatoes and sauté for an additional 30 seconds. Add the chicken breasts and cilantro. Pour in the water, chicken broth, and lime juice. Add the cinnamon stick and season with the salt and pepper. Select Cancel. Lock the lid. Select Manual and cook at high pressure for 15 minutes. When the cook time is complete, allow the pressure to release naturally. Remove the lid. Ladle the soup into bowls. Garnish with avocado, queso fresco, a drizzling of Mexican crema, fried tortilla strips, and a squeeze of fresh lime juice. Serve with warm tortillas (if using).

Tortilla Soup

SERVES 6 to 8 | PREP TIME: 10 minutes | MANUAL: 15 minutes high pressure | RELEASE: Natural | TOTAL TIME: 30 minutes

½ medium white onion, peeled	Chopped avocado, for garnish
2 garlic cloves, peeled	Chopped queso fresco, for garnish
2 cups chicken broth	
2 pounds boneless, skinless chicken breasts, cut into 2-inch pieces	Mexican crema, for garnish
	Fried tortilla strips, for garnish
4 cilantro sprigs	Freshly squeezed lime juice, for garnish
3 cups water	
1 cup red enchilada sauce	Warm corn or flour tortillas, for serving (optional)
1 cup tomato sauce	
1½ teaspoons coarse salt	

In a blender, puree the onion, garlic, and chicken broth until smooth. In the Instant Pot, arrange the chicken breast pieces and cilantro sprigs. Pour in the onion puree, water, enchilada sauce, and tomato sauce. Season with the salt. Lock the lid. Select Manual and cook at high pressure for 15 minutes. When the cook time is complete, allow the pressure to release naturally. Remove the lid. Ladle the soup into bowls. Garnish with avocado, queso fresco, a drizzling of Mexican crema, fried tortilla strips, and a squeeze of fresh lime juice. Serve with warm tortillas (if using).

Chicken Potpie Soup

SERVES 6 | PREP TIME: 10 minutes | SAUTÉ: 10 minutes | MANUAL: 3 minutes | RELEASE: Natural for 10 minutes, then Quick | TOTAL TIME: 42 minutes

2 tablespoons extra-virgin olive oil

3 pounds boneless, skinless chicken breasts, cut into 1- to 1½-inch bite-size pieces

1 small onion, chopped

3 medium celery stalks, cut into ½-inch pieces

4 garlic cloves, minced

3 medium russet potatoes, peeled and cut into 1-inch cubes

12 ounces frozen mixed vegetables (peas, carrots, corn, and green beans)

3½ cups chicken broth

2 teaspoons dried sage

2 teaspoons Italian seasoning

2 teaspoons freshly ground black pepper

1 teaspoon dried thyme

3 ounces cream cheese, cubed

½ cup freshly grated Parmesan cheese

1 cup heavy (whipping) cream

Select Sauté, and when the Instant Pot is hot, pour in the oil. Stir in the chicken, onion, and celery and cook until the chicken turns white on the outside, 3 to 5 minutes. Add the garlic and cook until fragrant, about 1 minute. Then add the potatoes, frozen veggies, broth, sage, Italian seasoning, pepper, and thyme. Lock the lid. Select Manual and cook at high pressure for 3 minutes. When the cook time is complete, let the pressure release naturally for 10 minutes, then quick-release any remaining pressure. Turn the Sauté function back on and add the cream cheese, Parmesan, and cream. Stir well. Turn the pressure cooker off and let the soup sit for 5 minutes to thicken.

Mexican-Style Chicken Soup

SERVES 6 | PREP TIME: 10 minutes | MANUAL: 20 minutes high pressure | RELEASE: Natural | TOTAL TIME: 50 minutes

2¼ pounds boneless, skinless chicken breast or thighs, cut into large chunks

1 medium onion, roughly chopped

3 whole garlic cloves, peeled

1 serrano chile, stemmed and split in half lengthwise

6 cilantro sprigs

2 bay leaves

1½ teaspoons coarse salt

½ teaspoon freshly ground black pepper

½ teaspoon crushed dried Mexican oregano

2 ears corn, husks removed and cut into 2-inch pieces

2 celery stalks, cut into large chunks

4 medium carrots, cut into large chunks

1 cup green beans, trimmed

3 medium Yukon Gold potatoes, peeled and cut into quarters

2 medium Mexican calabacitas or zucchini, cut into large chunks

Salsa, for serving

Freshly squeezed lime juice, for serving

Warm corn tortillas, for serving (optional)

In the Instant Pot, combine the chicken, onion, garlic, chile, cilantro, bay leaves, salt, black pepper, and oregano. Top with the corn pieces, celery, carrots, green beans, potatoes, and calabacitas. Pour in enough water to reach the two-thirds mark inside the Instant Pot. Lock the lid. Select Manual and cook at high pressure for 20 minutes. When the cook time is complete, allow the pressure to release naturally. Remove the lid. Remove and discard the bay leaves. Ladle the soup into bowls. Serve with your favorite salsa, a squeeze of fresh lime juice, and warm corn tortillas (if using).

Tlalpeño-Style Chicken and Chickpea Soup

SERVES 6 to 8 | PREP TIME: 10 minutes | MANUAL: 15 minutes high pressure | RELEASE: Natural | TOTAL TIME: 45 minutes

½ medium white onion, quartered

2 garlic cloves, peeled

2 to 4 canned chipotle chiles in adobo sauce

2 cups chicken broth

2 pounds boneless, skinless chicken breasts, cut into 2-inch pieces

2 (15-ounce) cans chickpeas, drained

1 epazote leaf or 3 cilantro sprigs

4 cups water

1½ teaspoons coarse salt

Diced avocado, for garnish

Diced queso fresco, for garnish

Freshly squeezed lime juice, for garnish

Warm corn tortillas, for serving (optional)

In a blender, puree the onion, garlic, 2 chipotle chiles, and the chicken broth until smooth. If desired, add the remaining 2 chipotles and process until smooth. In the Instant Pot, combine the chicken, chickpeas, and epazote. Pour in the onion puree and water. Season with the salt. Lock the lid. Select Manual and cook at high pressure for 15 minutes. When the cook time is complete, allow the pressure to release naturally. Remove the lid. Ladle the soup into bowls. Garnish with avocado, queso fresco, and a squeeze of fresh lime juice. Serve with warm tortillas (if using).

Lasagna Soup

SERVES 6 | PREP TIME: 10 minutes | SAUTÉ: 7 minutes | MANUAL: 5 minutes high pressure | RELEASE: Quick | TOTAL TIME: 36 minutes

1 pound mild ground Italian sausage	3 cups water, divided
½ teaspoon salt	4 cups dry mini lasagna noodles
½ teaspoon Italian seasoning	1 (25-ounce) jar marinara sauce
¼ teaspoon freshly ground black pepper	1 cup ricotta cheese
1 small onion, diced	1 cup shredded mozzarella cheese
3 garlic cloves, minced	

Turn on the Sauté function, and when the Instant Pot is hot, put in the sausage, salt, Italian seasoning, and pepper. Cook, stirring to break up the sausage, until it starts to brown lightly. Add the onion and garlic. Cook until the meat is thoroughly browned, 5 to 7 minutes. Add 1 cup of water and deglaze the pot, stirring to scrape up the browned bits from the bottom of the pot. Add the noodles, marinara sauce, and remaining 2 cups of water. Use the back of a spoon to gently push down any noodles that are not submerged, but do not stir. Lock the lid. Select Manual and cook at high pressure for 5 minutes. When the cook time is complete, quick-release the pressure. Remove the lid and stir in the ricotta. Add the mozzarella and replace the lid. Allow the pot to sit undisturbed for 5 minutes to melt the cheese, then serve.

Meatball Soup in Tomato Broth

SERVES 6 | PREP TIME: 10 minutes | MANUAL: 20 minutes high pressure | RELEASE: Quick | TOTAL TIME: 30 minutes

FOR THE MEATBALLS

½ pound ground beef	¼ medium white onion, finely chopped
½ pound ground pork	
2 tablespoons long-grain rice	1 serrano chile, finely chopped (optional)
2 tablespoons plain dry breadcrumbs	1 garlic clove, minced
2 tablespoons old-fashioned oats	¾ teaspoon coarse salt
1 large egg	¼ teaspoon freshly ground black pepper
1 large Roma tomato, finely chopped	¼ teaspoon crushed dried Mexican oregano

FOR THE SOUP

5 cups water	2 medium Yukon Gold potatoes, peeled and diced
2 cups tomato sauce	
3 medium carrots, thinly sliced	2 medium Mexican calabacitas or zucchini, cut into bite-size pieces

4 cilantro sprigs	Chopped fresh cilantro, for garnish
½ teaspoon coarse salt, plus more for seasoning (optional)	Freshly squeezed lime juice, for garnish
¼ teaspoon freshly ground black pepper	Warm corn tortillas (optional)
¼ teaspoon crushed dried Mexican oregano	

TO MAKE THE MEATBALLS

In a large bowl, combine the beef, pork, rice, breadcrumbs, oats, egg, tomato, onion, chile, garlic, salt, pepper, and oregano, mixing until the mixture comes together. Divide and shape into 1½- to 2-inch meatballs.

TO MAKE THE SOUP

Pour the water and tomato sauce into the Instant Pot. Add the carrots, potatoes, *calabacitas*, and cilantro sprigs. Carefully drop the meatballs, one at a time, into the broth. (Do not stir beyond this point!) Season the broth with the salt, pepper, and oregano. Lock the lid. Select Manual and cook at high pressure for 20 minutes. When the cook time is complete, quick-release the pressure. Remove the lid. Season with additional salt, if necessary. Ladle the soup into bowls. Garnish with chopped cilantro and a squeeze of fresh lime juice. Serve with warm corn tortillas (if desired).

Sausage, White Bean, and Kale Soup

SERVES 6 | PREP AND FINISHING: 10 minutes | SAUTÉ: 5 minutes | MANUAL: 10 minutes high pressure | RELEASE: Natural for 10 minutes, then Quick | TOTAL TIME: 45 minutes

2 tablespoons extra-virgin olive oil	1 pound spicy sausage, cut into ¾-inch-thick pieces
1 medium yellow onion, diced	6 cups chicken broth
3 garlic cloves, minced	1 (5-ounce) bag baby kale
4 carrots, chopped	2 (15-ounce) cans white beans, drained and rinsed
3 celery stalks, sliced	Juice of 1 lemon

Select Sauté and pour in the olive oil. Once the oil is hot, add the onion, garlic, carrots, celery, and sausage and cook for 3 minutes. Select Cancel and pour in the broth. Using a wooden spoon, scrape up any browned bits stuck to the bottom of the pot. Add the kale and beans and stir to combine. Lock the Lid. Select Manual and cook at high pressure for 10 minutes. When the cook time is complete, naturally release the pressure for 10 minutes, then quick-release any remaining pressure. Remove the lid. Using an immersion blender, blend the soup about halfway so the beans and vegetables are still chunky. Stir in the lemon juice. Serve immediately.

Beef and Brown Rice Soup

SERVES 4 to 6 | PREP TIME: 5 minutes | SAUTÉ:
15 minutes | MANUAL: 20 minutes high pressure |
RELEASE: Natural for 10 minutes, then Quick | TOTAL
TIME: 1 hour

2 tablespoons canola oil
1 pound beef chuck, cut
   into 1-inch cubes
Salt
Freshly ground
   black pepper
2 cups brown rice
2 carrots, diced
1 yellow onion, diced
2 celery stalks, diced

¼ cup minced
   fresh parsley
1 teaspoon minced garlic
1 teaspoon minced
   fresh thyme
1 teaspoon minced fresh
   rosemary
½ cup dry red wine
   (optional)
8 cups beef broth

Select Sauté and heat the oil in the Instant Pot until
it shimmers. Pat the beef dry with paper towels and
season generously with salt and pepper. Add the
beef to the pot and sear until it is gently browned
on all sides, about 10 minutes. Add the rice, carrots,
onion, celery, parsley, garlic, thyme, and rosemary.
Continue to sauté for 1 minute, until the rice smells
toasted. Add the red wine (if using) and scrape up
any browned bits from the bottom of the pot. Add the
broth. Stir to combine. Select Cancel. Lock the lid and
cook on high pressure for 20 minutes. When the cook
time is complete, let the pressure naturally release for
10 minutes, then quick-release any remaining pressure. Serve.

Beef and Barley Soup

SERVES 4 | PREP TIME: 10 minutes | MANUAL:
30 minutes high pressure | RELEASE: Natural | TOTAL
TIME: 1 hour

4 cups beef broth
1 pound beef chuck roast,
   cut into ¾-inch pieces
¾ cup barley
2 carrots, chopped
2 celery stalks, chopped
1 yellow onion, diced
4 garlic cloves, minced

2 tablespoons double con-
   centrated tomato paste
¾ teaspoon kosher salt
½ teaspoon freshly ground
   black pepper
¼ cup fresh parsley,
   chopped

In the Instant Pot, combine the broth, beef, barley, carrots, celery, onion, garlic, tomato paste, salt, and pepper.
Lock the lid. Select Manual and cook at high pressure
for 30 minutes. When the cook time is complete, let
the pressure release naturally for 10 minutes, then
quick-release any remaining pressure. Remove the lid
and stir in the parsley.

Mexican-Style Beef Soup

SERVES 8 | PREP TIME: 10 minutes | MANUAL:
60 minutes high pressure | RELEASE: Natural | TOTAL
TIME: 1 hour 30 minutes

3½ pounds beef stew meat
2 ears corn, each cut into
   3 pieces each
1 medium white
   onion, halved
3 whole garlic
   cloves, peeled
6 cilantro sprigs
1½ teaspoons coarse salt
½ teaspoon freshly ground
   black pepper
4 medium carrots, cut into
   bite-size pieces

1 cup green beans, cut into
   1-inch pieces
3 medium Yukon Gold
   potatoes, cut into eighths
2 medium chayote squash,
   peeled, pitted, and cut
   into eighths
¼ head cabbage,
   roughly chopped
Freshly squeezed lime
   juice, for garnish
Salsa, for garnish
Warm corn tortillas, for
   serving (optional)

In the Instant Pot, combine the beef, corn, onion, garlic,
and cilantro. Season with the salt and pepper. Add the
carrots, green beans, potatoes, chayote squash, and
cabbage. Fill the Instant Pot with enough water to reach
the two-thirds mark. Lock the lid. Select Manual and
cook at high pressure for 60 minutes. When the cook
time is complete, allow the pressure to release naturally.
Remove the lid. Ladle the soup into bowls. Garnish with
a squeeze of fresh lime juice and your favorite salsa.
Serve with warm corn tortillas (if using).

Beef, Bean, and Hominy Soup

SERVES 6 to 8 | PREP TIME: 10 minutes | SAUTÉ:
11 minutes | MANUAL: 60 minutes high pressure |
RELEASE: Natural | TOTAL TIME: 1 hour 15 minutes

1 tablespoon vegetable oil
2¼ pounds oxtails
½ medium white
   onion, diced
3 Hungarian wax peppers,
   thinly sliced
2 whole garlic
   cloves, peeled
2 cups dried pinto beans
6 cups water
1 (29-ounce) can white
   hominy, drained

1 bay leaf
1 teaspoon crushed dried
   Mexican oregano
Coarse salt
Chopped red onion,
   for garnish
Chopped fresh cilantro,
   for garnish
Freshly squeezed lime
   juice, for garnish
Warm flour tortillas, for
   serving (optional)

Select Sauté and adjust to More for high. Heat the
vegetable oil in the pot, add the oxtails, and sauté for
6 to 8 minutes, flipping once, until lightly browned on
both sides. Stir in the onion, peppers, and garlic. Sauté
for 2 to 3 minutes, or until the onion is translucent. Add
the water, pinto beans, hominy, bay leaf, and oregano.
Select Cancel. Lock the lid. Select Manual and cook at
high pressure for 60 minutes. When the cook time is

complete, allow the pressure to release naturally. Season the soup with salt. Remove and discard the bay leaf. To serve, ladle the soup into bowls. Garnish with chopped red onion, cilantro, and a squeeze of fresh lime juice. Serve with warm flour tortillas (if using).

Tripe Soup

SERVES 8 | PREP TIME: 5 minutes | MANUAL: 1 hour 15 minutes high pressure | RELEASE: Natural | TOTAL TIME: 1 hour 45 minutes

1 pound blanket/flat tripe, cut into 2- to 3-inch pieces

1 pound honeycomb tripe, cut into 2- to 3-inch pieces

1 pound book tripe, cut into 2- to 3-inch pieces

6 cups water

1½ cups red enchilada sauce

1½ teaspoons coarse salt, plus more for seasoning (optional)

Chopped white onion, for garnish

Crushed dried Mexican oregano, for garnish

Red pepper flakes or árbol chile flakes, for garnish

Freshly squeezed lime juice, for garnish

Warm corn tortillas, for serving (optional)

In the Instant Pot, combine all the tripe, the water, enchilada sauce, and salt. Lock the lid. Select Manual and cook at high pressure for 1 hour, 15 minutes. When the cook time is complete, allow the pressure to release naturally. Remove the lid. Stir the soup gently to combine; season with additional salt, if desired. Ladle into bowls and garnish with a heaping tablespoon of chopped onion, a pinch of dried Mexican oregano, a dash of red pepper flakes, and a squeeze of fresh lime juice. Serve with warm corn tortillas (if desired).

Vegetarian Chili

SERVES 8 | PREP TIME: 10 minutes | SAUTÉ: 3 minutes | MANUAL: 20 minutes high pressure | RELEASE: Natural | TOTAL TIME: 1 hour

2 tablespoons extra-virgin olive oil

1 medium white onion, chopped

3 garlic cloves, minced

3 Hungarian wax peppers, seeded and finely chopped

3 medium carrots, chopped

2 celery stalks, chopped

3 Roma tomatoes, seeded and chopped

2 medium Mexican calabacitas or zucchini, chopped

1 yellow squash, chopped

1 pound dried lentils

1 (15-ounce) can black beans, drained and rinsed

1 (15½-ounce) can golden corn kernels, drained

5 cilantro sprigs

6¼ cups water, divided

1 (12-ounce) bottle Mexican beer

2 bay leaves

2 tablespoons ancho chile powder

1 teaspoon crushed dried Mexican oregano

1 teaspoon ground cumin

½ teaspoon freshly ground black pepper

3 tablespoons masa harina

1 to 1½ teaspoons coarse salt

Mexican crema or sour cream, for garnish

Shredded Colby Jack cheese, for garnish

Chopped red onion, for garnish

Finely chopped fresh cilantro, for garnish

Select Sauté and adjust to More for high. Heat the olive oil in the pot, add the onion, garlic, and wax peppers, and sauté for 2 to 3 minutes, or until the onion is translucent. Stir in the carrots, celery, tomatoes, *calabacitas*, squash, lentils, black beans, corn, and cilantro. Add 6 cups of water, the beer, bay leaves, ancho chile powder, oregano, cumin, and black pepper. Select Cancel. Lock the lid. Select Manual and cook at high pressure for 20 minutes. When the cook time is complete, allow the pressure to release naturally. Remove the lid. Remove and discard the bay leaves. In a small bowl, dissolve the masa harina in the remaining ¼ cup of water; stir it into the chili. Season the chili with the salt. Lightly mash some of the lentils to help thicken the chili. Ladle the chili into bowls. Garnish with a dollop of Mexican crema, shredded Colby Jack cheese, chopped red onion, and cilantro.

Red Quinoa and Black Bean Chili

SERVES 4 to 6 | PREP TIME: 10 minutes | SAUTÉ: 3 to 5 minutes | MANUAL: 7 minutes high pressure | RELEASE: Natural for 10 minutes, then Quick | TOTAL TIME: 35 minutes

1 large onion, diced

2 red bell peppers, seeded and diced

4 garlic cloves, minced

1 tablespoon chili powder

2 teaspoons ground cumin

2 cups water

2 (14½-ounce) cans black beans, drained and rinsed

1 (28-ounce) can diced tomatoes

½ cup red quinoa

1 tablespoon vegan Worcestershire sauce

Freshly ground black pepper

Salt (optional)

Select Sauté. Sauté the onion and bell peppers for 3 to 5 minutes, adding water as needed, a tablespoon at a time, to prevent sticking. Add the garlic, chili powder, and cumin and stir for 30 seconds, until fragrant. Add the water, black beans, tomatoes, quinoa, and Worcestershire sauce and season to taste with pepper and salt (if using). Select Cancel. Lock the lid. Select Manual and cook at high pressure for 7 minutes. When the cook time is complete, let the pressure release naturally for 10 minutes, then quick-release any remaining pressure. Remove the lid. Stir and serve immediately.

White Bean Chili Verde

SERVES 4 to 6 | PREP TIME: 10 minutes | SAUTÉ: 6 to 10 minutes | MANUAL: 45 minutes high pressure | RELEASE: Natural for 10 minutes, then Quick | TOTAL TIME: 1 hour 20 minutes

1 large onion, diced
4 celery stalks, diced
6 cups vegetable broth, divided
2 jalapeño peppers, minced
5 garlic cloves, minced
1 tablespoon ground cumin
2 teaspoons dried oregano
1 pound dried great northern beans (about 2 cups), rinsed and sorted
2 (7-ounce) cans diced green chiles
5 ounces fresh baby spinach
Freshly ground black pepper
Salt (optional)

Select Sauté. Sauté the onion and celery for 3 to 5 minutes, until translucent, adding broth as needed to prevent sticking. Add the jalapeños, garlic, cumin, and oregano and stir for 30 seconds, until fragrant. Add the remaining broth, the beans, and green chiles. Stir to combine, scraping up any browned bits from the bottom of the pot. Sauté for 3 to 5 minutes, then press Cancel. Lock the lid. Select Manual and cook at high pressure for 45 minutes. When the cook time is complete, let the pressure release naturally for 10 minutes, then quick-release any remaining pressure. Remove the lid. Using an immersion blender, puree some of the chili to thicken it, leaving some in chunks. Stir in the spinach until wilted. Season to taste with pepper and salt (if using). Serve immediately.

Black Bean, Sweet Potato, and Chorizo Chili

SERVES 8 | PREP TIME: 10 minutes | SAUTÉ: 10 minutes | MANUAL: 60 minutes high pressure | RELEASE: Natural | TOTAL TIME: 1 hour 45 minutes

1 tablespoon vegetable oil
1 pound Mexican pork chorizo
2 green bell peppers, seeded and diced
1 large white onion, diced
4 garlic cloves, minced
2 medium sweet potatoes, peeled and diced
3 Roma tomatoes, diced
1 pound dried black beans
6 cups water
1 (12-ounce) bottle dark Mexican beer
1 (3-ounce) tablet Mexican chocolate, cut into eighths
1½ tablespoons chipotle chile powder
1 teaspoon crushed dried Mexican oregano
½ teaspoon ground cumin
½ teaspoon freshly ground black pepper
1 to 1½ teaspoons coarse salt
Sour cream, for garnish
Crumbled queso cotija, for garnish

Select Sauté and adjust to More for high. Heat the vegetable oil in the pot, add the chorizo, and sauté for 5 to 7 minutes, or until cooked through. Add the bell peppers, onion, and garlic. Sauté for 2 to 3 minutes, or until the onion is translucent. Stir in the sweet potatoes, tomatoes, and black beans. Add the water, beer, chocolate, chipotle powder, oregano, cumin, and pepper. Lock the lid. Select Manual and cook at high pressure for 60 minutes. When the cook time is complete, allow the pressure to release naturally. Remove the lid. Season the chili with the salt and ladle into bowls. Garnish with a dollop of sour cream and crumbled queso cotija.

Tex-Mex Chili

SERVES 8 to 10 | PREP TIME: 10 minutes | SAUTÉ: 11 minutes | MANUAL: 20 minutes high pressure | RELEASE: Natural | TOTAL TIME: 55 minutes

1 tablespoon vegetable oil
2¼ pounds lean (93 percent) ground beef
1 medium white onion, chopped
2 serrano chiles, finely chopped
2 roasted poblano peppers, peeled, seeded, and cut into thin strips
4 garlic cloves, minced
4 Roma tomatoes, chopped
1 (15½-ounce) can black beans, drained and rinsed
1 (15½-ounce) can pinto beans, drained and rinsed
1 tablespoon ancho chile powder
1 tablespoon California chile powder
1½ teaspoons coarse salt, plus more for seasoning (optional)
1 teaspoon paprika
1 teaspoon ground cumin
1 teaspoon crushed dried Mexican oregano
½ teaspoon freshly ground black pepper
2½ cups water, divided
1 cup beef broth
6 to 8 cilantro sprigs
3 tablespoons masa harina
Sour cream, for garnish
Chopped tomato, for garnish
Chopped onion, for garnish
Chopped fresh cilantro, for garnish
Crumbled queso cotija, for garnish

Select Sauté and adjust to More for high. Heat the vegetable oil in the pot, add the ground beef, and sauté for 6 to 8 minutes, breaking it up with the back of a wooden spoon, until no longer pink. Add the onion, chiles, roasted pepper strips, and garlic. Sauté for an additional 2 to 3 minutes, or until the onion is translucent. Stir in the tomatoes, black beans, and pinto beans. Season with the chile powders, salt, paprika, cumin, oregano, and pepper. Pour in 2 cups of water and the beef broth. Add the cilantro sprigs. Select Cancel. Lock the lid. Select Manual and cook at high pressure for 20 minutes. When the cook time is complete, allow the pressure to release naturally. Remove the lid. In a small bowl, dissolve the masa harina in the remaining ½ cup of water; immediately stir into the hot chili. Season with more salt, if desired. Ladle the chili into bowls. Garnish with a dollop of sour cream and chopped tomato, onion, and cilantro. Sprinkle a little crumbled queso cotija on top.

Ranch White Chicken Chili

SERVES 8 | PREP TIME: 10 minutes | MANUAL:
20 minutes | RELEASE: Natural for 10 minutes, then
Quick | TOTAL TIME: 47 minutes

2 large boneless, skinless
  chicken breasts
1 (15-ounce) can black
  beans, drained
  and rinsed
1 (15-ounce) can white
  beans, drained
  and rinsed
1 medium onion, chopped
2 cups frozen corn

1 (10-ounce) can
  diced tomatoes and
  green chiles
1 cup chicken broth
1 teaspoon chili powder
1 teaspoon ground cumin
1 (½-ounce) packet ranch
  dressing mix
8 ounces cream cheese,
  cut into 6 pieces

In the Instant Pot, combine the chicken, black beans, white beans, onion, corn, tomatoes with their juices, and chicken broth. Add the chili powder, cumin, and ranch dressing mix and stir well. Lock the lid. Select Manual and cook at high pressure for 20 minutes. When the cook time is complete, let the pressure release naturally for 10 minutes, then quick-release any remaining pressure. Transfer the chicken to a plate and shred it with a fork. Add the cream cheese to the bean mixture and stir until the cheese is melted and combined. Return the chicken to the pot and stir well.

Ratatouille

SERVES 8 | PREP AND FINISHING: 5 minutes | SAUTÉ:
7 minutes | MANUAL: 10 minutes high pressure |
RELEASE: Natural for 3 minutes, then Quick |
TOTAL TIME: 42 minutes

2 tablespoons extra-virgin
  olive oil
3 garlic cloves,
  finely chopped
1 medium onion, cut into
  ¼-inch slices
2 small zucchini, cut into
  ¼-inch slices
1 small eggplant, cut into
  ¼-inch slices
1 yellow bell pepper,
  seeded and cut into
  ¼-inch slices

1 small butternut squash,
  peeled, seeded, and cut
  into ¼-inch slices
1 tablespoon dried thyme
10 fresh basil leaves,
  finely chopped
2 teaspoons kosher salt
1 teaspoon freshly ground
  black pepper
3 medium tomatoes, cut
  into ¼-inch slices
3 cups vegetable broth

Select Sauté and pour in the olive oil. Once hot, add the garlic and onion and sauté for about 5 minutes. Add the zucchini, eggplant, bell pepper, butternut squash, thyme, basil, salt, and pepper. Sauté for another 4 minutes. Select Cancel. Transfer the vegetables to a baking sheet and set them aside until cool to the touch. Using an 8-inch round, 2-inch deep ceramic dish, arrange the sautéed vegetables and tomatoes in a pattern. Alternatively,

place the slices upright, along the edge, until the dish is covered. Place the dish inside the Instant Pot. Pour the broth over the vegetables. Lock the Lid. Select Manual and cook at high pressure for 10 minutes. When the cook time is complete, quick-release the pressure. Carefully remove the dish from the Instant Pot and serve immediately.

Quinoa and Vegetable Stew

SERVES 4 | PREP AND FINISHING: 10 minutes | SAUTÉ:
5 minutes | MANUAL: 8 minutes high pressure |
RELEASE: Natural | TOTAL TIME: 35 minutes

2 teaspoons corn oil
1 yellow onion,
  finely chopped
3 Roma tomatoes,
  finely chopped
½ cup chopped red
  bell pepper
1½ cups broccoli florets
1 zucchini, cut into
  1-inch chunks
¼ cup frozen corn ker-
  nels, thawed to room
  temperature

¼ cup (½-inch pieces)
  diced carrot
4 cups vegetable broth
½ cup quinoa, rinsed
2 teaspoons kosher salt
1 teaspoon ground
  coriander
½ teaspoon paprika
½ teaspoon ground cumin
¼ cup finely chopped fresh
  cilantro, divided

Select Sauté and pour in the oil. Once hot, add the onion and cook until translucent, about 5 minutes. Add the tomatoes, bell pepper, broccoli, zucchini, corn, and carrot, and mix well. Add the broth, quinoa, salt, coriander, paprika, and cumin. Add 2 tablespoons of cilantro and mix thoroughly. Select Cancel. Lock the Lid. Select Manual and cook at high pressure for 8 minutes. When the cook time is complete, naturally release the pressure. Remove the lid. Stir in the remaining 2 tablespoons of cilantro and serve hot.

Nepali-Style Mixed Bean Stew

SERVES 8 | PREP AND FINISHING: 10 minutes, plus
2 hours to soak | SAUTÉ: 10 minutes, divided | MANUAL:
30 minutes high pressure | RELEASE: Natural |
TOTAL TIME: 3 hours

2 cups mixed dried beans
  and lentils
3 teaspoons corn
  oil, divided
1 yellow onion,
  roughly chopped
3 garlic cloves
2 teaspoons finely
  chopped fresh ginger
3 tomatoes,
  roughly chopped
1 teaspoon fennel seeds

1 teaspoon carom seeds
1 teaspoon cumin seeds
1 teaspoon ground
  coriander
1 teaspoon chili powder
½ teaspoon ground
  turmeric
2 cups water
1 tablespoon chopped
  fresh cilantro

In a large bowl, cover the beans and lentils with 2 to 3 inches of cold water. Soak at room temperature for 2 hours. Drain them and rinse. Select Sauté and pour in 1½ teaspoons of oil. Once hot, add the onion, garlic, ginger, and tomatoes. Sauté for 5 minutes or until the onion is translucent, stirring occasionally. Select Cancel. Let cool for 5 minutes. Transfer the onion mixture to a blender. Blend to make a coarse paste. Select Sauté and pour in the remaining 1½ teaspoons of oil. Once hot, add the fennel, carom, and cumin seeds and sauté for 30 seconds. Add the onion paste, coriander, chili powder, and turmeric. Cook, stirring frequently, for 1 minute. Add the water and deglaze the pot, scraping up any browned bits from the bottom of the pot. Add the beans to the inner pot. Select Cancel. Lock the Lid. Press Manual and cook at high pressure for 30 minutes. When the cook time is complete, naturally release the pressure. Remove the lid. Stir in the cilantro and serve hot.

Vegetable Jambalaya

SERVES 8 | PREP AND FINISHING: 10 minutes, plus 15 minutes to cool | SAUTÉ: 10 minutes | MANUAL: 12 minutes low pressure | RELEASE: Natural | TOTAL TIME: 55 minutes

2 tablespoons corn oil
1 dried bay leaf
1 onion, finely chopped
2 garlic cloves, finely chopped
1 green serrano chile, finely chopped
4 tomatoes, finely chopped
1½ teaspoons kosher salt
1 teaspoon dried oregano
½ teaspoon cayenne pepper
½ teaspoon paprika
½ teaspoon dried thyme
½ teaspoon sugar
2 teaspoons soy sauce

1 cup chopped red bell pepper
1 cup halved mushrooms
3 celery stalks, cut into 1-inch pieces
1 medium carrot, cut into 1-inch pieces
1 cup cooked black beans
¼ cup finely chopped fresh cilantro, divided
3 cups vegetable broth
1½ cups short grain white rice
½ cup shredded Mexican-blend cheese

Select Sauté and pour in the oil. Once hot, add the bay leaf, onion, garlic, and chile. Sauté for 3 to 4 minutes or until the onion is translucent. Add the tomatoes, salt, oregano, cayenne pepper, paprika, thyme, and sugar and stir well. Loosely place the lid on top and cook for 3 minutes or until the tomatoes are soft. Add the soy sauce, bell pepper, mushrooms, celery, carrot, beans, and 2 tablespoons of cilantro. Mix in the broth and rice. Select Cancel. Lock the Lid. Select Rice and cook on low pressure for 12 minutes. When the cook time is complete, naturally release the pressure. Remove the lid. Let the rice cool for 15 minutes, then remove the bay leaf. Use a fork to gently fluff the rice. Stir in the

cheese and the remaining 2 tablespoons of cilantro and serve hot.

White Bean and Swiss Chard Stew

SERVES 4 to 6 | PREP TIME: 6 minutes | SAUTÉ LOW: 5 minutes | MANUAL: 4 minutes high pressure | RELEASE: Quick | TOTAL TIME: 15 minutes

1 tablespoon extra-virgin olive oil
2 carrots, sliced, with the thicker end cut into half-moons
1 celery stalk, sliced
½ onion, large dice
2 or 3 garlic cloves, minced
2 cups cooked great northern beans
3 tomatoes, chopped
¼ to ½ teaspoon red pepper flakes

½ teaspoon dried rosemary
½ teaspoon dried oregano
¼ teaspoon dried basil
½ teaspoon salt, plus more as needed
Pinch freshly ground black pepper, plus more as needed
1 small bunch Swiss chard leaves, chopped
Nutritional yeast, for sprinkling (optional)

Select Sauté Low. When the display reads HOT, pour in the oil and heat until it shimmers. Add the carrots, celery, and onion. Cook for 2 to 3 minutes, stirring occasionally. Add the garlic and cook for 30 seconds more. Select Cancel. Stir in the beans, tomatoes, red pepper flakes, rosemary, oregano, basil, salt, and pepper. Lock the lid. Select Manual and cook at high pressure for 4 minutes. When the cook time is complete, quick-release the pressure. Remove the lid and stir in the Swiss chard. Let it wilt for 2 to 3 minutes. Taste and season with salt and pepper, as needed, and sprinkle the nutritional yeast over individual servings (if using).

African-Style Peanut Stew

SERVES 4 to 6 | PREP TIME: 7 minutes | SAUTÉ LOW: 5 minutes | MANUAL: 3 minutes high pressure | RELEASE: Quick | TOTAL TIME: 15 minutes

1 tablespoon roasted walnut oil
1 small onion, large dice
1 red bell pepper, seeded and large dice
1 jalapeño pepper, diced
3 garlic cloves, minced
3 tomatoes, large dice
1 sweet potato, peeled and large dice
2 tablespoons peeled and minced fresh ginger
1½ teaspoons ground cumin
½ teaspoon chili powder

½ teaspoon salt, plus more as needed
2 cups vegetable broth, divided
½ cup creamy all-natural peanut butter
1 small bunch collard green leaves, chopped
Freshly ground black pepper
½ cup chopped roasted peanuts

Select Sauté Low, and when the display reads HOT, pour in the oil and heat until it shimmers. Add the onion, bell pepper, and jalapeño. Cook for 2 to 3 minutes, stirring frequently. Select Cancel and add the garlic. Cook for 30 seconds, stirring. Stir in the tomatoes, sweet potato, ginger, cumin, chili powder, and salt. Let it rest for a few minutes. While the stew rests, in a large measuring cup, whisk 1 cup of broth and peanut butter until smooth. Pour this into the Instant Pot. Use the remaining 1 cup of broth to rinse out the measuring cup, making sure you get as much of the peanut butter as possible. Add this to the pot. Lock the lid. Select Manual and cook at high pressure for 3 minutes. When the cook time is complete, quick-release the pressure. Remove the lid, stir in the collard greens, and let them wilt for 1 to 2 minutes. Taste and season with salt and pepper, as needed, and serve topped with chopped peanuts.

Chickpea, Farro, and Tomato Stew

SERVES 4 to 6 | PREP TIME: 10 minutes | SAUTÉ: 3 to 5 minutes | MANUAL: 10 minutes high pressure | RELEASE: Natural for 10 minutes, then Quick | TOTAL TIME: 50 minutes

1 medium onion, diced
5 garlic cloves, minced
1 tablespoon Italian seasoning
¼ to ½ teaspoon red pepper flakes
3 cups vegetable broth or water
1 cup pearled farro
1 (28-ounce) can diced tomatoes

1 (15-ounce) can chickpeas, drained and rinsed
5 ounces baby spinach
Zest and juice of 1 lemon
Freshly ground black pepper
Salt (optional)
Plant-based Parmesan (optional), for serving

Select Sauté. Sauté the onion for 3 to 5 minutes, adding water as needed, a tablespoon at a time, to prevent sticking. Add the garlic, Italian seasoning, and red pepper flakes to taste and stir for 30 seconds, until fragrant. Select Cancel. Add the broth, farro, tomatoes, and chickpeas. Lock the lid. Select Manual and cook at high pressure for 10 minutes. When the cook time is complete, let the pressure release naturally for 10 minutes, then quick-release any remaining pressure. Remove the lid. Stir in the spinach and lemon zest and juice, allowing the residual heat from the stew to wilt the spinach. Season to taste with pepper and salt (if using). Serve immediately with a sprinkle of Parmesan (if using).

Coconut-Cabbage Stew

SERVES 4 to 6 | PREP TIME: 10 minutes | SAUTÉ: 3 to 5 minutes | MANUAL: 3 minutes high pressure | RELEASE: Natural for 5 minutes, then Quick | TOTAL TIME: 30 minutes

1 medium onion, diced
8 ounces shiitake or cremini mushrooms, chopped
4 garlic cloves, minced
1 (1-inch) knob fresh ginger, peeled and grated, or 1 teaspoon dried ginger
3 large carrots, diced
2 or 3 medium yellow potatoes, chopped into 1-inch chunks

1 tablespoon gluten-free soy sauce
2½ to 3 cups vegetable broth
1 small head green or Napa cabbage, sliced
1 (14-ounce) can full-fat coconut milk
Freshly ground black pepper

Select Sauté. Sauté the onion and mushrooms for 3 to 5 minutes, until the onion is translucent, adding water as needed to prevent sticking. Add the garlic and ginger and stir for 30 seconds, until fragrant. Select Cancel. Add the carrots, potatoes, and soy sauce. Stir in 2½ cups of broth and add more as needed to just cover the vegetables. Place the cabbage on top. Lock the lid. Select Manual and cook at high pressure for 3 minutes. When the cook time is complete, let the pressure release naturally for 5 minutes, then quick-release any remaining pressure. Remove the lid. Stir in the coconut milk until heated through and season to taste with pepper. Serve immediately.

Barley, Mushroom, and Kale Stew

SERVES 4 to 6 | PREP TIME: 10 minutes | SAUTÉ: 3 to 5 minutes | MANUAL: 20 minutes high pressure | RELEASE: Natural for 10 minutes, then Quick | TOTAL TIME: 1 hour

1 medium onion, diced
4 celery stalks, diced
1 pound cremini mushrooms, sliced
3 garlic cloves, minced
2 tablespoons tomato paste
1 tablespoon poultry seasoning
6 cups vegetable broth or water

1 cup pearled barley
2 tablespoons balsamic vinegar
1 tablespoon chickpea miso paste
1 bunch kale, stemmed and chopped
Freshly ground black pepper
Salt (optional)

Select Sauté. Sauté the onion, celery, and mushrooms for 3 to 5 minutes, until the onion is translucent, adding water as needed to prevent sticking. Add the garlic, tomato paste, and poultry seasoning and stir for 30 seconds, until fragrant. Stir in the broth, barley, vinegar, and miso, scraping up any browned bits from the bottom of the pot. Place the kale on top. Select Cancel. Lock the lid. Select Manual and cook at high pressure for 20 minutes. When the cook time is complete, let the pressure release naturally for 10 minutes, then quick-release any remaining pressure. Remove the lid. Stir well and season to taste with pepper and salt (if using). Serve immediately.

Red Lentil Dal with Kale

SERVES 4 to 6 | PREP TIME: 10 minutes | SAUTÉ:
3 to 5 minutes | MANUAL: 7 minutes high pressure |
RELEASE: Natural for 10 minutes, then Quick | TOTAL
TIME: 40 minutes

1 large onion, diced
4 garlic cloves, minced
1 (1-inch) knob fresh ginger, peeled and grated
1 tablespoon garam masala
¼ teaspoon red pepper flakes (optional)
3 cups water
1½ cups dry red lentils, rinsed and sorted
1 large carrot, diced
1 Roma tomato, diced
3 or 4 fresh kale leaves, stemmed and chopped
1 (14-ounce) can full-fat coconut milk
Zest and juice of 1 lemon
Freshly ground black pepper
Salt (optional)
Fresh cilantro (optional)

Select Sauté. Sauté the onion for 3 to 5 minutes, until translucent, adding water as needed to prevent sticking. Add the garlic, ginger, garam masala, and red pepper flakes (if using) and stir for 30 seconds, until fragrant. Select Cancel. Add the water, lentils, carrot, and tomato and stir well to combine. Place the kale on top. Lock the lid. Select Manual and cook at high pressure for 7 minutes. When the cook time is complete, let the pressure release naturally for 10 minutes, then quick-release any remaining pressure. Remove the lid. Stir in the coconut milk and lemon zest and juice, then season to taste with pepper and salt (if using). Serve immediately, topped with cilantro (if using).

Ciambotta

SERVES 4 to 6 | PREP TIME: 5 minutes | SAUTÉ LOW:
4 minutes | MANUAL: 8 minutes high pressure |
RELEASE: Natural for 10 minutes, then Quick | TOTAL
TIME: 27 minutes

1 to 2 tablespoons extra-virgin olive oil
2 leeks, white and very light green parts only, cleaned well, halved lengthwise, cut into half-moons
1 sweet onion, large dice
1 carrot, halved lengthwise and cut into half-moons
1 celery stalk, sliced
1 cup sliced white mushrooms
1 small eggplant, large dice
3 garlic cloves, minced
3 Yukon Gold potatoes, peeled and cut into bite-size pieces
3 Roma tomatoes, large dice
4 cups vegetable broth
1 teaspoon dried oregano
½ teaspoon salt, plus more as needed
2 cups torn kale leaves
Freshly ground black pepper
Fresh basil, for garnish

Select Sauté Low. When the display reads HOT, pour in the oil and heat until it shimmers. Add the leeks, onion, carrot, celery, mushrooms, and eggplant. Cook for about

2 minutes, stirring occasionally. Add the garlic. Cook for 30 seconds more. Select Cancel and add the potatoes, tomatoes, broth, oregano, and salt. Lock the lid. Select Manual and cook at high pressure for 8 minutes. When the cook time is complete, let the pressure release naturally for 10 minutes, then quick-release any remaining pressure. Remove the lid and stir in the kale. Taste and season with more salt, as needed, and pepper. If there's too much liquid, select Sauté Low again and cook for a few minutes to evaporate. Serve garnished with basil.

American Goulash

SERVES 6 | PREP TIME: 5 minutes | SAUTÉ: 7 minutes |
MANUAL: 5 minutes high pressure | RELEASE: Quick |
TOTAL TIME: 26 minutes

1 tablespoon vegetable oil
1 pound lean (93 percent) ground beef
1 large onion, chopped
3 garlic cloves, minced
2½ cups water
3 cups elbow noodles, uncooked
2 (15-ounce) cans diced tomatoes
2 (15-ounce) cans tomato sauce
3 tablespoons soy sauce
2 tablespoons Italian seasoning
3 bay leaves
Salt
Freshly ground black pepper

Select Sauté, and when the Instant Pot is hot, pour in the oil. Add the beef, onion, and garlic and cook until the meat is browned, 5 to 7 minutes. If necessary, drain any fat from the pot. Stir in the water, scraping up any browned bits from the bottom of the pot. Add the noodles, diced tomatoes with their juices, tomato sauce, soy sauce, Italian seasoning, and bay leaves. Season with salt and pepper. Do not stir. Select Cancel. Lock the lid. Select Manual and cook at high pressure for 5 minutes. When the cook time is complete, quick-release the pressure. Remove the lid. Discard the bay leaves and give everything a good stir. If the sauce looks too thin, cover the pot and let it sit for 1 to 2 minutes to thicken.

Beef Stew

SERVES 8 | PREP TIME: 10 minutes | SAUTÉ: 18 minutes |
MANUAL: 30 minutes high pressure | RELEASE:
Natural for 10 minutes, then Quick | TOTAL TIME: 1 hour
16 minutes

3 tablespoons extra-virgin olive oil
2½ pounds beef chuck roast, cut into 1½-inch pieces
1 large onion, diced
1½ cups chopped celery
2 tablespoons minced garlic
¼ cup balsamic vinegar
3 cups beef broth
3 tablespoons tomato paste
4 cups halved baby potatoes
1½ cups chopped carrots
2 teaspoons salt

2 teaspoons freshly ground
    black pepper
1 teaspoon dried thyme

1 teaspoon dried rosemary
1 teaspoon dried oregano

Select Sauté, and when the Instant Pot is hot, pour in the oil. Add the meat, working in batches if necessary, and brown it for 2 to 3 minutes on each side. Don't try to cook it through; you are just searing it at this point. Add the onion and celery and cook until the onion is translucent, 3 to 4 minutes. Add the garlic and cook until fragrant, about 1 minute. Pour in the balsamic vinegar and deglaze the pot, stirring to scrape up the browned bits from the bottom of the pot. Add the potatoes, carrots, salt, pepper, thyme, rosemary, and oregano. Lock the lid. Select Manual and cook at high pressure for 30 minutes. When the cook time is complete, let the pressure release naturally for 10 minutes, then quick-release any remaining pressure. Scoop into bowls and serve.

Pork and Bean Stew

SERVES 8 to 10 | **PREP TIME:** 15 minutes | **SAUTÉ:** 17 minutes | **MANUAL:** 60 minutes high pressure | **RELEASE:** Natural | **TOTAL TIME:** 1 hour 55 minutes

6 bacon slices, cut into
    1-inch pieces
4 ounces Mexican pork
    chorizo, casings removed
2 boneless smoked
    pork chops, cut into
    bite-size pieces
4 slices deli ham, chopped
4 pork hot dog franks, cut
    into 1-inch slices
½ medium white
    onion, chopped

2 serrano chiles,
    finely chopped
3 garlic cloves, minced
3 Roma tomatoes, chopped
1 pound dried pinto beans
Handful cilantro sprigs
1 teaspoon crushed dried
    Mexican oregano
1½ teaspoons coarse salt
Warm tortillas, for serving
    (optional)

Select Sauté and adjust to More for high. Fry the bacon in the pot for 4 to 6 minutes, or until cooked through. Add the chorizo and smoked pork chops; sauté for 3 to 5 minutes, or until cooked through. Add the ham and hot dog franks; sauté for an additional 3 minutes. Stir in the onion, chiles, and garlic. Sauté for 2 to 3 minutes, or just until the onion is translucent. Add the tomatoes, beans, cilantro, oregano, and enough water to reach the two-thirds mark on the inside of the Instant Pot. Select Cancel. Lock the lid. Select Manual and cook at high pressure for 60 minutes. When the cook time is complete, allow the pressure to release naturally. Remove the lid. Season the beans with the coarse salt, ladle into bowls, and serve with warm tortillas (if desired).

Green Chicken Pozole

SERVES 8 | **PREP TIME:** 5 minutes | **MANUAL:** 20 minutes high pressure | **RELEASE:** Natural | **TOTAL TIME:** 50 minutes

3 pounds boneless chicken
    breasts or thighs, cut into
    large chunks
1 medium onion, halved
3 garlic cloves, minced
4 cilantro sprigs
1 (29-ounce) can white
    hominy, drained
3 cups salsa verde
3 cups water
2 cups chicken broth
½ teaspoon coarse salt,
    plus more for seasoning
    (optional)

½ teaspoon crushed dried
    Mexican oregano
Chopped red onion,
    for garnish
Shredded cabbage or
    lettuce, for garnish
Sliced radishes, for garnish
Freshly squeezed lime
    juice, for garnish
Tostada shells or tortilla chips, for serving
    (optional)

In the Instant Pot, combine the chicken, onion, garlic, cilantro, hominy, and salsa verde. Add the water, chicken broth, salt, and oregano. Lock the lid. Select Manual and cook at high pressure for 20 minutes. When the cook time is complete, allow the pressure to release naturally. Remove the lid. Season the pozole with more salt, if necessary. Ladle into bowls and garnish with chopped onion, shredded cabbage, sliced radishes, and a squeeze of fresh lime juice. Serve with tostada shells or tortilla chips (if using).

White Pozole

SERVES 8 | **PREP TIME:** 5 minutes | **MANUAL:** 55 minutes high pressure | **RELEASE:** Natural | **TOTAL TIME:** 1 hour 30 minutes

3½ pounds pork stew
    meat
3 (15-ounce) cans white
    hominy, drained
2 Hungarian wax peppers,
    seeded and thinly sliced
1 medium white onion,
    thinly sliced
5 garlic cloves, minced
6 cilantro sprigs
2 bay leaves
1½ teaspoons coarse salt,
    plus more for seasoning
    (optional)

1 teaspoon dried
    Mexican oregano
½ teaspoon freshly ground
    black pepper
Chopped red onion,
    for garnish
Shredded cabbage or
    lettuce, for garnish
Sliced radishes, for
    garnish
Lime wedges, for garnish
Salsa, for garnish (optional)

In the Instant Pot, combine the pork, hominy, wax peppers, onion, garlic, and cilantro. Add the bay leaves, salt, oregano, and pepper. Pour in enough water to reach the two-thirds mark inside the pot. Lock the lid. Select Manual and cook at high pressure for 55 minutes. When the cook time is complete, allow the pressure to release naturally. Remove the lid. Remove and discard the bay leaves. Season the pozole with more salt, if desired. Ladle into bowls and garnish with red onion, cabbage, radishes, lime wedges, and salsa (if using).

Traditional Red Pork Pozole

SERVES 6 to 8 | PREP TIME: 10 minutes | MANUAL: 60 minutes high pressure | RELEASE: Natural | TOTAL TIME: 1 hour 35 minutes

3 pounds boneless pork leg, cut into 2-inch pieces
3 (15-ounce) cans white hominy, drained
1 medium white onion, halved
3 garlic cloves, minced
Handful cilantro sprigs
2 cups red enchilada sauce
2 dried bay leaves
1½ teaspoons coarse salt, plus more for seasoning (optional)
1 teaspoon crushed dried Mexican oregano
¼ teaspoon freshly ground black pepper
Freshly squeezed lime juice, for garnish
Shredded cabbage, for garnish
Chopped onion, for garnish
Sliced radishes, for garnish
Cucumber salsa or your favorite bottled hot sauce, for garnish
Tostada shells, for serving (optional)

In the Instant Pot, combine the pork, hominy, onion, garlic, and cilantro. Add the enchilada sauce, bay leaves, salt, oregano, and pepper. Pour in enough water to reach the two-thirds mark inside the Instant Pot. Lock the lid. Select Manual and cook at high pressure for 60 minutes. When the cook time is complete, allow the pressure to release naturally. Remove the lid. Remove and discard the bay leaves. Stir the pozole gently to combine. Season with additional salt, if desired. Ladle into bowls. Garnish with a squeeze of fresh lime juice, cabbage, onion, radishes, and a heaping tablespoon of cucumber salsa. Serve with tostada shells (if using).

VEGETABLE SIDES AND MAINS

Steamed Artichokes

SERVES 2 to 4 | PREP TIME: 5 minutes | MANUAL: 10 minutes high pressure | RELEASE: Quick | TOTAL TIME: 15 minutes

4 or 5 artichokes, rinsed
1 large lemon
1 cup water
2 garlic cloves, peeled

With a sharp knife, cut about 1 inch off the top (petal end) of one artichoke. Remove the tough outer leaves (usually one or two layers), and trim off the stem. Repeat with the remaining artichokes. Cut half of the lemon into ¼-inch-thick round slices. Cut the other half into wedges. Rub the lemon wedges over the entire outside of the artichokes, focusing on the cut edges. In the Instant Pot, combine the water, lemon slices, and garlic. Place a trivet into the pot and put the artichokes on the trivet in a single layer, stem-side down. Lock the lid. Select Manual and cook at high pressure for 10 minutes. When the cook time is complete, quick-release the pressure. Remove the lid. Using tongs, remove the artichokes and serve warm. Enjoy by dipping each leaf in your favorite dipping sauce and pulling out the artichoke meat with your teeth.

Green Bean Stir-Fry

SERVES 4 | PREP AND FINISHING: 20 minutes | MANUAL: Steam 1 minute high pressure | SAUTÉ: 3 minutes | RELEASE: Quick | TOTAL TIME: 35 minutes

12 ounces green beans, trimmed
1 cup water
2 tablespoons corn oil
2 garlic cloves, finely chopped
3 tablespoons crushed peanuts
2 tablespoons soy sauce
¼ teaspoon kosher salt
½ teaspoon cane sugar
2 teaspoons red pepper flakes

Place the beans in the steamer basket. Pour the water into the Instant Pot and place the trivet inside. Place the basket on the trivet. Lock the lid. Select Manual and steam at high pressure for 1 minute. When the cook time is complete, quick-release the pressure. Remove the lid. Drain the beans and wipe the inner pot dry. Select Sauté and pour in the oil. Once hot, add the garlic and sauté for 1 minute. Add the peanuts and soy sauce and sauté for 2 minutes more. In a large bowl, combine the green beans, garlic, peanuts, salt, and sugar. Mix until the sugar and salt are dissolved. Sprinkle with red pepper flakes and serve hot.

Green Beans with Shallots and Bacon

SERVES 4 to 6 | PREP TIME: 10 minutes | SAUTÉ: 7 minutes | MANUAL: 2 minutes high pressure | RELEASE: Quick | TOTAL TIME: 40 minutes

1 cup water
1 pound green beans, trimmed
2 slices bacon, chopped
2 shallots, chopped
½ teaspoon salt

Pour the water into the Instant Pot and insert a steamer basket or trivet. Place the green beans in the steamer basket or on the trivet. Lock the lid. Select Manual and cook at high pressure for 2 minutes. When the cook time is complete, quick-release the pressure. Remove the lid. Remove the steamer or trivet with green beans and pour the water out of the pot. Return the pot to the Instant Pot and select Sauté. Add the bacon, shallots, and salt. Sauté for about 5 minutes, or until the bacon crisps up and the shallots are browned. Add the bacon-shallot mixture (including the bacon fat) to the green beans. Serve hot.

Creamy Green Beans with Mushrooms

SERVES 6 | PREP AND FINISHING: 15 minutes | MANUAL: 6 minutes low pressure, divided | SAUTÉ: 9 minutes | RELEASE: Quick | TOTAL TIME: 30 minutes

8 ounces mushrooms
2 tablespoons unsalted butter
½ teaspoon kosher salt, divided
1 pound green beans, trimmed and cut into 1-inch lengths
2 garlic cloves, minced
½ cup heavy (whipping) cream
Freshly ground black pepper

Cut the stems off the mushrooms and cut them into quarters if small or eighths if large. Put them in the Instant Pot with the butter and ¼ teaspoon of salt. Pour in enough water to just barely cover the mushrooms. Lock the lid. Select Manual and cook at low pressure for 4 minutes. When the cook time is complete, quick-release the pressure. Remove the lid. With the mushrooms still in the pot, put the green beans in a steamer basket and put the basket in the pot. (The mushrooms will be around the feet of the basket.) Lock the lid. Select Manual and cook at low pressure for 2 minutes. When the cook time is complete, quick-release the pressure. Remove the lid and carefully remove the steamer basket. Sprinkle the beans with the remaining ¼ teaspoon of salt and set them aside. Select Sauté and adjust to More for high heat. Bring the liquid to a boil and cook until the water has completely evaporated, leaving the butter and mushrooms in the bottom of the pot. Add the garlic to the mushrooms and cook, stirring occasionally, until the mushrooms are browned, about 4 minutes. Leaving the pot on Sauté, add the cream and cook for a few minutes, just until the cream has thickened. Add the beans and stir to coat and heat through. Taste and adjust the seasoning, adding the remaining salt and some black pepper. Spoon into a serving dish and serve.

Braised Green Beans with Bacon

SERVES 4 | PREP AND FINISHING: 15 minutes | SAUTÉ: 9 minutes | MANUAL: Steam 3 minutes low pressure | RELEASE: Quick | TOTAL TIME: 20 minutes

4 bacon slices, chopped
1 small onion, chopped
½ teaspoon kosher salt, divided
1 pound green beans, trimmed and cut into 1½-inch lengths
⅓ cup chicken broth or vegetable broth

Select Sauté and adjust to Normal for medium heat. Cook the bacon until most of the fat has rendered and the bacon is crisp, about 6 minutes. Use a slotted spoon to remove the bacon and drain on paper towels, leaving the rendered fat in the pot. Add the onion and ¼ teaspoon of salt. Cook, stirring frequently, until the onion pieces separate and soften, 2 to 3 minutes. Add the beans to the pressure cooker and sprinkle with the remaining ¼ teaspoon of salt. Stir to coat the beans with the onion and fat. Add the broth to the pot. Lock the lid. Select Manual and steam at low pressure for 3 minutes. When the cook time is complete, quick-release the pressure. Remove the lid. Spoon the beans into a serving dish, drizzling them with a little of the braising liquid. Top with the bacon and serve.

Szechuan-Style Honey-Glazed Asparagus

SERVES 4 | PREP AND FINISHING: 15 minutes | MANUAL: 1 minute high pressure | RELEASE: Quick | TOTAL TIME: 25 minutes

2 bunches asparagus (about 24), woody ends removed
1 tablespoon extra-virgin olive oil
½ teaspoon kosher salt
½ teaspoon freshly ground black pepper
1 cup water
2 tablespoons honey
1 tablespoon szechuan sauce

Place the asparagus in a large bowl. Drizzle with the olive oil, salt, and pepper and toss to combine. Place the asparagus in the steamer basket. Pour the water into the Instant Pot and place the trivet inside. Place the steamer basket on the trivet. Lock the lid. Select Manual and cook at high pressure for 1 minute. (For firm and crunchy asparagus, set the time to 0 minutes.) When the cook time is complete, quick-release the pressure. Remove the lid. Using tongs, transfer the asparagus to a serving bowl. In a small bowl, combine the honey and Szechuan sauce. Drizzle over the asparagus and serve hot.

Candied Carrots

SERVES 4 to 6 | PREP TIME: 3 minutes | MANUAL: 2 minutes high pressure | RELEASE: Quick | TOTAL TIME: 5 minutes

1 (1-pound) bag baby carrots
1 cup water
3 tablespoons vegan butter
3 tablespoons packed light brown sugar
½ to 1 teaspoon salt

Put the carrots in a steamer basket and place the basket into the Instant Pot. Pour in the water. Lock the lid. Select Manual and cook at high pressure for 2 minutes. When the cook time is complete, quick-release the pressure. Remove the lid and add the butter, letting it melt into the carrots for 1 minute or so. Add the brown sugar and ½ teaspoon of salt. Stir until the carrots are coated. Taste and add more salt if needed.

Creole Carrots

SERVES 4 | PREP AND FINISHING: 10 minutes | SAUTÉ:
8 minutes, divided | MANUAL: 2 minutes low pressure |
RELEASE: Quick | TOTAL TIME: 20 minutes

3 tablespoons unsalted
  butter, divided
1 pound carrots, cut into
  sticks about 2 inches long
  and ½ inch on each side
½ teaspoon kosher salt

¼ cup chicken broth
1 tablespoon freshly
  squeezed lemon juice
1 tablespoon Creole
  mustard or other
  whole-grain mustard

Select Sauté and adjust to More for high heat. Put
2 tablespoons of butter in the pot to melt. When the butter
has just begun to brown, add the carrots and salt. Stir to
coat with the butter and then arrange them into a single
layer as much as possible. Cook without stirring until the
carrots just start to brown, about 2 minutes. Stir to expose
another side of the carrots to the heat and repeat until that
side begins to brown. Select Cancel. Add the broth to the
Instant Pot. Lock the lid. Select Manual and cook at low
pressure for 2 minutes. When the cook time is complete,
quick-release the pressure. Remove the lid. Select Sauté
and adjust to More for high heat. Bring the liquid to a boil
and cook until almost all the broth has evaporated, about
4 minutes. Add the lemon juice, mustard, and the remaining 1 tablespoon of butter and stir to coat. Serve.

Lemon Ginger Asparagus

SERVES 4 to 6 | PREP TIME: 5 minutes | MANUAL:
0 minutes low pressure | RELEASE: Quick | TOTAL TIME:
5 minutes

1 bunch asparagus, tough
  ends removed, halved
  if remaining pieces are
  longer than 4 inches
1 cup water
2 tablespoons extra-virgin
  olive oil

1½ teaspoons to
  1 tablespoon freshly
  squeezed lemon juice
½ to 1 teaspoon salt
½ to ¾ teaspoon peeled
  and grated fresh ginger

Place the asparagus in a steamer basket and put the
basket into the Instant Pot. Add the water. Lock the lid.
Select Manual and cook at low pressure for 0 minutes.
When the cook time is complete, quick-release the pressure. In a serving bowl, stir together the oil, lemon juice,
½ teaspoon of salt, and ½ teaspoon of ginger. Remove the
lid and add the asparagus to the bowl. Toss to combine.
Taste and add the remaining lemon juice and/or ginger,
as needed.

Garlicky Lemon Broccoli

SERVES 2 to 4 | PREP TIME: 5 minutes | MANUAL:
0 minutes high pressure | RELEASE: Quick |
TOTAL TIME: 5 minutes

1 cup water
4 garlic cloves,
  roughly chopped
6 cups chopped broccoli

Juice of 1 lemon
½ to 1 teaspoon salt
Zest of 1 lemon

In the Instant Pot, combine the water and garlic. Place
the broccoli in a steamer basket and put the basket into
the Instant Pot. Pour the lemon juice over the broccoli so
it runs down into the water. Lock the lid. Select Manual
and cook at high pressure for 0 minutes. When the cook
time is complete, quick-release the pressure. Remove the
lid and remove the broccoli. Sprinkle the salt and lemon
zest over the broccoli. Stir well.

Collard Greens

SERVES 6 | PREP TIME: 5 minutes | MANUAL: 60 minutes
high pressure | RELEASE: Quick | TOTAL TIME: 1 hour
15 minutes

5 cups chicken broth
1 smoked turkey leg (or
  ham hock)
1 (2-pound) bag fresh collard greens

3 garlic cloves, minced
¼ teaspoon red
  pepper flakes

In the Instant Pot, combine the broth, turkey leg, collard
greens, garlic, and red pepper flakes. You may need to
pack in the collard greens. Lock the lid. Select Manual
and cook at high pressure for 60 minutes (50 minutes if
you prefer a firmer bite to the greens). When the cook
time is complete, quick-release the pressure. Remove the
turkey leg and shred the meat, discarding the bones and
skin. Return the meat to the greens, stir well, and serve.

Gingered Collard Greens

SERVES 4 to 6 | PREP TIME: 10 minutes | MANUAL:
10 minutes high pressure | RELEASE: Quick | TOTAL
TIME: 25 minutes

1½ pounds collard
  greens, stemmed,
  leaves chopped
1½ cups vegetable broth

3 tablespoons rice vinegar
3 garlic cloves, minced
1 (2-inch) knob fresh ginger,
  peeled and grated

In the Instant Pot, combine the collard greens, broth,
vinegar, garlic, and ginger. Lock the lid. Select Manual and
cook at high pressure for 10 minutes. When the cook time
is complete, quick-release the pressure. Remove the lid.

Always Perfect Beets

SERVES 4 to 6 | PREP TIME: 5 minutes | MANUAL:
20 minutes high pressure | RELEASE: Quick | TOTAL
TIME: 25 minutes

6 beets, roughly 6 inches in circumference, leafy greens (if attached) and roots trimmed

1 cup water

Scrub the beets under cold running water. The skin will be thick and bumpy in parts; just make sure all the dirt is gone. Pour the water into the Instant Pot and place a steamer basket inside. Place the beets in the basket in a single layer (or with as little overlap as possible). Lock the lid. Select Manual and cook at high pressure for 20 minutes. When the cook time is complete, quick-release the pressure. Remove the lid. Using tongs, remove the beets. If you want to peel them, place the beets in a colander and rub the skins while running them under cold water. Cut them into quarters and season as desired.

Green Chile Chickpeas

SERVES 4 to 6 | PREP TIME: 5 minutes | MANUAL: 45 minutes high pressure | SAUTÉ LOW: 4 minutes | RELEASE: Natural for 20 minutes, then Quick | TOTAL TIME: 1 hour 14 minutes

6 cups water

2 cups dried chickpeas, rinsed

1 small tomato, diced

1 cup diced roasted green chiles (freshly roasted or from a can)

2 teaspoons freshly squeezed lemon juice

1 teaspoon ground cumin

½ teaspoon chili powder, plus more as needed

½ to 1 teaspoon salt

½ teaspoon garlic powder

½ teaspoon red pepper flakes

½ teaspoon smoked paprika

½ teaspoon onion powder

¼ teaspoon dried oregano

¼ teaspoon freshly ground black pepper

In the Instant Pot, combine the chickpeas and water. Lock the lid. Select Manual and cook at high pressure for 45 minutes. When the cook time is complete, let the pressure release naturally for 20 minutes, then quick-release any remaining pressure. Remove the lid and drain the chickpeas, reserving 1 to 2 tablespoons of the cooking water. Return the chickpeas to the Instant Pot. Stir in the tomato, green chiles, lemon juice, cumin, chili powder, salt, garlic powder, red pepper flakes, paprika, onion powder, oregano, and black pepper. If they're too dry, add the reserved cooking water. Select Sauté Low and cook for 3 to 4 minutes. You may need to turn the Instant Pot off if anything starts to burn at the bottom. Put the lid back on and turn on the Keep Warm function. Let the chickpeas sit for 5 minutes.

Red Thai-Style Curry Cauliflower

SERVES 4 to 6 | PREP TIME: 10 minutes | MANUAL: 2 minutes high pressure | RELEASE: Quick | TOTAL TIME: 12 minutes

1 (14-ounce) can full-fat coconut milk

½ to 1 cup water

2 tablespoons red curry paste

1 teaspoon garlic powder

1 teaspoon salt, plus more as needed

½ teaspoon ground ginger

½ teaspoon onion powder

¼ teaspoon chili powder (Thai is great, or cayenne pepper)

1 bell pepper, any color, seeded and thinly sliced

1 small to medium head cauliflower, cut into bite-size pieces (3 to 4 cups)

1 (14-ounce) can diced tomatoes

Freshly ground black pepper

Cooked rice or other grain, for serving (optional)

In the Instant Pot, stir the coconut milk, water, red curry paste, garlic powder, salt, ginger, onion powder, and chili powder. Add the bell pepper, cauliflower, and tomatoes with their juices and stir again. Lock the lid. Select Manual and cook at high pressure for 2 minutes. When the cook time is complete, quick-release the pressure. Remove the lid and stir. Taste and season with more salt and pepper, as needed. Serve with rice or another grain (if using).

Green Beans in Red Chile Sauce

SERVES 6 | PREP TIME: 5 minutes | SAUTÉ: 4 minutes | MANUAL: 5 minutes high pressure | RELEASE: Natural | TOTAL TIME: 24 minutes

1 tablespoon vegetable oil

¼ medium white onion, thinly sliced

2 tablespoons masa harina

1½ cups red enchilada sauce

1 cup water

12 ounces green beans, cut into 2-inch pieces

Select Sauté and adjust to More for high. Heat the vegetable oil in the pot, add the onion, and sauté for 2 to 3 minutes, or until translucent. Sprinkle the masa harina over the onion and sauté for an additional 30 seconds. Whisk in the enchilada sauce and water until the masa harina dissolves completely. Add the green beans. Select Cancel. Lock the lid. Select Manual and cook at high pressure for 5 minutes. When the cook time is complete, allow the pressure to release naturally. Remove the lid. Stir the beans gently to combine. Serve immediately.

Mexican-Style Zucchini

SERVES 6 | PREP TIME: 5 minutes | SAUTÉ: 3 minutes | MANUAL: 5 minutes high pressure | RELEASE: Quick | TOTAL TIME: 15 minutes

1 tablespoon vegetable oil

½ medium white onion, finely chopped

1 serrano chile, seeded and finely chopped

5 medium calabacitas or zucchini, cut into 1-inch slices

3 Roma tomatoes, finely chopped

1 (15-ounce) can golden
corn kernels, drained
Coarse salt
Freshly ground
black pepper
1 cup crumbled
queso cotija

Select Sauté and adjust to More for high. Heat the vegetable oil in the pot, add the onion and chile, and sauté for 2 to 3 minutes, or until the onion is translucent. Stir in the calabacitas, tomatoes, and corn. Season lightly with salt and pepper. Select Cancel. Lock the lid. Select Manual and cook at high pressure for 5 minutes. When the cook time is complete, quick-release the pressure. Remove the lid. Sprinkle the crumbled queso cotija over the cooked calabacitas.

Steamed Broccoli and Carrots

SERVES 6 | PREP AND FINISHING: 10 minutes | MANUAL: 2 minutes high pressure | RELEASE: Quick | TOTAL TIME: 22 minutes

1 medium head broc-
coli, cut into florets
(about 2 cups)
1 pound carrots, cut into
1-inch-long chunks
1 cup water

Place the broccoli florets and carrots in a steamer basket. Pour the water into the Instant Pot, then set the steamer basket inside. Lock the lid. Select Manual and cook at high pressure for 2 minutes. When the cook time is complete, quick-release the pressure. Remove the lid. Serve immediately.

Brussels Sprouts with Sweet Dijon Vinaigrette

SERVES 4 to 6 | PREP TIME: 5 minutes | MANUAL: 1 minute high pressure | RELEASE: Quick | TOTAL TIME: 15 minutes

1 pound fresh
Brussels sprouts
1 cup water
2 garlic cloves, smashed
3 tablespoons apple
cider vinegar
2 tablespoons
Dijon mustard
1 tablespoon maple syrup
Freshly ground
black pepper

In the Instant Pot, combine the Brussels sprouts, water, and garlic. Lock the lid. Select Manual and cook at high pressure for 1 minute. In a small bowl, whisk together the vinegar, mustard, and maple syrup. When the cook time is complete, quick-release the pressure. Remove the lid. Drain the water and mince the garlic. Add the dressing to the sprouts and garlic and toss to coat. Season with pepper and serve immediately.

Brown Butter Fingerling Potatoes

SERVES 4 | PREP TIME: 5 minutes | SAUTÉ: 10 minutes | MANUAL: 7 minutes high pressure | RELEASE: Natural for 10 minutes, then Quick | TOTAL TIME: 45 minutes

2 tablespoons
unsalted butter
1½ pounds small fingerling
potatoes, each pricked
twice with a small knife
½ cup vegetable broth
1 fresh rosemary sprig
(leaves only), minced
Salt
Freshly ground
black pepper

Select Sauté. Put the butter in the Instant Pot. Once the butter is mostly melted, add the potatoes. Stir to coat the potatoes. Cook, stirring occasionally, for about 10 minutes, or until the skins start to get crispy and the butter is browned but not burned. Add the broth and rosemary. Select Cancel. Lock the lid. Select Manual and cook at high pressure for 7 minutes. When the cook time is complete, allow the pressure to naturally release for 10 minutes, then quick-release any remaining pressure. Season with salt and pepper.

Yukon Gold Potatoes

SERVES 6 | PREP AND FINISHING: 10 minutes | MANUAL: 10 minutes high pressure | RELEASE: Natural for 10 minutes, then Quick | TOTAL TIME: 40 minutes

1 cup water
2 pounds Yukon Gold
potatoes

Place the trivet in the Instant Pot, then pour in the water. Place the potatoes on the trivet. Lock the lid. Select Manual and cook at high pressure for 10 minutes. When the cook time is complete, naturally release the pressure for 10 minutes, then quick-release any remaining pressure. Remove the lid. Using tongs, transfer the potatoes to a serving plate or bowl. Serve immediately.

Scalloped Potatoes

SERVES 4 to 6 | PREP TIME: 15 minutes | MANUAL: 27 minutes high pressure | RELEASE: Quick | TOTAL TIME: 50 minutes

1 cup unsweetened
plant-based milk
½ cup vegetable broth
2 scallions, white and green
parts, chopped
2 tablespoons nutri-
tional yeast
1 tablespoon arrow-
root powder
1 teaspoon garlic powder
1 teaspoon minced fresh
rosemary
1 teaspoon mus-
tard powder
Freshly ground
black pepper
Salt (optional)
1½ pounds russet potatoes
(4 or 5 medium), peeled
1 cup water

In a large mixing bowl, whisk together the milk, broth, scallions, nutritional yeast, arrowroot powder, garlic powder, rosemary, and mustard powder. Season to taste with pepper and salt (if using). Using a mandoline, the slicing blade on a food processor, or the slicing side of a box grater, slice the potatoes *very* thinly. In a 7-inch-round ovenproof baking dish, arrange a 1-inch layer of potatoes, followed by enough of the sauce to just cover the potatoes. Continue layering until all the potatoes are submerged under the sauce in the dish. Pour the water into the Instant Pot and insert the trivet. Place the dish on the trivet. Lock the lid. Select Manual and cook at high pressure for 27 minutes. When the cook time is complete, quick-release the pressure. Remove the lid and the dish. Serve immediately.

Garlic-Herb Baby Potatoes

SERVES 4 to 6 | PREP TIME: 5 minutes | MANUAL: 7 minutes high pressure | SAUTÉ: 3 to 4 minutes | RELEASE: Quick | TOTAL TIME: 20 minutes

2 pounds baby red-skinned potatoes
1 cup water
3 tablespoons plant-based butter, melted, or extra-virgin olive oil
1 teaspoon garlic powder
1 teaspoon dried thyme
1 teaspoon dried rosemary, crushed
1 teaspoon salt
Freshly ground black pepper

Pierce the potatoes with a fork and slice any larger potatoes in half. In the Instant Pot, combine the potatoes and water. Lock the lid. Select Manual and cook at high pressure for 7 minutes. When the cook time is complete, quick-release the pressure. Remove the lid. Drain the water and Select Sauté. Add the butter, garlic powder, thyme, rosemary, salt, and pepper to taste. Stir to combine and allow the potatoes to brown slightly for 3 to 4 minutes.

Loaded Buffalo Potato Skins

SERVES 4 | PREP TIME: 10 minutes | SAUTÉ: 3 minutes | MANUAL: 7 minutes high pressure | RELEASE: Quick | TOTAL TIME: 25 minutes

1 cup water
4 small red potatoes
¼ cup blue cheese or ranch salad dressing
2 tablespoons Buffalo wing sauce
¼ cup shredded Cheddar cheese
2 scallions, white and green parts, chopped

Set the trivet in the Instant Pot and pour in the water. Place the potatoes on the trivet and lock the lid. Select Manual and cook at high pressure for 7 minutes. When the cook time is complete, quick-release the pressure. Let the potatoes cool, then cut them in half and scoop out the flesh, leaving a ½-inch rim around the edge on the potato. Discard the inner potato or save it for another use. Brush the inside of each potato half with salad dressing and wing sauce. Divide the cheese evenly among the potato skins. Remove the trivet from the Instant Pot and wipe the inner pot dry. Return the potatoes to the pot, cut-sides up. Select Sauté and replace the lid. Cook for 2 to 3 minutes, until the cheese is melted. Sprinkle with the scallions.

Creamy Mashed Potatoes

SERVES 6 | PREP TIME: 5 minutes | MANUAL: 10 minutes high pressure | RELEASE: Quick | TOTAL TIME: 20 minutes

1 cup chicken broth
1 teaspoon salt, plus more as needed
3 pounds russet potatoes, peeled and quartered
½ cup whole milk
6 tablespoons (¾ stick) unsalted butter, at room temperature

Set the trivet in the Instant Pot and pour in the broth and the salt. Place the potatoes on the trivet, adding the biggest pieces first so that the others don't fall through. Lock the lid. Select Manual and cook at high pressure for 10 minutes. When the cook time is complete, quick-release the pressure. Remove the lid. Remove the trivet, leaving the potatoes inside the pot. Mash the potatoes with a potato masher, then add the milk and butter. Continue to mash until all the lumps have been removed, and season with additional salt if desired.

Sweet Potato Gratin

SERVES 8 | PREP AND FINISHING: 20 minutes, plus 1 hour to cool | MANUAL: 30 minutes high pressure | RELEASE: Natural | TOTAL TIME: 2 hours

2 medium sweet potatoes, peeled and thinly sliced (about 1 pound)
2 tablespoons extra-virgin olive oil
1 teaspoon kosher salt
1 teaspoon freshly ground black pepper
1 tablespoon dried basil
1 tablespoon dried thyme
1 tablespoon butter, melted
½ cup heavy (whipping) cream
1 cup Mexican-blend shredded cheese
2 tablespoons panko breadcrumbs
1 cup water

In a large bowl, drizzle the olive oil over the sweet potato slices. Season with the salt, pepper, basil, and thyme. Mix thoroughly to coat the sweet potatoes. Set it aside. In a small bowl, mix the butter and cream. In a springform pan that will fit in the Instant Pot, arrange a single layer of sweet potatoes. Spread about 2 tablespoons of the cream-butter mixture on top, and sprinkle with 4 to 5 tablespoons of cheese. Repeat these steps until all the sweet potato slices have been used, about three layers. After the last layer, sprinkle the breadcrumbs on top. Cover the pan with foil. Pour the water into the Instant Pot and place the trivet inside. Place the springform pan on the trivet. Lock the lid. Select Manual and cook at high pressure for 30 minutes. When the cook time is complete, naturally release the pressure. Remove the lid. Carefully remove the pan. Let the sweet potatoes cool for at least 1 hour before serving so the cheese sets.

Mashed Sweet Potatoes with Toasted Almonds

SERVES 4 | PREP AND FINISHING: 15 minutes | SAUTÉ: 9 minutes, divided | MANUAL: 8 minutes high pressure | RELEASE: Natural for 10 minutes, then Quick | TOTAL TIME: 40 minutes

¼ cup unsalted butter, divided
½ cup raw whole almonds, very coarsely chopped
2 large or 4 small sweet potatoes (about 1½ pounds), quartered

1 cup water
¼ cup half-and-half
½ teaspoon kosher salt
¼ teaspoon freshly grated nutmeg

Select Sauté and adjust to More for high heat. Put 1 tablespoon of butter in the pot to melt. When the butter has stopped foaming, add the almonds. Cook, stirring, until the almonds are golden brown and fragrant, about 6 minutes. Select Cancel. Transfer the almonds to a small bowl and wipe out the pot. Pile the sweet potatoes in a steamer basket and place the basket in the Instant Pot. Add the water to the pot. Lock the lid. Select Manual and cook at high pressure for 8 minutes. When the cook time is complete, let the pressure release naturally for 10 minutes, then quick-release any remaining pressure. Remove the lid. Remove the steamer from the pot and set the potatoes aside. Pour the water out of the pot and wipe it dry. Select Sauté and adjust to Less for low heat. Pour in the half-and-half and add the remaining 3 tablespoons of butter. Remove the skins from the potatoes. Using a ricer, press the potatoes into the pot and stir to combine with the cream and butter. (If you don't have a ricer, mash the potatoes into the cream and butter with a potato masher or large fork.) Season with the salt. Spoon the potatoes into a serving dish. Top with the toasted almonds, sprinkle with the nutmeg, and serve.

Candied Yams

SERVES 6 to 8 | PREP TIME: 5 minutes | MANUAL: 25 minutes high pressure | RELEASE: Natural | TOTAL TIME: 55 minutes

2¼ pounds sweet potatoes, cut into 2-inch slices
2 cups water

2 (3-inch) cinnamon sticks
2 piloncillo cones

In the Instant Pot, combine the sweet potatoes and water. Top with the cinnamon sticks and piloncillo cones. Lock the lid. Select Manual and cook at high pressure for 25 minutes. When the cook time is complete, allow the pressure to release naturally. Remove the lid. Serve immediately.

Sweet Potatoes

SERVES 6 | PREP AND FINISHING: 5 minutes | MANUAL: 15 minutes high pressure | RELEASE: Natural for 10 minutes, then Quick | TOTAL TIME: 40 minutes

1 cup water   6 medium sweet potatoes

Place a trivet or steamer basket inside the Instant Pot, then pour in the water. Arrange the sweet potatoes in the basket. Lock the lid. Select Manual and cook at high pressure for 15 minutes. When the cook time is complete, naturally release the pressure for 10 minutes, then quick-release any remaining pressure. Remove the lid. Serve the sweet potatoes immediately.

Spiced Sweet Potatoes

SERVES 4 to 6 | PREP TIME: 10 minutes | MANUAL: 9 minutes high pressure | RELEASE: Quick | TOTAL TIME: 25 minutes

4 or 5 medium sweet potatoes (about 2 pounds), peeled and cut into 1-inch chunks
1 cup freshly squeezed orange juice
2 garlic cloves, minced
1 (1-inch) knob fresh ginger, peeled and grated, or 1 teaspoon ground ginger

1 (1-inch) knob fresh turmeric, peeled and grated, or 1 teaspoon ground turmeric
½ teaspoon ground cinnamon
1 tablespoon maple syrup

In the Instant Pot, combine the sweet potatoes, orange juice, garlic, ginger, turmeric, and cinnamon. Lock the lid. Select Manual and cook at high pressure for 9 minutes. When the cook time is complete, quick-release the pressure. Remove the lid. Add the maple syrup and mash the potatoes with a handheld potato masher or a large fork. Stir to blend and serve immediately.

Sweet Potato Casserole

SERVES 6 | PREP TIME: 10 minutes | MANUAL: 14 minutes high pressure | RELEASE: Natural for 15 minutes, then Quick | TOTAL TIME: 44 minutes

1 cup water
2 pounds sweet potatoes, washed and cut in half lengthwise
⅔ cup heavy (whipping) cream, plus more as needed
¼ cup (½ stick) unsalted butter
2 tablespoons dark brown sugar

2 teaspoons ground cinnamon
½ teaspoon salt
½ teaspoon ground nutmeg
Mini marshmallows, for topping (optional)
Walnuts, for topping (optional)

Set the trivet in the Instant Pot and pour in the water. Place the sweet potatoes, cut-side up, on the trivet, stacking them if needed. Lock the lid. Select Manual and cook at high pressure for 14 minutes. When the cook time is complete, let the pressure release naturally for 15 minutes, then quick-release any remaining pressure. Remove the lid and trivet and drain the water. Select Sauté and scoop the sweet potato flesh into the Instant Pot. Add the cream, butter, brown sugar, cinnamon, salt, and nutmeg. Mash the potatoes with a hand mixer and stir everything to combine. Select Cancel. Top the sweet potatoes with mini marshmallows (if using) and walnuts (if using). Return the cover to the pot and let sit for 2 to 3 minutes for the marshmallows to soften.

Corn on the Cob

SERVES 6 | PREP TIME: 5 minutes | MANUAL: 2 minutes | RELEASE: Quick | TOTAL TIME: 17 minutes

4 cups water
½ cup heavy (whipping) cream or 1 cup half-and-half
¼ cup (½ stick) unsalted butter
6 ears corn, shucked and halved crosswise

In the Instant Pot, combine the water, cream, and butter and stir well. Then place the corn in the pot, standing the cobs vertically to fit. Lock the lid. Select Manual and cook at high pressure for 2 minutes. When the cook time is complete, quick-release the pressure. Remove the corn and let it sit for 5 minutes before serving.

Mini Corn on the Cob with Tofu Crema

SERVES 4 to 6 | PREP TIME: 5 minutes | MANUAL: 6 minutes high pressure | RELEASE: Quick | TOTAL TIME: 15 minutes

1 cup water
4 to 6 frozen mini corncobs
1 (14-ounce) package silken tofu, drained
1 tablespoon freshly squeezed lemon juice
1 tablespoon apple cider vinegar
1 teaspoon ground cumin
Salt (optional)
1 lime, cut into wedges
1 tablespoon chili powder

Pour the water into the Instant Pot and place the trivet inside. Set the corn on the trivet. Lock the lid. Select Manual and cook at high pressure for 6 minutes. In a blender or food processor, combine the tofu, lemon juice, vinegar, cumin, and salt to taste (if using). Blend well and set it aside. When the cook time is complete, quick-release the pressure. Remove the lid. Rub each cob with a lime wedge, then slather it with a generous amount of crema. Sprinkle ¼ to ½ teaspoon of chili powder on each cob. Serve immediately.

Cajun-Style Creamed Corn

SERVES 6 | PREP AND FINISHING: 10 minutes | MANUAL: 3 minutes high pressure | SAUTÉ: 5 minutes | RELEASE: Quick | TOTAL TIME: 20 minutes

2½ cups frozen corn
½ cup chopped onion (½ medium onion)
⅓ cup chopped red bell pepper (¼ medium pepper)
2 garlic cloves, minced
1 jalapeño, seeded and minced
½ cup chicken broth
2 tablespoons unsalted butter
½ teaspoon Cajun seasoning
½ teaspoon kosher salt, plus more as needed
¼ cup heavy (whipping) cream
1 very small tomato, seeded and diced (about ¼ cup)
¼ cup thinly sliced scallions, white and green parts

In the Instant Pot, combine the corn, onion, bell pepper, garlic, jalapeño, broth, butter, Cajun seasoning, and salt. Lock the lid. Select Manual and cook at high pressure for 3 minutes. When the cook time is complete, quick-release the pressure. Remove the lid. Select Sauté and adjust to More for high heat. Bring the liquid to a boil and simmer until most of it has evaporated, about 3 minutes. Add the cream and cook until the cream has thickened slightly, 1 to 2 minutes. Add the tomato and scallions and cook just to warm through. Taste and add more salt if needed. Spoon into a serving dish and serve.

Sesame Chickpeas and Veggies

SERVES 4 to 6 | PREP TIME: 5 minutes | SAUTÉ: 5 to 7 minutes | TOTAL TIME: 20 minutes

1⅓ cups vegetable broth, divided
½ cup tamari, coconut aminos, or low-sodium gluten-free soy sauce
3 tablespoons arrowroot powder or cornstarch
3 tablespoons maple syrup
1 tablespoon rice vinegar
2 tablespoons toasted sesame oil (optional)
1 (12-ounce) bag frozen stir-fry vegetables
2 teaspoons garlic powder
2 teaspoons ground ginger
1 (15-ounce) can chickpeas, drained and rinsed
Hot cooked rice, for serving (optional)
2 tablespoons toasted sesame seeds
3 scallions, white and green parts, diced (optional)

In a medium bowl, whisk 1 cup of broth, the tamari, cornstarch, maple syrup, and vinegar. Set it aside. Select Sauté and heat the oil (if using). Sauté the vegetables, adding 2 to 4 tablespoons of the broth as needed to prevent sticking, until they are heated through, 5 to 7 minutes. Stir in the garlic and ginger. When the vegetables are cooked, remove them to a large bowl. Add the tamari mixture and chickpeas to the pot. Stir until boiling and thickened. Return the vegetables to the pot and toss to combine. Serve over hot cooked rice (if using) with sesame seeds and scallions (if using) on top.

Yellow Split Pea and Broccoli Curry

SERVES 4 to 6 | PREP TIME: 10 minutes | SAUTÉ: 3 minutes | MANUAL: 5 minutes high pressure | RELEASE: Natural for 5 minutes, then Quick | TOTAL TIME: 30 minutes

1 medium onion, diced
3 garlic cloves, minced
1 (1-inch) knob ginger, peeled and grated
2 teaspoons curry powder
½ teaspoon red pepper flakes (optional)
2½ cups water
1 (15-ounce) can diced tomatoes

1 cup yellow split peas, rinsed and sorted
2 heads broccoli florets, chopped into bite-size pieces
Zest and juice of 2 limes
Freshly ground black pepper
Salt (optional)
Hot cooked rice, for serving (optional)

Select Sauté. Sauté the onion for 3 minutes, adding water as needed to prevent sticking. Add the garlic, ginger, curry powder, and red pepper flakes (if using) and stir for 30 seconds, until fragrant. Select Cancel. Stir in the water, tomatoes, and split peas. Lock the lid. Select Manual and cook at high pressure for 5 minutes. When the cook time is complete, let the pressure release naturally for 5 minutes, then quick-release any remaining pressure. Remove the lid. Stir in the broccoli, close the lid, and let steam for 5 minutes. Stir in the lime zest and juice and season to taste with pepper and salt (if using). Serve immediately over hot cooked rice (if using).

Turmeric-Spiced Cabbage, Potatoes, and Carrots

SERVES 4 to 6 | PREP TIME: 10 minutes | SAUTÉ: 3 minutes | MANUAL: 2 minutes high pressure | RELEASE: Quick | TOTAL TIME: 25 minutes

1 medium onion, diced
1 (1-inch) knob ginger, peeled and grated
1 teaspoon paprika
1 teaspoon ground cumin
½ teaspoon ground turmeric
3 medium yellow potatoes, cut into 1-inch chunks (about 3 cups)

3 or 4 medium carrots, cut into 2-inch pieces (about 3 cups)
1 cup water
½ large head cabbage, chopped (5 to 6 cups)
Freshly ground black pepper
Salt (optional)

Select Sauté. Sauté the onion for 3 minutes, adding water as needed to prevent sticking. Add the ginger, paprika, cumin, and turmeric and stir for 30 seconds, until fragrant. Stir in the potatoes and carrots. Select Cancel. Pour in the water, stirring well. Place the cabbage on top but do not stir.

Lock the lid. Select Manual and cook at high pressure for 2 minutes. When the cook time is complete, quick-release the pressure. Remove the lid. Stir and season to taste with pepper and salt (if using). Serve immediately.

Autumn Acorn Squash

SERVES 4 | PREP TIME: 5 minutes | MANUAL: 5 minutes high pressure | RELEASE: Natural | TOTAL TIME: 20 minutes

2 acorn squash
4 teaspoons coconut oil
4 teaspoons pure maple syrup

¼ teaspoon ground cinnamon
¼ teaspoon kosher salt
1 cup water

Cut the squash in half through the root, then scoop out and discard the seeds. Divide the coconut oil, maple syrup, cinnamon, and salt evenly among the centers of each squash half. Pour the water into the Instant Pot and insert the trivet. Stack the squash, cut-side up, on top of the trivet. Lock the lid. Select Manual and cook at high pressure for 5 minutes. When the cook time is complete, let the pressure release naturally for 5 minutes, then quick-release any remaining pressure. Remove the lid and serve.

Spinach-Stuffed Mushrooms

SERVES 6 | PREP TIME: 10 minutes | SAUTÉ: 3 minutes | MANUAL: 5 minutes | RELEASE: Quick | TOTAL TIME: 23 minutes

12 white mushrooms
1 tablespoon unsalted butter
2 cups baby spinach, chopped

1 tablespoon minced shallot
⅓ cup grated Pecorino Romano cheese
1 teaspoon lemon juice

Remove the stems from the mushroom caps. Finely chop the stems. Select Sauté and melt the butter. When the butter has melted, add the spinach and shallot and cook until the spinach is wilted, 2 to 3 minutes. Stir in the mushroom stems, cheese, and lemon juice. Divide the spinach mixture evenly among the mushroom caps. Set the trivet in the Instant Pot and pour in 1 cup of water. Place the mushrooms, filling-side up, on the trivet. Lock the lid. Select Manual and cook at high pressure for 5 minutes on manual high pressure. When the cook time is complete, quick-release the pressure.

Sweet and Sour Glazed Brussels Sprouts

SERVES 4 | PREP AND FINISHING: 20 minutes | SAUTÉ: 12 minutes, divided | MANUAL: 1 minute high pressure | RELEASE: Quick | TOTAL TIME: 33 minutes

2 or 3 bacon slices, diced

½ cup chopped onion (½ medium onion)

½ cup chopped peeled
    apple (½ medium apple)
½ cup apple juice or cider
¼ cup chicken broth
1 pound Brussels sprouts,
    trimmed and halved

½ teaspoon kosher salt
2 tablespoons apple
    cider vinegar
1 tablespoon brown sugar

Select Sauté and adjust to Normal for medium heat. Cook the bacon until most of the fat has rendered and the bacon is crisp, about 6 minutes. Use a slotted spoon to remove the bacon, and drain on paper towels, leaving the rendered fat in the pot. Add the onion and apple and cook, stirring frequently, until the onion pieces separate and soften, 2 to 3 minutes. Select Cancel. Add the apple juice and broth to the pot. Put the sprouts in a steamer basket and put the basket in the pot. Lock the lid. Select Manual and cook at high pressure for 1 minute. When the cook time is complete, quick-release the pressure. Remove the lid. Carefully remove the steamer basket from the pot. Sprinkle the Brussels sprouts with the salt. Select Sauté and adjust to More for high heat. Bring the liquid to a boil and cook until it has reduced to a glaze (it will be thickened and shiny), about 3 minutes. Stir in the vinegar and brown sugar and bring back to a boil. Add the Brussels sprouts and stir to coat with the sauce and heat through. Transfer to a bowl, sprinkle with the bacon, and serve.

Broccoli and Cauliflower with Cheese Sauce

SERVES 4 | PREP AND FINISHING: 10 minutes | MANUAL: 1 minute low pressure | SAUTÉ: 5 minutes | RELEASE: Quick | TOTAL TIME: 15 minutes

2 cups broccoli florets
2 cups cauliflower florets
1 cup water
¾ cup evaporated milk
1 tablespoon
    unsalted butter

2 cups grated sharp
    Cheddar cheese (about
    8 ounces)
1 teaspoon cornstarch
1 teaspoon Dijon
    mustard

Combine the broccoli and cauliflower in a steamer basket. Pour the water into the Instant Pot and place the steamer basket inside. Lock the lid. Select Manual and cook at low pressure for 1 minute. When the cook time is complete, quick-release the pressure. Remove the lid. Use tongs or a potholder to remove the steamer basket. Tent the vegetables loosely with foil to keep warm. Discard the cooking water in the pot and wipe it dry. Select Sauté and adjust to More for high heat. Pour in the evaporated milk, add the butter, and bring to a simmer. While the milk heats, toss the cheese with the cornstarch in a bowl. Add the cheese a handful at a time, stirring to melt the cheese before adding the next handful. When all the cheese is melted, stir in the mustard. Transfer the vegetables to a serving bowl, pour the cheese sauce over, and serve.

Pickled Beets

SERVES 6 | PREP AND FINISHING: 15 minutes | MANUAL: 10 minutes high pressure | SAUTÉ: 3 minutes | RELEASE: Quick | TOTAL TIME: 30 minutes, plus 2 hours to chill

2 pounds medium beets
    (about 2 inches across),
    trimmed but not peeled
1 cup water
1 medium orange
¾ cup red wine vinegar
½ cup dry red wine
⅓ cup sugar

1 teaspoon whole cloves
1 teaspoon whole all-
    spice berries
¼ teaspoon whole black
    peppercorns
1 tablespoon prepared
    horseradish

Pile the beets in a steamer basket and place the basket in the Instant Pot. Add the water to the pot. Lock the lid. Select Manual and cook at high pressure for 10 minutes. When the cook time is complete, quick-release the pressure. Remove the lid and carefully remove the steamer basket from the pot. As soon as the beets are cool enough to handle, remove and discard the skin and cut them into ¼-inch slices, then cut the slices in half to form half-moons. Set aside in a medium bowl or in several mason jars. Pour the water out of the pot. Peel the zest from the orange into the pot, then juice the orange and add the juice to the pot. Add the vinegar, wine, sugar, cloves, allspice berries, and peppercorns to the pot. Select Sauté and adjust to More for high heat. Bring the liquid to a boil and cook until the sugar has dissolved, 2 to 3 minutes. Turn off the heat and stir in the horseradish. Pour the hot pickling liquid over the beets. Let cool to room temperature, then refrigerate. The beets can be eaten after a couple of hours.

Black-Eyed Peas and Greens

SERVES 4 | PREP AND FINISHING: 15 minutes | MANUAL: 53 minutes high pressure, divided | RELEASE: Natural for 15 minutes, divided, then Quick | TOTAL TIME: 1 hour 30 minutes, plus overnight to soak

1 tablespoon kosher salt,
    plus more for seasoning
2 quarts water, divided
8 ounces dried
    black-eyed peas
1 or 2 smoked turkey
    wings or legs
1 small onion, peeled
    and halved
1 bay leaf

½ teaspoon dried thyme
½ teaspoon freshly ground
    black pepper, plus more
    for seasoning
¼ teaspoon red
    pepper flakes
8 cups chopped col-
    lard greens
1 tablespoon red
    wine vinegar

In a large bowl, dissolve the salt in 1 quart of water. Add the black-eyed peas and soak at room temperature for 8 to 24 hours. Drain them and rinse. Put the turkey wing(s) in the Instant Pot and add the remaining 1 quart of water. Lock the lid. Select Manual (or Soup) and cook at high pressure for 35 minutes. When the cook time is complete, naturally release the pressure for 10 minutes, then quick-release any remaining pressure. Remove the lid. Remove the wing(s) from the pressure cooker and let them cool. Pour the cooking liquid into a bowl or large container and reserve. Shred the meat and set aside. Put the drained black-eyed peas in the Instant Pot, along with the onion halves, bay leaf, thyme, black pepper, and red pepper flakes. Put the greens on top of the beans and pour in the reserved turkey cooking liquid. Lock the lid. Select Manual and cook at high pressure for 18 minutes. When the cook time is complete, naturally release the pressure for 5 minutes, then quick-release any remaining pressure. Remove the lid. Remove the bay leaf and onion halves, then stir in the reserved meat and the vinegar. Let simmer for a minute to warm the meat through. Taste and adjust the seasoning with more salt and black pepper if needed. If the peas or greens aren't done to your liking, select Sauté and simmer for a few minutes. Ladle into bowls and serve.

Cauliflower Mashed Potatoes

SERVES 6 | **PREP TIME:** 10 minutes | **MANUAL:** 8 minutes high pressure | **RELEASE:** Quick | **TOTAL TIME:** 25 minutes

2 cups water	¼ cup unsweetened
1 pound potatoes, peeled and cubed	nondairy milk, such as almond or coconut
2 cups fresh or frozen cauliflower florets	¼ teaspoon kosher salt
4 garlic cloves	½ teaspoon freshly ground black pepper

Pour the water into the Instant Pot and insert the trivet or a steamer basket. Add the potatoes, cauliflower, and garlic. Lock the lid. Select Manual and cook at high pressure for 8 minutes. When the cook time is complete, quick-release the pressure. Remove the lid and drain the water. Return the vegetables to the pot and add the milk, salt, and pepper. Use a potato masher to mash the potatoes and cauliflower to your desired consistency, then serve.

Tempeh Sloppy Janes

SERVES 4 to 6 | **PREP TIME:** 10 minutes | **SAUTÉ LOW:** 6 minutes | **MANUAL:** 2 minutes high pressure | **RELEASE:** Quick | **TOTAL TIME:** 18 minutes

1 tablespoon extra-virgin olive oil	1 (15-ounce) can vegan refried beans
1 (8-ounce) package unflavored tempeh	1 (10-ounce) can diced tomatoes with green chiles
1 teaspoon smoked paprika	½ cup vegetable broth
½ teaspoon salt, plus more as needed	2 tablespoons vegan Worcestershire sauce

1 tablespoon Dijon mustard	Sliced onion, for serving
½ teaspoon garlic powder	Sliced bell pepper, for serving
1 or 2 pinches chili powder	Pickles, for serving
Freshly ground black pepper	Vegan cheese, for serving
¼ cup quick cook oats	Barbecue sauce, for serving
4 to 6 buns or rolls, for serving	

Select Sauté Low. When the display reads HOT, pour in the oil and heat until it shimmers. Crumble in the tempeh and add the paprika and salt. Cook for 4 to 5 minutes, stirring occasionally. Select Cancel. Add the refried beans, tomatoes and green chiles with their juices, broth, Worcestershire sauce, mustard, garlic powder, and chili powder, and season to taste with black pepper. Lock the lid. Select Manual and cook at high pressure for 2 minutes. When the cook time is complete, quick-release the pressure. Remove the lid and stir in the oats. There will likely be too much liquid; if so, select Sauté medium and cook, uncovered, for 2 to 3 minutes, or until the extra liquid evaporates. Serve on buns, topped as desired.

Arancini Casserole

SERVES 6 | **PREP TIME:** 5 minutes | **SAUTÉ:** 4 minutes | **MANUAL:** 20 minutes high pressure | **RELEASE:** Quick | **TOTAL TIME:** 40 minutes

1 tablespoon extra-virgin olive oil	1 cup water
1 yellow onion, diced	2 cups shredded mozzarella
1 cup short-grain brown rice	¼ cup panko breadcrumbs (optional)
1 cup frozen cauliflower rice	Nonstick cooking spray (optional)
2 cups marinara or other pasta sauce	

Select Sauté and pour in the olive oil. When the oil is hot, add the onion and cook for 3 to 4 minutes, stirring occasionally, until softened. Stir in the brown rice. Select Cancel. Add the cauliflower rice, marinara, and water. Lock the lid. Select Manual and cook at high pressure for 20 minutes. When the cook time is complete, quick-release the pressure. Remove the lid and stir. Top the rice with the mozzarella, then replace the lid and let it sit for 2 to 3 minutes, until the cheese has melted. Serve as is or preheat the oven to broil. Transfer the casserole to a small (9-by-6-inch) baking dish. Top it with a thin layer of panko breadcrumbs (if using) and spritz with nonstick spray. Broil for 2 to 3 minutes, until toasted and golden brown. Cut into six slices and serve.

Spaghetti Squash with Pesto

SERVES 6 | PREP AND FINISHING: 25 minutes | MANUAL: 12 minutes high pressure | RELEASE: Natural 10 minutes, then Quick | TOTAL TIME: 1 hour

1½ cups plus 3 tablespoons water, divided	1 (roughly 3-pound) spaghetti squash, pierced with a knife about 10 times
	¼ cup pesto

Pour 1½ cups of water into the Instant Pot and place the trivet inside. Place the squash on the trivet. Lock the lid. Select Manual and cook at high pressure for 12 minutes. When the cook time is complete, release the pressure naturally for 10 minutes, then quick-release any remaining pressure. Remove the lid. Using tongs, carefully transfer the squash to a cutting board to cool for about 10 minutes. Halve the spaghetti squash lengthwise. Using a spoon, scoop out and discard the seeds. Using a fork, scrape the flesh of the squash and shred into long "noodles." Place the noodles in a medium serving bowl. In a small bowl, mix the pesto with the remaining 3 tablespoons of water. Drizzle over the squash, toss to combine, and serve warm.

Ethiopian-Style Vegetable Curry

SERVES 6 | PREP AND FINISHING: 20 minutes | MANUAL: Steam 5 minutes high pressure | RELEASE: Quick | SAUTÉ: 7 minutes | TOTAL TIME: 40 minutes

2 medium carrots, cut into 1-inch pieces	1 garlic clove, finely chopped
3 cups roughly shredded green cabbage	1 teaspoon peeled and freshly grated ginger
2 Yukon Gold potatoes, cut into 1-inch pieces (about ½ pound)	1 tablespoon mild curry powder
1 cup water	1¼ teaspoons kosher salt
2 teaspoons corn oil	1 tablespoon finely chopped fresh cilantro, for garnish
½ onion, finely chopped	

Place the carrots, cabbage, and potatoes in the steamer basket. Pour the water into the Instant Pot and place the trivet inside. Place the steamer basket on the trivet. Lock the lid. Select Manual and steam at high pressure for 5 minutes. When the cook time is complete, quick-release the pressure. Remove the lid. Place the vegetables in a colander. Discard the water. Wipe the inside of the pot dry and return it to its place. Select Sauté and pour in the oil. Once hot, add the onion, garlic, and ginger and sauté until the onion turns translucent, about 3 minutes. Add the curry powder and salt and sauté for 2 minutes. Add the steamed vegetables and cook, stirring frequently, for about 2 minutes. Transfer the curry to a serving platter, garnish with the cilantro, and serve hot.

Kung Pao Broccoli with Tofu

SERVES 4 | PREP AND FINISHING: 20 minutes | SAUTÉ: 3 minutes | MANUAL: 1 minute high pressure | RELEASE: Quick | TOTAL TIME: 35 minutes

1¼ cups water	1 teaspoon freshly ground black pepper
1 tablespoon cornstarch	
1 tablespoon rice vinegar	3 whole cloves
1 tablespoon soy sauce	2 cups broccoli florets, cut into bite-size pieces (about 10 ounces)
1 tablespoon sriracha	
1 teaspoon sugar	
½ teaspoon kosher salt	¾ cup bite-size pieces red and green bell pepper mix
2 tablespoons peanut oil	
10 scallions, chopped, white and green parts separated	
	½ cup (1-inch cubes) extra-firm tofu, pressed to remove water
1 garlic clove, finely chopped	
	¼ cup peanuts
3 dried Thai red chiles	

In a small mixing bowl, stir together the water and cornstarch. Mix thoroughly and set aside. In a medium bowl, mix the vinegar, soy sauce, sriracha, sugar, and salt. Set it aside. Select Sauté and pour in the oil. Once hot, add the white parts of the scallions and the garlic, chiles, pepper, and cloves. Sauté for 2 minutes. Add the broccoli, bell pepper, tofu, peanuts, and sauce. Mix thoroughly. Add the slurry and stir constantly until everything is well combined. Select Cancel. Lock the lid. Select Manual and cook at high pressure for 1 minute. When the cook time is complete, quick-release the pressure. Remove the lid. Stir the kung pao once before transferring to a serving bowl. Do not keep the kung pao in Keep Warm mode, as the broccoli might become soft and mushy. Garnish with the green parts of the scallions and serve hot.

Kung Pao Cauliflower

SERVES 4 | PREP TIME: 10 minutes | MANUAL: 2 minutes high pressure | SAUTÉ: 6 minutes | RELEASE: Quick | TOTAL TIME: 25 minutes

½ cup water	¼ cup coconut aminos or tamari
4 cups fresh cauliflower florets	
	2 tablespoons honey
1 teaspoon sesame oil	⅛ teaspoon kosher salt
2 garlic cloves, minced	¼ cup peanuts, chopped
2 teaspoons red pepper flakes	2 scallions, greens parts only, sliced

Pour the water into the Instant Pot and insert the trivet. Place the cauliflower on top of the trivet. Lock the lid. Select Manual and cook at high pressure for 2 minutes. When the cook time is complete, quick-release the pressure. Remove the lid and remove the cauliflower from the pot. Pour out any remaining water and wipe the pot dry. Select Sauté and pour in the sesame oil. When the oil is hot, add the garlic and red pepper flakes. Cook for 1 to

2 minutes, stirring occasionally, until fragrant. Add the coconut aminos, honey, and salt. Cook for 3 to 4 minutes, stirring constantly, until reduced to a thick sauce. Select Cancel. Return the cauliflower to the pot and stir to coat with sauce. Sprinkle with peanuts and scallions and serve.

Brazilian-Style Vegetable Curry

SERVES 8 | PREP AND FINISHING: 20 minutes | SAUTÉ: 5 minutes | MANUAL: 8 minutes high pressure, divided | RELEASE: Quick | TOTAL TIME: 45 minutes

3 Roma tomatoes, chopped
½ cup water
½ cup roughly chopped yellow onion
1 Thai green chile, chopped
1 dried red chile
2 garlic cloves, finely chopped
1 teaspoon peeled and finely chopped fresh ginger
2 teaspoons corn oil

2 cups (1-inch cubes) butternut squash
1 (14-ounce) can full-fat coconut milk
1¼ teaspoons kosher salt
1 medium eggplant, cut into bite-size pieces
1 cup chopped red, orange, or yellow bell pepper or a mix
2 tablespoons chopped fresh cilantro

In a blender, roughly grind the tomatoes, water, onion, green chile, red chile, garlic, and ginger. Select Sauté and pour the oil into the Instant Pot. Once hot, slowly pour in the tomato paste mixture. Sauté for about 5 minutes, until the onions are translucent. Add the butternut squash, coconut milk, and salt. Select Cancel. Lock the lid. Select Manual and cook at high pressure for 5 minutes. When the cook time is complete, quick-release the pressure. Remove the lid. Scrape the bottom of the pot with a wooden spoon, ensuring nothing is sticking to the bottom. Add the eggplant and bell pepper. Lock the lid. Select Manual and cook at high pressure for 3 minutes. When the cook time is complete, quick-release the pressure. Remove the lid. Stir the curry and garnish with the cilantro. Serve hot.

Thai-Style Vegetable Curry

SERVES 6 | PREP AND FINISHING: 20 minutes | SAUTÉ: 3 minutes | MANUAL: 2 minutes high pressure | RELEASE: Natural 5 minutes, then Quick | TOTAL TIME: 40 minutes

FOR THE THAI CURRY PASTE

3 dried red Thai chiles
2 garlic cloves
¼ cup chopped onion
3 tablespoons water
1 tablespoon finely chopped fresh cilantro
1 tablespoon finely chopped fresh ginger

1 tablespoon sliced lemongrass
1 teaspoon coriander seeds
½ teaspoon cumin seeds
½ teaspoon whole black peppercorns

FOR THE VEGETABLE CURRY

2 teaspoons corn oil
½ cup (1-inch pieces) chopped carrots
½ cup (1-inch cubed) peeled potatoes
5 fresh snap peas
5 fresh baby corn ears, cut into bite-size pieces
1 teaspoon kosher salt
1 teaspoon sugar

¼ teaspoon ground turmeric
1 (12-ounce) can full-fat coconut milk
½ cup (½-inch cubes) extra-firm tofu, pressed to remove water
6 fresh basil leaves, roughly chopped

TO MAKE THE THAI CURRY PASTE

In a blender, blend the chiles, garlic, onion, water, cilantro, ginger, lemongrass, coriander seeds, cumin seeds, and peppercorns into a smooth paste.

TO MAKE THE VEGETABLE CURRY

Select Sauté and pour in the oil. Once hot, add the carrots, potatoes, snap peas, baby corn, salt, sugar, and turmeric and sauté for 1 minute. Add the curry paste and sauté for 2 minutes more. Add the coconut milk, tofu, and half of the basil and mix thoroughly. Select Cancel. Lock the lid. Select Manual and cook at high pressure for 2 minutes. When the cook time is complete, naturally release the pressure for 5 minutes, then quick-release any remaining pressure. Remove the lid. Serve, garnished with the remaining basil.

Mixed Vegetable Korma

SERVES 6 | PREP AND FINISHING: 20 minutes | MANUAL: 5 minutes high pressure, divided | SAUTÉ: 2 minutes | RELEASE: Quick | TOTAL TIME: 35 minutes

½ cup chopped onion
10 raw cashews
1 green Thai chile, finely chopped
1 cup water, divided
1 large carrot, chopped into 1-inch cubes (about ¾ cup)
1 medium potato, peeled and cut into 1-inch cubes (about ½ cup)
1¼ cups cauliflower florets (about ½ pound)

¼ cup frozen peas
⅓ cup heavy (whipping) cream
1 teaspoon curry powder
½ teaspoon ground allspice
1 teaspoon kosher salt
2 tablespoons finely chopped fresh cilantro
1 tablespoon roughly chopped fresh mint leaves
Naan bread, for serving

In the Instant Pot, combine the onion, cashews, green chile, and ½ cup of water. Lock the lid. Select Manual and cook at high pressure for 2 minutes. When the cook time is complete, quick-release the pressure. Remove the lid. Use an immersion blender to puree the mixture. Select Sauté. Once hot, add the carrot, potato, cauliflower, peas, cream, curry powder, allspice, salt, and remaining ½ cup of water to the onion-cashew paste. Mix thoroughly and sauté for 2 minutes. Select Cancel. Lock the lid. Select Manual and cook at high pressure for 3 minutes. When the cook time is complete, quick-release the pressure. Remove the lid. Add the chopped cilantro and mint leaves, then stir the korma one last time. Serve hot with naan bread.

Chana Masala

SERVES 6 | **PREP AND FINISHING:** 10 minutes, plus at least 8 hours to soak | **SAUTÉ:** 7 minutes | **MANUAL:** 30 minutes high pressure | **RELEASE:** Natural | **TOTAL TIME:** 9 hours

1 cup dried chickpeas
1 tablespoon corn oil
1 tablespoon cumin seeds
1 (1-inch) cinnamon stick
1 yellow onion, finely chopped
3 tomatoes, finely chopped
2 teaspoons ground coriander
1 teaspoon chili powder
½ teaspoon ground turmeric
½ tablespoon salt
2½ cups water
3 tablespoons finely chopped fresh cilantro, divided

In a large bowl, cover the chickpeas with 2 to 3 inches of cold water. Soak at room temperature for 8 hours or overnight. Drain them and rinse. Select Sauté and pour in the oil. Once hot, add the cumin seeds and cinnamon stick and cook for 30 seconds. Add the onion and sauté until translucent, about 5 minutes. Add the tomatoes, coriander, chili powder, turmeric, and salt. Cook, stirring frequently, until the tomatoes are soft, about 2 minutes. Pour the water into the Instant Pot, then add the chickpeas and 1½ tablespoons of cilantro. Select Cancel. Lock the lid. Select Manual and cook at high pressure for 30 minutes. When the cook time is complete, naturally release the pressure. Remove the lid. Stir the curry. Sprinkle the remaining 1½ tablespoons of cilantro on top and serve hot.

Mixed-Vegetable Dal

SERVES 6 | **PREP AND FINISHING:** 10 minutes | **SAUTÉ:** 5 minutes | **MANUAL:** 15 minutes high pressure | **RELEASE:** Natural | **TOTAL TIME:** 40 minutes

1 tablespoon butter
1 tablespoon cumin seeds
1 teaspoon peeled and finely chopped fresh ginger
2 green Thai chiles, finely chopped
½ cup (1-inch chunks) chopped carrot
½ cup (1-inch cubes) chopped butternut squash
½ cup (1-inch chunks) chopped zucchini
2 cups broccoli florets
2 teaspoons kosher salt
½ teaspoon ground turmeric
¼ teaspoon ground allspice
3 cups water
1 cup dried red lentils, rinsed and drained
3 tablespoons chopped fresh cilantro

Select Sauté and melt the butter. Add the cumin seeds, ginger, and chiles and sauté for 1 minute. Add the carrot, butternut squash, zucchini, broccoli, salt, turmeric, and allspice and mix well. Pour the water into the Instant Pot and mix in the lentils. Select Cancel. Lock the lid. Select Manual and cook at high pressure for 15 minutes. When the cook time is complete, naturally release the pressure. Remove the lid. Using the back of a ladle, mash the lentils and vegetables. Stir in the cilantro and serve hot.

Pinto Bean and Vegetable Tacos

SERVES 6 | **PREP AND FINISHING:** 10 minutes, plus 4 hours to soak | **MANUAL:** 8 minutes high pressure | **RELEASE:** Natural 10 minutes, then Quick | **SAUTÉ:** 12 minutes | **TOTAL TIME:** 4 hours 50 minutes

1 cup dried pinto beans
2 cups water
2 tablespoons corn oil
1 yellow onion, finely chopped
10 white mushrooms, halved
¼ cup chopped bell peppers
1 zucchini, cut into 1-inch chunks
1 medium carrot, cut into 1-inch chunks
2 teaspoons kosher salt
1 teaspoon ground cumin
1 teaspoon taco seasoning
½ teaspoon chili powder
6 corn tortillas, warmed
½ cup Mexican-blend shredded cheese
1 tablespoon finely chopped fresh cilantro

In a large bowl, cover the pinto beans with 2 to 3 inches of cold water. Soak at room temperature for 4 hours. Drain and rinse. Pour the water into the Instant Pot and add the beans. Lock the lid. Select Manual and cook at high pressure for 8 minutes. When the cook time is complete, naturally release the pressure for 10 minutes, then quick-release any remaining pressure. Drain the beans. Wipe the inner pot dry. Select Sauté and pour in the oil. Once hot, add the onion and sauté until translucent, about 5 minutes. Add the mushrooms, bell pepper, zucchini, carrot, salt, cumin, taco seasoning, and chili powder. Mix and cook for 5 minutes, until the bell pepper becomes tender, stirring every 2 minutes. Add the beans and continue cooking and stirring for another 2 minutes. Fill the warmed tortillas with the beans and vegetables, garnish with shredded cheese and cilantro, and serve.

Korean-Style Barbecue Chickpea Tacos

SERVES 4 to 6 | **PREP TIME:** 10 minutes | **MANUAL:** 45 minutes high pressure | **SAUTÉ LOW:** 7 minutes | **RELEASE:** Natural for 15 minutes, then Quick | **TOTAL TIME:** 1 hour 17 minutes

1 cup dried chickpeas, rinsed
1 to 2 cups plus 3 tablespoons water, divided
3 tablespoons cornstarch
2 to 3 tablespoons gochujang (Korean hot pepper paste)

⅓ cup packed light
  brown sugar
⅓ cup soy sauce
2 tablespoons hot chili oil
2 teaspoons rice
  wine vinegar
½ teaspoon onion powder
½ teaspoon garlic powder
2 cups pineapple chunks
1 teaspoon sriracha, plus
  more as needed
6 to 8 taco shells

In the Instant Pot, combine the chickpeas with enough water to cover. Lock the lid. Select Manual and cook at high pressure for 45 minutes. When the cook time is complete, let the pressure release naturally for 15 minutes, then quick-release any remaining pressure. Remove the lid and pour the contents into a colander to drain. Return the chickpeas to the inner pot. In a small bowl, whisk the cornstarch and 3 tablespoons of water. Set it aside. Select Sauté Low. To the chickpeas, add the gochujang, brown sugar, soy sauce, chili oil, vinegar, onion powder, and garlic powder. Cook until it starts to bubble. Stir in the cornstarch slurry. Simmer for 4 to 5 minutes more, stirring frequently, until the sauce thickens and the chickpeas are nice and coated. In a medium bowl, stir together the pineapple and sriracha. Taste before adding more sauce. Fill the taco shells with the chickpeas and top with the pineapple.

Gobi Masala

SERVES 4 to 6 | PREP TIME: 5 minutes | SAUTÉ LOW: 6 minutes | MANUAL: 1 minute high pressure | RELEASE: Quick | TOTAL TIME: 12 minutes

1 tablespoon extra-virgin
  olive oil
1 teaspoon cumin seeds
1 white onion, diced
1 garlic clove, minced
1 head cauli-
  flower, chopped
1 cup water
1 tablespoon ground
  coriander
1 teaspoon ground cumin
½ teaspoon garam masala
½ teaspoon salt
Hot cooked rice, for serving
  (optional)

Select Sauté Low. When the display reads HOT, pour in the oil and heat until it shimmers. Add the cumin seeds. Cook for 30 seconds, stirring nearly constantly. Add the onion. Cook for 2 to 3 minutes. Select Cancel and add the garlic. Cook for about 30 seconds, stirring frequently. Add the cauliflower, water, coriander, cumin, garam masala, and salt. Lock the lid. Select Manual and cook at high pressure for 1 minute. When the cook time is complete, quick-release the pressure. Remove the lid and serve with hot rice (if using).

Roasted Poblano Pepper Tacos

SERVES 6 to 8 | PREP TIME: 8 minutes | SAUTÉ: 3 minutes | MANUAL: 8 minutes high pressure | RELEASE: Quick | TOTAL TIME: 20 minutes

2 tablespoons vegetable oil
1 medium white onion,
  thinly sliced
2 garlic cloves, minced
8 roasted poblano pep-
  pers, peeled, seeded, and
  cut into thin strips
2 Roma tomatoes, seeded
  and thinly sliced
1 cup Mexican crema or
  sour cream
¼ cup whole milk
2 medium Yukon Gold
  potatoes, peeled
  and diced
1 (15¼-ounce) can
  golden corn ker-
  nels, drained
Coarse salt
Freshly ground
  black pepper
Corn tortillas, for serving
Crumbled queso cotija,
  for garnish

Select Sauté and adjust to More for high. Heat the vegetable oil in the pot, add the onion and garlic, and sauté for 2 to 3 minutes, or until the onion is translucent. Stir in the roasted poblano pepper strips, tomatoes, Mexican crema, milk, potatoes, and corn. Season with salt and pepper. Select Cancel. Lock the lid. Select Manual and cook at high pressure for 8 minutes. When the cook time is complete, quick-release the pressure. Remove the lid. Stir gently to combine. Heat the corn tortillas on a comal or griddle until soft and pliable. Stack two warm corn tortillas for each taco. Spoon a couple of heaping tablespoons of the poblano pepper mixture down the center of each tortilla stack. Top with crumbled queso cotija.

Cauliflower Tinga

SERVES 6 to 8 | PREP TIME: 5 minutes | SAUTÉ: 3 minutes | MANUAL: 10 minutes high pressure | RELEASE: Quick | TOTAL TIME: 20 minutes

4 Roma tomatoes
2 to 4 chipotle chiles in
  adobo sauce
1 cup water
1 tablespoon
  vegetable oil
1 medium onion, diced
2 garlic cloves, minced
1 head cauliflower,
  roughly chopped
Coarse salt
Freshly ground
  black pepper
Corn tortillas, for
  serving
Pickled red onions,
  for garnish
Chopped fresh cilantro,
  for garnish

In a blender, puree the tomatoes, chipotle chiles, and water until smooth. Select Sauté and adjust to More for high. Heat the vegetable oil in the pot, add the onion and garlic, and sauté for 2 to 3 minutes, or until the onion is translucent. Stir in the cauliflower and tomato-chipotle puree. Season with salt and pepper. Select Cancel. Lock the lid. Select Manual and cook at high pressure for 10 minutes. When the cook time is complete, quick-release the pressure. Remove the lid. Spoon the cauliflower tinga onto corn tortillas. Garnish with pickled red onions and chopped cilantro.

Cauliflower Fried Rice

SERVES 4 | PREP TIME: 10 minutes | SAUTÉ: 3 minutes | MANUAL: 1 minute high pressure | RELEASE: Natural for 5 minutes, then Quick | TOTAL TIME: 29 minutes

2 teaspoons canola or vegetable oil
1 medium onion, chopped
1 medium green or red bell pepper, seeded and diced
2 teaspoons peeled and grated fresh ginger
2 garlic cloves, finely minced
1 cup frozen edamame
1 cup frozen or fresh corn
½ cup fresh or frozen green peas

1 (12-ounce) bag frozen cauliflower rice (no need to thaw) or 3½ cups fresh
1 tablespoon soy sauce
¾ teaspoon salt
¼ teaspoon red pepper flakes
⅛ teaspoon freshly ground black pepper
2 tablespoons water (only if using fresh cauliflower rice)
2 teaspoons freshly squeezed lime or lemon juice (optional)

Select Sauté, and once the pot is hot, pour in the oil. Add the onion, bell pepper, ginger, and garlic and cook for 2 to 3 minutes, until the onion turns translucent. Add the edamame, corn, peas, cauliflower rice, soy sauce, salt, red pepper flakes, black pepper, and water (if using fresh cauliflower rice). Mix well, breaking up any big pieces of frozen cauliflower rice, and make sure to scrape the bottom of the pot to loosen any browned bits. Select Cancel. Lock the lid. Select Manual and cook at high pressure for 1 minute. When the cook time is complete, naturally release the pressure for 5 minutes, then quick-release any remaining pressure. Remove the lid and stir in the lime juice (if using). If there is excess liquid, select Sauté and cook for 1 to 2 minutes to evaporate it. Serve hot.

Green Thai Coconut Curry with Tofu

SERVES 6 | PREP AND FINISHING: 10 minutes | SAUTÉ: 5 Minutes | MANUAL: 5 minutes high pressure | RELEASE: Natural for 10 minutes, then Quick | TOTAL TIME: 40 minutes

2 tablespoons extra-virgin olive oil
1 medium yellow onion, chopped
3 garlic cloves, minced
1 cup vegetable broth
1 (13½-ounce) can full-fat coconut milk
1 medium zucchini, chopped (about 1 cup)
2 red bell peppers, seeded and sliced

10 ounces extra-firm tofu, cubed
1 tablespoon Thai green curry paste
½ teaspoon ground ginger
½ teaspoon fine sea salt
Juice of 1 lime

Select Sauté and pour the olive oil into the Instant Pot. Once the oil is hot, add the onion and garlic and cook for about 3 minutes, or until the onion starts to soften. Select Cancel. Pour in the broth and coconut milk. Using a wooden spoon, scrape up any browned bits stuck to the bottom of the pot. Add the zucchini, bell peppers, tofu, curry paste, and ginger and stir to combine. Lock the lid. Select Manual and cook at high pressure for 5 minutes. When the cook time is complete, naturally release the pressure for 10 minutes, then quick-release any remaining pressure. Remove the lid. Stir in the salt and lime juice. Serve immediately.

Chickpea Salad Lettuce Wraps

SERVES 4 to 6 | PREP TIME: 5 minutes | MANUAL: 52 minutes high pressure | RELEASE: Natural | TOTAL TIME: 1 hour 20 minutes

FOR THE TOFU MAYO

1 (8-ounce) package silken tofu
1 teaspoon freshly squeezed lemon juice
1 teaspoon white wine vinegar

¾ teaspoon salt
½ teaspoon nutritional yeast
½ teaspoon mustard powder

FOR THE CHICKPEAS

4 cups water
1 cup dried chickpeas, rinsed and sorted
½ medium onion, roughly chopped
¾ teaspoon poultry seasoning, divided
2 celery stalks, diced

¼ cup finely chopped onion
Freshly ground black pepper
Salt (optional)
8 to 12 lettuce leaves, such as butter or romaine

TO MAKE THE TOFU MAYO

In a blender or food processor, combine the tofu, lemon juice, vinegar, salt, nutritional yeast, and mustard. Blend well and refrigerate it until needed.

TO MAKE THE CHICKPEAS

In the Instant Pot, combine the water, chickpeas, roughly chopped onion, and ¼ teaspoon of poultry seasoning. Lock the lid. Select Manual and cook at high pressure for 52 minutes. When the cook time is complete, let the pressure release naturally. Remove the chickpeas to a large mixing bowl and let them cool. Mash the cooled chickpeas with a fork or potato masher, leaving most beans partially intact. Add the finely chopped onion, celery, the remaining ½ teaspoon of poultry seasoning, and ½ cup of the tofu mayo. Stir well to combine. Season to taste with pepper and salt (if using). Portion about ¼ cup onto each lettuce leaf. Roll and serve immediately.

Southwestern Taco Bowls

SERVES 4 to 6 | PREP TIME: 5 minutes | MANUAL:
16 minutes high pressure | RELEASE: Quick | TOTAL
TIME: 30 minutes

4 cups vegetable broth
2 cups long-grain
   brown rice
2 cups green or brown lentils, rinsed and sorted
½ cup salsa
2 teaspoons fennel seeds

1 tablespoon chili powder
2 teaspoons onion powder
Juice of 4 limes, divided
Salt (optional)
8 to 12 cups shred-
   ded lettuce
2 avocados, diced

In the Instant Pot, stir together the broth, rice, lentils, salsa, fennel, chili powder, and onion powder.
Lock the lid. Select Manual and cook at high pressure for 16 minutes. When the cook time is complete,
quick-release the pressure. Remove the lid. Add half the
lime juice and salt to taste (if using). Fluff with a fork to
combine. Toss the lettuce with the remaining lime juice.
For serving, add about 2 cups of the lettuce to each bowl,
top with the rice and lentils, and garnish with the diced
avocado.

Indian-Style Burrito Bowls

SERVES 4 | PREP TIME: 5 minutes | SAUTÉ: 4 minutes |
PRESSURE BUILD: 10 minutes | MANUAL: 5 minutes high
pressure | RELEASE: Natural for 10 minutes, then Quick |
TOTAL TIME: 34 minutes

1 cup basmati rice, rinsed
   and drained
1¼ cups water
2 tablespoons canola or
   vegetable oil
1 medium onion, chopped
1 medium red or green
   bell pepper, seeded
   and diced
2 teaspoons grated
   fresh ginger
2 garlic cloves,
   finely minced
1 cup canned tomato puree
1 teaspoon salt
1 teaspoon cay-
   enne pepper

1 teaspoon ground
   coriander
1 teaspoon chaat masala
½ teaspoon garam masala
1 (15-ounce) can red
   kidney beans, rinsed
   and drained
1 cup grated Cheddar or
   pepper Jack cheese
   (optional)
Plain Greek yogurt,
   for serving
Sliced avocado, for serving
Chopped tomato,
   for serving

In a bowl, combine the rice and water. Set aside. Select
Sauté and pour in the oil. Once the pot is hot, add the
onion, bell pepper, ginger, and garlic and cook until
the onion is lightly browned around the edges, 3 to
4 minutes. Add the tomato puree, salt, cayenne pepper,
coriander, chaat masala, garam masala, and beans.
Stir well, scraping the bottom of the pot to loosen any
browned bits. Add the rice along with the soaking water.
Lock the lid and close the steam valve, then cook on high

for 5 minutes on high pressure. When the cook time is
complete, release the pressure naturally for 10 minutes,
then quick-release any remaining pressure. Remove the
lid and, if using, sprinkle the cheese evenly on top and
cover for 5 minutes to let it melt. Gently fluff the rice and
serve topped with yogurt, avocado, and tomato.

Potato and Kale Curry

SERVES 4 to 6 | PREP TIME: 10 minutes | SAUTÉ: 5 to
7 minutes, divided | MANUAL: 6 minutes high pressure |
RELEASE: Natural for 5 minutes, then Quick | TOTAL
TIME: 30 minutes

1 medium onion, diced
4 garlic cloves, minced
2 tablespoons
   curry powder
½ teaspoon red pepper
   flakes (optional)
2¼ cups water, divided
1 (14-ounce) can full-fat
   coconut milk
2 pounds red or yellow
   potatoes, cut into
   1-inch pieces

1 tablespoon maple syrup
   (optional)
1 bunch Tuscan
   kale, stemmed
1 (15-ounce) can chickpeas,
   drained and rinsed
3 tablespoons arrow-
   root powder
Freshly ground
   black pepper
Salt (optional)

Select Sauté. Sauté the onion for 3 minutes, adding
water as needed to prevent sticking. Add the garlic, curry
powder, and red pepper flakes (if using) and stir for
30 seconds, until fragrant. Select Cancel. Stir in 2 cups
of water, the coconut milk, potatoes, and maple syrup (if
using). Place the kale on top. Lock the lid. Select Manual
and cook at high pressure for 6 minutes. When the cook
time is complete, let the pressure release naturally for
5 minutes, then quick-release any remaining pressure.
Remove the lid. Stir in the chickpeas. In a small bowl,
whisk together the arrowroot and the remaining ¼ cup
of water. Select Sauté and stir in the arrowroot slurry
until thickened, 2 to 4 minutes. Season to taste with
pepper and salt (if using).

Creamy Spaghetti Squash with Spinach, Olives, and Roasted Red Peppers

SERVES 4 to 6 | PREP TIME: 10 minutes | MANUAL:
8 minutes high pressure | RELEASE: Quick | TOTAL
TIME: 30 minutes

1 cup water
1 (2- to 4-pound) spa-
   ghetti squash, halved
   and seeded
¾ cup unsweetened
   plant-based milk
1 cup canned white beans,
   drained and rinsed
2 garlic cloves, smashed

2 tablespoons nutri-
   tional yeast
Zest and juice of 1 lemon
Freshly ground
   black pepper
Salt (optional)
5 ounces fresh
   baby spinach

1 (6-ounce) jar pitted kalamata olives, drained and chopped

2 or 3 jarred roasted red peppers, chopped

¼ cup chopped fresh flat-leaf parsley

Pour the water into the Instant Pot and insert the trivet. Place the squash on the trivet. Lock the lid. Select Manual and cook at high pressure for 8 minutes. In a blender or food processor, combine the milk, beans, garlic, nutritional yeast, lemon zest, and lemon juice and season to taste with pepper and salt (if using). Blend well. Set it aside. When the cook time is complete, quick-release the pressure. Remove the lid. Drain the squash. Using a fork, remove the pulp of the squash, shredding it into long spaghetti-like strands. Discard the skin. Add the spinach, olives, red peppers, and sauce and toss to combine. Stir in half the parsley and serve.

Spaghetti Squash with Feta, Tomatoes, and Pine Nuts

SERVES 4 | PREP AND FINISHING: 10 minutes | MANUAL: Steam 7 minutes high pressure | RELEASE: Quick | TOTAL TIME: 25 minutes

1 small spaghetti squash (3 to 4 pounds), halved and seeded

1 cup water

¼ cup extra-virgin olive oil

2 tablespoons freshly squeezed lemon juice

¼ teaspoon kosher salt

⅛ teaspoon freshly ground black pepper

1 pint cherry tomatoes, halved

½ cup crumbled feta cheese

3 tablespoons toasted pine nuts

2 tablespoons chopped fresh parsley

Place the squash halves, cut-side down, on a trivet. Pour the water into the Instant Pot and place the trivet inside. Lock the lid. Select Manual and steam at high pressure for 7 minutes. When the cook time is complete, quick-release the pressure. Remove the lid. While the squash cooks, combine the olive oil, lemon juice, salt, and pepper in a small jar with a tight-fitting lid. Shake until well combined. Use tongs to remove the squash halves from the pot. Let them cool slightly, then scrape out the flesh with a fork to form long strands. Transfer to a serving bowl and let cool until just warm. Add the tomatoes and feta cheese. Drizzle with the dressing and toss to coat. Top with the pine nuts and parsley.

Garlicky Lemon-Parmesan Spaghetti Squash

SERVES 4 | PREP TIME: 10 minutes | MANUAL: 10 minutes high pressure | SAUTÉ: 3 minutes | RELEASE: Quick | TOTAL TIME: 30 minutes

2 small (2½- to 3-pound) spaghetti squash

1 cup water

¼ cup extra-virgin olive oil6 garlic cloves, sliced

Zest and juice of 1 lemon

½ cup shredded Parmesan cheese

¼ cup fresh parsley, chopped

½ teaspoon kosher salt

½ teaspoon freshly ground black pepper

Halve the spaghetti squash crosswise and discard the seeds. Pour the water into the Instant Pot and insert the trivet. Place the squash on top of the trivet, stacking the halves to fit if necessary. Lock the lid. Select Manual and cook at high pressure for 10 minutes. When the cook time is complete, quick-release the pressure. Remove the lid. Remove the squash and discard any remaining water. Let the squash rest for about 5 minutes. When it is cool enough to handle, use a fork to scrape the flesh into spaghetti-like strands. Return the inner pot to the Instant Pot. Select Sauté and pour in the olive oil. When the oil is hot, add the garlic and lemon zest. Cook for 2 to 3 minutes, stirring frequently, until softened and fragrant. Select Cancel. Stir in the lemon juice. Return the squash strands to the pot and stir to coat. Stir in the Parmesan and parsley. Season with salt and pepper.

Eggplant Parmesan

SERVES 4 | PREP TIME: 10 minutes | MANUAL: 10 minutes high pressure | RELEASE: Quick | TOTAL TIME: 30 minutes

2 medium eggplants

½ cup water

2 cups marinara sauce

1 cup shredded mozzarella cheese

Cut the top and bottom off each eggplant, then slice the eggplants lengthwise into ¼-inch planks. Pour the water into the Instant Pot. Stir in ½ cup of marinara sauce. Add two or three pieces of eggplant to form a single layer. Spread ½ cup of marinara sauce over the eggplant and sprinkle with ¼ cup of cheese. Repeat this process for four total layers of eggplant, sauce, and cheese. Lock the lid. Select Manual and cook at high pressure for 10 minutes. When the cook time is complete, quick-release the pressure. Remove the lid and serve.

Chickpea Tikka Masala

SERVES 6 | PREP TIME: 5 minutes | SAUTÉ: 13 minutes | MANUAL: 2 minutes high pressure | RELEASE: Quick | TOTAL TIME: 25 minutes

1 tablespoon unsalted butter

½ cup chopped onion

1 medium red bell pepper, seeded and chopped

2 (15-ounce) cans chopped tomatoes

2 (15-ounce) cans chickpeas, drained

6 garlic cloves, chopped

4 teaspoons garam masala

Salt

Freshly ground black pepper

1 cup full fat coconut milk

4 cups fully cooked white rice (optional)

Select Sauté, and when the Instant Pot is hot, melt the butter. Stir in the onion and bell pepper and cook until the onion is translucent, about 5 minutes. Add the tomatoes with their juices, chickpeas, garlic, and garam masala and season with salt and pepper. Select Cancel. Lock the lid. Select Manual and cook at high pressure for 2 minutes. When the cook time is complete, quick-release the pressure. Remove the lid. Select Sauté. Add the coconut milk and heat until the mixture boils. Serve over rice (if using).

Jackfruit Masala

SERVES 4 | PREP TIME: 10 minutes | SAUTÉ: 8 minutes | PRESSURE BUILD: 8 minutes | MANUAL: 6 minutes high pressure | RELEASE: Natural for 10 minutes, then Quick | TOTAL TIME: 42 minutes

1 (20-ounce) can jackfruit in brine or water, rinsed and drained	½ green serrano chile, chopped
1 tablespoon canola or vegetable oil	2 medium tomatoes, chopped
½ teaspoon cumin seeds	1 teaspoon salt
1 large onion, finely chopped	1 teaspoon cayenne pepper
1 teaspoon grated fresh ginger	1 teaspoon garam masala
2 garlic cloves, finely minced	¼ teaspoon ground turmeric
	½ cup water
	½ cup full-fat coconut milk

Cut the jackfruit into bite-size pieces, then use a fork to shred the pieces. Select Sauté, and once the pot is hot, pour in the oil. Add the cumin seeds and cook for about 30 seconds, until the seeds start to sputter. Add the onion, ginger, garlic, and chile and cook for 3 to 4 minutes, until the onion turns translucent. Stir in the tomatoes, salt, cayenne pepper, garam masala, and turmeric and cook for 2 to 3 minutes, until the tomatoes are very soft. Add the water and jackfruit. Mix well, scraping the bottom to loosen any browned bits. Lock the lid and close the steam valve. Set the timer for 6 minutes on high pressure. When the timer sounds, natural-release the steam for 10 minutes, then quick-release the remainder. Open the lid and stir in the coconut milk. Cover for 5 minutes. Serve hot.

Italian-Style Chickpea Stew with Pesto

SERVES 4 | PREP AND FINISHING: 15 minutes | SAUTÉ: 3 minutes | MANUAL: 10 minutes high pressure | RELEASE: Natural for 10 minutes, then Quick | TOTAL TIME: 40 minutes, plus overnight to soak

FOR THE PESTO

1½ packed cups fresh basil leaves (about ¾ ounce)	1 garlic clove, minced
¼ cup extra-virgin olive oil, plus more as needed	1 tablespoon toasted pine nuts
¼ cup grated Parmesan cheese (about 1 ounce)	

FOR THE CHICKPEAS

1 tablespoon plus ½ teaspoon kosher salt, divided	2 medium carrots, chopped (about ¾ cup)
1 quart water	1 (14-ounce) can diced tomatoes
12 ounces dried chickpeas	4 cups chicken broth
2 tablespoons extra-virgin olive oil	¼ cup grated Parmesan or similar cheese
1 small onion, chopped (about ¾ cup)	

TO MAKE THE PESTO

In a small food processor or blender, combine the basil, oil, cheese, garlic, and pine nuts. Pulse until a coarse paste forms, adding a tablespoon or two of water or more olive oil, if necessary to get a loose enough consistency. Set aside ⅓ cup of pesto for this recipe.

TO MAKE THE CHICKPEAS

In a large bowl, dissolve 1 tablespoon of kosher salt in the water. Add the chickpeas and soak at room temperature for 8 to 24 hours. Drain and rinse. Select Sauté and adjust to More for high heat. Pour in the olive oil and heat until it shimmers. Add the onion and ¼ teaspoon of salt. Cook, stirring, until the onion pieces separate and soften, 2 to 3 minutes. Select Cancel. Add the chickpeas, carrots, tomatoes with their juices, broth, and remaining ¼ teaspoon of salt. Lock the lid. Select Manual and cook at high pressure for 10 minutes. When the cook time is complete, naturally release the pressure for 10 minutes, then quick-release any remaining pressure. Remove the lid. Ladle into bowls and top each with a spoonful of pesto. Sprinkle with the cheese and serve.

Brown and Wild Rice–Stuffed Peppers

SERVES 4 | PREP AND FINISHING: 15 minutes | SAUTÉ: 4 minutes | MANUAL: 28 minutes high pressure, divided | BROIL: 2 minutes | RELEASE: Natural for 15 minutes, divided, then Quick | TOTAL TIME: 1 hour

2 cups warm water	1½ cups vegetable broth
½ cup wild rice	1 bay leaf
4 red or green bell peppers	1 fresh thyme sprig or ¼ teaspoon dried thyme
1 tablespoon extra-virgin olive oil	1 cup water
1 small onion, diced (about ¾ cup)	½ cup panko breadcrumbs
¼ teaspoon kosher salt, plus more as needed	3 tablespoons grated Parmesan or similar cheese
1 garlic clove, minced	1 tablespoon unsalted butter, melted
½ cup brown rice	

In a small bowl, combine the warm water and wild rice. Let sit for 15 to 20 minutes, while you prep the remaining ingredients. Drain. Cut about ⅓-inch off the top of each pepper, setting the tops aside. Remove the seeds and pith from the peppers, leaving a hollow shell. Stem the pepper tops and chop the flesh. Select Sauté and adjust to More for high heat. Heat the oil until it shimmers. Add the onion and diced bell pepper and salt. Cook, stirring frequently, until the onion pieces separate and soften, 2 to 3 minutes. Add the garlic and cook until fragrant, another 1 minute or so. Select Cancel. Add the drained wild rice, brown rice, broth, bay leaf, and thyme to the pot. Lock the lid. Select Manual and cook at high pressure for 20 minutes. When the cook time is complete, naturally release the pressure for 10 minutes, then quick-release any remaining pressure. Remove the lid. Adjust the seasoning and remove and discard the bay leaf and thyme sprig (if using). Spoon the filling into the hollowed-out bell peppers, mounding it up slightly. Wipe out the pot, making sure no rice is stuck to the bottom. Place the steamer trivet in the pot and pour in 1 cup of water. Place the peppers on the trivet. Lock the lid. Select Manual and cook at high pressure for 8 minutes. When the cook time is complete, naturally release the pressure for 5 minutes, then quick-release any remaining pressure. Remove the lid. Preheat the broiler. Carefully remove the peppers from the pot and place them on a baking sheet or in a baking dish. In a small bowl, mix the panko, Parmesan cheese, and melted butter and sprinkle the mixture over the top of the peppers and filling. Broil the peppers until the tops are golden brown and crisp, 2 to 4 minutes. Serve.

Spicy Tofu Curry with Rice

SERVES 4 | PREP AND FINISHING: 15 minutes | SAUTÉ: 3 minutes | MANUAL: 4 minutes high pressure | RELEASE: Quick | TOTAL TIME: 25 minutes

1 tablespoon extra-virgin olive oil	1 tablespoon freshly squeezed lime juice
1 medium onion, chopped	1 teaspoon Thai red curry paste
3 garlic cloves, finely minced	1 teaspoon curry powder
1 small red bell pepper, seeded and chopped	1 teaspoon sugar
½ teaspoon kosher salt, divided	1 pound firm or extra-firm tofu, drained and cut into ½-inch cubes
1 (14-ounce) can diced tomatoes, drained	2 cups cooked white rice, for serving
¾ cup vegetable broth	2 scallions, both white and green parts, sliced, for garnish
2 tablespoons tomato paste	

Select Sauté and adjust to More for high heat. Heat the oil until it shimmers. Add the onion, garlic, and bell pepper and ¼ teaspoon of salt. Cook, stirring frequently, until the onion pieces separate and begin to soften, 2 to 3 minutes. Select Cancel. Stir in the tomatoes, vegetable broth, and tomato paste and stir to break up the tomato paste. Add the lime juice, curry paste, curry powder, and sugar and stir to combine. Add the tofu. Lock the lid. Select Manual and cook at high pressure for 4 minutes. When the cook time is complete, quick-release the

pressure. Remove the lid. Stir the curry, then let it sit for 2 to 3 minutes. Serve over rice and garnish with the scallions.

Smoky Black Bean Tacos

SERVES 4 | PREP AND FINISHING: 20 minutes | SAUTÉ: 3 minutes | MANUAL: 15 minutes high pressure | RELEASE: Natural for 10 minutes | TOTAL TIME: 50 minutes, plus overnight to soak

1 tablespoon plus 1 teaspoon kosher salt, divided	2 medium garlic cloves, minced
1 quart water	2½ cups vegetable broth
12 ounces dried black beans	2 tablespoons ancho chile sauce
1 tablespoon extra-virgin olive oil	1 teaspoon pureed canned chipotles
1 small onion, chopped (about ¾ cup)	1 teaspoon ground cumin
1 medium jalapeño, seeded and diced	½ teaspoon dried oregano
½ small red bell pepper, chopped (about ¼ cup)	8 to 12 corn or flour tortillas, warmed
½ small green bell pepper, chopped (about ¼ cup)	1 cup crumbled queso fresco or shredded Monterey Jack cheese

FOR THE PICO DE GALLO

1 large tomato, seeded and diced	2 tablespoons chopped fresh cilantro
½ very small onion, chopped (about ⅓ cup)	⅛ teaspoon ground cumin
1 large jalapeño, seeded and chopped (about 3 tablespoons)	½ teaspoon kosher salt, plus more as needed
	1 to 2 teaspoons freshly squeezed lime juice, divided

In a large bowl, dissolve 1 tablespoon of kosher salt in the water. Add the beans and soak at room temperature for 8 to 24 hours. Drain and rinse. Select Sauté and adjust to More for high heat. Heat the olive oil until it shimmers. Add the onion, jalapeño, red and green bell peppers, and garlic. Cook, stirring occasionally, until the onion is soft, 2 to 3 minutes. Add the vegetable broth and stir, scraping the bottom of the pot to dissolve any browned bits. Stir in the chile sauce, chipotle puree, cumin, oregano, and remaining 1 teaspoon of salt. Select Cancel. Add the drained beans to the pot. Lock the lid. Select Manual and cook at high pressure for 15 minutes. When the cook time is complete, naturally release the pressure for 10 minutes, then quick-release any remaining pressure. Remove the lid.

TO MAKE THE PICO DE GALLO
While the beans are cooking, in a small bowl, gently toss together the tomato, onion, jalapeño, cilantro, cumin, salt, and 1 teaspoon of lime juice. Taste and adjust the

seasoning, adding the remaining 1 teaspoon of lime juice if necessary. If the beans are too soupy, select Sauté and adjust to Normal for medium heat. Simmer until the sauce has thickened to the consistency you want. Taste and add more salt if necessary. To serve, spoon some beans into a warmed tortilla and top with the cheese and pico de gallo.

Everyday Potato Curry

SERVES 4 | **PREP TIME:** 10 minutes | **SAUTÉ:** 5 minutes | **MANUAL:** 2 minutes high pressure | **RELEASE:** Natural for 5 minutes, then Quick | **TOTAL TIME:** 30 minutes

1 tablespoon canola or vegetable oil
½ teaspoon mustard seeds
1 medium onion, thinly sliced
½ green serrano chile, finely minced
1 medium tomato, chopped
1 teaspoon salt
½ teaspoon cayenne pepper
¼ teaspoon ground turmeric
3 medium potatoes (about 1 pound), peeled and cut into ½-inch pieces
½ cup water

Select Sauté, and once the pot is hot, pour in the oil. Add the mustard seeds and cook for about 30 seconds, until they start to sputter. Add the onion and chile and cook for 2 to 3 minutes, until the onion turns translucent. Add the tomato, salt, cayenne pepper, and turmeric and cook for about 1 minute, until the tomato is soft. Stir in the potatoes and water. Select Cancel. Lock the lid. Select Manual and cook at high pressure for 2 minutes. When the cook time is complete, naturally release the pressure for 5 minutes, then quick-release any remaining pressure. Remove the lid and stir. Serve hot.

Vegetable Biryani

SERVES 4 to 6 | **PREP TIME:** 15 minutes | **SAUTÉ:** 6 minutes | **MANUAL:** 5 minutes high pressure | **RELEASE:** Natural for 10 minutes, then Quick | **TOTAL TIME:** 46 minutes

2½ cups water
2 cups basmati rice, rinsed and drained
3 tablespoons ghee, canola oil, or vegetable oil
4 whole cloves (optional)
4 cardamom pods (optional)
1 (2-inch) cinnamon stick (optional)
1 teaspoon cumin seeds
2 bay leaves
2 tablespoons chopped raw cashews
1 large onion, thinly sliced
1 tablespoon peeled and grated fresh ginger
4 large garlic cloves, finely minced
1 medium carrot, cut into 1-inch pieces
1 large potato, peeled and cut into 1-inch pieces
1 cup fresh or frozen green peas
½ cup chopped green beans
1 small red or green bell pepper, seeded and chopped

1 medium tomato, chopped
½ cup plain Greek yogurt
2 teaspoons salt
1½ teaspoons cayenne pepper
1 teaspoon ground coriander
1 teaspoon garam masala
¼ cup chopped fresh mint
¼ cup chopped fresh cilantro

In a medium bowl, combine the water and rice. Set it aside. Select Sauté, and when the pot is hot, melt the ghee or oil. Then add the cloves (if using), cardamom pods (if using), cinnamon stick (if using), cumin seeds, bay leaves, and cashews. Cook for about 1 minute, until the spices are fragrant. Add the onion and cook for 3 to 4 minutes, until the edges begin to caramelize slightly. Stir in the ginger and garlic and cook for about 1 minute, until they are fragrant. Add the carrot, potato, peas, green beans, bell pepper, tomato, yogurt, salt, cayenne pepper, coriander, and garam masala. Mix well, then add the rice along with the soaking water, mint, and cilantro. Stir to combine, making sure to scrape the bottom of the pot to loosen any browned bits. Select Cancel. Lock the lid. Select Manual and cook at high pressure for 5 minutes. When the cook time is complete, naturally release the pressure for 10 minutes, then quick-release any remaining pressure. Remove the lid and gently fluff the rice. Serve hot.

Mushroom Masala

SERVES 4 | **PREP TIME:** 10 minutes | **SAUTÉ:** 6 minutes | **MANUAL:** 4 minutes high pressure | **RELEASE:** Natural for 5 minutes, then Quick | **TOTAL TIME:** 33 minutes

1 tablespoon canola or vegetable oil
1 medium onion, chopped
1 teaspoon grated fresh ginger
2 garlic cloves, finely minced
½ cup canned tomato puree
¾ teaspoon salt
¾ teaspoon cayenne pepper
½ teaspoon garam masala
8 ounces cremini or white button mushrooms, chopped
1 cup frozen or fresh green peas
¼ cup water
¼ cup full-fat coconut milk

Select Sauté, and once the pot is hot, pour in the oil. Add the onion, ginger, and garlic and cook for 3 to 4 minutes, until the onion is lightly browned around the edges. Stir in the tomato puree, salt, cayenne pepper, and garam masala and cook for 1 to 2 minutes, until simmering. Add the mushrooms, peas, and water and mix well, making sure to scrape the bottom of the pot to loosen any browned bits. Select Cancel. Lock the lid. Select Manual and cook at high pressure for 4 minutes. When the cook time is complete, naturally release the pressure for 5 minutes, then quick-release any remaining pressure. Remove the lid and stir in the coconut milk. Cover for 5 minutes, then serve hot.

Aloo Gobi

SERVES 4 | PREP TIME: 10 minutes | SAUTÉ: 8 minutes | MANUAL: 1 minute high pressure | RELEASE: Quick | TOTAL TIME: 27 minutes

2 tablespoons canola or vegetable oil
1 teaspoon cumin seeds
1 medium onion, chopped
2 teaspoons peeled and grated fresh ginger
2 garlic cloves, finely minced
2 medium potatoes, peeled and cubed
¾ cup water, divided

2 medium tomatoes, chopped
1¼ teaspoons salt
1 teaspoon cayenne pepper
½ teaspoon ground turmeric
¼ teaspoon red pepper flakes (optional)
3 cups fresh or frozen cauliflower florets

Select Sauté, and once the pot is hot, pour in the oil. Add the cumin seeds and cook for about 30 seconds, until the seeds start to sputter. Add the onion, ginger, garlic, and potatoes and cook, stirring occasionally, for about 2 minutes, until the onion turns translucent. Add ½ cup of water and mix well. Cover the pot and cook until the potatoes are slightly tender, 3 to 4 minutes. Add the tomatoes, salt, cayenne pepper, turmeric, and red pepper flakes and cook until the tomatoes are soft, about 1 minute. Stir in the remaining ¼ cup of water and scrape the bottom of the pot to loosen any browned bits. Add the cauliflower florets right on top. Do not stir. Select Cancel. Lock the lid. Select Manual and cook at high pressure for 1 minute. When the cook time is complete, quick-release the pressure. Remove the lid and stir the cooked cauliflower into the curry. If there is any excess liquid, select Sauté and cook for 1 to 2 minutes to reduce the mixture. Serve hot.

Tofu and Sweet Potato Vindaloo

SERVES 4 to 6 | PREP TIME: 15 minutes | SAUTÉ: 9 minutes, divided | MANUAL: 3 minutes high pressure | RELEASE: Quick | TOTAL TIME: 35 minutes

4 garlic cloves
1 (1-inch) piece ginger, peeled and roughly chopped
2 teaspoons sugar
1¼ teaspoons salt
1 teaspoon cayenne pepper
1 teaspoon ground cumin
1 teaspoon ground coriander
½ teaspoon ground turmeric
½ teaspoon freshly ground black pepper

¼ teaspoon ground cardamom
Pinch ground cloves (optional)
¾ cup water, divided
2 tablespoons white wine vinegar or distilled white vinegar
3 tablespoons canola or vegetable oil, divided
1 medium onion, finely chopped
2 medium sweet potatoes, peeled and cut into 1-inch pieces

2 cups fresh or frozen cauliflower florets
1 cup canned tomato puree

2 cups extra-firm cubed tofu (about 7 ounces)
1 cup fresh or frozen green peas

In a blender or food processor, combine the garlic, ginger, sugar, salt, cayenne pepper, cumin, coriander, turmeric, black pepper, cardamom, cloves (if using), ¼ cup of water, the vinegar, and 1 tablespoon of oil. Blend to a smooth paste. Set it aside. Select Sauté, and once the pot is hot, pour in the remaining 2 tablespoons of oil. Add the onion and cook for 3 to 4 minutes, until lightly browned around the edges. Add the spice paste and cook for 1 to 2 minutes. Add the sweet potatoes, cauliflower, tomato puree, and remaining ½ cup of water. Stir to combine. Select Cancel. Lock the lid. Select Manual and cook at high pressure for 3 minutes. When the cook time is complete, quick-release the pressure. Remove the lid and stir in the cubed tofu and peas. Select Sauté and cook for 2 to 3 minutes to heat through. Serve immediately.

Millet Burrito Bowls

SERVES 4 | PREP TIME: 5 minutes | SAUTÉ: 4 minutes | MANUAL: 9 minutes high pressure | RELEASE: Natural for 10 minutes, then Quick | TOTAL TIME: 30 minutes

1 tablespoon extra-virgin olive oil
1 yellow onion, finely diced
1 red bell pepper, seeded and sliced
1 (15½-ounce) can black beans, drained and rinsed

2 cups frozen corn
1 cup millet, rinsed well and drained
1 cup salsa
¾ cup vegetable broth
½ teaspoon kosher salt
¼ cup fresh cilantro, chopped

Select Sauté on the Instant Pot and pour in the olive oil. When the oil is hot, add the onion and bell pepper. Cook for 3 to 4 minutes, stirring occasionally, until softened. Select Cancel. Add the beans, corn, millet, salsa, broth, and salt. Stir to combine. Lock the lid. Select Manual and cook at high pressure for 9 minutes. When the cook time is complete, let the pressure release naturally for 10 minutes, then quick-release any remaining pressure. Remove the lid and stir. Top with the cilantro and serve.

Jackfruit al Pastor Tacos

SERVES 6 to 8 | PREP TIME: 10 minutes | SAUTÉ: 3 minutes | MANUAL: 10 minutes high pressure | RELEASE: Natural | TOTAL TIME: 45 minutes

1 tablespoon vegetable oil
1 medium white onion, thinly sliced
2 garlic cloves, minced

1 (7- to 8-pound) jackfruit, peeled, quartered, cored, and seeded, flesh scooped out by hand

1 (30-ounce) can crushed
   pineapple
Juice of 1 orange
1 tablespoon white vinegar
1½ tablespoons ancho
   chile powder
½ tablespoon chipotle
   chile powder
1 teaspoon coarse salt
1 teaspoon crushed dried
   Mexican oregano

1 teaspoon ground cumin
½ teaspoon freshly ground
   black pepper
¼ teaspoon ground cloves
Corn tortillas
Chopped red onion,
   for garnish
Chopped fresh cilantro,
   for garnish
Salsa, for garnish

Select Sauté and adjust to More for high. Heat the vegetable oil in the pot, add the onion and garlic, and sauté for 2 to 3 minutes, or until the onion is translucent. Add the jackfruit, pineapple with its juices, and the orange juice. Add the vinegar, chile powders, salt, oregano, cumin, pepper, and cloves. Select Cancel. Lock the lid. Select Manual and cook at high pressure for 10 minutes. When the cook time is complete, allow the pressure to release naturally. Remove the lid. Stir gently to combine. Heat the corn tortillas on a griddle over medium-high heat until soft and pliable. Stack two tortillas per taco. Top with a couple of heaping tablespoons of the jackfruit. Garnish with chopped red onion, cilantro, and your favorite salsa.

FISH AND SEAFOOD

Steamed Crab Legs with Dipping Sauce

SERVES 4 | PREP TIME: 5 minutes | MANUAL: 4 minutes | RELEASE: Quick | TOTAL TIME: 14 minutes

1 cup water
2 pounds snow crab legs
   (4 clusters)
1 teaspoon Old Bay
   seasoning
¼ cup (½ stick)
   unsalted butter

2 garlic cloves, minced
½ tablespoon lemon juice
1 teaspoon chopped fresh
   flat-leaf parsley
¼ teaspoon salt
¼ teaspoon freshly ground
   black pepper

Set the trivet in the Instant Pot and pour in the water. Place the crab legs on the trivet, folding them at the joint to fit. Sprinkle evenly with the Old Bay seasoning. In a small ramekin, combine the butter, garlic, lemon juice, parsley, salt, and pepper. Cover tightly with foil and place in the center of the crab legs. Lock the lid. Select Manual and cook at high pressure for 4 minutes. When the cook time is complete, quick-release the pressure. Uncover the dipping sauce and mix well. Serve the legs and sauce immediately.

Coconut-Lime Mussels

SERVES 4 | PREP TIME: 5 minutes, plus 15 minutes to soak | MANUAL: 3 minutes high pressure | RELEASE: Quick | TOTAL TIME: 35 minutes

1 (13½-ounce) can
   full-fat unsweetened
   coconut milk
2 cups water
1 (1-inch) knob fresh ginger,
   peeled and grated

Zest and juice of 1 lime
3 pounds fresh mussels,
   soaked and scrubbed
¼ cup fresh
   cilantro, chopped

In the Instant Pot, combine the coconut milk, water, ginger, lime zest, and lime juice. Stir well. Add the mussels to the pot. Lock the lid. Select Manual and cook at high pressure for 3 minutes. When the cook time is complete, quick-release the pressure. Remove the lid and stir in the cilantro before serving.

Mussels with Red Pepper–Garlic Sauce

SERVES 4 | PREP AND FINISHING: 15 minutes | SAUTÉ: 1 minute | MANUAL: 1 minute high pressure | RELEASE: Quick | TOTAL TIME: 20 minutes

1 tablespoon extra-virgin
   olive oil
4 garlic cloves, minced
1 large roasted red
   bell pepper, minced
   or pureed
¾ cup fish broth, clam
   juice, or water
½ cup dry white wine

⅛ teaspoon red
   pepper flakes
3 pounds mussels, cleaned
   and debearded
2 tablespoons heavy
   (whipping) cream
3 tablespoons coarsely
   chopped fresh parsley

Select Sauté and adjust to Normal for medium heat. Heat the olive oil until it shimmers. Add the garlic and cook, stirring frequently, until it is fragrant, about 1 minute. Add the roasted red pepper, fish broth, wine, and red pepper flakes. Stir to combine. Select Cancel. Add the mussels to the pot. Lock the lid. Select Manual and cook at high pressure for 1 minute. When the cook time is complete, quick-release the pressure. Remove the lid. Check the mussels; if they are not opened, replace the lid but don't lock it into place. Let the mussels steam for another 1 minute, until they've opened. (Discard any that do not open.) Stir in the cream and parsley and serve with the cooking liquid.

Creamy Corn Chowder with Smoked Trout

SERVES 4 | PREP AND FINISHING: 15 minutes | MANUAL: 5 minutes high pressure | RELEASE: Natural for 5 minutes, then Quick | TOTAL TIME: 35 minutes

1 tablespoon
   unsalted butter
2 large scallions, white and
   green parts, chopped
   (about ⅓ cup)
½ teaspoon kosher salt,
   plus more as needed
1 tablespoon
   all-purpose flour

¼ cup dry white wine
3 cups whole milk
2 small or 1 medium Yukon
   Gold potato, peeled and
   cut into ½-inch cubes
   (about 2 cups)
1½ cups frozen corn
2 tablespoons sour cream

2 teaspoons prepared
horseradish
1 teaspoon grated
lemon zest
4 ounces hot-smoked
trout, chopped or flaked
into small chunks

Freshly ground
black pepper
2 tablespoons chopped
fresh chives

Select Sauté and adjust to Normal for medium heat. Put the butter in the pot to melt. When it has stopped foaming, add the scallions and salt. Cook, stirring frequently, until softened, about 1 minute. Stir in the flour and cook until it turns a very light tan color, 2 to 3 minutes. Add the wine, whisking to combine with the flour mixture, and cook until the mixture has thickened, about 2 minutes. Add the milk and whisk until the mixture is smooth. Select Cancel. Add the potatoes and corn. Lock the lid. Select Manual and cook at high pressure for 5 minutes. When the cook time is complete, naturally release the pressure for 5 minutes, then quick-release any remaining pressure. Remove the lid. Add the sour cream, horseradish, and lemon zest. Stir and taste, adding more salt and black pepper if necessary. Stir in the trout and ladle the soup into bowls. Top with the chives and serve.

Seafood Gumbo

SERVES 6 | PREP AND FINISHING: 10 minutes | SAUTÉ: 5 minutes | MANUAL: 5 minutes high pressure | RELEASE: Natural for 5 minutes, then Quick | TOTAL TIME: 35 minutes

2 tablespoons extra-virgin
olive oil
1 medium yellow
onion, diced
2 garlic cloves, minced
2 celery stalks, diced
2 cups chicken broth
1 (14-ounce) can diced
tomatoes
1 pound halibut fillets,
patted dry and cut into
2-inch cubes

1 pound medium shrimp,
peeled and deveined,
tails left on
½ teaspoon cay-
enne pepper
1 teaspoon dried oregano
1 teaspoon dried thyme
2 teaspoon paprika
½ teaspoon fine sea salt
½ teaspoon freshly ground
black pepper

Select Sauté and pour in the olive oil the Instant Pot. Once the oil is hot, add the onion, garlic, and celery and sauté for 3 minutes, stirring occasionally. Select Cancel. Add the broth and diced tomatoes with their juices into the pot. Using a wooden spoon, scrape up any browned bits stuck to the bottom of the pot. Add the halibut, shrimp, cayenne pepper, oregano, thyme, paprika, salt, and pepper. Stir to combine. Lock the lid. Select Manual and cook at high pressure for 5 minutes. When the cook time is complete, naturally release the pressure for 5 minutes, then quick-release any remaining pressure. Remove the lid. Stir the gumbo. Serve immediately.

Seafood Cioppino

SERVES 6 | PREP TIME: 10 minutes | SAUTÉ: 4 minutes | MANUAL: 3 minutes high pressure | RELEASE: Natural | TOTAL TIME: 30 minutes

1 tablespoon extra-virgin
olive oil
1 yellow onion,
finely chopped
2 garlic cloves, thinly sliced
1 pound firm, skinless white
fish (such as halibut), cut
into 1-inch pieces
1 pound large shrimp,
peeled and deveined

1 pound littleneck clams
2 cups marinara sauce
1½ cups seafood broth
2 celery stalks,
finely chopped
1 green bell pepper, seeded
and finely chopped
1 teaspoon dried oregano

Select Sauté on the Instant Pot and pour in the olive oil. When the oil is hot, add the onion and garlic. Cook for 3 to 4 minutes, stirring occasionally, until soft. Select Cancel. Add the white fish, shrimp, clams, marinara sauce, seafood broth, celery, bell pepper, and oregano. Lock the lid. Select Manual and cook at high pressure for 3 minutes. When the cook time is complete, let the pressure release naturally for 5 minutes, then quick-release any remaining pressure. Remove the lid and serve.

Fisherman's Stew (Bouillabaisse)

SERVES 4 | PREP AND FINISHING: 15 minutes | SAUTÉ: 1 minute | MANUAL: 10 minutes high pressure, plus 1 minute low pressure | RELEASE: Natural for 5 minutes, then Quick | TOTAL TIME: 35 minutes

FOR THE STEW

2 tablespoons extra-virgin
olive oil
½ small onion, chopped
(about ½ cup)
½ small fennel bulb,
trimmed and chopped
(about ½ cup)
1 small garlic clove, minced
1 (14-ounce) can diced
tomatoes, undrained
3 cups fish stock, clam
juice, or water
½ cup dry white wine
Zest and juice of 1 orange
(zest removed in
large strips)
1 bay leaf

½ teaspoon kosher
salt (1 teaspoon if
using water)
¼ teaspoon freshly ground
black pepper
3 or 4 saffron threads
(optional)
12 ounces firm white fish
fillets, such as cod, halibut, or snapper
12 ounces peeled
medium-large (36/40)
frozen shrimp
2 tablespoons chopped
fresh parsley
Toasted baguette slices,
for serving

FOR THE ROUILLE

3 tablespoons mayonnaise
1 tablespoon extra-virgin
olive oil

¼ cup finely chopped
roasted red pepper
½ teaspoon minced garlic

TO MAKE THE STEW

Select Sauté and adjust to Normal for medium heat. Heat the olive oil until it shimmers. Add the onion, fennel, and garlic and cook, stirring frequently, until the garlic is fragrant, about 1 minute. Add the tomatoes with their juice, fish stock, wine, orange zest and juice, bay leaf, salt, pepper, and saffron (if using). Stir to combine. Lock the lid into place. Select Manual; adjust the pressure to High and the time to 10 minutes. When the cooking time is done, naturally release the pressure for 5 minutes, then quick release any remaining pressure. Unlock and remove the lid. Add the fish fillets and shrimp to the soup. Lock the lid into place. Select Manual; adjust the pressure to Low and the time to 1 minute. When the cooking time is done, quick-release the pressure. Unlock and remove the lid.

TO MAKE THE ROUILLE

While the soup base is cooking, combine the mayonnaise, oil, red pepper, and garlic in a deep narrow container and blend with an immersion blender. (If you don't have an immersion blender, simply whisk together the ingredients in a small bowl—the sauce won't be as smooth, but it will taste fine.) Remove and discard the bay leaf and strips of orange zest from the stew. Stir in the parsley. Ladle the stew into bowls and top each with a spoonful of rouille. Serve with toasted baguette slices.

Cheesy Tuna Noodle Casserole

SERVES 8 | PREP TIME: 5 minutes | SAUTÉ: 4 minutes | MANUAL: 3 minutes | RELEASE: Quick | TOTAL TIME: 21 minutes

3 tablespoons unsalted butter	2 (6-ounce) cans chunk white tuna in water, drained
1 small onion, diced	
3 cups chicken broth	1 (12-ounce) bag frozen peas
½ teaspoon salt	
½ teaspoon freshly ground black pepper	12 ounces wide egg noodles, uncooked
2 garlic cloves, minced	2 (10½-ounce) cans condensed cream of mushroom soup
1 teaspoon onion powder	
1 cup whole milk	
	2 cups shredded mild Cheddar cheese

Select Sauté, and when the Instant Pot is hot, melt the butter. Stir in the onion and cook until translucent, about 4 minutes. Select Cancel. Add the broth, salt, pepper, garlic, and onion powder and stir. Then add the milk, tuna, peas, and noodles, but do not stir. Spread the mushroom soup evenly over the noodles. Do not stir. Lock the lid. Select Manual and cook at high pressure for 3 minutes. When the cook time is complete, quick-release the pressure. Stir in the cheese and serve.

Peel-and-Eat Shrimp with Two Sauces

SERVES 4 | PREP AND FINISHING: 15 minutes | MANUAL: Steam 1 minute low pressure | RELEASE: Quick | TOTAL TIME: 20 minutes

1 cup water	2 pounds frozen jumbo (16/25) shrimp, shell on

FOR THE COCKTAIL SAUCE

½ cup ketchup	½ teaspoon Worcestershire sauce
1 tablespoon prepared horseradish	
1 tablespoon freshly squeezed lemon juice	Dash hot pepper sauce, such as Tabasco
	⅛ teaspoon celery salt

FOR THE REMOULADE

¼ cup plain yogurt	½ teaspoon Worcestershire sauce
¼ cup mayonnaise	
2 tablespoons ketchup	2 scallions, roughly chopped
2 tablespoons Creole mustard or other grainy mustard	
	2 tablespoons fresh parsley leaves
2 teaspoons prepared horseradish	

Fill a large bowl about halfway with cold water. Add several handfuls of ice cubes. Set it aside. Pour the water into the Instant Pot. Arrange the frozen shrimp in a single layer (as much as possible) in a steamer basket and place it inside. Lock the lid. Select Manual and steam at low pressure for 1 minute. When the cook time is complete, quick-release the pressure. Remove the lid and take the steamer basket out. Transfer the shrimp to the ice bath.

TO MAKE THE COCKTAIL SAUCE

In a small bowl, mix the ketchup, horseradish, lemon juice, Worcestershire sauce, hot sauce, and celery salt. Whisk until smooth and adjust the seasoning, if necessary.

TO MAKE THE REMOULADE

In a small food processor, combine the yogurt, mayonnaise, ketchup, mustard, horseradish, Worcestershire sauce, scallions, and parsley. Process until mostly smooth, scraping down the sides of the bowl as necessary. (If you don't have a food processor, whisk together the yogurt, mayonnaise, ketchup, mustard, horseradish, and Worcestershire sauce. Finely mince the scallions and parsley and stir into the sauce.) Arrange the shrimp on a large platter with the dipping sauces in ramekins. Provide a bowl for the shells—and lots of napkins.

Spicy Shrimp and Grits

SERVES 6 | PREP AND FINISHING: 15 minutes | SAUTÉ: 10 minutes | MANUAL: 10 minutes high pressure | RELEASE: Natural for 10 minutes, then Quick | TOTAL TIME: 55 minutes

2 tablespoons extra-virgin
   olive oil
1 pound medium shrimp,
   peeled and deveined,
   tails left on
2 garlic cloves, minced
½ teaspoon chili powder

1 cup chicken broth
4 cups water
2 cups cornmeal grits
1 tablespoon
   unsalted butter
½ teaspoon fine sea salt

¼ cup chopped fresh
   flat-leaf parsley
1 teaspoon salt
¼ teaspoon freshly ground
   black pepper
¼ teaspoon red
   pepper flakes

Juice of 1 medium lemon
¼ teaspoon saffron
1 pound frozen wild shrimp
   (16–20 count), shells and
   tails on
½ cup frozen peas, thawed

Select Sauté and add the olive oil to the Instant Pot. Once the oil is hot, add the shrimp, garlic, and chili powder and sauté for about 5 minutes, stirring occasionally so the shrimp are cooked through on both sides. Select Cancel. Using a slotted spoon, transfer the shrimp and garlic to a serving plate. Cover to keep warm. Pour the broth into the pot. Using a wooden spoon, scrape up any browned bits stuck to the bottom of the pot. Add the water, grits, butter, and salt to the pot. Lock the lid. Select Manual and cook at high pressure for 10 minutes. When the cook time is complete, naturally release the pressure for 10 minutes, then quick-release any remaining pressure. Remove the lid. Stir the grits. Divide the grits among individual serving plates and top with the shrimp.

Shrimp Boil

SERVES 4 | PREP TIME: 5 minutes | MANUAL: 7 minutes, high pressure, divided | RELEASE: Quick | TOTAL TIME: 20 minutes

1 cup chicken broth
1 pound baby red pota-
   toes, halved
4 links all-natural
   Cajun-style
   sausage, sliced
4 ears fresh corn, shucked
   and halved crosswise

1 tablespoon Cajun
   seasoning
1 pound frozen
   peel-and-eat shrimp
¼ cup fresh
   parsley, chopped
1 lemon, cut into wedges

In the Instant Pot, combine the broth, potatoes, sausage, corn, and Cajun seasoning. Lock the lid. Select and cook at high pressure for 5 minutes. When the cook time is complete, quick-release the pressure. Remove the lid and add the shrimp. Lock the lid. Select Manual and cook at high pressure for 2 minutes. When the cook time is complete, quick-release the pressure. Remove the lid and stir in the parsley. Serve with lemon wedges.

Shrimp Paella

SERVES 4 | PREP TIME: 5 minutes | SAUTÉ: 5 minutes | MANUAL: 5 minutes | RELEASE: Quick | TOTAL TIME: 21 minutes

¼ cup (½ stick)
   unsalted butter
1 medium red bell pepper,
   seeded and diced

4 garlic cloves, minced
1½ cups chicken broth
1 cup jasmine rice, rinsed

Select Sauté, and when the Instant Pot is hot, melt the butter. Stir in the bell pepper and garlic and cook until the peppers start to soften, about 4 minutes. Add just enough broth to deglaze the pot, stirring to scrape up the browned bits from the bottom. Select Cancel. Add the rice, parsley, salt, black pepper, red pepper flakes, lemon juice, saffron, and remaining chicken broth to the pot and place the shrimp on top. Do not stir. Lock the lid. Select Manual and cook at high pressure for 5 minutes. When the cook time is complete, quick-release the pressure. Remove the lid. Gently remove the cooked shrimp from the rice and peel them. Return the shrimp to the rice. Stir in the peas and serve.

Shrimp Scampi

SERVES 6 | PREP TIME: 5 minutes | SAUTÉ: 5 minutes | MANUAL: 5 minutes | RELEASE: Quick | TOTAL TIME: 20 minutes

2 tablespoons extra-virgin
   olive oil
3 tablespoons
   unsalted butter
3 garlic cloves, minced
¼ cup finely chopped
   flat-leaf parsley
½ cup dry white wine
   (such as Pinot Grigio,
   Sauvignon Blanc, or
   Chardonnay)
½ teaspoon red
   pepper flakes

½ teaspoon salt
½ teaspoon freshly ground
   black pepper
1 (15-ounce) can
   chicken broth
Juice of ½ lemon
2 pounds frozen medium
   shrimp (36/40 count),
   peeled and deveined
12 ounces angel hair pasta
Lemon wedges, for serving
   (optional)

Select Sauté and put the oil and butter in the Instant Pot. When it is hot, stir in the garlic and parsley and cook until fragrant, 1 to 2 minutes. Add the wine, red pepper flakes, salt, and black pepper and cook for about 3 minutes. Add the broth and lemon juice, stirring to scrape up any browned bits from the bottom of the pot. Select Cancel. Add the shrimp to the pot. Break the pasta in half and layer it in the pot on top of the shrimp. Make sure the pasta is completely submerged in the liquid. Use tongs to lightly push the pasta down, if necessary, but do not stir. Lock the lid. Select Manual and cook at high pressure for 5 minutes. When the cook time is complete, quick-release the pressure. Remove the lid. Stir well and serve with lemon wedges (if using).

Bang Bang Shrimp Pasta

SERVES 4 | PREP TIME: 5 minutes | SAUTÉ: 1 minute | MANUAL: 5 minutes | RELEASE: Quick | TOTAL TIME: 21 minutes

2 tablespoons extra-virgin olive oil

3 garlic cloves, minced, divided

16 ounces spaghetti, broken in half

3 cups water

1 pound medium shrimp (36/40 count), shells and tails left on

1 teaspoon paprika

¾ tablespoon lime juice

½ cup mayonnaise

⅓ cup Thai sweet chile sauce

2 teaspoons sriracha

¼ teaspoon red pepper flakes

Select Sauté, and when the Instant Pot is hot, pour in the oil. Stir in the garlic and sauté until fragrant, about 1 minute. Layer the noodles in a crisscross pattern and then add the water. Gently push all the noodles down so that they are covered by water. Select Cancel. Put the shrimp in the middle of a piece of foil. Sprinkle the shrimp with the paprika and lime juice. Fold the foil into a parcel and place it on top of the noodles. Lock the lid. Select Manual and cook at high pressure for 5 minutes. When the cook time is complete, quick-release the pressure. While the pasta is cooking, in a small bowl, mix the mayonnaise, chile sauce, sriracha, and red pepper flakes and set it aside. Remove the lid. Unfold the shrimp parcel and dump the juices into the pasta. Peel the shrimp and add them to the pasta. Stir well, breaking up any noodle clumps. Stir in the sauce until everything is well combined.

Coconut Fish Curry

SERVES 6 | PREP AND FINISHING: 10 minutes | SAUTÉ: 5 minutes | MANUAL: 4 minutes high pressure | RELEASE: Natural for 10 minutes, then Quick | TOTAL TIME: 39 minutes

2 tablespoons extra-virgin olive oil

1 white onion, sliced

1½ pounds mahi mahi fillets (about 4 fillets), cut into 2-inch cubes

1 tablespoon green curry paste

1 (13.5-ounce) can full-fat coconut milk

2 tablespoons reduced-sodium soy sauce

1 tablespoon packed light brown sugar

½ teaspoon ground ginger

2 red bell peppers, seeded and sliced

Juice of 1 lime

Select Sauté and pour in the olive oil to the Instant Pot. Once the oil is hot, add the onion, fish, and green curry paste. Sauté for about 4 minutes, stirring occasionally, until the fish is browned on all sides. Select Cancel. Add the coconut milk, soy sauce, brown sugar, and ginger. Using a wooden spoon, scrape up any browned bits stuck to the bottom of the pot. Add the

bell peppers and stir to combine. Lock the lid. Select Manual and cook at high pressure for 4 minutes. When the cook time is complete, naturally release the pressure for 10 minutes, then quick-release any remaining pressure. Remove the lid. Stir in the lime juice. Serve immediately.

Maple-Mustard Salmon with Asparagus

SERVES 4 | PREP TIME: 10 minutes | MANUAL: 3 minutes high pressure, divided | RELEASE: Quick | TOTAL TIME: 20 minutes

1 tablespoon pure maple syrup

1 tablespoon Dijon mustard

⅛ teaspoon kosher salt

4 (6-ounce) salmon fillets

1 cup water

1 pound asparagus, trimmed

1 cup cherry tomatoes, halved

In a small bowl, combine the maple syrup, mustard, and salt. Spread the sauce onto the salmon fillets. Pour the water into the Instant Pot and insert the trivet. Place the salmon fillets on the trivet. Lock the lid. Select Manual and cook at high pressure for 2 minutes. When the cook time is complete, quick-release the pressure. Remove the lid and add the asparagus. Lock the lid. Select Manual and cook at high pressure for 1 minute. When the cook time is complete, quick-release the pressure. Remove the lid. Remove the asparagus from the pot and mix it with the tomatoes. Serve alongside the salmon.

Poached Salmon with Mustard Cream Sauce

SERVES 4 | PREP AND FINISHING: 15 minutes | MANUAL: 5 minutes low pressure | RELEASE: Quick | TOTAL TIME: 25 minutes

1 (20- to 24-ounce) center-cut salmon fillet

1 teaspoon kosher salt, divided

½ teaspoon freshly ground black pepper, divided

2 cups water or fish broth

½ cup dry white wine

Zest and juice of 1 small lemon

1 bay leaf

⅓ cup heavy (whipping) cream

1 tablespoon Dijon mustard

3 tablespoons minced fresh dill, divided

Season the salmon with ½ teaspoon of salt and ¼ teaspoon of black pepper. In the Instant Pot, combine the water, wine, lemon zest, lemon juice, and bay leaf. Place a steamer trivet or basket in the pot and place the salmon on top of it. The fish should be partially submerged in the liquid. Lock the lid. Select Manual and cook at low pressure for 5 minutes. When the cook time is complete, quick-release the pressure. Remove the lid. While the fish is cooking, pour the cream into a small bowl and beat with a hand mixer or vigorously whisk by hand just until the cream has thickened. Stir in the mustard, the remaining ½ teaspoon of salt and ¼ teaspoon of pepper, and 2 tablespoons of dill. Carefully remove the steamer trivet from the pot. With a large, slotted spatula, transfer the fish to a platter. Spoon the sauce over the fish, garnish it with the remaining 1 tablespoon of dill, and serve.

Salmon with Lemon Butter and Dill

SERVES 4 | PREP TIME: 5 minutes | SAUTÉ: 5 minutes | MANUAL: 3 minutes | RELEASE: Quick | TOTAL TIME: 18 minutes

¾ cup dry white wine	Salt
3 tablespoons minced shallot	Freshly ground black pepper
2 tablespoons lemon juice	1 cup water
½ cup (1 stick) unsalted butter, cut into pieces	4 (6-ounce) skin-on salmon fillets (¾ to 1 inch thick)
1½ tablespoons chopped fresh dill	1 medium lemon, sliced

Select Sauté, and when the Instant Pot is hot, pour in the white wine and add the shallots and lemon juice. Cook until the shallots are soft, about 3 minutes. Select Cancel. Add the butter, whisking constantly. When the butter is melted, add the dill and salt and pepper to taste. Transfer the sauce to a bowl and set it aside. Set the trivet in the Instant Pot and pour in the water. Place the salmon on the trivet, skin-side down. Sprinkle with salt and pepper and top with the lemon slices. Lock the lid. Select Manual and cook at high pressure for 3 minutes. When the cook time is complete, quick-release the pressure. Remove the lid. Spoon the buttery sauce over the salmon and serve.

Lemon and Dill Tilapia

SERVES 4 | PREP TIME: 10 minutes | MANUAL: 17 minutes high pressure | RELEASE: Quick | TOTAL TIME: 35 minutes

2 medium zucchini, sliced	1 teaspoon butter
4 (4-ounce) frozen tilapia fillets	2 tablespoons freshly chopped dill
1 lemon, cut into 8 slices	1 cup water

Place a sheet of parchment paper on your counter. Position one-quarter of the zucchini slices in the center of the parchment and top them with 1 tilapia fillet, 2 lemon slices, ¼ teaspoon of butter, and ½ tablespoon of dill. Fold the parchment over the fish and crimp the edges to create a sealed packet. Repeat three times for a total of four packets. Pour the water into the Instant Pot and insert the trivet. Stack the packets on top of the trivet. Lock the lid. Select Manual and cook at high pressure for 17 minutes. When the cook time is complete, quick-release the pressure. Remove the lid and remove the packets from the pot. Unfold the parchment and serve.

Tilapia with Parsley-Caper Sauce

SERVES 4 | PREP AND FINISHING: 15 minutes | MANUAL: 2 minutes low pressure | SAUTÉ: 3 minutes | RELEASE: Quick | TOTAL TIME: 25 minutes

4 (4- to 5-ounce) frozen tilapia fillets	½ cup vegetable broth
½ teaspoon kosher salt	1 tablespoon dry white wine
Nonstick cooking spray	2 tablespoons drained capers
2 tablespoons extra-virgin olive oil	¼ cup chopped fresh parsley
1 large garlic clove, minced	
1 scallion, white and green parts, thinly sliced	

Season both sides of the fillets with the salt. Spray a silicone steamer trivet with cooking spray and arrange the frozen fillets in a single layer (as much as possible) on it. Add the olive oil, garlic, scallion, broth, and wine to the Instant Pot. Place the trivet with the fish in the pot. Lock the lid. Select Manual and cook at low pressure for 2 minutes. When the cook time is complete, quick-release the pressure. Remove the lid. Carefully remove the trivet and loosely tent the fish with foil to keep it warm. Select Sauté and adjust to Normal for medium heat. Simmer the sauce until most of the liquid has evaporated, about 3 minutes. Stir in the capers and parsley. Arrange the fillets on a serving platter and spoon the sauce over them. Serve.

Tilapia with Tomato-Olive Sauce

SERVES 4 | PREP AND FINISHING: 15 minutes | MANUAL: 2 minutes low pressure | SAUTÉ: 3 minutes | RELEASE: Quick | TOTAL TIME: 28 minutes

4 (4- to 5-ounce) frozen tilapia fillets	1 tablespoon dry white wine
½ teaspoon kosher salt	1 (14-ounce) can diced tomatoes
Nonstick cooking spray	¼ cup sliced green olives
2 tablespoons extra-virgin olive oil	1 tablespoon chopped fresh parsley
1 large garlic clove, minced	
1 large shallot, sliced, or ¼ cup sliced onion	

Season both sides of the fillets with the salt. Spray a silicone steamer trivet with cooking spray and arrange the frozen fillets in a single layer (as much as possible) on it. Add the olive oil, garlic, shallot, wine, and tomatoes with their juices to the pot. Place the trivet with the fish in the pot. Lock the lid. Select Manual and cook at low pressure for 2 minutes. When the cook time is complete, quick-release the pressure. Remove the lid. Carefully remove the trivet and loosely tent the fish with foil to keep it warm. Select Sauté and adjust to Normal for medium heat. Simmer the sauce until about half of the liquid has evaporated. Stir in the olives and parsley. Arrange the fillets on a serving platter and spoon the sauce over them. Serve.

Tilapia with Mustard-Chive Sauce

SERVES 4 | PREP AND FINISHING: 15 minutes | MANUAL: 2 minutes low pressure | SAUTÉ: 3 minutes | RELEASE: Quick | TOTAL TIME: 28 minutes

4 (4- to 5-ounce) frozen tilapia fillets
½ teaspoon kosher salt
Nonstick cooking spray
2 tablespoons unsalted butter
1 large garlic clove, minced
1 large shallot, sliced, or ¼ cup sliced onion
¼ cup heavy (whipping) cream
¼ cup vegetable broth
1 tablespoon dry white wine
2 tablespoons Dijon mustard
2 tablespoons minced fresh chives

Season both sides of the fillets with the salt. Spray a silicone steamer trivet with cooking spray and arrange the frozen fillets in a single layer (as much as possible) on it. Combine the butter, garlic, shallot, cream, broth, and wine in the pot. Place the trivet with the fish in the pot. Lock the lid. Select Manual and cook at low pressure for 2 minutes. When the cook time is complete, quick-release the pressure. Remove the lid. Carefully remove the trivet and loosely tent the fish with foil to keep it warm. Select Sauté and adjust to Normal for medium heat. Stir in the mustard and chives. Arrange the fillets on a serving platter and spoon the sauce over them. Serve.

Steamed Cod with Ginger-Garlic Broth and Snow Peas

SERVES 4 | PREP AND FINISHING: 10 minutes | MANUAL: 2 minutes low pressure | RELEASE: Quick | TOTAL TIME: 20 minutes

4 (6- to 8-ounce) cod fillets
¼ teaspoon kosher salt
¼ teaspoon freshly ground black pepper
1 cup fish broth or vegetable broth
2 tablespoons unseasoned rice vinegar
2 tablespoons soy sauce
2 tablespoons dry sherry or rice wine
1 tablespoon peeled and minced fresh ginger
2 or 3 large garlic cloves, minced (about 1 tablespoon)
8 ounces snow peas, trimmed
2 scallions, white and green parts, thinly sliced
1 tablespoon toasted sesame oil

Season the cod on both sides with the salt and pepper. In the Instant Pot, combine the broth, vinegar, soy sauce, sherry, ginger, and garlic. Place a steamer trivet or basket in the pot and place the cod on it. Scatter the snow peas over the fillets. Lock the lid. Select Manual and cook at low pressure for 2 minutes. When the cook time is complete, quick-release the pressure. Remove the lid. Carefully remove the steamer trivet from the pot. With a large, slotted spatula, divide the fish and snow peas among four shallow bowls. Spoon the broth over the fish. Top with the scallions, drizzle with the sesame oil, and serve.

POULTRY

Chicken with Mushrooms

SERVES 4 | PREP TIME: 10 minutes | SAUTÉ: 15 minutes | MANUAL: 15 minutes high pressure | RELEASE: Quick | TOTAL TIME: 50 minutes

4 bone-in, skinless chicken breasts (2 to 2½ pounds)
1 teaspoon salt
¼ teaspoon freshly ground black pepper
2 tablespoons extra-virgin olive oil, divided
1 pound cremini mushrooms, thinly sliced
1 onion, diced
1 cup chicken broth
1 tablespoon Italian seasoning

Season the chicken breasts with the salt and pepper. Select Sauté. Heat 1 tablespoon of oil in the Instant Pot until it shimmers. Add the chicken and cook on one side for about 5 minutes, or until browned. Transfer the chicken to a plate and set it aside. Put the remaining 1 tablespoon of oil in the pot, along with the mushrooms and onion. Sauté for 8 to 10 minutes, or until softened. Add the broth and Italian seasoning. Deglaze, mixing well and scraping up any browned bits on the bottom of the pot. Return the chicken to the pot. Select Cancel. Lock the lid. Select Manual and cook at high pressure for 15 minutes. When the cook time is complete, quick-release the pressure. Remove the lid. Transfer the chicken to a serving dish. If desired, select Sauté mode again and simmer the sauce until your desired consistency is reached.

Chicken and Biscuits

SERVES 4 | PREP AND FINISH TIME: 30 minutes | MANUAL: 5 minutes high pressure | RELEASE: Quick | TOTAL TIME: 40 minutes

¼ cup all-purpose flour
½ teaspoon kosher salt
⅛ teaspoon freshly ground black pepper
⅛ teaspoon cayenne pepper
1¼ pounds boneless, skinless chicken thighs
¼ cup unsalted butter
3 cups chicken broth
3 large carrots, peeled and cut into 1-inch pieces
2 large celery stalks, cut into ½-inch slices
1 cup frozen pearl onions
1 bay leaf
⅔ cup frozen peas, thawed
1½ cups self-rising flour
¾ cup heavy (whipping) cream

In a shallow dish, mix the flour, salt, black pepper, and cayenne pepper. Dredge the chicken thighs in the flour, lightly coating both sides. Gently shake off any excess flour and set the flour aside. Select Sauté and adjust to More for high heat. Put the butter in the Instant Pot to melt. When it has stopped foaming, add the chicken in a single layer (you may need to do two batches). Cook, undisturbed, until golden brown, 4 to 5 minutes. Flip the chicken and cook until browned on the other side, 3 to

4 minutes. Transfer the chicken to a plate and let cool for a few minutes, then cut into bite-size pieces. With the pot still on Sauté, add the remaining flour mixture to the butter in the pot. Cook, stirring constantly, until the roux (a smooth, paste-like mixture) is golden brown. Add about 1 cup of broth, whisking until it is combined with the roux. Add the remaining 2 cups of broth and stir, scraping up any browned bits from the bottom of the pot, until the sauce has thickened slightly to the consistency of a light gravy. Add more chicken broth if the sauce is too thick. Add the chicken, carrots, celery, pearl onions, and bay leaf to the Instant Pot. Lock the lid. Select Manual and cook on high pressure for 5 minutes. When the cook time is complete, quick-release the pressure. Remove the lid, add the peas, and stir to warm them through. While the chicken cooks, preheat the oven to 400°F. In a medium bowl, make the biscuit dough by whisking the flour and cream until the mixture holds together. Spoon the chicken mixture into a shallow baking dish. Scoop the biscuit dough into balls about 1½ inches in diameter and place them evenly over the chicken mixture. Bake until the biscuits are golden brown, 12 to 14 minutes. Remove the bay leaf and serve.

Tuscan-Style Chicken Stew

SERVES 4 to 6 | PREP TIME: 10 minutes | SAUTÉ: 6 minutes | MANUAL: 10 minutes high pressure | RELEASE: Natural for 15 minutes | TOTAL TIME: 50 minutes

2 tablespoons extra-virgin olive oil	1 cup chicken broth
1 onion, chopped	6 bone-in, skinless chicken thighs and/or drumsticks
2 celery stalks, chopped	1 teaspoon dried oregano
2 carrots, chopped	Large pinch red pepper flakes
4 garlic cloves, minced	
1 pound small red or white potatoes, halved	Salt
1 (14½-ounce) can chopped or crushed tomatoes	Freshly ground black pepper
1 (15-ounce) can red kidney beans, rinsed and drained	2 tablespoons chopped fresh parsley leaves
	1 tablespoon balsamic vinegar

Select Sauté. Heat the oil in the Instant Pot until it shimmers. Add the onion, celery, and carrots and stir. Cook for 5 minutes, until the onion is translucent. Add the garlic and cook for 1 minute more. Add the potatoes, tomatoes with their juices, kidney beans, broth, chicken, oregano, and red pepper flakes. Season with salt and black pepper and mix gently. Select Cancel. Lock the lid. Select Manual and cook at high pressure for 10 minutes. When the cook time is complete, natural release the pressure for 15 minutes. Remove the lid and remove the chicken. Pull the meat off the bones and return it to the pot. Stir in the parsley and vinegar. Taste for seasoning and serve.

Jamaican-Style Jerk Chicken

SERVES 4 to 6 | PREP TIME: 10 minutes | MANUAL: 10 minutes high pressure | RELEASE: Natural for 5 minutes, then Quick | TOTAL TIME: 35 minutes

1 (12-ounce) bottle gluten-free Jamaican jerk sauce	2 garlic cloves, smashed
	Zest of 1 lime
2 cups low-sodium chicken broth	4 cups cooked white rice, for serving
2 pounds bone-in, skinless chicken thighs	Juice of 1 lime
4 shallots, peeled and sliced lengthwise	½ bunch cilantro, roughly chopped
	2 scallions, white and green parts, thinly sliced

In the Instant Pot, combine the jerk sauce, broth, chicken, shallots, garlic, and lime zest. Lock the lid. Select Manual and cook at high pressure for 10 minutes. When the cook time is complete, allow the pressure to naturally release for 5 minutes, then quick-release any remaining pressure. Serve the jerk chicken over white rice, and top with the lime juice, cilantro, and scallions.

Cuban-Style Chicken

SERVES 4 to 6 | PREP TIME: 10 minutes | SAUTÉ: 6 minutes | MANUAL: 10 minutes high pressure | RELEASE: Natural for 5 minutes, then Quick | TOTAL TIME: 40 minutes

2 tablespoons extra-virgin olive oil	Juice and zest of 1 orange
2 pounds boneless, skinless chicken thighs, cut into 2-inch pieces	½ cup pepper-stuffed olives
	¼ cup raisins
2 green bell peppers, seeded and sliced	1 pound Yukon Gold potatoes, cut into 2-inch pieces
1 onion, halved and sliced	2 cups low-sodium chicken broth
8 garlic cloves, smashed	
½ cup minced fresh parsley	Salt
2 teaspoons dried oregano	Freshly ground black pepper
Juice and zest of 1 lime	1 cup frozen peas

Select Sauté. Heat the oil in the Instant Pot until it shimmers. Sear the chicken for 2 minutes on each side, until it begins to brown. Add the bell peppers, onion, garlic, parsley, and oregano and sauté for 2 minutes, just until fragrant and the vegetables begin to soften. Add the lime juice and zest, orange juice and zest, olives, raisins, potatoes, and chicken broth to the pot. Season generously with salt and pepper. Select Cancel. Lock the lid. Select Manual and cook at high pressure for 10 minutes. When the cook time is complete, naturally release the pressure for 5 minutes, then quick-release any remaining pressure. Remove the lid. Stir in the peas, adjust the seasoning, and serve warm.

Arroz con Pollo

SERVES 6 | PREP TIME: 15 minutes | SAUTÉ: 10 minutes | MANUAL: 12 minutes high pressure | RELEASE: Natural | TOTAL TIME: 1 hour 5 minutes

1 tablespoon California chili powder

1 teaspoon ground cumin

1 teaspoon crushed dried Mexican oregano

1 teaspoon coarse salt, plus more for seasoning

½ teaspoon freshly ground black pepper

½ teaspoon onion powder

½ teaspoon garlic powder

6 boneless chicken thighs

3 tablespoons vegetable oil, divided

1 cup long-grain or jasmine rice

½ medium white onion, finely chopped

2 garlic cloves, minced

4 Roma tomatoes, finely chopped

1 cup chicken broth

1 (8-ounce) can tomato sauce

4 cilantro sprigs

Pico de gallo, for garnish (optional)

Pimiento-stuffed olives, sliced, for garnish (optional)

In a small bowl, combine the chili powder, cumin, oregano, salt, pepper, onion powder, and garlic powder. Sprinkle the spice mixture over the chicken thighs. Select Sauté and adjust to More for high heat. Heat 2 tablespoons of vegetable oil in the pot, add the chicken thighs, and fry for 5 to 7 minutes, or until golden brown. Transfer the chicken to a heatproof plate. In the Instant Pot, heat the remaining 1 tablespoon of vegetable oil. Sauté the rice until light golden brown. Add the onion and garlic and sauté for 2 to 3 minutes, or just until the onion is translucent. Stir in the tomatoes. Pour in the chicken broth and tomato sauce and season lightly with salt. Return the chicken to the Instant Pot. Top with the cilantro. Select Cancel. Lock the lid. Select Manual and cook at high pressure for 12 minutes. When the cook time is complete, allow the pressure to release naturally. Remove the lid. Discard the cilantro. Serve immediately, garnished with pico de gallo (if using) and pimiento-stuffed olive slices (if using).

Chicken Barbacoa

SERVES 6 to 8 | PREP TIME: 5 minutes | MANUAL: 15 minutes high pressure | RELEASE: Natural | TOTAL TIME: 45 minutes

2½ pounds boneless, skinless chicken breast

3 garlic cloves, minced

1 cup red enchilada sauce

1 cup chicken broth

2 tablespoons white vinegar

1 teaspoon coarse salt

1 teaspoon crushed dried Mexican oregano

1 teaspoon ground cumin

½ teaspoon ground cinnamon

¼ teaspoon ground cloves

Pickled red onions, for garnish

Chopped fresh cilantro, for garnish

In the Instant Pot, combine the chicken breast and garlic. Pour in the enchilada sauce, broth, and vinegar. Season with the salt, oregano, cumin, cinnamon, and cloves. Lock the lid. Select Manual and cook at high pressure for 15 minutes. When the cook time is complete, allow the pressure to release naturally. Remove the lid. Use two forks to shred the chicken breast in the pot. Serve immediately, garnished with pickled red onions and cilantro.

Chicken Carnitas

SERVES 6 to 8 | PREP TIME: 5 minutes | SAUTÉ: 8 minutes | MANUAL: 15 minutes high pressure | RELEASE: Natural | TOTAL TIME: 50 minutes

2 tablespoons manteca (pork lard) or vegetable oil

3 pounds boneless, skinless chicken breasts, cut into 2-inch pieces

1 cup freshly squeezed orange juice

¼ cup freshly squeezed lime juice

1½ teaspoons coarse salt

1 teaspoon crushed dried Mexican oregano

½ teaspoon freshly ground black pepper

1 medium white onion, thinly sliced

3 garlic cloves, minced

6 cilantro sprigs

Warm corn or flour tortillas, for serving (optional)

Lime wedges, for garnish

Select Sauté and adjust to More for high. Heat the *manteca* in the pot, add the chicken, and fry, stirring occasionally, for 6 to 8 minutes, or until golden brown. Pour in the orange juice and lime juice. Season with the salt, oregano, and pepper. Top with the onion, garlic, and cilantro. Select Cancel. Lock the lid. Select Manual and cook at high pressure for 15 minutes. When the cook time is complete, allow the pressure to release naturally. Remove the lid. Using two forks, shred the chicken in the pot. Serve with warm tortillas (if using) and garnish with lime wedges.

Chipotle-Glazed Wings

SERVES 6 to 8 | PREP TIME: 10 minutes | SAUTÉ: 15 minutes | MANUAL: 10 minutes high pressure | BAKE: 8 minutes | RELEASE: Quick | TOTAL TIME: 35 minutes

3 pounds chicken wings

2 tablespoons vegetable oil

1 tablespoon chipotle chili powder

¾ teaspoon coarse salt

¼ teaspoon freshly ground black pepper

Nonstick cooking spray

⅔ cup guava jam

4 to 6 tablespoons pureed canned chipotle

Cut the chicken wings into three pieces, separating them at the joint; discard the wing tips. Select Sauté and adjust to More for high. Heat the vegetable oil in the pot. Working in batches, add the chicken wings and sauté, flipping once, for 6 to 8 minutes, or until light golden brown. As each batch of wings finishes cooking, transfer to a heatproof plate. Season the wings with the chipotle powder, salt, and pepper. Select Cancel. Pour 1 cup of water into the Instant Pot. Place the trivet inside. Arrange the chicken wings on the trivet. Lock the lid. Select Manual and cook at high pressure for 10 minutes. While the wings are cooking, preheat the oven to 425°F. Lightly grease a baking sheet with cooking spray. In a small bowl, mix the guava jam and chipotle puree. When the cook time is complete, quick-release the pressure. Remove the lid. Arrange the chicken wings in a single layer on the prepared baking sheet. Brush them with the guava-chipotle glaze. Bake the wings for 6 to 8 minutes, or until golden and crisp.

Teriyaki Chicken and Rice

SERVES 6 | PREP AND FINISHING: 10 minutes | SAUTÉ: 5 minutes | MANUAL: 8 minutes high pressure | RELEASE: Natural for 10 minutes, then Quick | TOTAL TIME: 43 minutes

2 tablespoons extra-virgin olive oil

1½ pounds boneless, skinless chicken breasts (4 or 5 breasts)

2 garlic cloves, minced

¼ cup reduced-sodium soy sauce

1¾ cups low-sodium chicken broth

1½ cups white rice, rinsed

2 carrots, sliced (about 1 cup)

2 tablespoons pure maple syrup

½ teaspoon ground ginger

1 tablespoon white wine vinegar

Select Sauté and pour in the olive oil to the Instant Pot. Once the oil is hot, add the chicken and garlic and sauté for 4 minutes, turning the chicken once so it browns on both sides. Use a spoon to transfer the chicken and garlic to a plate. Select Cancel and add the soy sauce. Using a wooden spoon, scrape up any browned bits stuck to the bottom of the pot. Add the broth, rice, carrots, maple syrup, and ginger to the pot. Stir to combine. Place the chicken on top, but don't stir. Select Cancel. Lock the lid. Select Manual and cook at high pressure for 8 minutes. When the cook time is complete, naturally release the pressure for 10 minutes, then quick-release any remaining pressure. Remove the lid. Stir in the vinegar. Serve immediately.

Kung Pao Chicken

SERVES 6 | PREP AND FINISHING: 10 minutes | SAUTÉ: 10 minutes, divided | MANUAL: 8 minutes high pressure | RELEASE: Natural for 10 minutes, then Quick | TOTAL TIME: 48 minutes

½ cup water

2 tablespoons cornstarch

1 tablespoon extra-virgin olive oil

2 pounds boneless, skinless chicken breasts (5 or 6 breasts), cut into bite-size pieces

2 garlic cloves, minced

1 onion, diced

1 cup chicken broth

2 red bell peppers, seeded and sliced

¼ cup reduced-sodium soy sauce or tamari

2 tablespoons packed light brown sugar

¼ teaspoon ground ginger

¼ teaspoon red pepper flakes

2 tablespoons rice vinegar

¼ cup chopped roasted peanuts

In a small bowl, make a slurry by whisking together the water and cornstarch. Set it aside. Select Sauté and add the olive oil to the Instant Pot. Once hot, add the chicken, garlic, and onion and sauté for 2 minutes, stirring occasionally. Turn the chicken over and let the chicken and vegetables cook for 2 minutes more. Select Cancel. Pour the broth into the pot and use a wooden spoon to scrape up any browned bits stuck to the bottom of the pot. Add the bell peppers, soy sauce, brown sugar, ginger, and red pepper flakes and stir to combine. Select Cancel. Lock the lid. Select Manual and cook at high pressure for 8 minutes. When the cook time is complete, let naturally release the pressure for 10 minutes, then quick-release any remaining pressure. Remove the lid. Using a slotted spoon, transfer the chicken to a plate. Select Sauté. Once the liquid starts bubbling, whisk in the cornstarch slurry and vinegar. Whisk consistently for 2 minutes or until the sauce starts to thicken. Serve immediately, garnished with chopped peanuts.

Honey Sesame Chicken

SERVES 6 | PREP AND FINISHING: 10 minutes | SAUTÉ: 10 minutes, divided | MANUAL: 8 minutes high pressure | RELEASE: Natural for 10 minutes, then Quick | TOTAL TIME: 48 minutes

½ cup water

2 tablespoons cornstarch

1 tablespoon extra-virgin olive oil

2 pounds boneless, skinless chicken breasts (5 or 6 breasts), cut into bite-size pieces

2 garlic cloves, minced

1 medium yellow onion, diced

1 cup low-sodium chicken broth

¼ cup reduced-sodium soy sauce

¼ cup honey

2 teaspoons toasted sesame oil

In a small bowl, make a slurry by whisking together the water and cornstarch. Set it aside. Select Sauté and pour in the olive oil to the Instant Pot. Once the oil is hot, add the chicken, garlic, and onion and sauté for 2 minutes, stirring occasionally. Turn the chicken over and let it cook for 2 minutes more. Select Cancel. Pour the broth into the pot and use a wooden spoon to scrape up any browned bits stuck to the bottom of the pot. Add the soy sauce and honey and stir to combine. Lock the lid. Select Manual and cook at high pressure for 8 minutes. When the cook time is complete, naturally release the pressure for 10 minutes, then quick-release any remaining pressure. Remove the lid. Using a slotted spoon, transfer the chicken to a plate. Select Sauté. Once the liquid starts bubbling, whisk in the cornstarch slurry and sesame oil. Whisk consistently for 2 minutes or until the sauce starts to thicken. Serve immediately.

Indian-Style Butter Chicken

SERVES 6 | PREP AND FINISHING: 10 minutes | SAUTÉ: 5 minutes | MANUAL: 10 minutes high pressure | RELEASE: Natural for 10 minutes, then Quick | TOTAL TIME: 45 minutes

1 tablespoon extra-virgin olive oil
2 garlic cloves, minced
1 medium yellow onion, diced
1 tablespoon garam masala
¼ teaspoon ground ginger
1 cup chicken broth
1 (6-ounce) can tomato paste

1 medium head cauliflower, cut into florets (about 3 cups)
2 pounds boneless, skinless chicken breasts (5 or 6 breasts)
2 tablespoons unsalted butter, cut into small pieces
½ cup full-fat canned coconut milk
½ teaspoon fine sea salt

Select Sauté on the Instant Pot and pour in the olive oil. Once the oil is hot, add the garlic, onion, garam masala, and ginger and sauté for 3 minutes, stirring occasionally. Select Cancel and pour the broth into the pot. Using a wooden spoon, scrape up any browned bits stuck to the bottom of the pot. Add the tomato paste, cauliflower, and chicken to the pot, but do not stir. Top the chicken with the butter pieces. Lock the lid. Select Manual and cook at high pressure for 10 minutes. When the cook time is complete, naturally release the pressure for 10 minutes, then quick-release any remaining pressure. Remove the lid. Using a slotted spoon, transfer the chicken to a cutting board. Use two forks to shred the chicken, then return it to the pot. Stir in the coconut milk and salt. Serve immediately.

Greek-Inspired Chicken and Quinoa

SERVES 4 | PREP TIME: 5 minutes | SAUTÉ: 4 minutes | MANUAL: 10 minutes high pressure | RELEASE: Natural | TOTAL TIME: 35 minutes

2 tablespoons extra-virgin olive oil
1 red onion, finely chopped
1 red bell pepper, seeded and finely chopped
1 cup chicken broth
1½ pounds boneless, skinless chicken breast, cubed
¾ cup quinoa, rinsed well
1 teaspoon dried oregano
½ teaspoon kosher salt

½ teaspoon freshly ground black pepper
1 cup grape or cherry tomatoes, halved
½ cup pitted kalamata olives
¼ cup crumbled feta cheese
2 tablespoons freshly squeezed lemon juice

Select Sauté on the Instant Pot and pour in the olive oil. When the oil is hot, add the onion and bell pepper. Cook for 3 to 4 minutes, stirring occasionally, until softened. Select Cancel. Add the broth, chicken, quinoa, oregano, salt, and pepper. Lock the lid. Select Manual and cook at high pressure for 10 minutes. When the cook time is complete, let the pressure release naturally for 10 minutes, then quick-release any remaining pressure. Remove the lid and stir in the tomatoes, olives, feta, and lemon juice before serving.

Chicken Cacciatore

SERVES 4 | PREP AND FINISHING: 20 minutes | SAUTÉ: 13 minutes, divided | MANUAL: 10 minutes high pressure | RELEASE: Natural for 10 minutes, then Quick | TOTAL TIME: 45 minutes

4 to 6 bone-in, skin-on chicken thighs and/or drumsticks
½ teaspoon kosher salt, plus more as needed
2 tablespoons extra-virgin olive oil
1 small onion, sliced
2 garlic cloves, minced
8 ounces cremini or white button mushrooms, cleaned and sliced

⅓ cup dry red wine
½ cup chicken broth
1 (14-ounce) can diced tomatoes
1 teaspoon dried oregano
2 tablespoons chopped fresh parsley
2 tablespoons drained capers

Sprinkle the chicken pieces on both sides with the salt. Select Sauté and adjust to More for high heat. Heat the oil until it shimmers. Add the chicken, skin-side down, and cook, undisturbed, until the skin is dark golden brown and most of the fat under the skin has rendered out, about 5 minutes. Do not crowd, work in batches if necessary. Flip the chicken and cook until light golden brown on the other side, about 3 minutes. Transfer the chicken to a plate. Carefully pour off almost all the fat, leaving just enough to cover the bottom of the pot with a thick coat (about 1 tablespoon). Add the onion and garlic and cook, stirring frequently, until the onion begins to brown, about 3 minutes. Add the mushrooms and cook until they begin to soften, 1 to 2 minutes. Add the wine and scrape the bottom of the pot to release the browned bits. Boil until the liquid reduces by about half. Add the broth, tomatoes with their juices, and oregano. Add the chicken pieces, skin-side up, to the pot. Select Cancel. Lock the lid. Select Manual and cook at high pressure for 10 minutes. When the cook time is complete, naturally release the pressure for 10 minutes, then quick-release any remaining pressure. Transfer the chicken to a plate. Strain the sauce into a fat separator and let it rest until the fat rises to the surface. (If you don't have a fat separator, let the sauce sit for a few minutes, then spoon or blot off any excess fat from the top of the sauce.) Pour the defatted sauce back into the pot and select Keep Warm. If you prefer a thicker sauce, select Sauté and adjust to Less. Let the sauce simmer for several minutes until it's reduced to the consistency you like. Adjust the seasoning, adding more salt if necessary, and stir in the parsley and capers. Serve the chicken topped with the sauce.

Mexican-Style Chicken Cacciatore

SERVES 6 | PREP TIME: 10 minutes | SAUTÉ: 16 minutes | MANUAL: 15 minutes high pressure | RELEASE: Natural | TOTAL TIME: 1 hour 5 minutes

¼ cup butter
6 chicken leg quarters
Coarse salt
Freshly ground
  black pepper
1 medium white onion,
  thinly sliced
2 Hungarian wax peppers
2 garlic cloves, minced

4 medium
  calabacitas or zucchini,
  cut into 1-inch slices
4 cilantro sprigs
1½ cups tomato sauce
1 cup chicken broth
Cooked rice, for serving
Finely chopped fresh
  cilantro, for garnish

Select Sauté and adjust to More for high. Heat the butter in the pot until completely melted. Add the chicken leg quarters, two or three at a time, and fry, flipping once, for 8 minutes, or until golden brown on both sides. Season generously with salt and pepper. As each batch of chicken pieces finishes cooking, transfer them to a heatproof plate. Return all the chicken pieces to the Instant Pot. Top with the onion, wax peppers, garlic, calabacitas, and cilantro sprigs. Select Cancel. Pour in the tomato sauce and chicken broth. Lock the lid. Select Manual and cook at high pressure for 15 minutes. When the cook time is complete, allow the pressure to release naturally. Remove the lid. Discard the cilantro sprigs. Serve immediately with rice and garnished with chopped cilantro.

Poblano Chicken

SERVES 6 | PREP TIME: 10 minutes | SAUTÉ: 13 minutes | MANUAL: 12 minutes high pressure | RELEASE: Quick | TOTAL TIME: 35 minutes

1 tablespoon extra-virgin
  olive oil
1 tablespoon butter
4 boneless, skinless
  chicken breasts, cut into
  thin strips
Coarse salt
Freshly ground
  black pepper
4 roasted poblano pep-
  pers, peeled, seeded, and
  cut into thin strips

1 medium onion,
  thinly sliced
3 garlic cloves, minced
8 ounces button mush-
  rooms, sliced
1 (15½-ounce) can golden
  corn kernels, drained
1 cup Mexican crema or
  sour cream
⅓ cup whole milk
Crumbled queso añejo or
  cotija, for garnish

Select Sauté and adjust to More for high. Heat the olive oil and butter in the pot until the butter has melted completely. Add the chicken and sauté for 6 to 8 minutes, or until it is no longer pink. Season generously with salt and pepper. Stir in the poblano peppers, onion, garlic, and mushrooms. Sauté for 3 to 5 minutes, or until the onion is translucent. Select Cancel. Stir in the corn, Mexican crema, and milk. Lock the lid. Select Manual and cook at high pressure for 12 minutes. When the cook time is complete, quick-release the pressure. Remove the lid. Stir the chicken gently to combine. Garnish with crumbled queso añejo. Serve immediately.

Adobo Chicken and Potatoes

SERVES 6 to 8 | PREP TIME: 5 minutes | MANUAL: 35 minutes high pressure | RELEASE: Natural | TOTAL TIME: 1 hour 5 minutes

3 pounds bone-in chicken
  breasts or thighs
6 medium Yukon
  Gold potatoes, cut
  into wedges
2 medium green bell
  peppers, seeded and
  roughly chopped
1 medium white onion,
  roughly chopped
3 garlic cloves, minced

1½ teaspoons coarse salt
1 teaspoon ground cumin
½ teaspoon freshly ground
  black pepper
1½ cups red
  enchilada sauce
1 cup freshly squeezed
  orange juice
Pickled jalapeño peppers,
  for garnish
Cooked rice, for serving

In the Instant Pot, combine the chicken, potatoes, bell peppers, onion, and garlic, then season with the salt, cumin, and pepper. Stir in the enchilada sauce and orange juice, making sure all the chicken and potato pieces are completely coated. Lock the lid. Select Manual and cook at high pressure for 35 minutes. When the cook time is complete, allow the pressure to release naturally. Remove the lid. To serve, garnish with pickled jalapeños. Serve with rice.

Chicken Fried Rice

SERVES 4 | PREP TIME: 5 minutes | SAUTÉ: 3 minutes | MANUAL: 3 minutes high pressure | RELEASE: Natural 10 minutes | TOTAL TIME: 26 minutes

2 teaspoons vegetable
  oil, divided
2 large eggs, whisked
3 garlic cloves, minced
1¼ cups chicken broth
1 pound boneless, skinless
  chicken breasts, cubed
1 cup diced carrots

1½ cups jasmine
  rice, rinsed
3 tablespoons soy sauce
½ teaspoon toasted
  sesame oil
½ cup frozen peas, thawed
Sesame seeds, for garnish
  (optional)

Select Sauté and pour in 1 teaspoon of oil. When the oil is hot, add the eggs and push them around with a spatula to scramble them until they are fully cooked. Transfer the eggs to a plate and set them aside. Bits of egg will be stuck to the bottom of the pot, but that's okay. Pour in the remaining 1 teaspoon of oil, then add the garlic. Sauté until fragrant, about 1 minute. Select Cancel. Add the chicken broth and stir to scrape up all the browned bits from the bottom of the pot. Add the chicken, carrot, and rice. Do not stir; just press the rice down to submerge it. Lock the lid. Select Manual and cook at high pressure for 3 minutes. When the cook time is complete, let the pressure release naturally for 10 minutes, then quick-release any remaining pressure. Stir in the soy sauce and sesame oil until the rice is well coated. Add the peas and scrambled eggs and stir to combine. Place the lid back on the Instant Pot and let it sit undisturbed for 5 minutes to warm the peas and eggs. Toss with sesame seeds (if using) and serve immediately.

Basil Chicken with Green Beans

SERVES 4 | PREP TIME: 5 minutes | SAUTÉ: 3 minutes | MANUAL: 2 minutes high pressure | RELEASE: Quick | TOTAL TIME: 20 minutes

2 teaspoons extra-virgin olive oil	½ cup water
1½ pounds ground chicken	1 tablespoon coconut aminos or tamari
1 red bell pepper, seeded and sliced	1 tablespoon gluten-free fish sauce
1 shallot, finely chopped	½ pound fresh green beans
1 tablespoon chile pepper paste	1 cup whole fresh basil leaves

Select Sauté on the Instant Pot and pour in the olive oil. When the oil is hot, add the chicken and cook for 2 to 3 minutes to brown, stirring occasionally to break up the meat. Select Cancel. Add the bell pepper, shallot, chile pepper paste, water, coconut aminos, and fish sauce. Stir to combine. Lock the lid. Select Manual and cook at high pressure for 2 minutes. When the cook time is complete, quick-release the pressure. Remove the lid and add the green beans. Select Keep Warm, return the lid to the pot, and let it sit for 5 minutes, until the green beans are steamed. Remove the lid and stir in the basil before serving.

Cheesy Chicken, Broccoli, and Rice Casserole

SERVES 4 | PREP TIME: 5 minutes | SAUTÉ: 6 minutes | MANUAL: 5 minutes high pressure | RELEASE: Natural for 5 minutes, then Quick | TOTAL TIME: 26 minutes

2 tablespoons unsalted butter	¾ teaspoon freshly ground black pepper
2 pounds boneless, skinless chicken breasts, cubed	1 teaspoon garlic powder
	1⅓ cups long-grain rice
1 small onion, diced	½ cup whole milk
2 garlic cloves, minced	2 cups shredded mild Cheddar cheese
1⅓ cups chicken broth	2 cups frozen broccoli florets, thawed
1 teaspoon salt	

Select Sauté, and when the Instant Pot is hot, melt the butter. Add the chicken and onion and cook until the onion starts to turn translucent, about 5 minutes. Add the garlic and cook until fragrant, about 1 minute. Add the broth, salt, pepper, and garlic powder. Stir to combine. Add the rice; do not stir but press down to make sure it's submerged. Select Cancel. Lock the lid. Select Manual and cook at high pressure for 5 minutes. When the cook time is complete, let the pressure release naturally for 5 minutes, then quick-release any remaining pressure. Stir in the milk and cheese, then add the broccoli and stir again. Cover the pot and let sit for 2 or 3 minutes to melt the cheese and heat the broccoli.

Chicken Burrito Bowls

SERVES 5 | PREP TIME: 5 minutes | SAUTÉ: 5 minutes | MANUAL: 10 minutes high pressure | RELEASE: Natural for 5 minutes, then Quick | TOTAL TIME: 32 minutes

2 tablespoons extra-virgin olive oil	2 pounds boneless, skinless chicken thighs, cubed
1 medium onion, diced	
3 garlic cloves, minced	1 (15-ounce) can black beans, drained and rinsed
1½ tablespoons chili powder	
1½ teaspoons ground cumin	1 cup frozen corn
	1 (16-ounce) jar chunky salsa
1 cup chicken broth	
Salt	1 cup long-grain white rice
Freshly ground black pepper	

Select Sauté, and when the Instant Pot is hot, pour in the oil. Stir in the onion and garlic and cook until the onion is translucent, about 4 minutes. Add the chili powder and cumin and cook until fragrant, about 1 minute. Add the broth and stir to scrape up the browned bits from the bottom. Evenly sprinkle salt and pepper over the chicken, then place it in the pot. Add the beans, corn, and salsa. Stir well to combine. Sprinkle the rice over the mixture and gently press it down with a spoon to submerge, but do not stir. Select Cancel. Lock the lid. Select Manual and cook at high pressure for 10 minutes. When the cook time is complete, let the pressure release naturally for 5 minutes, then quick-release any remaining pressure. Stir everything to combine.

Chicken-and-Rice Porridge

SERVES 6 | PREP TIME: 10 minutes | SAUTÉ: 5 minutes | MANUAL: 10 minutes high pressure | RELEASE: Natural for 25 minutes, then Quick | TOTAL TIME: 1 hour 10 minutes

¼ cup vegetable oil	2 knobs fresh ginger, peeled and cut into matchsticks

3 garlic cloves, minced
1 large onion, chopped
3 carrots, cubed
3 celery stalks, sliced
2 tablespoons fish sauce
2 to 3 pounds boneless, skinless chicken thighs
1¼ cups jasmine rice, rinsed

1½ tablespoons salt
1½ teaspoons freshly ground black pepper
2 bay leaves
8 cups chicken broth
6 hard-boiled eggs, peeled, for serving (optional)
Lemon slices, for serving (optional)

Select Sauté, and when the Instant Pot is hot, pour in the oil. Stir in the ginger, garlic, onion, carrot, and celery and sauté for about 5 minutes, or until the celery is starting to soften. Add the fish sauce and stir. Add the chicken, rice, salt, pepper, bay leaves, and broth. Do not stir. Select Cancel. Lock the lid. Select Manual and cook at high pressure for 10 minutes. When the cook time is complete, let the pressure release naturally for 25 minutes, then quick-release any remaining pressure. Remove the lid. Remove the chicken and shred it; then stir it back into the pot. Discard the bay leaves. Serve with an egg (if using) and a slice of lemon (if using).

Chicken Alfredo

SERVES 4 | PREP TIME: 5 minutes | MANUAL: 5 minutes high pressure | RELEASE: Natural for 7 minutes, then Quick | TOTAL TIME: 26 minutes

1½ cups chicken broth
1½ cups heavy (whipping) cream
3 garlic cloves, minced
Salt
Freshly ground black pepper

8 ounces linguine pasta, broken in half
5 chicken tenderloins
1 cup shredded Parmesan cheese

In the Instant Pot, combine the broth, cream, and garlic and season with salt and pepper. Layer in the pasta, arranging it in a crisscross pattern to keep it from clumping together. Do not stir but use the back of a spoon to push the noodles down, ensuring they are covered by the liquids. Place the chicken on the pasta and season with salt and pepper. Lock the lid. Select Manual and cook at high pressure for 5 minutes. When the cook time is complete, let the pressure release naturally for 7 minutes, then quick-release any remaining pressure. Remove the lid. Remove the chicken and set it aside. Slowly add the Parmesan and stir the pasta around. Dice the chicken and stir it into the sauce.

Buffalo Chicken Pasta

SERVES 6 | PREP TIME: 5 minutes | MANUAL: 14 minutes high pressure | RELEASE: Quick | TOTAL TIME: 29 minutes

1 pound boneless, skinless chicken breasts

4 cups water, divided
1 cup hot sauce

¼ cup (½ stick) unsalted butter
1 pound penne pasta
8 ounces cream cheese, cubed

1 cup prepared ranch or blue cheese dressing
¾ cup shredded Monterey Jack cheese

In the Instant Pot, combine the chicken, 1 cup of water, the hot sauce, and butter. Lock the lid. Select Manual and cook at high pressure for 10 minutes. When the cook time is complete, quick-release the pressure. Do not drain the liquid. Transfer the chicken to a plate and shred it. Put the pasta in the pot and lay the shredded chicken on top. Add the cream cheese, dressing, and the remaining 3 cups of water. Lock the lid. Select Manual and cook at high pressure for 4 minutes. When the cook time is complete, quick-release the pressure. Stir in the Monterey Jack cheese.

Chicken and Gravy

SERVES 4 | PREP TIME: 5 minutes | SAUTÉ: 8 minutes | MANUAL: 5 minutes high pressure | RELEASE: Natural for 5 minutes, then Quick | TOTAL TIME: 30 minutes

1 (1-ounce) packet ranch seasoning mix (such as Hidden Valley)
2 pounds boneless, skinless chicken breasts

1 tablespoon extra-virgin olive oil
1½ cups chicken broth
2 tablespoons cornstarch
2 tablespoons cold water

Sprinkle the ranch seasoning onto both sides of the chicken. Select Sauté, and when the Instant Pot is hot, pour in the oil. Cook the chicken until browned, about 3 minutes per side. Transfer the chicken to a plate. Add the chicken broth to the Instant Pot and scrape up any browned bits stuck to the bottom of the pot. Place the trivet in the pot and place the chicken on the trivet. Lock the lid. Select Manual and cook at high pressure for 5 minutes. When the cook time is complete, let the pressure release naturally for 5 minutes, then quick-release any remaining pressure. While the chicken is cooking, mix the cornstarch and cold water to form a slurry. When the cook time is up, remove the chicken and slice it. Select Sauté and whisk in the slurry. Simmer for a minute or two until it thickens and then turn off the pressure cooker. Serve the gravy over the chicken.

Chicken Curry

SERVES 4 | PREP TIME: 5 minutes | SAUTÉ: 15 minutes, divided | MANUAL: 5 minutes high pressure | RELEASE: Natural for 15 minutes, then Quick | TOTAL TIME: 45 minutes

2 pounds boneless, skinless chicken breasts, cubed
Salt

Freshly ground black pepper
2 tablespoons extra-virgin olive oil

1 medium onion, diced

6 garlic cloves, minced

1 tablespoon peeled and minced fresh ginger

3 tablespoons curry powder

½ teaspoon cayenne pepper

2 tablespoons tomato paste

1 tablespoon soy sauce

1 cup chicken broth

½ cup coconut milk

Dry the chicken thoroughly with paper towels and season with salt and pepper. Select Sauté, and when the Instant Pot is hot, pour in the oil. Place the chicken in the pot and brown on each side for about 4 minutes. Transfer the chicken to a plate and set aside. Add the onion and sauté until beginning to soften, about 3 minutes. Stir in the garlic, ginger, curry powder, cayenne, tomato paste, and soy sauce and sauté for another 2 minutes. Add the chicken broth, stirring to scrape up the browned bits from the bottom of the pot. Return the chicken and any juices to the pot. Select Cancel. Lock the lid. Select Manual and cook at high pressure for 5 minutes. When the cook time is complete, let the pressure release naturally for 15 minutes, then quick-release any remaining pressure. Select Sauté and add the coconut milk. Cook for about 2 minutes, until warmed through.

Chipotle Chicken Meatballs

SERVES 6 to 8 | PREP TIME: 10 minutes | MANUAL: 15 minutes high pressure | RELEASE: Natural | TOTAL TIME: 45 minutes

2 pounds ground chicken

½ cup plain dried breadcrumbs

⅓ cup long-grain or jasmine rice

⅓ cup old-fashioned oats

1 large egg

½ medium white onion, finely chopped

2 garlic cloves, minced

1 teaspoon coarse salt

½ teaspoon freshly ground black pepper

½ teaspoon crushed dried Mexican oregano

3 cups tomato sauce

2 cups chicken broth

2 to 4 tablespoons canned chipotle puree

Cooked rice, for serving

Warm corn or flour tortillas, for serving (optional)

In a large bowl, mix the ground chicken, breadcrumbs, rice, oats, egg, onion, garlic, salt, pepper, and oregano until well combined. Divide and shape the mixture into 2-inch meatballs; set them aside. In the Instant Pot, combine the tomato sauce and chicken broth. Stir in 2 to 4 tablespoons of the chipotle puree, as desired. Carefully drop the meatballs into the sauce. Do not stir! Lock the lid. Select Manual and cook at high pressure for 15 minutes. When the cook time is complete, allow the pressure to release naturally. Remove the lid. Stir gently to combine. Ladle into bowls over rice. Serve with warm tortillas (if using).

Salsa Verde Shredded Chicken Taquitos

SERVES 6 to 8 | MANUAL: 15 minutes high pressure | FRY: 6 minutes | RELEASE: Natural | TOTAL TIME: 45 minutes

2¼ pounds boneless, skinless chicken breasts

½ medium white onion, finely chopped

2 garlic cloves, minced

4 cilantro sprigs

1½ cups green enchilada sauce

1 cup chicken broth

1 teaspoon coarse salt

12 to 16 corn tortillas

1 cup vegetable oil

Shredded lettuce, for garnish

Guacamole, for garnish

Crumbled queso cotija, for garnish

In the Instant Pot, combine the chicken, onion, garlic, and cilantro. Pour the salsa verde and chicken broth on top and season with the salt. Lock the lid. Select Manual and cook at high pressure for 15 minutes. When the cook time is complete, allow the pressure to release naturally. Remove the lid. Discard the cilantro sprigs. Using two forks, shred the chicken in the pot. Heat the corn tortillas on a griddle over medium-high heat until soft and pliable. Spoon 2 to 3 heaping tablespoons of the shredded chicken mixture down the center of each tortilla. Roll the taquitos up tightly, securing with a toothpick if necessary. Heat the vegetable oil in a medium skillet over high heat. Fry the taquitos, 3 to 4 at a time, until golden and crisp, about 1 minute per side. As you finish frying each batch, transfer the taquitos to a paper towel–lined plate to drain any excess oil. To serve, arrange two or three taquitos per plate. Garnish with shredded lettuce, guacamole, and queso cotija.

Perfect Chicken Breast with Creamy Pesto Sauce

SERVES 4 | PREP AND FINISHING: 10 minutes | MANUAL: 5 minutes low pressure | SAUTÉ: 2 minutes | RELEASE: Natural for 8 minutes, then Quick | TOTAL TIME: 30 minutes

2 (14- to 16-ounce) boneless, skinless chicken breasts

½ teaspoon kosher salt, plus more as needed

⅓ cup heavy (whipping) cream

¼ cup chicken broth

1 tablespoon dry white wine

¼ cup pesto, divided

Season the chicken on both sides with the salt. Pour the cream, broth, and wine into the Instant Pot. Stir in 3 tablespoons of pesto. Put the chicken breasts on a trivet or shallow steamer basket and place in the pot. Lock the lid. Select Manual and cook at low pressure for 5 minutes. When the cook time is complete, naturally release the pressure for 8 minutes, then quick-release any remaining pressure. Remove the lid. Transfer the chicken breasts to a plate or rack. Use a thermometer to check their internal temperature; the breasts should register 150°F in the center. Select Sauté and adjust to Normal for medium heat. Simmer until the sauce thickens slightly, 1 to 2 minutes. Stir in the remaining 1 tablespoon of pesto and add more salt if necessary. While the sauce simmers, slice the chicken against the grain and divide among four plates. Top the chicken with the sauce and serve.

Perfect Chicken Breast with Romesco Sauce

SERVES 4 | PREP AND FINISHING: 10 minutes | MANUAL: 5 minutes low pressure | SAUTÉ: 2 minutes | RELEASE: Natural for 8 minutes, then Quick | TOTAL TIME: 30 minutes

2 (14- to 16-ounce) boneless, skinless chicken breasts
½ teaspoon kosher salt, plus more as needed
1 large roasted red pepper, pureed (about ½ cup)
⅓ cup strained tomatoes or tomato sauce
¼ cup chicken broth

1 tablespoon extra-virgin olive oil
½ teaspoon smoked or regular paprika
½ teaspoon kosher salt
¼ teaspoon cayenne pepper
1 teaspoon sherry vinegar or apple cider vinegar
¼ cup toasted slivered almonds

Season the chicken on both sides with the salt. Pour the red pepper puree, tomatoes, broth, and oil into the Instant Pot. Add the paprika, salt, and cayenne and stir to combine. Put the chicken breasts on a trivet or shallow steamer basket and place in the pot. Lock the lid. Select Manual and cook at low pressure for 5 minutes. When the cook time is complete, naturally release the pressure for 8 minutes, then quick-release any remaining pressure. Remove the lid. Transfer the chicken breasts to a plate or rack. Use a thermometer to check their internal temperature; the breasts should register 150°F in the center. Select Sauté and adjust to Normal for medium heat. Add the vinegar and simmer until the sauce thickens slightly, 1 to 2 minutes. While the sauce simmers, slice the chicken against the grain and divide among four plates. Top the chicken with the sauce, garnish with the toasted almonds, and serve.

Perfect Chicken Breast with Coconut-Curry Sauce

SERVES 4 | PREP AND FINISHING: 10 minutes | MANUAL: 5 minutes low pressure | SAUTÉ: 2 minutes | RELEASE: Natural for 8 minutes, then Quick | TOTAL TIME: 30 minutes

2 (14- to 16-ounce) boneless, skinless chicken breasts
½ teaspoon kosher salt, plus more as needed

½ cup coconut milk
¼ cup chicken broth
1 teaspoon Thai red curry paste
½ teaspoon curry powder

1 tablespoon freshly squeezed lime juice
1 teaspoon sugar

¼ cup roasted unsalted peanuts, crushed
1 tablespoon minced fresh basil

Season the chicken on both sides with the salt. Pour the coconut milk and broth into the Instant Pot. Add the curry paste and curry powder and stir to combine. Put the chicken breasts on a trivet or shallow steamer basket and place in the pot. Lock the lid. Select Manual and cook at low pressure for 5 minutes. When the cook time is complete, naturally release the pressure for 8 minutes, then quick-release any remaining pressure. Remove the lid. Transfer the chicken breasts to a plate or rack. Use a thermometer to check their internal temperature; the breasts should register 150°F in the center. Select Sauté and adjust to Normal for medium heat. Add the lime juice and sugar and simmer until the sauce thickens slightly, 1 to 2 minutes. While the sauce simmers, slice the chicken against the grain and divide among four plates. Top the chicken with the sauce, garnish with the peanuts and basil, and serve.

Thai-Style Cashew Chicken

SERVES 4 | PREP AND FINISHING: 20 minutes | SAUTÉ: 9 minutes | MANUAL: 5 minutes high pressure | RELEASE: Natural for 5 minutes, then Quick | TOTAL TIME: 35 minutes

¼ cup all-purpose flour
1 teaspoon kosher salt
1 pound boneless, skinless chicken thighs
3 tablespoons vegetable oil
½ cup chicken broth
2 tablespoons soy sauce
1 tablespoon fish sauce
1 tablespoon freshly squeezed lime juice
2 teaspoons sugar
1 teaspoon red pepper flakes

½ small onion, sliced thin (about ½ cup)
1 small red bell pepper, seeded and cut into 1-inch pieces
1 medium jalapeño, seeded and cut into thin half-moons
2 teaspoons cornstarch
1 tablespoon water
1 cup roasted unsalted cashews

In a shallow dish, mix the flour and salt. Dredge the chicken thighs in the flour, lightly coating both sides. Gently shake off any excess flour. Select Sauté and adjust to More for high heat. Heat the oil until it shimmers. Add the chicken in a single layer (you may want to do two batches or use a skillet on the stove). Let cook, undisturbed, until golden brown, 4 to 5 minutes. Flip the thighs and cook until browned on the other side, 3 to 4 minutes. Transfer the thighs to a plate and let cool for a few minutes, then cut into bite-size pieces. While the chicken cools, pour any accumulated fat out of the pot. While the pot is still hot, pour in the chicken broth and stir, scraping up any browned bits from the bottom of the pot. Simmer the broth until it reduces by about half. Add the soy sauce, fish sauce, lime juice, sugar, and red pepper flakes to the pot and stir to combine. Select Cancel. Add the chicken, onion, bell pepper, and jalapeño to the pot. Lock the lid. Select Manual and cook at high pressure for 5 minutes. When the cook time is complete, naturally release the pressure for 5 minutes, then quick-release any remaining pressure. Remove the lid. In a small bowl, whisk together the cornstarch and water until the mixture is smooth. Stir this into the sauce and cook until the sauce thickens, 2 to 3 minutes. Taste and adjust the seasoning, if necessary. Add the cashews and mix gently. Serve.

Orange Chicken

SERVES 4 | PREP AND FINISHING: 20 minutes | SAUTÉ: 11 minutes | MANUAL: 5 minutes high pressure | RELEASE: Natural for 5 minutes, then Quick | TOTAL TIME: 35 minutes

¼ cup all-purpose flour	2 tablespoons soy sauce
1 teaspoon kosher salt	1 tablespoon rice vinegar
1½ pounds boneless, skin- less chicken thighs	1 tablespoon orange juice concentrate
3 tablespoons vegetable oil	1 teaspoon red pepper flakes
2 teaspoons peeled and minced ginger	3 scallions, sliced, greens and whites separated
1 garlic clove, minced	
¼ cup chicken broth	2 teaspoons cornstarch
1 teaspoon grated orange zest	1 tablespoon water
¼ cup freshly squeezed orange juice	2 teaspoons toasted sesame oil
	Steamed rice, for serving

In a shallow dish, mix the flour and salt. Dredge the chicken thighs in the flour, lightly coating both sides, and shake off any excess flour. Select Sauté and adjust to More for high heat. Heat the oil until it shimmers. Add the chicken in a single layer (you may want to do two batches or use a skillet on the stove). Let cook, undisturbed, until golden brown, 4 to 5 minutes. Flip the chicken and cook until browned on the other side, 3 to 4 minutes. Transfer the chicken to a plate and let cool for a few minutes, then cut into bite-size pieces. While the chicken cools, pour most of the fat out of the pot, leaving a thin coat. With the pot still on Sauté, add the ginger and garlic and cook, stirring, until fragrant, 1 to 2 minutes. Pour in the chicken broth and stir, scraping up any browned bits from the bottom of the pot. Simmer the broth until it reduces by about half. Add the orange zest and juice, soy sauce, rice vinegar, orange juice concentrate, and red pepper flakes and stir to combine. Add the chicken and the white parts of the scallions to the Instant Pot. Select Cancel. Lock the lid. Select Manual and cook at high pressure for 5 minutes. When the cook time is complete, naturally release the pressure for 5 minutes, then quick-release any remaining pressure. Remove the lid. In a small bowl, whisk together the cornstarch and water until the mixture is smooth. Stir this into the sauce and cook until the sauce thickens,

2 to 3 minutes. Taste and adjust the seasoning, if necessary. Drizzle with the sesame oil and top with the green parts of the scallions. Serve over rice.

Milk-Braised Chicken with Lemon-Garlic Sauce

SERVES 4 | PREP AND FINISHING: 25 minutes | SAUTÉ: 16 minutes | MANUAL: 12 minutes low pressure | RELEASE: Natural for 8 minutes, then Quick | TOTAL TIME: 50 minutes

1 (4- to 4½-pound) whole chicken, giblets removed	½ cup chicken broth
	1½ cups whole milk
1 teaspoon kosher salt	Zest of 1 lemon (grated or in strips)
2 tablespoons extra-virgin olive oil or vegetable oil	
	10 garlic cloves, peeled

Sprinkle the chicken all over with the salt. Select Sauté and adjust to More for high heat. Heat the oil until it shimmers. Blot the chicken dry and place it in the Instant Pot, breast-side down. Let it cook, undisturbed, until the skin is dark golden brown, about 5 minutes. Turn the chicken over and brown the other side, about 5 minutes. Use tongs to turn the chicken on one side for 2 to 3 minutes more, then repeat on the other side. Transfer the chicken to a plate. Pour off all the fat and add the broth and scrape the bottom of the pot to release the browned bits. Select Cancel. Pour the milk into the pot. Place the chicken, breast-side up, in the pot and add the zest and garlic. Lock the lid. Select Manual and cook at low pressure for 12 minutes. When the cook time is complete, naturally release the pressure for 8 minutes, then quick-release any remaining pressure. Remove the chicken from the pot and place it on a rack set over a baking sheet. The temperature of the chicken breast should be just under 150°F, with the thigh meat at about 165°F. If the temperature is much lower than that, return the chicken to the pot and put the lid on, but don't lock it. Keep the chicken on warm for a few minutes until it registers the proper temperatures. Let the chicken rest on the rack while you finish the sauce. If your zest is in strips, remove and discard them. For a smoother sauce, blend it with an immersion blender. Cut the chicken into serving pieces, spoon the sauce over, and serve.

Red Chicken Enchiladas

SERVES 4 | PREP AND FINISHING: 30 minutes | MANUAL: 10 minutes high pressure | Bake: 16 minutes | RELEASE: Natural for 10 minutes, then Quick | TOTAL TIME: 50 minutes

1 pound boneless, skinless chicken thighs	3 tablespoons vegetable oil or nonstick cooking spray
2 cups ancho chile sauce	½ cup crumbled queso fresco
½ cup chopped onion	
12 corn tortillas	

Put the chicken thighs in the Instant Pot. Pour in the ancho chile sauce. Lock the lid. Select Manual and cook at high pressure for 10 minutes. When the cook time is complete, naturally release the pressure for 10 minutes, then quick-release any remaining pressure. Remove the lid. Transfer the chicken to a bowl and let it cool for a few minutes. Keep the sauce warm. When the chicken is just cool enough to handle, cut or pull it into bite-size chunks. Mix in about ⅔ cup of the warm sauce; the chicken should be well coated with sauce but not drowning. Put the onion in a small bowl. Preheat the oven to 350°F. Place 6 tortillas on a baking sheet in a single layer. Brush the tortillas lightly with the oil (or spray with cooking spray), then turn them over and repeat on the other side. Bake just until the tortillas are warm and pliable, about 3 minutes. Remove from the oven and place the tortillas in a stack on a plate. Cover with foil to keep warm. Repeat with the remaining 6 tortillas. Leave the oven on. Spoon about ½ cup of warm sauce into a 9-by-13-inch baking dish. Place one tortilla in the sauce and flip it so it's lightly coated on both sides, then place 2 tablespoons of chicken and 2 teaspoons of chopped onion on the tortilla. Roll the tortilla up and place it at the end of the dish, seam-side down. Repeat with the remaining tortillas. When all the enchiladas are filled and rolled, pour enough sauce over them to just cover them (they should not be swimming in sauce). Bake until warmed through, 8 to 10 minutes. Sprinkle the queso fresco over the enchiladas and serve.

Sesame-Soy Chicken Wings

SERVES 4 | PREP AND FINISHING: 15 minutes | MANUAL: 10 minutes high pressure | SAUTÉ: 4 minutes | RELEASE: Quick | TOTAL TIME: 30 minutes

12 whole chicken wings or 24 wing segments (drumettes and/or flats)

1½ cups water, plus more as needed

½ cup soy sauce

2 tablespoons toasted sesame oil

2 or 3 slices peeled ginger

3 garlic cloves, lightly smashed

2 tablespoons sugar

1 teaspoon Chinese five-spice powder

2 tablespoons minced fresh cilantro, basil, or scallion greens, for garnish

If you have whole wings, cut off the tips and save for another use or discard. Cut each wing at the joint into a drumette and a flat segment. Pour the water and soy sauce into the Instant Pot. Add the sesame oil, ginger, garlic, sugar, and five-spice powder and stir to combine. Add the chicken wings and stir to coat with the liquid. The wings should be mostly submerged; if necessary, add a little more water. Lock the lid. Select Manual and cook at high pressure for 10 minutes. When the cook time is complete, quick-release the pressure. Remove the lid. Using a spider or skimmer, remove the wings from the pot and set them aside on a plate. Select Sauté and adjust to More for high heat. Bring the sauce to a boil and let it reduce by about

half, about 4 minutes. Return the wings to the sauce and stir to coat. Transfer the wings to a deep platter or bowl and pour the sauce over. Garnish with the cilantro and serve.

Chicken Tinga

SERVES 4 | PREP AND FINISHING: 15 minutes | SAUTÉ: 9 minutes, divided | MANUAL: 10 minutes high pressure | RELEASE: Natural for 10 minutes, then Quick | TOTAL TIME: 40 minutes

2 tablespoons extra-virgin olive oil

8 ounces tomatillos (2 to 3 large), husked and quartered

1 medium onion, chopped (about 1 cup)

2 garlic cloves, minced

½ cup chicken broth

1 (14-ounce) can fire-roasted tomatoes

1 teaspoon dried oregano

½ teaspoon kosher salt, plus more as needed

¼ teaspoon ground cumin

1 pound boneless, skinless chicken thighs

1 teaspoon chili paste

Select Sauté and adjust to More for high heat. Heat the olive oil until it shimmers. Add the tomatillos in a single layer and cook, undisturbed, until browned, about 2 minutes. Add the onion and garlic and cook, stirring occasionally, until the onion is browned, about 4 minutes. Add the chicken broth and stir, scraping the bottom of the pot to get up any browned bits. Add the tomatoes with their juices, oregano, salt, and cumin. Stir to combine. Select Cancel. Add the chicken to the pot. Lock the lid. Select Manual and cook at high pressure for 10 minutes. When the cook time is complete, naturally release the pressure for 10 minutes, then quick-release any remaining pressure. Transfer the chicken to a plate and let cool. When it's cool enough to handle, chop or pull the chicken into bite-size pieces. Use an immersion blender to puree the sauce. Stir in the chili paste. Select Sauté and adjust to Normal for medium heat. Simmer until the sauce has thickened to the consistency of gravy, about 3 minutes. Taste and adjust the seasoning, adding more salt if necessary. Add the chicken to the sauce and stir to warm it through. Serve.

Honey Mustard-Garlic Wings

SERVES 4 | PREP AND FINISHING: 15 minutes | MANUAL: 10 minutes high pressure | BROIL: 7 to 12 minutes | RELEASE: Quick | TOTAL TIME: 37 minutes

12 whole chicken wings or 24 wing segments (drumettes and/or flats)

1 cup water

⅓ cup honey

⅓ cup Dijon mustard

4 garlic cloves, minced

If you have whole wings, cut off the tips and save for another use or discard. Cut each wing at the joint into a drumette and a flat segment. Place the chicken wings in a steamer basket. Pour the water into the Instant Pot and place the basket in the pot. Lock the lid. Select Manual and cook at high pressure for 10 minutes. When the cook time is complete, quick-release the pressure. Remove the lid. Remove the wings from the pot and transfer them to a rack set over a baking sheet. Preheat the broiler. In a small bowl, mix the honey, mustard, and garlic. Baste the wings with about half of the sauce. Broil the wings until browned, 4 to 6 minutes. Flip the wings and baste them with the remaining sauce. Broil until the second side is browned, 3 to 6 minutes. Serve.

Chicken and Orzo with Lemon Sauce

SERVES 4 | PREP AND FINISHING: 15 minutes | MANUAL: 4 minutes low pressure | SAUTÉ: 2 minutes | RELEASE: Natural for 5 minutes, then Quick | TOTAL TIME: 30 minutes

4 cups chicken broth, plus more as needed

6 ounces orzo

2 large boneless, skinless chicken breasts

¼ teaspoon kosher salt, plus more as needed

1 large egg

2 tablespoons freshly squeezed lemon juice

Freshly ground black pepper

Pour the broth into the Instant Pot and stir in the orzo. Place the chicken breasts on top of the orzo and sprinkle them with the salt. Lock the lid. Select Manual and cook at low pressure for 4 minutes. When the cook time is complete, naturally release the pressure for 5 minutes, then quick-release any remaining pressure. Remove the lid. Transfer the chicken breasts to a plate or cutting board and set aside to cool for a minute, then cut into bite-size pieces. Don't worry if the center of the chicken isn't quite done; it will cook again. In a small bowl, thoroughly beat the egg. Whisk in the lemon juice. Select Sauté and adjust to Normal for medium heat. Slowly add about 1 cup of the warm chicken broth to the egg and lemon mixture, whisking constantly. (If there is not enough broth in the pot to ladle out 1 cup, add more broth and bring it to a simmer.) Add the chicken pieces and simmer for 1 to 2 minutes, or until the chicken is cooked. Turn off the heat and add the egg-and-broth mixture to the pot. Stir to combine. Adjust the seasoning if necessary and serve.

Brazilian-Style Chicken Thighs with Dark Beer

SERVES 4 | PREP AND FINISHING: 20 minutes | SAUTÉ: 14 minutes, divided | MANUAL: 10 minutes high pressure | RELEASE: Natural for 10 minutes, then Quick | TOTAL TIME: 45 minutes

4 to 6 bone-in, skin-on chicken thighs

½ teaspoon kosher salt, plus more as needed

2 tablespoons extra-virgin olive oil

1 large onion, sliced

3 large garlic cloves, minced

1 cup dark beer, such as a porter or stout

¼ cup chicken broth

1 teaspoon smoked or regular paprika

½ teaspoon dried oregano

½ teaspoon dried basil

½ teaspoon red pepper flakes

¼ teaspoon freshly ground black pepper, plus more as needed

Sprinkle the chicken thighs on both sides with the salt. Select Sauté and adjust to More for high heat. Heat the oil until it shimmers. Add the chicken thighs, skin-side down, and let them cook, undisturbed, until the skin is dark golden brown and most of the fat under the skin has rendered out, about 5 minutes. Do not crowd the thighs; if necessary, work in batches. Flip the thighs and cook until light golden brown on the other side, about 3 minutes. Transfer the thighs to a plate. Carefully pour off almost all the fat, leaving just enough to cover the pot with a thick coat (about 1 tablespoon). Add the onion and garlic and cook, stirring frequently, until the onion begins to brown, about 3 minutes. Add the beer and scrape the bottom of the pot to release the browned bits. Boil until the liquid reduces by about half, about 2 minutes. Add the broth, paprika, oregano, basil, red pepper flakes, and black pepper. Bring the sauce to a boil and cook for 1 minute. Select Cancel. Add the chicken thighs, skin-side up, to the pot. Lock the lid. Select Manual and cook at high pressure for 10 minutes. When the cook time is complete, naturally release the pressure for 10 minutes, then quick-release any remaining pressure. Remove the chicken thighs and place them on a rack set over a baking sheet. Let the chicken rest on the rack while you finish the sauce. Strain the sauce into a fat separator and let it rest until the fat rises to the surface. (If you don't have a fat separator, let the sauce sit for a few minutes, then spoon or blot off any excess fat from the top of the sauce.) Pour the defatted sauce back into the Instant Pot and select Keep Warm. If you prefer a thicker sauce, select Sauté and adjust to Less. Let the sauce simmer for several minutes until it's reduced to the consistency you like, about 3 minutes. Adjust the seasoning, adding more salt and black pepper if needed. Serve the chicken thighs topped with the sauce.

Chicken Fajitas

SERVES 4 | PREP TIME: 10 minutes | MANUAL: 12 minutes high pressure | RELEASE: Natural | TOTAL TIME: 35 minutes

2 red or yellow bell peppers, seeded and sliced

1 red onion, sliced

1 teaspoon extra-virgin olive oil

½ teaspoon chili powder

¼ teaspoon kosher salt

1¼ pounds boneless, skinless chicken breast, thinly sliced

12 cassava flour or corn tortillas

In the Instant Pot, combine the bell peppers, onion, olive oil, chili powder, and salt. Place the chicken slices on top of the vegetables. Lock the lid. Select Manual and cook at high pressure for 12 minutes. When the cook time is complete, let the pressure release naturally for 5 minutes, then quick-release any remaining pressure. Remove the lid. Use a slotted spoon to divide the filling evenly among the tortillas, leaving any liquid in the pot.

Whole Cooked Chicken

SERVES 10 | PREP AND FINISHING: 10 minutes | MANUAL: 30 minutes high pressure | RELEASE: Natural for 10 minutes, then Quick | TOTAL TIME: 60 minutes

1 cup water
1 (4½- to 5-pound) whole chicken, giblets removed
1 tablespoon extra-virgin olive oil
2 teaspoons fine sea salt
1 teaspoon dried thyme
½ teaspoon garlic powder

Place the trivet in the Instant Pot, then pour in the water. Place the chicken, breast-side down, on the trivet and drizzle it with the olive oil. Sprinkle the salt, thyme, and garlic powder over the chicken. Lock the lid. Select Manual and cook at high pressure for 30 minutes. When the cook time is complete, naturally release the pressure for 10 minutes, then quick-release any remaining pressure. Remove the lid. Using tongs, transfer the chicken to a serving plate. Serve immediately.

Parmesan Turkey Meatballs

SERVES 4 | PREP AND FINISHING: 15 minutes | SAUTÉ: 8 minutes, divided | MANUAL: 5 minutes high pressure | RELEASE: Natural for 5 minutes, then Quick | TOTAL TIME: 30 minutes

1 pound ground turkey
½ medium onion, finely chopped
3 garlic cloves, minced
½ cup grated Parmesan or similar cheese
2 tablespoons minced fresh parsley
½ teaspoon kosher salt
1 large egg
2 tablespoons whole milk
¼ cup breadcrumbs
2 tablespoons extra-virgin olive oil
½ cup chicken broth
1 (14-ounce) can diced tomatoes

In a large bowl, gently mix the ground turkey, onion, garlic, Parmesan cheese, parsley, and salt. In a small bowl, whisk together the egg and milk. Stir in the breadcrumbs. Add the egg-crumb mixture to the meat and gently mix until just evenly combined. Form meatballs using about 2 tablespoons of meat for each. You may find it easier to roll the balls if you moisten your hands with water. Select Sauté and adjust to More for high heat. Heat the oil until it shimmers. Add the meatballs in a single layer and let them cook, undisturbed, until browned on the bottom, 1 to 2 minutes. Turn the meatballs to brown on the opposite side. Move the meatballs to the sides of the pot (they may stack on top of one another) and pour in the chicken broth. Bring the liquid to a boil and scrape up any browned bits from the bottom of the pot. Add the tomatoes with their

juices and move the meatballs back into an even layer. Select Cancel. Lock the lid. Select Manual and cook at high pressure for 5 minutes. When the cook time is complete, naturally release the pressure for 5 minutes, then quick-release any remaining pressure. Remove the lid. Use a slotted spoon to transfer the meatballs to a bowl. Select Sauté and adjust to More for high heat. Bring the sauce to a boil and cook until it is very thick and chunky, about 4 minutes. Spoon the sauce over the meatballs and serve.

Savory Turkey Breast

SERVES 8 | PREP TIME: 15 minutes | SAUTÉ: 10 minutes, divided | MANUAL: 30 minutes high pressure | RELEASE: Natural for 15 minutes, then Quick | TOTAL TIME: 1 hour 15 minutes

3 tablespoons extra-virgin olive oil
1 tablespoon poultry seasoning
1 tablespoon paprika
1 teaspoon garlic powder
1 teaspoon salt
1 teaspoon freshly ground black pepper
½ teaspoon chili powder
½ teaspoon onion powder
½ teaspoon garlic powder
4 pounds boneless turkey breast, thawed if frozen
1 cup chicken broth
2 thyme sprigs
2 tablespoons unsalted butter (optional)
2 tablespoons all-purpose flour (optional)

In a small bowl, combine the oil, poultry seasoning, paprika, garlic powder, salt, pepper, chili powder, onion powder, and garlic powder. Pat the turkey breast dry with a paper towel and then coat it all over with the spice mixture. Select Sauté, and when the Instant Pot is hot, put the turkey breast in it and brown on all sides, 2 to 3 minutes per side. Remove the turkey breast and set it aside. Add the broth and deglaze the pot, stirring to scrape up the browned bits from the bottom. Select Cancel. Add the thyme to the broth and then set the trivet in the pot. Place the turkey on the trivet. Lock the lid. Select Manual and cook at high pressure for 30 minutes. When the cook time is complete, let the pressure release naturally for 15 minutes, then quick-release any remaining pressure. Use a meat thermometer to test the temperature of the turkey; make sure it reads 165°F at the thickest part of the breast before removing it from the pot. If it hasn't reached that temperature, lock the lid, select Manual and cook at high pressure for another 5 to 10 minutes. Transfer the turkey breast to a cutting board and let it rest for 15 minutes before cutting. While the turkey is resting, make the gravy (if using). Scoop out 2 cups of the drippings from the bottom of the pot. Discard the rest, along with the thyme sprigs. Select Sauté and heat the butter and flour. Whisk constantly for about 1 minute, or until the flour starts to turn golden. Add the drippings and cook until the gravy thickens, 2 to 3 minutes. Adjust the seasoning and transfer to a gravy boat. Slice the turkey breast and serve with the gravy (if using).

Turkey Lettuce Wraps

SERVES 4 | PREP TIME: 5 minutes | SAUTÉ: 3 minutes | MANUAL: 5 minutes high pressure | RELEASE: Natural | TOTAL TIME: 30 minutes

1 tablespoon extra-virgin olive oil	1 tablespoon rice vinegar
1 yellow onion, diced	1 (1-inch) knob fresh ginger, grated
2 garlic cloves, minced	1 (8-ounce) can water chestnuts, drained and diced
1 pound lean (93 percent) ground turkey	
⅓ cup water	2 scallions, white and light green parts, thinly sliced
2 tablespoons honey	
2 tablespoons coconut aminos or tamari	1 head butter lettuce

Select Sauté on the Instant Pot and pour in the olive oil. When the oil is hot, add the onion and garlic and cook for 2 to 3 minutes, stirring occasionally, until softened. Select Cancel. Add the ground turkey, water, honey, coconut aminos, vinegar, and ginger. Stir well to break up the meat. Lock the lid. Select Manual and cook at high pressure for 5 minutes. When the cook time is complete, let the pressure release naturally for 10 minutes, then quick-release any remaining pressure. Remove the lid and stir in the water chestnuts and scallions. If the sauce is too thin, select Keep Warm and simmer, uncovered, for 3 to 4 minutes, until thickened. Serve with lettuce for wrapping.

Turkey Dinner

SERVES 4 | PREP TIME: 10 minutes | MANUAL: 30 minutes high pressure, divided | RELEASE: Quick, then Natural for 10 minutes, then Quick | TOTAL TIME: 1 hour

1½ pounds turkey tenderloin	¼ teaspoon freshly ground black pepper
2 teaspoons extra-virgin olive oil, divided	2 cups cubed butternut squash
½ teaspoon poultry seasoning	4 celery stalks, sliced
½ teaspoon kosher salt	4 carrots, sliced
	1 cup water

Coat the turkey with 1 teaspoon of olive oil, then sprinkle it with the poultry seasoning, salt, and pepper. Set it aside. Place the squash, celery, and carrots on a piece of foil. Bring the sides of the foil up like a boat to contain the vegetables, but do not cover the top. Drizzle the vegetables with the remaining 1 teaspoon of olive oil, then set them aside. Pour the water into the Instant Pot and insert the trivet. Place the turkey on top of the trivet. Lock the lid. Select Manual and cook at high pressure for 20 minutes. When the cook time is complete, quick-release the pressure. Remove the lid and place the foil packet of vegetables directly on top of the turkey. Lock the lid. Select Manual and cook at high pressure for 10 minutes. When the cook time is complete, let the pressure release naturally for 10 minutes, then quick-release any remaining pressure. Remove the lid and lift out the foil packet of vegetables. Transfer the turkey to a cutting board and slice it before serving alongside the vegetables.

Turkey Bolognese

SERVES 6 | PREP AND FINISHING: 20 minutes | SAUTÉ: 10 minutes | MANUAL: 10 minutes high pressure | RELEASE: Natural for 10 minutes, then Quick | TOTAL TIME: 60 minutes

2 tablespoons extra-virgin olive oil	2 tablespoons tomato paste
1 medium yellow onion, chopped	½ cup red wine
2 garlic cloves, minced	2 pounds ground turkey
2 carrots, diced (about 1 cup)	1 (28-ounce) can crushed tomatoes
	½ cup water
	1 teaspoon dried oregano

Select Sauté on the Instant Pot and pour in the olive oil. Once the oil is hot, add the onion, garlic, carrots, and tomato paste. Sauté for 3 minutes or until the vegetables start to soften. Pour the wine into the pot. Using a wooden spoon, scrape up any browned bits stuck to the bottom of the pot. Add the ground turkey. Use the wooden spoon to break the meat apart as it cooks, about 3 minutes. Select Cancel and add the crushed tomatoes with their juices, water, and oregano. Lock the lid. Select Manual and cook at high pressure for 10 minutes. When the cook time is complete, naturally release the pressure for 10 minutes, then quick-release any remaining pressure. Remove the lid. Stir the sauce. If you want to thicken the sauce, select Sauté and let the sauce simmer for about 10 minutes. Serve immediately.

Turkey Mole

SERVES 4 | PREP TIME: 15 minutes | SAUTÉ: 15 minutes | MANUAL: 35 minutes high pressure | RELEASE: Natural | TOTAL TIME: 1 hour 30 minutes

3 tablespoons vegetable oil, divided	4 cups chicken broth
4 turkey legs	¼ cup sugar
Coarse salt	Cooked rice, for serving
Freshly ground black pepper	2 tablespoons toasted sesame seeds, for garnish
1 (8¼-ounce) jar mole paste	

Select Sauté and adjust to More for high. Heat 2 tablespoons of vegetable oil in the pot. Add the turkey legs, two at a time, and sauté, flipping a couple of times, for 6 to 8 minutes, or until light golden brown all over. Season generously with salt and pepper. As the turkey legs finish cooking, transfer them to a heatproof plate. Heat the remaining 1 tablespoon of vegetable oil in the Instant Pot. Add the mole paste and let it start to dissolve in the oil. Stir in the chicken broth, 1 cup at a time, until the mole paste has completely melted into the broth. Add the sugar and season with salt. Select Cancel. Return the turkey legs to the Instant Pot and stir to coat them with the mole. Lock the lid. Select Manual and cook at high pressure for 35 minutes. When the cook time is complete, allow the pressure to release naturally. Remove the lid. Serve the turkey mole with rice and garnish with the toasted sesame seeds.

Turkey Breast with Shallot Gravy

SERVES 4 | PREP TIME: 15 minutes | SAUTÉ: 8 minutes, divided | MANUAL: 25 minutes high pressure | RELEASE: Natural for 10 minutes, then Quick | TOTAL TIME: 1 hour

1 (1½-pound) boneless or bone-in turkey breast
½ teaspoon salt
½ teaspoon freshly ground black pepper
2 tablespoons unsalted butter

8 shallots, chopped
1 garlic clove, minced
1 teaspoon dried thyme
2 cups water
3 tablespoons cornstarch

Season the turkey breast with the salt and black pepper. Select Sauté. Melt the butter in the Instant Pot. Add the shallots, garlic, and thyme. Sauté for 2 minutes. Set a trivet in the pot and add the water. Place the turkey breast on the trivet. Select Cancel. Lock the lid. Select Manual and cook at high pressure for 25 minutes. When the cook time is complete, let the pressure release naturally for 10 minutes, then quick-release any remaining pressure. Remove the lid. Transfer the turkey to a serving dish and remove the trivet from the pot. Select Sauté. In a small bowl, whisk the cornstarch with 3 tablespoons of cooking liquid; return the mixture to the pot. Stir and cook for about 5 minutes to thicken the gravy. Slice the turkey. Serve the slices drizzled with gravy or pass the gravy separately in a gravy boat.

Cajun-Inspired Spiced Turkey Breast

SERVES 4 | PREP AND FINISHING: 15 minutes | MANUAL: 20 minutes low pressure | SAUTÉ: 4 minutes | RELEASE: Natural for 10 minutes, then Quick | TOTAL TIME: 50 minutes

¼ cup unsalted butter, at room temperature
1 teaspoon kosher salt, plus more as needed
½ teaspoon freshly ground black pepper, plus more as needed

½ teaspoon dried basil
½ teaspoon dried thyme
½ teaspoon garlic
¼ teaspoon cayenne pepper
1 small (about 5 pounds) whole turkey breast

1 cup chicken broth
2 tablespoons cornstarch

2 tablespoons water

In a small bowl, mix the butter, salt, black pepper, basil, thyme, garlic, and cayenne pepper. Use your hands to loosen the skin over the turkey breast and spread the spiced butter under the skin as evenly as possible. Pour the broth into the Instant Pot. Place the breast in the pot. Lock the lid. Select Manual and cook at low pressure for 20 minutes. When the cook time is complete, naturally release the pressure for 10 minutes, then quick-release any remaining pressure. Remove the lid. Transfer the turkey to a plate. Use a thermometer to check the temperature; the thickest part of the meat should register 150°F. In a small bowl, combine the cornstarch and water until the mixture is smooth. Select Sauté and adjust to Normal for medium heat. Bring the chicken broth to a simmer and add the cornstarch mixture. Cook until the gravy has thickened, about 4 minutes. Taste and adjust the seasoning, adding more salt and pepper if necessary. While the gravy simmers, remove the skin from the turkey. Cut the breast into ¼-inch-thick slices and spoon the gravy over them. Serve.

Turkey Tenderloins with Lemon-Caper Sauce

SERVES 4 | PREP AND FINISHING: 10 minutes | MANUAL: 8 minutes low pressure | SAUTÉ: 4 minutes | RELEASE: Natural for 8 minutes, then Quick | TOTAL TIME: 35 minutes

2 (14-ounce) turkey tenderloins
½ teaspoon kosher salt
¼ teaspoon freshly ground black pepper
½ cup chicken broth
3 tablespoons unsalted butter, divided

1 tablespoon freshly squeezed lemon juice
1 teaspoon grated lemon zest
1 tablespoon drained capers

Sprinkle the tenderloins on both sides with the salt and pepper. Pour the chicken broth into the Instant Pot and add 1 tablespoon of butter. Place the tenderloins in the pot. Lock the lid. Select Manual and cook at low pressure for 8 minutes. When the cook time is complete, naturally release the pressure for 8 minutes, then quick-release any remaining pressure. Remove the lid. Transfer the tenderloins to a plate. Use a thermometer to check the temperature; the tenderloins should register 150°F in the center. Select Sauté and adjust to Normal for medium heat. Bring the sauce to a simmer and add the lemon juice and lemon zest. Cook until the liquid has reduced by about half, about 4 minutes. Turn off the heat. One tablespoon at a time, whisk in the remaining 2 tablespoons of butter. Stir in the capers. While the sauce simmers, slice the turkey against the grain and divide among four plates. Top with the sauce and serve.

Beer-Braised Beef Roast

SERVES 6 to 8 | PREP TIME: 10 minutes | SAUTÉ: 8 minutes | MANUAL: 60 minutes high pressure | RELEASE: Natural | TOTAL TIME: 1 hour 30 minutes

3 tablespoons ancho chile powder

1½ teaspoons crushed dried Mexican oregano

1 teaspoon ground cumin

¾ teaspoon coarse salt

¾ teaspoon freshly ground black pepper

3 pounds beef chuck roast, cut into 3-inch pieces

2 tablespoons vegetable oil

1 large white onion, thinly sliced

3 garlic cloves, minced

5 cilantro sprigs

1 (12-ounce) bottle Mexican beer

¼ cup freshly squeezed lime juice

1 tablespoon Maggi Jugo seasoning sauce

1 tablespoon Worcestershire sauce

Chopped fresh cilantro, for garnish

Cooked rice, for serving

Refried beans, for serving

Flour tortillas, for serving (optional)

Chopped red onion, for garnish

In a small bowl, combine the chile powder, oregano, cumin, salt, and pepper. Sprinkle the spice rub over the chuck roast. Select Sauté and adjust to More for high. Heat the vegetable oil in the pot, add the meat, and fry for 6 to 8 minutes, or until lightly golden brown all over. Add the onion, garlic, and cilantro sprigs. Pour in the beer, lime juice, Maggi Jugo seasoning sauce, and Worcestershire sauce. Select Cancel. Lock the lid. Select Manual and cook at high pressure for 60 minutes. When the cook time is complete, allow the pressure to release naturally. Remove the lid. Using two forks, shred the meat in the pot. Serve with rice and beans, or if using, use the beef as a filling for tacos. Garnish with chopped red onion and cilantro.

Beef Burgundy

SERVES 8 | PREP AND FINISHING: 10 minutes | SAUTÉ: 5 minutes | MANUAL: 30 minutes high pressure | RELEASE: Natural for 10 minutes, then Quick | TOTAL TIME: 1 hour 5 minutes

2 pounds beef chuck roast, cut into 1-inch cubes

¼ cup all-purpose flour

2 tablespoons extra-virgin olive oil

2 garlic cloves, minced

1 medium yellow onion, diced

1 teaspoon dried thyme

1 teaspoon fine sea salt

½ teaspoon freshly ground black pepper

1 cup red wine

1 tablespoon tomato paste

4 carrots, peeled and sliced (about 1 cup)

Place the beef and flour in a zip-top bag. Seal the bag and then use your hands to make sure the beef gets coated with the flour. Select Sauté and put the olive oil in the

Instant Pot. Once the oil is hot, add the beef, garlic, onion, thyme, salt, and pepper. Sauté for 3 minutes, stirring occasionally. Select Cancel and pour in the wine. Use a wooden spoon to scrape up any browned bits stuck to the bottom of the pot. Add the tomato paste and carrots and stir to combine. Lock the lid with the steam release knob in the sealed position. Select Manual and cook at high pressure for 30 minutes. When the cook time is complete, naturally release the pressure for 10 minutes, then quick-release any remaining pressure. Remove the lid. Serve immediately.

Beef Shank Barbacoa

SERVES 6 | PREP TIME: 5 minutes | MANUAL: 45 minutes high pressure | RELEASE: Natural | TOTAL TIME: 1 hour 15 minutes

3 pounds beef shanks or boneless country-style beef ribs

¾ teaspoon coarse salt

½ teaspoon ground cumin

½ teaspoon freshly ground black pepper

¼ teaspoon crushed dried oregano

2 garlic cloves, thinly sliced

½ medium white onion, thinly sliced

1½ cups red enchilada sauce

1 (10½-ounce) can beef broth

Chopped onion, for garnish

Chopped fresh cilantro, for garnish

Warm corn tortillas, for serving (optional)

In the Instant Pot, combine the beef shanks, salt, cumin, pepper, and oregano. Top with the garlic and onion. Pour in the enchilada sauce, beef broth, and 1 cup of water. Lock the lid. Select Manual and cook at high pressure for 45 minutes. When the cook time is complete, allow the pressure to release naturally. Remove the lid. To serve, break up the beef shanks (or serve them whole) and ladle the chile broth over the meat. Garnish with chopped onion and cilantro. Serve with warm corn tortillas (if using).

Mexican-Style Ropa Vieja

SERVES 6 to 8 | PREP TIME: 10 minutes | SAUTÉ: 10 minutes | MANUAL: 30 minutes high pressure | RELEASE: Natural | TOTAL TIME: 1 hour 15 minutes

2½ pounds flank steak

1 teaspoon coarse salt

1 teaspoon paprika

½ teaspoon freshly ground black pepper

2 tablespoons vegetable oil

2 roasted poblano peppers, peeled, seeded, and cut into thin strips

2 Hungarian wax peppers, seeded and thinly sliced

2 Anaheim chiles, seeded and thinly sliced

1 medium white onion, thinly sliced

2 garlic cloves, minced

3 Roma tomatoes, seeded and thinly sliced

1 (8-ounce) can pitted black olives, drained

1 (10½-ounce) can beef broth

1½ cups tomato sauce
2 dried bay leaves
Cooked rice, for serving

Warm corn or flour tortillas, for serving (optional)

Season the flank steak with the salt, paprika, and black pepper. Select Sauté and adjust to More for high. Heat the vegetable oil in the pot, add the flank steak, and sauté, flipping once, for 5 to 7 minutes, or until golden brown. Transfer the steak to a heatproof plate. Add the poblano peppers, wax peppers, chiles, onion, and garlic to the pot. Sauté for 2 to 3 minutes, or just until the onion is translucent. Add the tomatoes, black olives, beef broth, and tomato sauce. Return the steak to the pot. Top with the bay leaves. Select Cancel. Lock the lid. Select Manual and cook at high pressure for 30 minutes. When the cook time is complete, allow the pressure to release naturally. Remove the lid. Remove and discard the bay leaves. Using two forks, shred the steak in the pot. Serve with rice and warm tortillas (if using).

Shredded Beef Chile Colorado Tamales

MAKES 24 tamales | PREP TIME: 20 minutes, plus 30 minutes for soaking the corn husks | MANUAL: 30 minutes high pressure | RELEASE: Natural | TOTAL TIME: 1 hour 15 minutes

24 dried corn husks
4 cups masa harina
1½ teaspoons
  baking powder
1 teaspoon coarse salt
1 cup manteca (pork lard)
  or shortening
3 cups very warm
  beef broth

2 cups water
4½ cups shredded beef
  chile Colorado
2 to 3 (6-ounce) cans pitted
  black olives, drained
2 cups tomato sauce or
  ranchero sauce
Shredded lettuce,
  for serving

In a large plastic container, soak the dried corn husks in enough boiling water to cover them. Place a heavy lid or pan on top of the corn husks to keep them submerged. Let them soak for at least 30 minutes, or until soft and pliable. Rinse the corn husks with cold water to remove any dirt and residue, then pat them dry with a kitchen towel. In a medium bowl, combine the masa harina, baking powder, and salt. Set it aside. In a large mixing bowl, cream the *manteca* with an electric mixer on medium-high speed until light and fluffy. With the mixer still on medium-high, slowly add the masa harina mixture, 1 cup at a time, until no dry bits are visible. The mixture will be grainy. Reduce the mixer speed to low and stir in the beef broth until it has all been absorbed. Using your hands, press the mixture together to form a dough. Add the water to the Instant Pot. Place the trivet inside. Spoon about ¼ cup of dough onto each corn husk, spreading it about ⅛ inch thick across two-thirds of the corn husk. Leave a ¼-inch space on

one side and at the top, and about a 3-inch space at the bottom. Place 2 to 3 tablespoons of the shredded beef filling down the center of the masa-covered corn husk. Top with 2 or 3 black olives. Starting at the ¼-inch edge, gently fold each tamale in thirds, then tuck in the ends. Place the wrapped tamales, seam-side down, on a large plate. Arrange the tamales vertically in the Instant Pot, with the open ends facing upward. Lock the lid. Select Manual and cook at high pressure for 30 minutes. While the tamales are steaming, warm the tomato sauce in a small saucepan until heated through. When the cook time is complete, allow the pressure to release naturally. Remove the lid. Let the tamales sit, uncovered, for 5 to 10 minutes before serving. To serve, remove the corn husks from the tamales. Top with shredded lettuce and ladle about ⅓ cup of the warmed tomato sauce or salsa over each tamale. Enjoy!

Korean-Style Beef Bowl

SERVES 6 | PREP AND FINISHING: 15 minutes | SAUTÉ: 10 minutes | MANUAL: 10 minutes high pressure | RELEASE: Natural for 5 minutes, then Quick | TOTAL TIME: 50 minutes

½ cup water
2 tablespoons cornstarch
1 tablespoon extra-virgin
  olive oil
2 pounds flank steak, cut
  into ½-inch-thick strips
3 garlic cloves, minced
½ cup beef broth
⅓ cup reduced-sodium
  soy sauce

¼ cup white wine vinegar
2 tablespoons honey
2 teaspoons sriracha sauce
¼ teaspoon ground ginger
1 medium cucumber, sliced
2 red bell peppers, seeded
  and sliced
4 scallions, white and light
  green parts only, sliced

In a small bowl, make a slurry by whisking together the water and cornstarch. Set it aside. Select Sauté on the Instant Pot and pour in the olive oil. Once the oil is hot, add the steak and garlic and sauté for 3 minutes, stirring occasionally so the beef starts to brown on all sides. Select Cancel and add the broth. Using a wooden spoon, scrape up any browned bits stuck to the bottom of the pot. Add the soy sauce, vinegar, honey, sriracha, and ginger. Stir to combine. Lock the lid. Select Manual and cook at high pressure for 10 minutes. When the cook time is complete, naturally release the pressure for 5 minutes, then quick-release any remaining pressure. Remove the lid. Select Sauté. Use a slotted spoon to transfer the beef to a serving plate. Once the liquid begins to bubble, whisk in the cornstarch slurry and let the sauce cook, uncovered, for 2 minutes or until it starts to thicken. Return the beef to the pot and stir to combine. Serve each bowl with a few slices of cucumber and red bell pepper and some sliced scallions on top.

All-in-One Meatloaf with Mashed Potatoes

SERVES 8 | PREP AND FINISHING: 10 minutes | MANUAL: 30 minutes high pressure | RELEASE: Natural for 10 minutes, then Quick | TOTAL TIME: 1 hour

1 pound medium russet or Yukon Gold potatoes
1 cup chicken broth
2 pounds 90 percent lean ground beef
½ medium yellow onion, chopped
2 garlic cloves, minced
1 large egg
2 teaspoons Worcestershire sauce
1 teaspoon Dijon mustard
2 tablespoons unsalted butter
1 teaspoon fine sea salt
½ teaspoon freshly ground black pepper

Place the potatoes and broth in the Instant Pot. In a large bowl, combine the ground beef, onion, garlic, egg, Worcestershire sauce, and mustard. Using your hands, mix the ingredients together thoroughly. Form the meat mixture into a loaf that will fit inside the Instant Pot. Tear off a 2-foot piece of foil and fold it in half. Turn up the edges so it makes the shape of a square basket that will fit inside the Instant Pot. Place the meatloaf in the foil basket and place it on top of the potatoes. Lock the lid. Select Manual and cook at high pressure for 30 minutes. When the cook time is complete, naturally release the pressure for 10 minutes, then quick-release the remaining pressure. Remove the lid. Carefully remove the meatloaf and the foil from the pot. Add the butter, salt, and pepper to the potatoes, then mash them to your liking with a potato masher or immersion blender. Serve immediately.

Garlicky Steak Bites

SERVES 4 | PREP TIME: 10 minutes | SAUTÉ: 4 minutes | MANUAL: 10 minutes high pressure | RELEASE: Natural for 10 minutes, then Quick | TOTAL TIME: 40 minutes

1½ pounds sirloin steak, cut into 1-inch cubes
⅛ teaspoon kosher salt
⅛ teaspoon freshly ground black pepper
2 tablespoons extra-virgin olive oil
4 garlic cloves, minced
½ cup beef broth
1 pound baby yellow potatoes
1 pint cremini mushrooms, quartered

Use a paper towel to pat the steak dry, then season it with the salt and pepper. Select Sauté and pour in the olive oil. When the oil is hot, add the steak cubes, working in batches if necessary to avoid crowding the pot. Cook for 3 to 4 minutes, stirring occasionally, until all sides are browned. Stir in the garlic. Select Cancel. Pour in the broth and scrape up any browned bits from the bottom of the pot. Add the potatoes and mushrooms. Lock the lid. Select Manual and cook at high pressure for 10 minutes. When the cook time is complete, let

the pressure release naturally for 10 minutes, then quick-release any remaining pressure. Remove the lid and serve.

Steamed Hamburgers

SERVES 6 | PREP TIME: 10 minutes | MANUAL: 15 minutes | RELEASE: Quick | TOTAL TIME: 30 minutes

2 pounds lean ground beef
2 teaspoons Worcestershire sauce
1 teaspoon salt
1 teaspoon garlic powder
½ teaspoon freshly ground black pepper
1 cup water
Cheese slices, for topping (optional)

In a medium bowl, mix the beef, Worcestershire sauce, salt, garlic powder, and pepper. Form six thick equal patties. Wrap each patty in foil, carefully sealing all the sides. Set the trivet in the Instant Pot and pour in the water. Stack the burgers evenly on the trivet. Lock the lid. Select Manual and cook at high pressure for 15 minutes. When the cook time is complete, quick-release the pressure. If you want to make cheeseburgers, unwrap the cooked burgers immediately, lay the cheese on top, and allow it to melt.

Barbecued Beef Sandwiches

SERVES 4 | PREP AND FINISHING: 15 minutes | MANUAL: 25 minutes high pressure | SAUTÉ: 4 minutes | RELEASE: Natural for 15 minutes, then Quick | TOTAL TIME: 1 hour

1 (2¼-pound) boneless beef chuck roast
½ teaspoon kosher salt, plus more as needed
2 cups barbecue sauce, divided
4 hoagie rolls or large hamburger buns, split

If the chuck roast is more than about 2½ inches thick, cut it into slices about 2 inches thick. Cut off any large chunks of fat. Sprinkle it all over with the salt. Put the beef in the Instant Pot and pour 1½ cups of barbecue sauce over it. Lock the lid. Select Manual and cook at high pressure for 25 minutes. When the cook time is complete, naturally release the pressure for 15 minutes, then quick-release any remaining pressure. Remove the lid and transfer the beef to a plate or baking sheet. Pour the liquid into a fat separator and allow the fat to rise to the surface, then return the sauce to the pot. (If you don't have a fat separator, spoon or blot off as much fat as possible.) Select Sauté and adjust to Normal for medium heat. Bring the sauce to a boil and let cook until reduced by about half, about 4 minutes; it should be the original consistency of the barbecue sauce. While the sauce reduces, shred the beef into small chunks, discarding any fat or gristle. Add the shredded beef and the remaining ½ cup of sauce to the pot. Cook, stirring, until the meat heats through. Taste and adjust the seasoning, adding more salt if necessary. Spoon the beef onto the bottom halves of the rolls and top with the remaining halves. Serve.

Beef Stroganoff

SERVES 4 | **PREP TIME:** 10 minutes | **SAUTÉ:** 10 minutes | **MANUAL:** 15 minutes high pressure, divided | **RELEASE:** Quick | **TOTAL TIME:** 40 minutes

¼ cup all-purpose flour	3 cups sliced portobello
Salt	mushrooms
Freshly ground	3 cups beef broth
black pepper	¼ cup cooking sherry
2 pounds beef stew meat,	1 tablespoon
cut into bite-size pieces	Worcestershire sauce
2 tablespoons	1 (12-ounce) package wide
unsalted butter	egg noodles
1 small onion, chopped	8 ounces sour cream
3 garlic cloves, minced	

In a large resealable plastic bag, mix the flour, salt, and pepper. Add the meat and shake until it's evenly coated. Select Sauté and melt the butter. Add the beef and cook for 3 to 5 minutes, or until browned on each side. Add the onion, garlic, and mushrooms and cook until the onion starts to soften, 2 to 4 minutes. Scoop out the beef with a slotted spoon and set aside. Add the broth, sherry, and Worcestershire sauce, stirring to scrape up the browned bits from the bottom of the pot. Select Cancel. Return the beef to the pot. Lock the lid. Select Manual and cook at high pressure for 10 minutes. When the cook time is complete, quick-release the pressure. Add the egg noodles and lock the lid. Select Manual and cook at high pressure for 5 minutes. When the cook time is complete, quick-release the pressure. Remove the lid and add the sour cream. Season with salt and pepper. Stir to combine.

Sunday Pot Roast

SERVES 8 | **PREP TIME:** 14 minutes | **SAUTÉ:** 20 minutes, divided | **MANUAL:** 1 hour 10 minutes, divided | **RELEASE:** Natural for 20 minutes, then Quick, divided | **TOTAL TIME:** 2 hours 10 minutes

3 pounds beef chuck roast	¾ tablespoon
1 teaspoon kosher salt	tomato paste
1 teaspoon freshly ground	1 tablespoon soy sauce
black pepper	5 medium carrots, cut into
1 teaspoon dried thyme	1-inch pieces
1 teaspoon extra-virgin	1½ pounds whole baby
olive oil	potatoes
1 large onion, chopped	2 tablespoons cornstarch
4 garlic cloves, minced	2 tablespoons water
1½ cups beef broth	

Cut the roast in half and sprinkle all sides with the salt, pepper, and thyme. Select Sauté, and pour in the oil.

Place the meat in the pot and brown all sides, about 4 minutes per side. Transfer the roast to a plate and set it aside. Add the onion and cook until translucent, 3 to 5 minutes. Add the garlic and cook until fragrant, about 1 minute. Add the broth and stir to scrape up the browned bits from the bottom of the pot. Add the tomato paste and soy sauce. Return the meat to the pot. Select Cancel. Lock the lid. Select Manual and cook at high pressure for 60 minutes. When the cook time is complete, let the pressure release naturally for 10 minutes, then quick-release any remaining pressure. Open the lid and put the carrots and potatoes on top of the meat. Lock the lid. Select Manual and cook at high pressure for 10 minutes. When the cook time is complete, let the pressure release naturally for 10 minutes, then quick-release any remaining pressure. Remove the meat, carrots, and potatoes and shred the meat into large chunks. In a small bowl, make a slurry by mixing the cornstarch and water. Select Sauté and add the slurry to the liquid in the pot. Cook for 2 minutes, stirring often, or until the sauce thickens into gravy. Spoon the gravy over the roast and serve with the potatoes and carrots on the side.

Southwestern Pot Roast

SERVES 6 | **PREP AND FINISHING:** 25 minutes | **SAUTÉ:** 14 minutes | **MANUAL:** 44 minutes high pressure, divided | **RELEASE:** Quick | **TOTAL TIME:** 1 hour 25 minutes

1 (3- to 3½-pound) bone-	¼ cup canned diced green
less chuck roast, about	chiles, drained
3 inches thick	1 teaspoon ground cumin
1½ teaspoons kosher salt	1 teaspoon dried oregano
2 tablespoons vegetable oil	1 pound red potatoes,
1 medium onion, quartered	quartered
3 large garlic cloves,	1 medium red bell pepper,
lightly smashed	seeded and cut into
¾ cup mild beer, such as a	1½-inch chunks
lager or pale ale	1 medium green bell
¾ cup beef broth	pepper, seeded and cut
2 tablespoons ancho	into 1½-inch chunks
chile sauce	1 large jalapeño, seeded
	and cut into half-moons

Sprinkle the beef on all sides with the salt. Select Sauté and adjust to More. Heat the oil until it shimmers. Blot the roast dry with paper towels and add it to the skillet. Let it cook, undisturbed, until deeply browned, about 3 minutes. Flip the roast and brown the other side for 3 minutes. Transfer the beef to a plate. Add the onion and garlic. Cook, without stirring, until the first side is darkly browned, even charred a bit, 2 to 3 minutes. Turn the onion and garlic over and repeat on the other side. Transfer it to the plate with the beef. Pour off the oil from the pot. Pour in the beer and stir, scraping the bottom of the pot to dissolve the browned bits. Bring the beer to a boil and cook until reduced by about a third, 1 to 2 minutes. Add the beef broth, ancho chile sauce, green chiles, cumin, and oregano. Stir to combine. Select Cancel. Add the beef with any accumulated juices, onion, and garlic to the pot. Lock the lid. Select Manual and cook at high pressure for 40 minutes. When the cook time is complete, quick-release the pressure. Remove the lid. Transfer the beef to a cutting board and tent with a piece of foil. Add the potatoes, bell peppers, and jalapeño to the pot. Lock the lid. Select Manual and cook at high pressure for 4 minutes. When the cook time is complete, quick-release the pressure. Remove the lid. While the vegetables are cooking, cut the beef against the grain into slices about ⅓ inch thick. Transfer them to a serving platter. When the vegetables are done, spoon them and the sauce over the beef and serve.

Lentils with Short Ribs

SERVES 4 | PREP AND FINISHING: 20 minutes | MANUAL: 55 minutes high pressure, divided | RELEASE: Natural for 20 minutes, then Quick, divided | TOTAL TIME: 1 hour 45 minutes

1½ pounds (2-inch) bone-in short ribs
1¾ teaspoons kosher salt, divided
¼ cup extra-virgin olive oil, divided, plus more as needed
1 medium onion, diced, divided
1 cup dry sherry, divided
2 cups beef broth
1 celery stalk, diced
1 carrot, diced
2 garlic cloves, minced
12 ounces green or brown lentils, rinsed

Season the short ribs on all sides with 1 teaspoon of salt. Select Sauté and adjust to More for high heat. Heat 2 tablespoons of oil until it shimmers. Add the short ribs in a single layer without crowding them. Brown the ribs on all sides, then remove and set aside, changing the cooker to medium heat or the Brown setting. Cook the onions. Add another coat of oil if the pot is dry and heat it until shimmering. Add half of the onion. Sprinkle with ¼ teaspoon of salt and stir until the onion pieces just start to brown, 3 to 4 minutes. Add ½ cup of sherry and cook until the liquid has reduced by about half, 2 to 3 minutes. Scrape the bottom of the pot to scrape up any browned bits. Select Cancel. Return the short ribs to the pot and add the broth. Lock the lid. Select Manual and cook at high pressure for 40 minutes. When the cook time is complete, naturally release the pressure for 10 minutes, then quick-release any remaining pressure. Remove the lid and transfer the ribs to a plate to cool. When they can be handled, remove the meat from the bones and shred it, discarding the fat and connective tissue. Set it aside. Strain the cooking liquid into a fat separator and set aside. (If you don't have a fat separator, let the sauce sit for a few minutes, then spoon or blot off any excess fat from the top of the sauce.) Discard the onion. Wipe out the pot. Select Sauté and adjust to More for high heat. Add the remaining 2 tablespoons

of oil to the pot and heat until it shimmers. Add the remaining onion, the celery, carrot, and garlic and cook, stirring frequently, until the vegetables start to soften, 2 to 3 minutes. Pour in the remaining ½ cup of sherry and cook until the raw alcohol smell is gone, 1 to 2 minutes more. Select Cancel. Add the lentils, the remaining ½ teaspoon of salt, and the defatted cooking liquid. Lock the lid. Select Manual and cook at high pressure for 15 minutes. When the cook time is complete, naturally release the pressure for 10 minutes, then quick-release any remaining pressure. Remove the lid. Taste and adjust the seasoning if needed. Stir in the reserved short rib meat. Let sit for a few minutes to warm the meat through, then serve.

Red Wine–Braised Short Ribs

SERVES 4 | PREP AND FINISHING: 25 minutes | SAUTÉ: 22 minutes, divided | MANUAL: 40 minutes high pressure | RELEASE: Natural for 20 minutes, then Quick | TOTAL TIME: 1 hour 30 minutes

½ teaspoon salt, plus more for seasoning
8 (2-inch) bone-in beef short ribs (about 4 pounds)
2 tablespoons extra-virgin olive oil, plus more as needed
2 small carrots, cut into ¼-inch rounds
1 medium onion, diced
1 garlic clove, minced
1 tablespoon tomato paste
½ cup dry red wine
1 cup beef broth
2 thyme sprigs or 1 teaspoon dried thyme, plus more for garnish (optional)
1 bay leaf
Freshly ground black pepper
1 teaspoon packed light brown sugar (optional)

Liberally salt the short ribs on all sides. Select Sauté and adjust to More for high heat. Heat the oil until it shimmers. Add the short ribs in a single layer without crowding them (work in batches if necessary). Brown the ribs for 3 to 4 minutes on each side, then transfer to a plate and set aside, leaving the cooker on high heat. Add another coat of oil if the pot is dry and heat it until shimmering. Add the carrots, onion, and garlic. Sprinkle with the salt and stir until the onion pieces separate and the vegetables begin to soften, 2 to 3 minutes. Stir in the tomato paste and cook for a few minutes, just until the paste begins to brown slightly. Add the wine and stir, scraping the bottom of the pot to dissolve the browned bits. Bring the liquid to a boil and cook until the wine has reduced by about a third, 2 to 3 minutes. Add the beef broth, thyme, and bay leaf. Add the ribs; the meat should be partially but not completely submerged in liquid. Select Cancel. Lock the lid. Select Manual and cook at high pressure for 40 minutes. When the cook time is complete, naturally release the pressure for 20 minutes, then quick-release any remaining pressure. Remove the lid. Carefully transfer the ribs to a plate or baking sheet. They'll be quite tender and will fall off the bones if you're not gentle. Tent lightly with foil to keep them warm while you finish the sauce. Strain the sauce mixture through a coarse strainer into a fat separator and discard the solids. When the fat has separated, pour the sauce back into the pot. (If you don't have a fat separator, strain the sauce and let it cool until any fat has risen to the top. Remove as much fat as possible with a spoon or use paper towels to blot it off, then return the sauce to the pot.) Select Sauté and adjust the heat to Normal. Bring the sauce to a simmer, stirring frequently to prevent it from scorching, until the sauce is the consistency of gravy, 8 to 10 minutes. Season with black pepper and taste. If the sauce is too acidic, add the brown sugar. Add more salt if necessary. Return the ribs to the pot and heat them for a minute or two. Serve and garnish, if using, with a few additional sprigs of thyme on each plate.

Chili Con Carne

SERVES 4 | PREP AND FINISHING: 20 minutes | SAUTÉ: 12 minutes | MANUAL 25 minutes high pressure | RELEASE Natural for 10 minutes, then Quick | TOTAL TIME: 1 hour

1 (2½-pound) boneless beef chuck roast
1 teaspoon kosher salt
2 tablespoons vegetable oil
1 medium onion, chopped (about 1 cup)
2 garlic cloves, minced
1 tablespoon ancho chile powder or similar
1 teaspoon ground cumin
½ teaspoon cayenne pepper

½ teaspoon dried oregano
½ cup mild beer, such as a lager or pale ale
½ cup beef broth
½ cup ancho chile sauce
2 tablespoons strained tomatoes or tomato sauce
1 teaspoon pureed canned chipotles

Cut the chuck roast into "steaks" about 1½ inches thick. Sprinkle them with the salt. Select Sauté and adjust to More for high heat. Heat the oil until it shimmers. Add the beef in a single layer without crowding (work in batches if necessary). Brown the beef for 3 minutes, then turn it over and brown the other side for 3 minutes. Transfer the beef to a plate or cutting board and set aside to cool slightly, then cut into 1-inch cubes. Add the onion and garlic. Cook, stirring occasionally, until the onion begins to brown, about 3 minutes. Add the chile powder, cumin, cayenne, and oregano and cook, stirring frequently, until fragrant, about 1 minute. Add the beer and stir, scraping the bottom of the pot to dissolve the browned bits. Bring to a boil and cook until the beer has reduced by about a third, 1 to 2 minutes. Add the beef broth, ancho chile sauce, strained tomatoes, and chipotle puree and stir to combine. Select Cancel. Add the beef cubes and any accumulated juices to the pot. Lock the lid. Select Manual and cook at high pressure for 25 minutes. When the cook time is complete, naturally release the pressure for 10 minutes, then quick-release any remaining pressure. Serve.

Beef Birria

SERVES 6 to 8 | PREP TIME: 10 minutes | MANUAL: 45 minutes high pressure | RELEASE: Natural | TOTAL TIME: 1 hour 15 minutes

2½ to 3 pounds beef chuck roast or shanks
1½ teaspoons coarse salt
½ teaspoon freshly ground black pepper
½ teaspoon crushed dried Mexican oregano
1 medium onion, quartered
3 garlic cloves, thinly sliced
6 cilantro sprigs

2 bay leaves
3 cups water
3 to 4 cups tomato sauce
Chopped white onion, for garnish
6 to 8 fresh serrano chiles, for garnish
Warm corn tortillas, for serving (optional)

If using beef chuck roast, cut into 2-inch slices and place inside the Instant Pot. Season with salt, pepper, and oregano. Add the onion, garlic, cilantro, and bay leaves. Pour in the water. Lock the lid. Select Manual and cook at high pressure for 45 minutes. When the cook time is complete, allow the pressure to release naturally. Remove the lid. Remove and discard the cilantro and bay leaves. In a small saucepan, heat the tomato sauce over medium heat until simmering. Remove from the heat. Using two forks, shred the beef. To serve, spoon the desired amount of shredded beef into bowls. Ladle at least ⅓ cup each of the cooking broth and tomato sauce into each bowl. Garnish with chopped white onion. Serve with a fresh serrano chile on the side and plenty of warm corn tortillas (if using).

Beef Tongue Tacos

SERVES 10 to 12 | PREP TIME: 5 minutes | MANUAL: 1 hour 10 minutes high pressure | RELEASE: Natural | TOTAL TIME: 1 hour 30 minutes

1 (3½- to 4-pound) beef tongue
3 cups water
6 cilantro sprigs
½ medium white onion, quartered
4 whole garlic cloves, peeled
2 serrano chiles, thinly sliced
1½ teaspoons coarse salt

1 teaspoon crushed dried Mexican oregano
½ teaspoon freshly ground black pepper
Corn tortillas, for serving
Chopped white onion, for garnish
Chopped fresh cilantro, for garnish
Lime wedges, for serving
Salsa, for serving

In the Instant Pot, arrange the beef tongue and add the water. Add the cilantro, onion, garlic, and chiles. Season with the salt, oregano, and pepper. Lock the lid. Select Manual and cook at high pressure for 1 hour 10 minutes. When the cook time is complete, allow the pressure to release naturally. Remove the lid. Using a slotted spoon, transfer the cooked beef tongue to a cutting board. Discard the outer layer of skin. Roughly chop the tongue into bite-size pieces. Heat the corn tortillas on a comal or griddle over medium heat until soft and pliable. Stack two corn tortillas per taco. Spoon 2 to 3 heaping tablespoons of chopped beef tongue down the center of each tortilla stack. Garnish with chopped onion and cilantro. Serve with lime wedges and your favorite salsa.

Beef Vindaloo

SERVES 4 | PREP AND FINISHING: 15 minutes | SAUTÉ: 6 minutes | MANUAL: 25 minutes high pressure | RELEASE: Natural for 15 minutes, then Quick | TOTAL TIME: 1 hour

¼ cup vegetable oil
1 medium onion, cut into slices (about 1 cup)
4 garlic cloves, minced
2 teaspoons cayenne pepper, plus more as needed
2 teaspoons curry powder
1 teaspoon smoked or regular paprika
1 teaspoon kosher salt, plus more as needed
½ teaspoon ground ginger

¼ teaspoon ground cinnamon
¼ teaspoon freshly ground black pepper, plus more as needed
½ cup chicken broth or beef broth
¼ cup rice vinegar
1 (2-pound) boneless beef chuck roast, trimmed and cut into 1½-inch cubes
Steamed rice, for serving

Select Sauté and adjust to More for high heat. (For a thicker sauce, adjust to Normal for medium heat.) Heat the oil until it shimmers. Add the onion and cook, stirring frequently, just until starting to brown, 2 to 3 minutes. Add the garlic and cook, stirring frequently, until fragrant, about 1 minute. Add the cayenne, curry powder, paprika, salt, ginger, cinnamon, and pepper and cook, stirring constantly, until a paste forms and darkens slightly, 1 to 2 minutes. Add the broth and vinegar and bring to a simmer. Scrape any browned bits from the bottom of the pot and reduce to your preferred consistency. Select Cancel. Add the beef to the Instant Pot. Lock the lid. Select Manual and cook at high pressure for 25 minutes. When the cook time is complete, naturally release the pressure for 15 minutes, then quick-release any remaining pressure. Remove the lid. Spoon or blot off any fat on the top of the sauce. For a thicker sauce, select Sauté and adjust to Normal for medium heat. Bring the sauce to a simmer and cook until reduced to your preferred consistency. Serve with rice.

Spicy Broccoli Beef

SERVES 4 | PREP AND FINISHING: 20 minutes | SAUTÉ: 11 minutes, divided | MANUAL: 1 minute low pressure | RELEASE: Quick | TOTAL TIME: 30 minutes

2 (12- to 14-ounce) top sirloin steaks, about 1 inch thick
½ teaspoon kosher salt

3 tablespoons vegetable oil, divided
¼ cup dry sherry
12 ounces broccoli florets (about 2 medium crowns)

½ cup beef broth
¼ cup water
¼ cup soy sauce
2 tablespoons oyster sauce
2 tablespoons rice vinegar
2 tablespoons orange juice concentrate
1 tablespoon Asian chili garlic sauce, plus more as needed

2 teaspoons cornstarch
1 tablespoon minced peeled ginger
1 tablespoon minced garlic
2 scallions, sliced, white and green parts separated
Steamed rice, for serving

Sprinkle the steaks on both sides with the salt. Heat a large cast-iron or other heavy skillet on the stove over high heat. Heat 2 tablespoons of oil until it shimmers. Add the beef in a single layer without crowding (work in batches if necessary). Sear the beef for 1½ minutes on each side, then transfer the beef to a rack or plate. Pour the oil out of the skillet or pot and pour in the sherry. Bring it to a simmer and cook, scraping the bottom of the pot to dissolve any browned bits, until the sherry has reduced by about half, about 4 minutes. Pour the reduced sherry into the Instant Pot. Select Cancel. Add the beef broth and water to the pot. Put the broccoli in a steamer basket or on a silicone steamer trivet and place the steaks on top of the broccoli. Place the steamer in the pot. Lock the lid. Select Manual and cook at low pressure for 1 minute. When the cook time is complete, quick-release the pressure. Remove the lid. Remove the steamer basket and transfer the steaks to a plate or cutting board. Pour the beef broth mixture from the pot into a small bowl. Add the soy sauce, oyster sauce, vinegar, orange juice concentrate, chili garlic sauce, and cornstarch and whisk together. Set aside. Select Sauté and adjust to Normal for medium heat. Heat the remaining 1 tablespoon of oil until it shimmers. Add the ginger, garlic, and the white parts of the scallions and cook, stirring frequently, until fragrant, about 2 minutes. Add the reserved beef broth mixture. Stir to combine and cook, stirring occasionally, until the sauce has thickened, 2 to 3 minutes. Adjust the heat to Less for low heat. While the sauce cooks, slice the steaks about ⅛ inch thick. If the slices are large, cut them into bite-size pieces. The steak might be raw in the center. Don't worry; it will cook again. Add the beef slices and broccoli to the sauce in the pot and stir to coat. Cook just long enough for the beef to finish cooking and the broccoli to warm through. (If the beef is quite raw in the center, add it first for a minute or so to cook further, then add the broccoli.) Serve with rice and garnish with the green parts of the scallions.

Sloppy Joes

SERVES 8 | PREP AND FINISHING: 5 minutes | SAUTÉ: 5 minutes | MANUAL: 10 minutes high pressure | RELEASE: Natural for 10 minutes, then Quick | TOTAL TIME: 40 minutes

1 tablespoon extra-virgin
olive oil
2 pounds 90 percent lean
ground beef
1 teaspoon onion powder
½ teaspoon garlic powder
1 teaspoon chili powder
1 (16-ounce) can
tomato puree
½ cup ketchup

2 tablespoons
reduced-sodium
soy sauce
1 tablespoon packed light
brown sugar
Purple slaw, for garnish
(optional)
Chopped fresh parsley, for
garnish (optional)

Select Sauté on the Instant Pot and pour in the olive
oil. Once the oil is hot, add the ground beef and cook for
3 minutes, using a spatula to break up the meat. Select
Cancel and add the onion powder, garlic powder, chili
powder, tomato puree, ketchup, soy sauce, and brown
sugar. Stir to combine. Lock the lid. Select Manual and
cook at high pressure for 10 minutes. When the cook
time is complete, naturally release the pressure for
10 minutes, then quick-release the remaining pressure.
Remove the lid. Stir the mixture to make sure it's well
combined. Serve immediately, garnished with purple
slaw (if using) and parsley (if using).

Stuffed Peppers

SERVES 4 | PREP TIME: 10 minutes | MANUAL: 10 minutes
high pressure | RELEASE: Natural for 10 minutes, then
Quick | TOTAL TIME: 40 minutes

4 red or orange
bell peppers
1 pound lean (93 percent)
ground beef
1 cup marinara sauce
1 cup cooked brown rice

1 tablespoon Italian
seasoning
½ teaspoon kosher salt
1 cup water
¼ cup shredded mozza-
rella cheese

Cut the top off each pepper and remove the seeds; set
them aside. In a large bowl, combine the ground beef,
marinara sauce, brown rice, Italian seasoning, and salt.
Spoon the filling evenly into the peppers (if you have
enough of the beef mixture, fill them to the top). Pour
the water into the Instant Pot and insert the trivet.
Arrange the peppers, filling-side up, on the trivet.
Lock the lid. Select Manual and cook at high pressure
for 10 minutes. When the cook time is complete, let
the pressure release naturally for 10 minutes, then
quick-release any remaining pressure. Remove the lid
and top the stuffed peppers with mozzarella. Replace the
lid and let the peppers steam for 3 to 4 minutes to melt
the cheese.

Sweet and Sour Meatballs

SERVES 6 | PREP TIME: 5 minutes | SAUTÉ: 10 minutes |
MANUAL: 5 minutes high pressure | RELEASE: Quick |
TOTAL TIME: 25 minutes

2¼ cups pineapple
juice, divided
½ cup packed light
brown sugar
½ cup rice vinegar
¼ cup ketchup
1 tablespoon sriracha

1 tablespoon soy sauce
1 (24-ounce) bag frozen
meatballs
1 tablespoon cornstarch
1 cup drained
pine-apple chunks

Select Sauté and add 2 cups of pineapple juice, the
brown sugar, vinegar, ketchup, sriracha, and soy sauce.
Stir and bring to a boil. Select Cancel and add the frozen
meatballs. Lock the lid. Select Manual and cook at high
pressure for 5 minutes. When the cook time is complete, quick-release the pressure. In a small bowl, whisk
together the remaining ¼ cup of pineapple juice and the
cornstarch until smooth to make a slurry. Select Sauté
and add the pineapple chunks and cornstarch slurry.
Mix well and cook until the sauce thickens, about
5 minutes.

Barbecue Little Smokies with Bacon

SERVES 6 | PREP TIME: 5 minutes | SAUTÉ: 5 minutes |
MANUAL: 3 minutes high pressure | RELEASE: Quick |
TOTAL TIME: 28 minutes

½ pound thick-cut
bacon, chopped
½ cup water
1 (28-ounce) bottle
barbecue sauce

1 (16-ounce) jar grape jelly
2 (14-ounce) packages
little smokies

Select Sauté, and when the Instant Pot is hot, cook the
bacon until crispy, about 5 minutes. Add the water and
deglaze the pot, stirring to scrape up the browned bits
from the bottom. Add the barbecue sauce and jelly.
Stir to combine and then add the little smokies. Make
sure the little smokies are covered with sauce. Select
Cancel. Lock the lid. Select Manual and cook at high
pressure for 3 minutes. When the cook time is complete,
quick-release the pressure. Remove the lid. Give everything a quick stir before serving.

Bacon and Portobello Fajitas

SERVES 6 | PREP TIME: 5 minutes | SAUTÉ: 9 minutes |
MANUAL: 5 minutes high pressure | RELEASE: Quick |
TOTAL TIME: 20 minutes

6 bacon slices, cut into
1-inch pieces
1 medium white onion,
thinly sliced
3 roasted poblano pep-
pers, peeled, seeded, and
cut into thin strips
2 red bell peppers, seeded
and thinly sliced

4 portobello mushrooms,
stemmed and
thinly sliced
1 teaspoon ground cumin
½ teaspoon freshly ground
black pepper
Coarse salt
1½ cups shredded
Manchego cheese

Warm flour tortillas, for
serving (optional)
Guacamole, for garnish

Sour cream, for garnish
Salsa, for garnish

Select Sauté and adjust to More for high. Fry the bacon in the pot for 4 to 6 minutes, or until golden and crisp. Add the onion, poblano peppers, and bell peppers. Sauté for 2 to 3 minutes, or until the onion is translucent. Add the portobello mushrooms and season with the cumin, black pepper, and salt. Select Cancel. Lock the lid. Select Manual and cook at high pressure for 5 minutes. When the cook time is complete, quick-release the pressure. Remove the lid. Sprinkle the Manchego cheese over the portobello mushrooms and peppers. Let set for 5 minutes, or until the cheese has melted completely. Serve with warm flour tortillas (if using). Garnish with guacamole, sour cream, and your favorite salsa.

Mexican-Style Wedding Pork Roast

SERVES 6 to 8 | PREP TIME: 10 minutes | SAUTÉ: 10 minutes | MANUAL: 30 minutes high pressure | RELEASE: Natural | TOTAL TIME: 1 hour 15 minutes

2 tablespoons lard or vegetable oil
2¼ pounds pork loin, cut into 2-inch pieces
1 (3-ounce) Mexican chocolate tablet, cut into 8 wedges
1¼ cups water, divided
2 cups red enchilada sauce
¼ cup sugar
1 tablespoon finely grated orange zest

1 teaspoon coarse salt
1 teaspoon ground cinnamon
½ teaspoon freshly ground black pepper
¼ teaspoon ground cloves
2 bay leaves
3 tablespoons masa harina
Cooked rice, for serving
Refried beans, for serving
Warm corn tortillas, for serving

Select Sauté and adjust to More for high. Heat the lard in the pot, add the pork loin, and sauté, stirring occasionally, for 6 to 8 minutes, or until light golden brown. Transfer the pork to a heatproof plate. In the Instant Pot, heat the chocolate for 1 to 2 minutes, or until it just starts to soften. Stir in 1 cup of water. Continue to cook, stirring constantly, until the chocolate has melted completely. Stir in the enchilada sauce, sugar, orange zest, salt, cinnamon, pepper, and cloves. Return the pork loin to the pot. Top with the bay leaves. Select Cancel. Lock the lid. Select Manual and cook at high pressure for 30 minutes. When the cook time is complete, allow the pressure to release naturally. Remove the lid. Remove and discard the bay leaves. In a small bowl, dissolve the masa harina in ¼ cup of water. Immediately stir into the pork mixture in the Instant Pot. Serve with rice, beans, and warm corn tortillas.

Pork Carnitas

SERVES 6 to 8 | PREP TIME: 10 minutes | SAUTÉ: 10 minutes | MANUAL: 25 minutes high pressure | RELEASE: Natural | TOTAL TIME: 1 hour 10 minutes

2 tablespoons manteca (pork lard) or vegetable oil
2¼ pounds pork shoulder roast or Boston butt, cut into 2-inch pieces
1 teaspoon coarse salt
1 teaspoon ground cumin

½ teaspoon freshly ground black pepper
1 cup freshly squeezed orange juice
¼ cup freshly squeezed lime juice
2 bay leaves

Select Sauté and adjust to More for high. Heat the manteca in the pot until completely melted. Add the pork and fry for 6 to 8 minutes, or until light golden brown. Season with the salt, cumin, and pepper. Add the orange and lime juices and top with the bay leaves. Lock the lid. Select Manual and cook at high pressure for 25 minutes. When the cook time is complete, allow the pressure to release naturally. Remove the lid. Remove and discard the bay leaves. Using two forks, shred the pork carnitas in the pot.

Pork Chile Colorado

SERVES 6 to 8 | PREP TIME: 10 minutes | SAUTÉ: 12 minutes | MANUAL: 25 minutes high pressure | RELEASE: Natural | TOTAL TIME: 1 hour 15 minutes

2 tablespoons manteca (pork lard) or vegetable oil
2¼ pounds pork loin, cut in 1-inch chunks
½ medium onion, thinly sliced
3 garlic cloves, minced
¾ teaspoon coarse salt
½ teaspoon freshly ground black pepper

1½ cups roughly chopped cooked nopales
1½ cups cooked pinto beans
¼ cup masa harina
1 cup water
2 cups enchilada sauce
Warm corn tortillas, for serving (optional)

Select Sauté and adjust to More for high. Heat the manteca in the pot until completely melted. Add the pork loin and fry for 6 to 8 minutes, or until lightly golden brown. Stir in the onion and garlic. Sauté for 2 to 3 minutes, or just until the onion is translucent. Season with the salt and pepper. Add the cooked nopales and pinto beans. In a small bowl, mix the masa harina with the water. Pour into the Instant Pot and add the enchilada sauce. Select Cancel. Lock the lid. Select Manual and cook at high pressure for 25 minutes. When the cook time is complete, allow the pressure to release naturally. Remove the lid. Serve the pork immediately with warm corn tortillas (if using).

Pork Chile Verde

SERVES 6 to 8 | PREP TIME: 10 minutes | SAUTÉ: 12 minutes | MANUAL: 25 minutes high pressure | RELEASE: Natural | TOTAL TIME: 1 hour 10 minutes

2 tablespoons manteca (pork lard) or vegetable oil

2 ½ pounds pork loin, cut into 2-inch pieces

¾ teaspoon coarse salt

¼ teaspoon freshly ground black pepper

½ medium white onion, thinly sliced

3 garlic cloves, minced

2 ears corn, husks removed, cut into 2-inch pieces

6 medium Mexican calabacitas, cut into 1-inch slices

2 cups green enchilada sauce

½ cup water

Warm corn tortillas, for serving (optional)

Refried beans, for serving (optional)

Select Sauté and adjust to More for high. Heat the manteca in the pot until completely melted. Add the pork and fry for 6 to 8 minutes, or until light golden brown. Season with the salt and pepper. Add the onion and garlic. Sauté for an additional 2 to 3 minutes, or just until the onion is translucent. Add the corn, calabacitas, enchilada sauce, and the water. Stir gently to combine. Lock the lid. Select Manual and cook at high pressure for 25 minutes. When the cook time is complete, allow the pressure to release naturally. Remove the lid. Serve the pork immediately with warm corn tortillas (if using) and refried beans (if using).

Honey Mustard Pork Tenderloin

SERVES 6 | PREP AND FINISHING: 10 minutes | SAUTÉ: 10 minutes, divided | MANUAL: 8 minutes high pressure | RELEASE: Natural for 10 minutes, then Quick | TOTAL TIME: 48 minutes

½ cup water

2 tablespoons cornstarch

2 tablespoons extra-virgin olive oil

2 pounds pork tenderloin

1 cup chicken broth

3 garlic cloves, minced

¼ cup honey

2 tablespoons Dijon mustard

½ teaspoon fine sea salt

¼ teaspoon freshly ground black pepper

In a small bowl, make a slurry by whisking together the water and cornstarch. Set it aside. Select Sauté on the Instant Pot and pour in the olive oil. Once the oil is hot, add the pork and brown it for 2 minutes per side. Select Cancel. Using tongs, transfer the pork to a plate. Pour the broth into the pot. Using a wooden spoon, scrape up any browned bits stuck to the bottom of the pot. Add the garlic, honey, mustard, salt, and pepper. Stir to combine. Place the trivet inside the pot. Use the tongs to place the pork on the trivet. Lock the lid. Select Manual and cook at high pressure for 8 minutes. When the cook time is complete, naturally release the pressure for 10 minutes,

then quick-release any remaining pressure. Remove the lid. Select Sauté. Using clean tongs, transfer the pork to a cutting board. Whisk the cornstarch slurry into the liquid and cook, uncovered, for about 5 minutes or until the sauce starts to thicken. Carefully pour the sauce into a small pitcher or glass bowl. Using a sharp knife, slice the pork into 6 servings. Serve the pork with the sauce.

Sweet and Sour Pork

SERVES 6 | PREP AND FINISHING: 15 minutes | SAUTÉ: 10 minutes, divided | MANUAL: 8 minutes high pressure | RELEASE: Natural for 10 minutes, then Quick | TOTAL TIME: 53 minutes

½ cup water

2 tablespoons cornstarch

1 tablespoon extra-virgin olive oil

2 pounds boneless pork shoulder, cut into 1-inch pieces

1 medium yellow onion, chopped

2 garlic cloves, minced

1¼ cups freshly squeezed orange juice

2 tablespoons tomato paste

⅓ cup reduced-sodium soy sauce

¼ cup white wine vinegar

¼ cup honey

2 red bell peppers, seeded and sliced

In a small bowl, make a slurry by whisking together the water and cornstarch. Set it aside. Select Sauté and pour in the olive oil. Once the oil is hot, add the pork, onion, and garlic and sauté for 3 minutes, stirring occasionally. Select Cancel and add the orange juice. Using a wooden spoon, scrape up any browned bits stuck to the bottom of the pot. Add the tomato paste, soy sauce, vinegar, honey, and bell peppers and stir to combine. Lock the lid. Select Manual and cook at high pressure for 8 minutes. When the cook time is complete, naturally release the pressure for 10 minutes, then quick-release any remaining pressure. Remove the lid. Select Sauté. Using a slotted spoon, transfer the pork and vegetables to a serving bowl. Whisk the cornstarch slurry into the liquid and let it simmer, uncovered, for 2 minutes or until the sauce starts to thicken. Place the pork and vegetables back in the pot and stir to combine. Serve immediately.

Tangy Vinegar Pork with Potatoes

SERVES 6 | PREP AND FINISHING: 15 minutes | SAUTÉ: 10 minutes, divided | MANUAL: 25 minutes high pressure | RELEASE: Natural for 10 minutes, then Quick | TOTAL TIME: 1 hour 10 minutes

½ cup water

2 tablespoons cornstarch

1 tablespoon extra-virgin olive oil

2 pounds boneless pork shoulder, cut into 1-inch cubes

2 garlic cloves, minced

1¼ cups chicken broth

⅓ cup reduced-sodium soy sauce

¼ cup white wine vinegar

2 tablespoons honey

½ teaspoon freshly ground black pepper	1 pound white potatoes, cut into 1-inch cubes

In a small bowl, make a slurry by whisking together the water and cornstarch. Set it aside. Select Sauté and pour in the olive oil. Once the oil is hot, add the pork and garlic and sauté for 3 minutes, stirring occasionally. Select Cancel and pour in the broth. Using a wooden spoon, scrape up any browned bits stuck to the bottom of the pot. Add the soy sauce, vinegar, honey, pepper, and potatoes to the pot and stir to combine. Lock the lid. Select Manual and cook at high pressure for 25 minutes. When the cook time is complete, naturally release the pressure for 10 minutes, then quick-release any remaining pressure. Remove the lid. Select Sauté. Using a slotted spoon, transfer the pork and potatoes to a serving plate. Once the liquid in the pot is bubbling, whisk in the cornstarch slurry. Let the sauce simmer, uncovered, for about 2 minutes or until the sauce starts to thicken. Return the pork and potatoes to the pot and stir to combine. Serve immediately.

Polish Sausage with Sauerkraut

SERVES 6 | PREP AND FINISHING: 10 minutes | SAUTÉ: 5 minutes | MANUAL: 10 minutes high pressure | RELEASE: Natural for 10 minutes, then Quick | TOTAL TIME: 45 minutes

1 tablespoon extra-virgin olive oil	1 (12-ounce) package fully cooked Polish sausage, cut into 1-inch-thick slices
1 medium yellow onion, chopped	
2 garlic cloves, minced	1 (32-ounce) jar sauerkraut
2 cups chicken broth	1 apple, chopped
	3 medium red potatoes, chopped into bite-size pieces

Select Sauté on the Instant Pot and pour in the olive oil. Once the oil is hot, add the onion and garlic and sauté for 3 minutes, stirring occasionally. Select Cancel and pour in the broth. Using a wooden spoon, scrape up any browned bits stuck to the bottom of the pot. Add the sausage slices, sauerkraut, apple, and potatoes and stir to combine. Lock the lid. Select Manual and cook at high pressure for 10 minutes. When the cook time is complete, naturally release the pressure for 10 minutes, then quick-release any remaining pressure. Remove the lid. Serve immediately.

Sausage and White Beans

SERVES 6 | PREP TIME: 10 minutes | SAUTÉ: 15 minutes | MANUAL: 40 minutes | RELEASE: Natural for 15 minutes, then Quick | TOTAL TIME: 1 hour 40 minutes

2 teaspoons extra-virgin olive oil	1 (4-inch) rosemary sprig
	¼ teaspoon dried oregano
2 pounds sweet Italian sausage	4 garlic cloves, pressed or minced
1 large onion, chopped	½ teaspoon freshly ground black pepper
1 large bay leaf	
4 carrots, chopped (about 1½ cups)	6 cups chicken broth
	3 tablespoons tomato paste
3 celery stalks, chopped (about 1 cup)	1 pound dried navy beans, rinsed and sorted
4 thyme sprigs or ½ teaspoon dried thyme	

Select Sauté and pour in the oil. When hot, add the sausage and cook until lightly browned on all sides, about 6 minutes. Add the onion, bay leaf, carrot, and celery and cook until the onion starts to turn translucent, about 5 minutes. Thoroughly scrape any browned bits from the bottom of the pot. Add the thyme, rosemary, oregano, and garlic. Cook until fragrant, about 1 minute. Add the pepper, broth, and tomato paste. Stir and bring to a simmer. Once simmering, add the beans and stir well. Select Cancel. Lock the lid. Select Manual and cook at high pressure for 40 minutes. When the cook time is complete, let the pressure release naturally for 15 minutes, then quick-release any remaining pressure. Taste a few beans for tenderness. If not yet tender enough, replace and lock the lid and cook for another 5 minutes. Remove the bay leaf and the thyme and rosemary sprigs and serve.

Brown Sugar Ham

SERVES 10 | PREP TIME: 5 minutes | MANUAL: 10 minutes | RELEASE: Quick | TOTAL TIME: 20 minutes

1 cup water	1 cup honey
1 (7½-pound) bone-in spiral ham	1 (20-ounce) can pineapple chunks in juice
1 cup packed light brown sugar	¼ teaspoon ground cloves

Place the trivet in the pot and then pour in the water. Place the ham on the trivet. In a small bowl, mix the brown sugar, honey, pineapple, and cloves to form a glaze. Brush the glaze onto the ham. Lock the lid. Select Manual and cook at high pressure for 10 minutes. When the cook time is complete, quick-release the pressure. Slice and serve.

Sweet and Smoky Ribs

SERVES 4 | PREP TIME: 5 minutes | MANUAL: 25 minutes high pressure | BROIL: 3 minutes | RELEASE: Natural for 15 minutes, then Quick | TOTAL TIME: 51 minutes

½ cup packed light brown sugar	1 tablespoon garlic powder
	1 tablespoon onion powder
1½ tablespoons paprika	1 tablespoon chili powder

1 tablespoon ground cumin
1 teaspoon freshly ground
   black pepper
2 teaspoons salt
1 rack (1½ to 2 pounds)
   baby back pork ribs

1½ cups apple juice
1 tablespoon liquid smoke
1 cup barbecue sauce
   of choice

In a small bowl, combine the brown sugar, paprika, garlic powder, onion powder, chili powder, cumin, pepper, and salt to make a dry rub. Mix well. Pat the ribs dry with a paper towel, then remove the thin silvery membrane from the back of the ribs by loosening it with a knife and peeling it off. Generously season both sides of the ribs with the dry rub. Set the trivet in the Instant Pot and pour in the apple juice and liquid smoke. Add the ribs, standing them vertically and curling them around the pot to fit. Lock the lid. Select Manual and cook at high pressure for 25 minutes. When the cook time is complete, let the pressure release naturally for 15 minutes, then quick-release any remaining pressure. Heat the broiler. Place the ribs on a foil-lined baking sheet and brush them with the barbecue sauce. Broil for about 3 minutes, or until slightly browned.

Root Beer Pulled Pork

SERVES 8 | PREP TIME: 5 minutes | SAUTÉ: 20 minutes | MANUAL: 50 minutes high pressure | RELEASE: Natural for 10 minutes, then Quick | TOTAL TIME: 1 hour 35 minutes

1 tablespoon salt
1 tablespoon onion powder
1 tablespoon garlic powder
1 tablespoon liquid smoke
1 (4-pound) pork
   shoulder roast

2 teaspoons extra-virgin
   olive oil
1 small onion, diced
2 cups root beer soda
1 cup barbecue sauce, plus
   more for serving
2 or 3 dashes hot sauce

In a small dish, mix the salt, onion powder, garlic powder, and liquid smoke. Pat the pork roast dry with paper towels and cut it into 4 large chunks, trimming off and discarding any large pieces of fat. Season the roast on all sides with the spice mix. Select Sauté, and when the Instant Pot is hot, pour in the oil. Sear the pork on all sides, about 3 minutes per side; then transfer it to a plate and set aside. Add the onion to the pot and cook until it starts to turn translucent, 3 to 5 minutes. Select Cancel and allow the pot to cool for 3 to 4 minutes. Return the pork to the pot. In a bowl, mix the root beer, barbecue sauce, and hot sauce, then pour over the pork. Lock the lid. Select Manual and cook at high pressure for 50 minutes. When the cook time is complete, let the pressure release naturally for 10 minutes, then quick-release any remaining pressure. Remove the pork and shred it with two forks. Spoon ½ cup of the cooking liquid over the pork and allow it to soak in.

Pork Tinga Tostadas

SERVES 6 to 8 | PREP TIME: 10 minutes | SAUTÉ: 10 minutes | MANUAL: 25 minutes high pressure | RELEASE: Natural | TOTAL TIME: 1 hour 10 minutes

1 (28-ounce) can mild green
   enchilada sauce
2 or 3 canned chipotles
   chiles in adobo sauce
1 tablespoon vegetable oil
8 ounces Mexican
   pork chorizo
1 medium white onion,
   thinly sliced
2 garlic cloves, minced

2¼ pounds pork loin, cut
   into 2-inch pieces
¾ teaspoon coarse salt
¼ teaspoon freshly ground
   black pepper
Tostada shells, for serving
Shredded lettuce,
   for garnish
Mexican crema, for garnish
Crumbled queso cotija,
   for garnish

In a blender, puree the enchilada sauce and chipotle chiles until smooth. Select Sauté and adjust to More for high. Heat the vegetable oil in the pot, add the chorizo, and fry for 5 to 7 minutes, breaking up the meat with the back of a wooden spoon, until cooked through. Stir in the onion and garlic and sauté for 2 to 3 minutes, or until the onion is translucent. Pour in the chipotle puree. Add the pork loin. Season with the salt and black pepper. Select Cancel. Lock the lid. Select Manual and cook at high pressure for 25 minutes. When the cook time is complete, allow the pressure to release naturally. Remove the lid. Using two forks, shred the pork meat. Spoon 3 or 4 heaping tablespoonfuls of pork atop each tostada shell. Garnish with shredded lettuce, Mexican crema, and crumbled queso cotija.

Pibil-Style Pork

SERVES 6 to 8 | PREP TIME: 10 minutes | MANUAL: 30 minutes high pressure | RELEASE: Natural | TOTAL TIME: 50 minutes

2 ounces ground achiote
1¼ cups freshly squeezed
   orange juice
½ cup freshly squeezed
   lime juice
3 tablespoons
   white vinegar
3 garlic cloves, minced
2¼ pounds pork loin, cut
   into 2-inch pieces
1 teaspoon coarse salt
1 teaspoon ground cumin

½ teaspoon freshly ground
   black pepper
½ teaspoon ground
   cinnamon
½ teaspoon dried oregano
1 medium onion,
   thinly sliced
1 banana leaf
Warm corn tortillas, for
   serving (optional)
Pickled red onions,
   for garnish

In a medium glass bowl, mix the ground achiote, orange juice, lime juice, vinegar, and garlic. Stir in the pork, mixing until completely coated with the marinade. Season with the salt, cumin, pepper, cinnamon, and oregano. Add the onion. Transfer the pork mixture to the Instant Pot. On a comal or griddle, warm the banana leaf over medium-high heat for 2 to 3 minutes, turning occasionally, until soft and pliable. Remove it from the heat. Arrange the banana leaf on top of the pork mixture. Lock the lid. Select Manual and cook at high pressure for 30 minutes. When the cook time is complete, allow the pressure to release naturally. Remove the lid. Carefully remove the banana leaf. Using two forks, shred the pork meat. Serve atop warm corn tortillas (if using). Garnish with pickled red onions.

Pork in Chile Sauce

SERVES 6 to 8 | PREP TIME: 10 minutes | SAUTÉ: 8 minutes | MANUAL: 30 minutes high pressure | RELEASE: Natural | TOTAL TIME: 1 hour 5 minutes

2 tablespoons manteca (pork lard) or vegetable oil	4 garlic cloves, minced
	6 cilantro sprigs
2¼ pounds pork loin, cut into 2-inch pieces	2 cups tomato sauce
	1½ cups spicy salsa
1½ teaspoons coarse salt	2 cups water
½ teaspoon freshly ground black pepper	Refried beans, for serving (optional)
½ medium white onion	Warm corn tortillas, for serving (optional)

Select Sauté and adjust to More for high. Heat the manteca in the pot until completely melted. Add the pork loin and sauté, stirring occasionally, for 6 to 8 minutes, or until light golden brown. Season with the salt and pepper. Add the onion, garlic, and cilantro. Stir in the tomato sauce, salsa, and water. Select Cancel. Lock the lid. Select Manual and cook at high pressure for 30 minutes. When the cook time is complete, allow the pressure to release naturally. Remove the lid. Stir gently to combine. Serve with beans (if using) and warm corn tortillas (if using).

Mole Pulled Pork Sliders

SERVES 6 to 8 | PREP TIME: 10 minutes | SAUTÉ: 5 minutes | MANUAL: 30 minutes high pressure | RELEASE: Natural | TOTAL TIME: 1 hour 10 minutes

2 tablespoons vegetable oil	¼ teaspoon ground cloves
1 (8¼-ounce) jar mole paste	¼ teaspoon ground cinnamon
2 cups chicken broth	2¼ pounds pork loin, cut into 3- to 4-inch pieces
2 cups water	Hawaiian rolls, for serving
6 tablespoons sugar	Pickled red onions, for garnish
1 teaspoon coarse salt	
½ teaspoon freshly ground black pepper	

Select Sauté and adjust to More for high. Heat the vegetable oil in the pot. Stir in the mole paste, stirring constantly for 3 to 5 minutes, or until completely melted into the oil. Whisk in the chicken broth and water until completely combined into a velvety sauce. Season with

the sugar, salt, pepper, cloves, and cinnamon. Add the pork loin, making sure each piece is coated with the mole sauce. Lock the lid. Select Manual and cook at high pressure for 30 minutes. When the cook time is complete, allow the pressure to release naturally. Remove the lid. Using two forks, shred the pork loin. Split the Hawaiian rolls in half crosswise. On a comal or griddle, toast the rolls over medium heat for 2 to 3 minutes, or until light golden brown. Spoon 2 or 3 heaping tablespoons of the mole pulled pork onto the bottom half of each roll. Garnish with pickled onions. Set the top half of the rolls in place and serve.

Pulled Pork Ragu

SERVES 6 | PREP TIME: 10 minutes | MANUAL: 45 minutes high pressure | RELEASE: Natural for 15 minutes, then Quick | TOTAL TIME: 1 hour 10 minutes

1 tablespoon extra-virgin olive oil	3 carrots, cut into ½-inch chunks
1½ pounds pork tenderloin, cut into 3-inch chunks	3 shallots or 1 small onion, chopped
1 (28-ounce) can crushed tomatoes	3 garlic cloves, minced
	1 tablespoon Italian seasoning
½ cup water	

In the Instant Pot, combine the olive oil, pork, crushed tomatoes with their juices, water, carrots, shallots, garlic, and Italian seasoning. Lock the lid. Select Manual and cook on high pressure for 45 minutes. When the cook time is complete, naturally release the pressure for at least 15 minutes, while the continues to cook, then quick-release any remaining pressure. Remove the lid, transfer the pork to a medium bowl, and shred it using two forks. Return the pork to the sauce and serve.

Southwestern Pork and Hominy Stew

SERVES 4 | PREP AND FINISHING: 20 minutes | MANUAL: 30 minutes high pressure | RELEASE: Natural for 10 minutes, then Quick | TOTAL TIME: 1 hour 10 minutes, plus overnight to soak

8 ounces dried hominy (pozole)	1 pound tomatillos, husked and diced (about 2 cups)
1½ pounds boneless country-style pork ribs, trimmed of excess fat	¼ cup canned diced green chiles, drained
	1 medium jalapeño, seeded and chopped
1½ teaspoons kosher salt, divided, plus more as needed	¼ teaspoon ground cumin
	4 cups chicken broth
2 tablespoons vegetable oil	1 avocado, peeled, pitted, and chopped
1 small onion, sliced (about 1 cup)	2 tablespoons chopped fresh cilantro
2 garlic cloves, minced	
½ cup mild beer, such as a lager or pale ale	

In a large bowl, cover the dried hominy with about 2 inches of water. Soak at room temperature for 8 to 24 hours. Drain and rinse, then drain again. Sprinkle the ribs on both sides with ½ teaspoon of salt. Select Sauté and adjust to More for high heat. Heat the oil until it shimmers. Add the ribs in a single layer and cook, undisturbed, until browned, about 3 minutes. Flip the ribs and repeat on the second side. Transfer the ribs to a plate. Add the onion and garlic and cook, stirring occasionally, until starting to brown, about 3 minutes. Add the beer and cook, scraping up any browned bits from the bottom of the pot. Let the beer simmer until it has reduced by about half, about 4 minutes. Select Cancel. Add the tomatillos, green chiles, jalapeño, cumin, remaining 1 teaspoon of salt, and broth to the pot. Add the hominy to the pot along with the browned ribs. Lock the lid. Select Manual and cook at high pressure for 30 minutes. When the cook time is complete, naturally release the pressure for 10 minutes, then quick-release any remaining pressure. Remove the lid. Remove the pork from the stew and shred it with two forks, discarding any fat or gristle. Return the meat to the pot. Blot or skim any fat from the surface of the stew. Taste and adjust the seasoning, adding more salt if necessary. Ladle the stew into bowls, top with the avocado and cilantro, and serve.

Pork Tenderloin with Cabbage and Noodles

SERVES 4 | PREP AND FINISHING: 20 minutes | SAUTÉ: 16 minutes | MANUAL: 4 minutes low pressure | RELEASE: Quick | TOTAL TIME: 40 minutes

3 bacon slices, chopped
1 medium pork tenderloin (about 1¼ pounds)
1½ teaspoons kosher salt, divided, plus more as needed
¼ teaspoon freshly ground black pepper, plus more as needed

1 teaspoon smoked or regular paprika
1 small onion, sliced (about 1 cup)
½ very small green cabbage, shredded (3 to 4 cups)
⅓ cup dry white wine
1¼ cups chicken broth
4 ounces wide egg noodles

Select Sauté and adjust to Normal for medium heat. Cook the bacon until most of the fat has rendered and the bacon is crisp, about 6 minutes. Use a slotted spoon to remove the bacon, and drain on paper towels, leaving the rendered fat in the pot. Cut the tenderloin in half crosswise. Sprinkle the halves with 1 teaspoon of salt, the pepper, and paprika. With the rendered fat in the pot, adjust to More for high heat. When the fat is hot, add the two pieces of pork tenderloin and sear, undisturbed, until browned, 2 to 3 minutes, then turn and sear the other sides. Transfer to a plate. Add the onion and cabbage to the pot and stir to coat with the remaining fat. Cook, stirring frequently, until the vegetables start to soften, about 2 minutes. Add the wine and bring

to a simmer, scraping up any browned bits from the bottom of the pot. Let the wine reduce slightly. Select Cancel. Add the chicken broth and noodles and stir to cover the noodles with the liquid (add more broth if the noodles are not submerged). Place the pork tenderloin halves on top of the vegetables and noodles. Lock the lid. Select Manual and cook at low pressure for 4 minutes. When the cook time is complete, quick-release the pressure. Remove the lid. Check the temperature of the pork; it should be about 145°F. If it is much lower than that, put it back with the noodles and put the lid on but don't lock it into place. Check it again in a couple of minutes. When it's done, transfer the pork to a cutting board and let it rest for a couple of minutes. Taste the noodles and cabbage and adjust the seasoning, adding more salt and pepper, if necessary, then spoon into a serving dish. Slice the pork and serve with the cabbage and noodles

Pork Loin Braised in Milk

SERVES 4 | PREP AND FINISHING: 25 minutes | SAUTÉ: 20 minutes, divided | MANUAL: 10 minutes low pressure | RELEASE: Natural for 12 minutes, then Quick | TOTAL TIME: 55 minutes

1 (2- to 2½-pound) pork loin
1 teaspoon kosher salt
½ teaspoon freshly ground black pepper
2 tablespoons vegetable oil
⅓ cup chicken broth
2 cups whole milk

¼ cup heavy (whipping) cream
½ teaspoon dried sage
3 small onions, quartered
2 large garlic cloves, peeled
2 tablespoons chopped fresh parsley

Select Sauté and adjust to More. Heat the oil until it shimmers. Add the pork to the pot, fat-side down. Let it cook, undisturbed, until the fat side is golden brown, about 4 minutes. Flip the pork and brown the other side for 3 minutes. Turn and brown the sides for about 2 minutes each. Transfer the pork to a plate. Pour off all the fat and pour in the chicken broth and scrape the bottom of the pot to release the browned bits. Pour the milk and cream into the Instant Pot. Stir in the sage. Add the pork, fat-side up, and the onion and garlic. Select Cancel. Lock the lid. Select Manual and cook at low pressure for 10 minutes. When the cook time is complete, naturally release the pressure for 12 minutes, then manually release any remaining pressure. Remove the lid. Check the temperature of the center of the pork. It should read between 110°F and 115°F. Select Sauté and adjust to Less for low heat. Bring the sauce to a simmer and cook the pork in the sauce for 3 to 5 minutes. Flip the pork and simmer for another 2 to 3 minutes, then check the temperature again. You're looking for a temperature of about 145°F in the center of the pork. Simmer a little longer if necessary until it reaches the correct temperature. Transfer the pork to a cutting board and allow it to rest for several minutes.

Finish the sauce by blending it until smooth with an immersion blender. Slice the pork and place it on a serving platter. Spoon the sauce over the slices, sprinkle with the parsley, and serve.

Smothered Pork Chops

SERVES 4 | PREP AND FINISHING: 20 minutes | SAUTÉ: 6 minutes | MANUAL: 1 minute low pressure | RELEASE: Natural for 4 minutes, then Quick | TOTAL TIME: 30 minutes

4 boneless pork loin chops, about 1½ inches thick
1½ teaspoons kosher salt, divided, plus more as needed
2 tablespoons vegetable oil
1 large onion, sliced thin (about 1½ cups)
8 ounces white button or cremini mushrooms, sliced

½ teaspoon dried thyme
¼ teaspoon freshly ground black pepper, plus more as needed
½ cup dry white wine
1 cup chicken broth
1 tablespoon all-purpose flour
2 teaspoons Worcestershire sauce
2 tablespoons sour cream

Sprinkle the pork chops on both sides with 1 teaspoon of salt. Heat a large, heavy skillet on the stove over medium-high heat. Heat the oil until it shimmers. Add the chops and let them cook, undisturbed, until golden brown, about 3 minutes. Flip the chops and brown the other side for 3 minutes. Transfer the chops to a plate. Add the onion to the pot and cook, stirring frequently, until the onion pieces start to separate and soften, 2 to 3 minutes. Add the mushrooms and sprinkle with the remaining ½ teaspoon of salt, the thyme, and the pepper. Cook, stirring occasionally, until the mushrooms are soft and starting to brown, 2 to 3 minutes. Add the wine and scrape the bottom of the pot to release the browned bits. Let the wine simmer until reduced by about half. Select Cancel. In a medium bowl, whisk together the chicken broth, flour, and Worcestershire sauce. Add to the Instant Pot and stir to combine with the onions and mushrooms. Transfer the chops to the pot and spoon some of the onion mixture over them. Lock the lid. Select Manual and cook at low pressure for 1 minute. When the cook time is complete, naturally release the pressure for 4 minutes, then quick-release any remaining pressure. Remove the lid. Transfer the pork chops to a serving platter. Add the sour cream to the sauce and stir to combine. Taste and adjust the seasoning, adding more salt or pepper if necessary. Spoon the sauce over the chops and serve.

Jerk Pork Shoulder

SERVES 4 | PREP AND FINISHING: 20 minutes | SAUTÉ: 11 minutes, divided | MANUAL: 25 minutes high pressure | RELEASE: Natural for 10 minutes, then Quick | TOTAL TIME: 1 hour

FOR THE PORK
2½ pounds boneless country-style pork ribs
1½ teaspoons kosher salt, plus more as needed

2 tablespoons vegetable oil
½ cup chicken broth

FOR THE JERK SAUCE
½ cup mild beer, such as a lager or pale ale
2 tablespoons sherry vinegar
1 habanero chile, seeded and minced
2 garlic cloves, minced
2 tablespoons grated peeled ginger

2 tablespoons packed light brown sugar
2 teaspoons ground allspice
1½ teaspoons kosher salt
1 teaspoon dried thyme
½ teaspoon ground cinnamon

TO MAKE THE PORK

Sprinkle the pork with the salt. Select Sauté and adjust to More for high heat. Heat the oil until it shimmers. Add the pork in a single layer and cook, undisturbed, until browned, about 3 minutes. Flip the meat and repeat on the other side. Transfer the pork to a plate.

TO MAKE THE JERK SAUCE

Pour the chicken broth into the pot and stir, scraping up any browned bits from the bottom of the pot. Select Cancel. In a small bowl, whisk the beer, vinegar, chile, garlic, ginger, brown sugar, allspice, salt, thyme, and cinnamon. Add the sauce along with the browned pork to the Instant Pot. Lock the lid. Select Manual and cook at high pressure for 25 minutes. When the cook time is complete, naturally release the pressure for 10 minutes, then quick-release any remaining pressure. Remove the lid.

Transfer the pork to a plate or cutting board and cut it into chunks, discarding any fat or gristle. Pour the sauce into a fat separator and let it rest until the fat rises to the surface. Pour the sauce back into the pot. (If you don't have a fat separator, let the sauce sit for a few minutes, then spoon or blot off any excess fat from the top of the sauce, then return the sauce to the pot.) Select Sauté and adjust to More for high heat. Bring the sauce to a boil and cook until it has thickened to a gravy consistency, about 5 minutes. Taste and adjust the seasoning, adding more salt if necessary. Return the pork to the pot and simmer t in the sauce for a few minutes to warm through. Serve.

Hawaiian Pineapple Pork

SERVES 6 | PREP AND FINISHING: 10 minutes | SAUTÉ: 5 minutes | MANUAL: 10 minutes high pressure | RELEASE: Natural for 10 minutes, then Quick | TOTAL TIME: 45 minutes

2 tablespoons extra-virgin olive oil

2 pounds pork loin, cut into 1-inch chunks

1 medium yellow onion, chopped

3 garlic cloves, minced

1 (20-ounce) can pineapple chunks in juice

2 red bell peppers, seeded and chopped

¼ cup reduced-sodium soy sauce

2 tablespoons packed light brown sugar

¼ teaspoon chili powder

Select Sauté pour in the olive oil. Once the oil is hot, add the pork, onion, and garlic. Sauté for 4 minutes, stirring occasionally to brown the pork on all sides. Select Cancel and add the pineapple with its juices. Using a wooden spoon, scrape up any browned bits stuck to the bottom of the pot. Add the bell peppers, soy sauce, brown sugar, and chili powder. Stir to combine. Lock the lid. Select Manual and cook at high pressure for 10 minutes. When the cook time is complete, naturally release the pressure for 10 minutes, then quick-release any remaining pressure. Remove the lid. Serve immediately.

Moroccan-Style Lamb Tagine

SERVES 6 to 8 | PREP TIME: 15 minutes | SAUTÉ: 10 minutes | MANUAL: 20 minutes high pressure | RELEASE: Natural for 15 minutes, then Quick | TOTAL TIME: 1 hour 15 minutes

2 tablespoons ground ginger

2 tablespoons packed light brown sugar

1 tablespoon ground cumin

1 tablespoon ground turmeric

2 teaspoons salt

1 teaspoon allspice

1 teaspoon ground cinnamon

½ teaspoon cayenne pepper

2 pounds boneless lamb shoulder, cut into 1-inch cubes

2 tablespoons canola oil

1 yellow onion, diced

2 carrots, diced

2 celery stalks, diced

½ cup sliced dried apricots

½ cup sliced dried figs

½ cup toasted slivered almonds

4 cups chicken or vegetable broth

In a shallow dish, combine the ginger, brown sugar, cumin, turmeric, salt, allspice, cinnamon, and cayenne. Pat the lamb shoulder dry with paper towels. Add it to the spice mixture and toss gently to coat the outside in the spice blend. Select Sauté. Heat the oil in the Instant Pot. Once hot, add the lamb and sear until browned on all sides, about 10 minutes. Add the onions, carrots, celery, apricots, figs, almonds, and broth to the pot. Stir to combine. Select Cancel. Lock the lid. Select Manual

and cook at high pressure for 20 minutes. When the cook time is complete, let the pressure naturally release for 15 minutes, then quick-release any remaining pressure. Remove the lid. Serve immediately.

Braised Lamb with Apricots

SERVES 6 | PREP TIME: 10 minutes | SAUTÉ: 8 minutes | MANUAL: 35 minutes | RELEASE: Natural for 10 minutes, then Quick | TOTAL TIME: 1 hour 10 minutes

1 tablespoon extra-virgin olive oil

1½ pounds lamb stew meat, cut into 1-inch cubes

2 tablespoons balsamic vinegar

1¼ cups water

1 (15½-ounce) can chickpeas, drained and rinsed

1 cup crushed tomatoes

½ cup unsulfured dried apricots, quartered

1 red onion, diced

1 lemon, thinly sliced

1 cinnamon stick

½ teaspoon kosher salt

½ teaspoon ground coriander

¼ cup fresh parsley, chopped

Select Sauté and pour in the olive oil. When the oil is hot, add the lamb and cook for 5 to 8 minutes, stirring occasionally, until browned. Stir in the vinegar and scrape up any browned bits from the bottom of the pot. Select Cancel. Add the water, chickpeas, tomatoes with their juices, apricots, onion, lemon, cinnamon stick, salt, and coriander. Lock the lid. Select Manual and cook at high pressure for 35 minutes. When the cook time is complete, let the pressure release naturally for 10 minutes, then quick-release any remaining pressure. Remove the lid and remove the cinnamon stick. Stir in the parsley and serve.

Lamb Gyros

SERVES 4 | PREP TIME: 15 minutes | MANUAL: 25 minutes high pressure | SAUTÉ: 6 minutes | RELEASE: Natural for 10 minutes, then Quick | TOTAL TIME: 1 hour

1 pound ground lamb

½ red onion, finely chopped

2 teaspoons dried marjoram

2 teaspoons dried crushed rosemary

2 teaspoons dried oregano

¾ teaspoon kosher salt, divided

½ cup water

1 cup full-fat plain Greek yogurt

1 tablespoon red wine vinegar

2 teaspoons freshly chopped dill

1 small cucumber, shredded

1 tablespoon extra-virgin olive oil

4 whole wheat pitas, warmed

In a medium bowl, combine the lamb, onion, marjoram, rosemary, oregano, and ½ teaspoon of salt. Press the meat mixture into a large square, about 5 inches wide and 1½ inches thick. Place the loaf on a piece of foil, then fold up the sides of the foil to catch the juices. Do not cover. Pour the water into the Instant Pot and insert the trivet. Place the foil with the lamb on top of the trivet and lock the lid in place. Select Manual and cook at high pressure for 25 minutes. Meanwhile, in a small bowl, combine the yogurt, vinegar, dill, and the remaining ¼ teaspoon of salt. Fold in the cucumber and set it aside. When the cook time is complete, let the pressure release naturally for 10 minutes, then quick-release any remaining pressure. Select Cancel. Remove the lid and lift out the gyro meat and foil. Empty the liquid from the bottom of the pot and wipe it dry. Select Sauté and adjust to More for high. Pour in the oil. When the oil is hot, add the gyro meat and cook for 3 minutes on each side, until browned. Remove the meat from the pot and slice it into very thin strips. Serve the sliced gyro meat in the pitas and top them with yogurt sauce.

Italian-Style Lamb Shanks with White Beans

SERVES 4 | PREP AND FINISHING: 25 minutes | SAUTÉ: 18 minutes, divided | MANUAL: 45 minutes high pressure, divided | RELEASE: Natural for 20 minutes, then Quick, divided | TOTAL TIME: 1 hour 35 minutes, plus overnight to soak

1 tablespoon plus 2 teaspoons kosher salt, divided	2 garlic cloves, minced
	2 large carrots, 1 quartered and 1 coarsely chopped
1 quart water	1 small fennel bulb, quartered, fronds reserved (optional)
8 ounces dried cannellini or great northern beans	
4 (10-ounce) lamb shanks	2 cups chicken broth, plus more as needed
2 tablespoons extra-virgin olive oil	1 medium tomato, seeded and chopped
½ cup dry white wine or dry white vermouth	Freshly ground black pepper
1 bay leaf	
1 medium onion, quartered	

In a large bowl, dissolve 1 tablespoon of salt in the water. Add the beans and soak at room temperature for 8 to 24 hours. Rinse and drain. Sprinkle the lamb shanks with 1½ teaspoons of salt. Cover with foil and let them sit at room temperature for 20 minutes to 2 hours. The longer they sit, the better. If they sit for 1 hour or less, it can be at room temperature. If they sit for longer than 1 hour, let them do so in the refrigerator. Select Sauté and adjust to More for high heat. Heat the oil until it shimmers. Blot the lamb shanks dry with a paper towel. Add two shanks to the pot and cook, undisturbed, until browned, about 5 minutes. Turn them over and repeat on the second side. Transfer the shanks to a plate and repeat with the remaining two shanks, transferring them to the plate when browned. Add the wine and cook, scraping to get up any browned bits from the bottom of the pot. Simmer the wine until it reduces by about half, about 4 minutes. Add the bay leaf, onion, garlic, carrot, and fennel (if using) to the pot. Transfer the browned shanks to the pot and pour in the broth. Select Cancel. Lock the lid. Select Manual and cook at high pressure for 35 minutes. When the cook time is complete, naturally release the pressure for 10 minutes, then quick-release any remaining pressure. Remove the lid. Transfer the shanks to a plate. Strain the sauce into a fat separator or bowl, discarding the vegetables. Let the fat rise for 5 minutes or so and then pour the sauce back into the pot, spooning off as much fat as possible if the sauce is in a bowl. Add the beans to the pot along with the chopped carrot and tomato. Make sure that the beans are covered by about 1 inch of liquid. If they are not, add more broth. Return the lamb to the pot. Lock the lid. Select Manual and cook at high pressure for 10 minutes. When the cook time is complete, naturally release the pressure for 10 minutes, then quick-release any remaining pressure. Remove the lid. Taste and adjust the seasoning, adding more salt if necessary and seasoning with pepper. If the beans are too soupy, select Sauté and adjust to Normal for medium heat. Simmer until the sauce thickens slightly, about 4 minutes. Serve the beans in bowls, each topped with a lamb shank and sprinkled with the fennel fronds (if using).

DESSERTS

Cinnamon Yogurt Custard

SERVES 4 | PREP AND FINISHING: 10 minutes, plus 4 hours to cool and chill | MANUAL: 25 minutes high pressure | RELEASE: Natural | TOTAL TIME: 4 hours 45 minutes

½ cup plain Greek yogurt	2 cups water
½ cup sweetened condensed milk	¼ cup chopped fruit or berries of your choice, for garnish
½ teaspoon ground cinnamon	

In a heatproof bowl that fits inside the Instant Pot, mix the yogurt, condensed milk, and cinnamon. Tightly cover the bowl with foil. Pour the water into the Instant Pot and place the trivet inside. Place the bowl on the trivet. Lock the lid. Select Manual and cook at high pressure for 25 minutes. When the cook time is complete, naturally release the pressure. Remove the lid. Carefully remove the bowl. Let it cool at room temperature for 30 minutes, then refrigerate, covered, for 3 to 4 hours. Serve garnished with the fruits of your choice.

Chocolate Pudding

SERVES 6 | PREP AND FINISHING: 15 minutes | MANUAL: 9 minutes high pressure | RELEASE: Natural for 10 minutes, then Quick | TOTAL TIME: 40 minutes, plus 2 hours to chill

2 large eggs

⅓ cup sugar

2 cups whole milk

⅓ cup unsweetened cocoa powder

2 teaspoons vanilla extract, divided

1 tablespoon cornstarch (optional)

Pinch salt

1 cup water

3 ounces bittersweet chocolate, chopped

¼ cup heavy (whipping) cream

Whipped cream, for serving (optional)

In a heatproof bowl that will fit in the Instant Pot, beat the eggs and sugar with a hand mixer until the sugar has mostly dissolved. Add half of the milk and half of the cocoa powder and beat to combine. Add the rest of the milk and cocoa powder, along with 1 teaspoon of vanilla, the cornstarch (if using), and salt. The mixture will probably appear grainy, but that's okay. Cover the bowl with foil. Pour the water into the Instant Pot. Place a trivet with handles in the pot and place the bowl on top. If your trivet doesn't have handles, use a foil sling to make removing the bowl easier. Lock the lid. Select Manual and cook at high pressure for 9 minutes. When the cook time is complete, let the pressure release naturally for 10 minutes, then quick-release any remaining pressure. Remove the lid. Carefully remove the bowl from the Instant Pot and remove the foil. The mixture will appear clumpy and curdled. While the pudding is cooking, combine the chocolate and cream in a small microwave-safe bowl and microwave for 25 seconds. Take the bowl out and stir the mixture. Repeat until the chocolate is mostly melted, another 10 to 15 seconds. With the hand mixer, blend the pudding until it begins to smooth out. Add the cream and chocolate and the remaining 1 teaspoon of vanilla and continue to beat until completely smooth. Spoon the pudding into 6 small (1 to 1½ cup) ramekins or custard cups. Refrigerate until set, 2 to 4 hours. Serve topped with whipped cream (if using).

Caramelized Banana Pudding

SERVES 6 | PREP AND FINISHING: 15 minutes | MANUAL: 6 minutes high pressure | RELEASE: Natural for 10 minutes | TOTAL TIME: 35 minutes, plus 2 hours to chill

2 tablespoons unsalted butter

2 or 3 large bananas, sliced into ¼-inch rounds

1 tablespoon packed light brown sugar

6 large egg yolks

⅔ cup granulated sugar

1 teaspoon vanilla extract

1 cup whole milk

1 cup heavy (whipping) cream

1 cup water

In a medium skillet, melt the butter over medium heat. When it has stopped foaming and is just starting to brown, add the banana slices in a single layer. Cook for 1 minute, then turn them over and cook for 1 minute more. Push the bananas to the sides of the skillet and

add the brown sugar. Let it cook, stirring, for 2 minutes, until melted and bubbling. Move the banana slices into the sugar and stir to coat. Remove the skillet from the heat and set aside. In a medium bowl, beat the egg yolks, granulated sugar, and vanilla with a hand mixer until the sugar is dissolved. Add the milk and cream and beat briefly to combine. Divide the bananas among 6 (1 to 1½-cup) ramekins or custard cups. Gently pour the custard over the bananas. Pour the water into the Instant Pot. Place a trivet in the pot and place the ramekins on top, stacking them if necessary. Drape a piece of foil over the ramekins to keep condensation off the top of the puddings. Lock the lid. Select Manual and cook at high pressure for 6 minutes. When the cook time is complete, let the pressure release naturally for 10 minutes, then quick-release any remaining pressure. Remove the lid. Carefully remove the foil and use tongs to remove the puddings from the pot. Let cool at room temperature for 20 minutes or so, then refrigerate until chilled, 1 to 2 hours, before serving.

Rice Pudding

SERVES 8 | PREP TIME: 5 minutes | SAUTÉ: 7 minutes | MANUAL: 13 minutes high pressure | RELEASE: Quick | TOTAL TIME: 32 minutes

1½ cups water

1 cup Arborio rice

¼ teaspoon kosher salt

2 cups whole milk, divided

½ cup sugar

2 large eggs, beaten

1 teaspoon vanilla extract

1 cup raisins (optional)

In the Instant Pot, combine the rice, water, and salt. Stir well. Lock the lid. Select Manual and cook at high pressure for 13 minutes. When the cook time is complete, quick-release the pressure. Add 1½ cups of milk and the sugar and stir to combine. Select Sauté and stir in the eggs, the remaining ½ cup of milk, and the vanilla. Cook until the rice pudding starts to boil and then turn off the pressure cooker. Stir in the raisins (if using) and serve.

Cinnamon-Apple Rice Pudding

SERVES 6 | PREP TIME: 10 minutes | MANUAL: 12 minutes high pressure | SAUTÉ: 3 minutes | RELEASE: Quick | TOTAL TIME: 40 minutes

2 cups whole milk

1 cup long-grain white rice

1 cup water

1 cup chopped peeled apples, such as Granny Smith

½ cup sugar

1 tablespoon pure vanilla extract

1 cinnamon stick

1 large egg

1 cup half-and-half

In the Instant Pot, combine the milk, rice, water, apples, sugar, vanilla, and cinnamon stick. Lock the lid. Select Manual and cook at high-pressure for 12 minutes, then quick-release any remaining pressure. Remove the lid. Select Cancel. In a small bowl, whisk the egg with ½ cup of the cooked rice mixture and add it to the pudding along with the half-and-half. Select Sauté and cook the pudding for 2 to 3 minutes, stirring the mixture well to thicken. Discard the cinnamon stick and serve warm.

Tres Leches Rice Pudding

SERVES 6 | PREP TIME: 5 minutes | MANUAL: 20 minutes high pressure | RELEASE: Natural | TOTAL TIME: 50 minutes

3 cups whole milk
1 (14-ounce) can sweetened condensed milk
1 (10-ounce) can evaporated milk
2 cups water
⅛ teaspoon coarse salt
1 cup long-grain rice
2 (3-inch) cinnamon sticks
Ground cinnamon, for serving

In the Instant Pot, combine the whole milk, condensed milk, evaporated milk, and water, whisking until combined. Season with the salt. Add the rice and cinnamon sticks. Lock the lid. Select Manual and cook at high pressure for 20 minutes. When the cook time is complete, allow the pressure to release naturally. Remove the lid. Discard the cinnamon sticks. Gently stir the rice to combine. Sprinkle with cinnamon just before serving.

Millet Vanilla Pudding

SERVES 4 to 6 | PREP TIME: 5 minutes | MANUAL: 15 minutes high pressure | RELEASE: Natural | TOTAL TIME: 30 minutes

2 cups water
1½ cups unsweetened plant-based milk, plus more for serving
1 cup millet
2 teaspoons pure vanilla extract
¼ cup maple syrup

In the Instant Pot, whisk together the water, milk, millet, and vanilla. Lock the lid. Select Manual and cook at high pressure for 15 minutes. When the cook time is complete, let the pressure release naturally. Remove the lid. Add the maple syrup and stir well to incorporate. Serve warm immediately, or chill for 3 to 4 hours and serve cold. The pudding will become thicker as it cools.

Tapioca Pudding

SERVES 4 | PREP TIME: 10 minutes | MANUAL: 6 minutes high pressure | RELEASE: Natural for 10 minutes, then Quick | TOTAL TIME: 30 minutes

3 cups water
1 cup medium tapioca pearls
2 cups whole milk
½ cup sugar
1 large egg, whisked
1 tablespoon pure vanilla extract
½ teaspoon salt

In the Instant Pot, combine the water and tapioca pearls. Lock the lid. Select Manual and cook at high-pressure for 6 minutes. After the cook time is complete, let the pressure naturally release for 10 minutes, then quick-release any remaining pressure. Remove the lid and stir in the milk, sugar, egg, vanilla, and salt while the tapioca is still piping hot. Allow to sit for 5 minutes to allow the egg to cook. You can serve this pudding warm or transfer it to an airtight container and chill in the refrigerator before enjoying.

Dulce de Leche

SERVES 4 | PREP AND FINISHING: 5 minutes, plus 30 minutes to cool | MANUAL: 45 minutes high pressure | RELEASE: Natural | TOTAL TIME: 1 hour 30 minutes

1 (14-ounce) can sweetened condensed milk
2 cups water
1 teaspoon sea salt
Chopped almonds, for topping (optional)
Chopped chocolate, for topping (optional)

Evenly divide the condensed milk among four (3-inch) ramekins. Tightly cover each with foil. Pour the water into the Instant Pot and place the trivet inside. Place the ramekins on the trivet, stacking them if needed. Lock the lid. Select Manual and cook at high pressure for 45 minutes. When the cook time is complete, naturally release the pressure. Remove the lid. Carefully remove the ramekins. Remove the foil, and sprinkle with the sea salt. Let cool for 30 minutes before topping with chopped almonds and chocolate (if using) and serving.

Crème Brûlée

SERVES 6 | PREP TIME: 15 minutes | MANUAL: 10 minutes high pressure | RELEASE: Natural for 15 minutes, then Quick | TOTAL TIME: 45 minutes, plus 4 hours to chill

6 tablespoons sugar, plus 4½ teaspoons, for topping
6 large egg yolks
2 cups heavy (whipping) cream
1½ teaspoons vanilla extract
⅛ teaspoon salt
1 cup water

In a medium bowl, whisk together 6 tablespoons of sugar and the egg yolks. While whisking constantly, add the cream, vanilla, and salt. Pour the mixture through a fine-mesh strainer into a pitcher. Divide and fill 6 (6-ounce) ramekins three-fourths full, then remove any air bubbles with the back of a spoon. Cover each ramekin tightly with foil. Set the trivet in the Instant Pot and pour in the water. Place four ramekins on the trivet and stack the remaining two on top. Lock the lid. Select Manual and cook at high pressure for 10 minutes on manual low pressure. When the cook time is complete, let the pressure release naturally for 15 minutes, then quick-release any remaining pressure. Remove the lid. Carefully transfer the ramekins to a baking sheet and let cool at room temperature for 30 minutes. Refrigerate until chilled, at least 4 hours and up to overnight. Spread ¾ teaspoon of sugar evenly on top of each cooked crème brûlée. Use a kitchen torch or broiler to caramelize the sugar and make a crispy top. Let them sit for 5 minutes before serving.

Baked Apples

SERVES 6 | **PREP TIME:** 15 minutes | **MANUAL:** 5 minutes high pressure | **RELEASE:** Quick | **TOTAL TIME:** 25 minutes

¾ cup rolled oats
⅓ cup packed light brown sugar
½ teaspoon ground allspice
¼ teaspoon ground cinnamon
¼ teaspoon ground nutmeg
3 tablespoons salted butter, melted
6 apples, cored
1 cup water

In a medium bowl, mix the oats, brown sugar, allspice, cinnamon, and nutmeg. Add the melted butter and stir until well combined. Fill the core of each apple with about 2 tablespoons of the oat mixture, using it all. Set the trivet in the Instant Pot and pour in the water. Place the apples on the trivet carefully so that they fit next to each other. Lock the lid. Select Manual and cook at high pressure for 5 minutes. When the cook time is complete, quick-release the pressure. Carefully remove each apple, place them on plates, and serve.

Vanilla Poached Pears with Caramel Sauce

SERVES 4 | **PREP TIME:** 10 minutes | **SAUTÉ LOW:** 2 minutes | **MANUAL:** 3 minutes high pressure | **RELEASE:** Quick | **TOTAL TIME:** 20 minutes

3 cups water
2 cups white wine
2 cups sugar
1 whole vanilla bean, split and scraped
1 cinnamon stick
4 Bosc pears, ripe but not soft
1 lemon, halved

Select Sauté Low. When the display reads HOT, pour in the water and white wine. Add the sugar, vanilla bean and seeds, and cinnamon stick, stirring well. Cook for 1 to 2 minutes, or until the sugar dissolves completely. Select Cancel and select Keep Warm. Gently peel the pears. If presentation is important, keep the stems intact. Rub the pears with the lemon halves to prevent browning and add the pears to the Instant Pot. Lock the lid. Select Manual and cook at high pressure for 3 minutes. When the cook time is complete, quick-release the pressure. Remove the lid and remove the pears. Set aside to cool. Save the sauce and pour it over the pears once cooled. Serve warm or at room temperature.

Apple Crisp

SERVES 5 | **PREP TIME:** 10 minutes | **MANUAL:** 5 minutes high pressure | **RELEASE:** Natural for 10 minutes, then Quick | **TOTAL TIME:** 33 minutes

5 Granny Smith apples (or another firm variety), peeled, cored, and cubed
½ cup water
2 tablespoons caramel sauce
1 tablespoon pure maple syrup
2 teaspoons ground cinnamon
¾ teaspoon ground nutmeg
¾ cup old-fashioned oats
⅓ cup packed light brown sugar
¼ cup (½ stick) salted butter, melted
¼ cup all-purpose flour
½ teaspoon sea salt

In the Instant Pot, combine the apples, water, caramel syrup, maple syrup, cinnamon, and nutmeg and stir well. In a small bowl, mix the oats, brown sugar, butter, flour, and salt. Sprinkle the topping mix over the apples. Lock the lid. Select Manual and cook at high pressure for 5 minutes. When the cook time is complete, let the pressure release naturally for 10 minutes, then quick-release any remaining pressure. Scoop and serve hot right from the pressure cooker.

Apple-Pear Crisp

SERVES 4 | **PREP AND FINISHING:** 10 minutes | **MANUAL:** 5 minutes high pressure | **RELEASE:** Quick | **SAUTÉ:** 4 minutes | **TOTAL TIME:** 30 minutes

½ cup packed light brown sugar
½ cup all-purpose flour
½ cup rolled oats
3 tablespoons butter, melted
1 teaspoon ground cinnamon
½ teaspoon freshly grated nutmeg
2 gala apples, peeled, cored, and sliced (about 2½ cups)
2 Asian pears, peeled, cored, and sliced (about 2½ cups)
½ cup water

In a small bowl, mix the brown sugar, flour, oats, butter, cinnamon, and nutmeg. In the Instant Pot, layer the apples and pears. Evenly spread the oat mixture on top of the fruit. Pour the water on top of the oat mixture. Lock the lid. Select Manual and cook at high pressure for 5 minutes. When the cook time is complete, quick-release the pressure. Remove the lid. Select Sauté and stir the crisp. Let it cook for 3 to 4 minutes, or until it bubbles, and serve warm.

Blueberry Cobbler

SERVES 4 to 6 | **PREP TIME:** 10 minutes | **MANUAL:** 7 minutes high pressure | **RELEASE:** Quick | **TOTAL TIME:** 30 minutes

¾ cup water
4 cups blueberries (fresh or frozen)
Zest and juice of 1 lemon
6 tablespoons maple syrup, divided
1 tablespoon arrowroot powder
1 cup gluten-free rolled oats
½ cup almond flour
½ cup shredded unsweetened coconut
¼ cup no-sugar-added applesauce
1 teaspoon ground cinnamon
1 teaspoon pure vanilla extract
2 tablespoons plant-based butter (optional)

Pour the water into the Instant Pot and insert the trivet. In a large mixing bowl, slightly mash together the berries, lemon zest, lemon juice, 2 tablespoons of maple syrup, and the arrowroot, keeping some berries intact. Pour the berry mixture into a 6-inch baking dish. In a medium bowl, stir together the oats, almond flour, coconut, applesauce, cinnamon, vanilla, remaining ¼ cup maple of syrup, and the butter (if using). Spread the topping over the blueberry mixture. Create a foil sling by folding a long piece of aluminum foil in half vertically two times, then use it to lower the baking dish into the pot. Lock the lid. Select Manual and cook at high pressure for 7 minutes. When the cook time is complete, quick-release the pressure. Remove the lid. Remove the pot and, if desired, place it under a broiler for 30 to 60 seconds to brown the topping. Serve immediately.

Peach Cobbler

SERVES 4 | PREP TIME: 5 minutes | MANUAL: 15 minutes high pressure | RELEASE: Natural for 10 minutes, then Quick | TOTAL TIME: 35 minutes

Nonstick cooking spray
1 (15¼-ounce) box yellow cake mix
½ cup (1 stick) unsalted butter, melted
½ teaspoon ground cinnamon
4 cups sliced peaches
1 teaspoon cornstarch
1 cup water

Spray a 7-inch cake pan with cooking spray. In a medium bowl, combine the cake mix, melted butter, and cinnamon. Add the sliced peaches to the prepared pan. Sprinkle with the cornstarch and mix well. Spread the cake mixture over the top; then wrap the whole pan in foil. Set the trivet in the Instant Pot and pour in the water. Place the pan on the trivet. Lock the lid. Select Manual and cook at high pressure for 15 minutes. When the cook time is complete, let the pressure release naturally for 10 minutes, then quick-release any remaining pressure.

New York Cheesecake

SERVES 8 | PREP TIME: 25 minutes | MANUAL: 25 minutes high pressure | RELEASE: Natural for 10 minutes, then Quick | TOTAL TIME: 1 hour 10 minutes, plus 4 hours to chill

4 ounces graham crackers, crushed into crumbs (about 1 cup crumbs)
2 tablespoons unsalted butter, melted
16 ounces cream cheese, at room temperature
½ cup sugar
⅔ cup plus 2 tablespoons sour cream, divided
2 tablespoons heavy (whipping) cream
1 teaspoon vanilla extract
1 teaspoon grated lemon zest
2 large eggs
1 cup water
1 tablespoon sugar

Preheat the oven to 350°F. In a small bowl, mix the graham cracker crumbs with the melted butter. Press the crumbs into the bottom of a 7-inch springform pan and up the sides about ½ inch. Bake until fragrant and set, 5 to 6 minutes. Let cool. In a medium bowl, beat the cream cheese with a hand mixer until very smooth. Add the sugar and beat until well blended. Add 2 tablespoons of sour cream, the heavy cream, vanilla, and lemon zest and beat to combine. Add the eggs, one at a time, and beat until incorporated. Pour the cheesecake mixture into the prepared crust. Gently smooth the top. Place a piece of foil over the top and be sure to crimp it over the sides of the pan. Pour the water into the Instant Pot. Place a trivet with handles in the pot and place the pan on top. If your trivet doesn't have handles, use a foil sling to make removing the pan easier. Lock the lid. Select Manual and cook at high pressure for 25 minutes. When the cook time is complete, let the pressure release naturally for 10 minutes, then quick-release any remaining pressure. Remove the lid. Carefully remove the cheesecake from the pot and remove the foil. The cheesecake should be set, with the center slightly softer than the edges. Mix the remaining ⅔ cup of sour cream and the sugar in a small bowl. Spread this mixture over the hot cheesecake. Let the cheesecake rest at room temperature for 15 to 20 minutes, then refrigerate until thoroughly chilled, 3 to 4 hours. Remove the sides of the springform pan. Serve.

Mango Cheesecake

SERVES 8 | PREP AND FINISHING: 20 minutes, plus at least 7 hours to cool and chill | MANUAL: 50 minutes high pressure | RELEASE: Natural | TOTAL TIME: 9 hours 20 minutes

1½ cups graham cracker crumbs
½ cup unsalted butter, melted, plus 1 tablespoon, at room temperature, divided
½ cup plus 2 tablespoons sugar, divided
2 mangos, peeled and roughly chopped, plus 1 mango, peeled and thinly sliced
2 cups plus 2 tablespoons water, divided
16 ounces cream cheese, at room temperature
2 tablespoons cornstarch

In a medium bowl, mix the graham cracker crumbs, melted butter, and 2 tablespoons of sugar. Reserve 2 tablespoons of the mixture to use as a garnish. Grease a springform pan that fits in the Instant Pot with the room-temperature butter. Add the crumb mixture to the pan and evenly press it down into the bottom. Place in the freezer for 15 minutes. Meanwhile, in a blender, combine the 2 chopped mangos and 2 tablespoons of water. Puree until smooth. This should make about 1 cup. In a large bowl, use a hand mixer to beat the cream cheese for 2 to 3 minutes or until light and fluffy. Add the remaining ½ cup of sugar and mix until well combined. Add the cornstarch and mango puree. Using a spoon, gently fold the mixture until well combined. Remove the springform pan from the freezer and pour the filling on top of the crust. Tightly cover the pan with foil. Pour the remaining 2 cups of water into the Instant Pot and place the trivet inside. Place the pan on top of the trivet. Lock the lid. Select Manual and cook at high pressure for 50 minutes. When the cook time is complete, naturally release the pressure. Remove the lid. Carefully remove the cake, then remove the foil. The center will be loose. Let it cool at room temperature for 1 hour, then cover the cheesecake again with foil and refrigerate for at least 6 hours. Before serving, sprinkle with the reserved crumb mixture and decorate with the sliced mangos.

Fruit and Pistachio Cheesecake

SERVES 8 | PREP TIME: 25 minutes | MANUAL: 25 minutes high pressure | RELEASE: Natural for 10 minutes, then Quick | TOTAL TIME: 1 hour 10 minutes, plus 4 hours to chill

4 ounces graham crackers, crushed into crumbs (about 1 cup crumbs)	1 teaspoon grated lemon zest
2 tablespoons unsalted butter, melted	2 large eggs
	½ cup toasted pistachios, divided
16 ounces cream cheese, at room temperature	1 cup water
½ cup sugar, plus 2 tablespoons	1 cup frozen raspberries, thawed
2 tablespoons sour cream	2 tablespoons raspberry liqueur
2 tablespoons heavy (whipping) cream	½ cup fresh raspberries
1 teaspoon vanilla extract	1 plum, sliced thin (optional)

Preheat the oven to 350°F. In a small bowl, mix the graham cracker crumbs with the melted butter. Press the crumbs into the bottom of a 7-inch springform pan and up the sides about ½ inch. Bake until fragrant and set, 5 to 6 minutes. Let cool. In a medium bowl, beat the cream cheese with a hand mixer until very smooth. Add ½ cup of sugar and beat until well blended. Add the sour cream, heavy cream, vanilla, and lemon zest and beat to combine. Add the eggs, one at a time, and beat until incorporated. Finely chop ¼ cup of the pistachios and gently fold them into the batter. Pour the cheesecake mixture into the prepared crust. Gently smooth the top. Place a piece of foil over the top and be sure to crimp it

over the sides of the pan. Pour the water into the Instant Pot. Place a trivet with handles in the pot and place the pan on top. If your trivet doesn't have handles, use a foil sling to make removing the pan easier. Lock the lid. Select Manual and cook at high pressure for 25 minutes. When the cook time is complete, let the pressure release naturally for 10 minutes, then quick-release any remaining pressure. Remove the lid. Carefully remove the cheesecake from the pot and remove the foil. The cheesecake should be set, with the center slightly softer than the edges. Let the cheesecake rest at room temperature for 15 to 20 minutes, then refrigerate until thoroughly chilled, 3 to 4 hours. Remove the sides of the springform pan. In a blender or small food processor, puree the frozen raspberries, raspberry liqueur, and the remaining 2 tablespoons of sugar. Strain into a small bowl or squeeze bottle. Drizzle over the top of the cheesecake. Top with the fresh raspberries, remaining ¼ cup of pistachios, and the plum (if using) and serve.

Lemon-Blueberry Cheesecake

SERVES 8 | PREP TIME: 25 minutes | MANUAL: 25 minutes high pressure | RELEASE: Natural for 10 minutes, then Quick | TOTAL TIME: 1 hour 10 minutes, plus 4 hours to chill

4 ounces graham crackers, crushed into crumbs (about 1 cup crumbs)	2 tablespoons heavy (whipping) cream
2 tablespoons unsalted butter, melted	1 teaspoon vanilla extract
	2 teaspoons lemon zest
16 ounces cream cheese, at room temperature	2 large eggs
	½ cup blueberries
½ cup sugar	1 cup water
2 tablespoons sour cream	1 cup lemon curd

Preheat the oven to 350°F. In a small bowl, mix the graham cracker crumbs with the melted butter. Press the crumbs into the bottom of a 7-inch springform pan and up the sides about ½ inch. Bake until fragrant and set, 5 to 6 minutes. Let cool. In a medium bowl, beat the cream cheese with a hand mixer until very smooth. Add the sugar and beat until well blended. Add the sour cream, heavy cream, vanilla, and lemon zest and beat to combine. Add the eggs, one at a time, and beat until incorporated. Pour half of the batter into the prepared crust and distribute the blueberries evenly over the top, then pour the remaining batter over the blueberries. Gently smooth the top. Place a piece of foil over the top and be sure to crimp it over the sides of the pan. Pour the water into the Instant Pot. Place a trivet with handles in the pot and place the pan on top. If your trivet doesn't have handles, use a foil sling to make removing the pan easier. Lock the lid. Select Manual and cook at high pressure for 25 minutes. When the cook time is complete, let the pressure release naturally for 10 minutes, then quick-release any remaining pressure. Remove the lid. Carefully remove the cheesecake from the pot and remove the foil. The cheesecake should be set, with the center slightly softer than the edges. Let the cheesecake rest at room temperature for 15 to 20 minutes, then refrigerate until thoroughly chilled, 3 to 4 hours. Remove the sides of the springform pan. Spread the lemon curd over the top of the cheesecake and serve.

Marbled Cream Cheese Pumpkin Pie

SERVES 6 | PREP TIME: 25 minutes | MANUAL: 30 minutes high pressure | RELEASE: Natural for 10 minutes, then Quick | TOTAL TIME: 1 hour 10 minutes, plus 4 hours to chill

4 ounces gingersnap cookies (about 10)	1 cup canned pumpkin puree (not pumpkin pie filling)
⅓ cup finely chopped pecans	½ teaspoon ground cinnamon
2 tablespoons unsalted butter, melted	¼ teaspoon ground ginger
8 ounces cream cheese, at room temperature	⅛ teaspoon ground cloves
	⅛ teaspoon ground allspice
6 tablespoons sour cream, at room temperature	⅛ teaspoon ground nutmeg
½ cup sugar	1 cup water
2 large eggs	Whipped cream, for garnish

Preheat the oven to 350°F. In a small food processor or in a zip-top bag using a rolling pin, crush the cookies into fine crumbs. You should have about 1 cup of crumbs. Transfer to a small bowl and stir in the pecans and melted butter. Press the crumbs into the bottom of a 7-inch springform pan and up the sides about ½ inch. Bake until fragrant and set, 5 to 6 minutes. Let cool. In a medium bowl, beat the cream cheese and sour cream with a hand mixer until very smooth. Add about half of the sugar and beat until well blended. Add the remaining sugar and beat again. Add the eggs and beat until they are just incorporated. Remove about ¼ cup of this cream cheese mixture and set aside. Add the pumpkin puree, cinnamon, ginger, cloves, allspice, and nutmeg to the cream cheese mixture in the bowl and beat until well blended. Pour the pumpkin mixture into the prepared crust. Depending on the depth of your pan, you may not need quite all of it. It should come up to about an inch from the top of the pan. Drop spoonfuls of the reserved cream cheese mixture evenly on top of the pumpkin filling. Run the tip of a small knife or a skewer through the filling to form a swirled ("marbleized") pattern on the top of the pie. Pour the water into the Instant Pot. Place a trivet with handles in the pot and place the pan on top. If your trivet doesn't have handles, use a foil sling to make removing the pan easier. Lay a piece of foil over the top of the bowl to prevent condensation from forming on top of the pie. Lock the lid. Select Manual and cook at high

pressure for 30 minutes. When the cook time is complete, let the pressure release naturally for 10 minutes, then quick-release any remaining pressure. Remove the lid. Carefully remove the pie from the pot and remove the foil. The pie should be set fully. Let the pie rest at room temperature for 10 to 20 minutes, then refrigerate until chilled, 3 to 4 hours. Remove the sides of the pan, garnish with the whipped cream, and serve.

Chocolate Chip Banana Bread

SERVES 6 | PREP TIME: 10 minutes | MANUAL: 50 minutes high pressure | RELEASE: Natural for 10 minutes, then Quick | TOTAL TIME: 1 hour 15 minutes

Nonstick cooking spray	2 very ripe bananas, mashed
½ cup (1 stick) unsalted butter, at room temperature	2 cups all-purpose flour
	1½ teaspoons baking soda
½ cup packed light brown sugar	½ teaspoon salt
2 large eggs, at room temperature	½ teaspoon ground cinnamon
1 teaspoon vanilla extract	½ cup semisweet chocolate chips
	1 cup water

Spray a 7-inch cake pan with cooking spray. In a large bowl and using a hand mixer, cream the butter and brown sugar together. Add the eggs and vanilla and mix to combine. Add the bananas and blend until just combined. In a medium bowl, mix the flour, baking soda, salt, and cinnamon. Pour the dry ingredients into the wet ingredients and stir them together until you see no more streaks of flour. Stir in the chocolate chips until combined. Pour the batter into the prepared pan, smooth the top, cover the pan loosely with a paper towel, and wrap it in foil. Set the trivet in the Instant Pot and pour in the water. Place the pan on the trivet. Lock the lid. Select Manual and cook at high pressure for 50 minutes. When the cook time is complete, let the pressure release naturally for 10 minutes, then quick-release any remaining pressure. Remove the lid. Remove the foil and let the bread sit for at least 10 minutes before slicing.

Banana Cake

SERVES 6 | PREP AND FINISHING: 10 minutes, plus at least 30 minutes to cool | MANUAL: 30 minutes high pressure | RELEASE: Natural | TOTAL TIME: 1 hour 20 minutes

1½ cups all-purpose flour	½ cup sugar
1½ teaspoons baking powder	¼ cup milk
½ teaspoon baking soda	¼ cup corn oil, plus more to grease the pan
2 medium very ripe bananas	10 pecans, crushed, divided

10 walnuts,
  crushed, divided
2 cups water

1 cup vanilla cream cheese
  frosting

In a large bowl, sift together the flour, baking powder, and baking soda. In a blender, puree the bananas until smooth. Set aside 1 cup of the puree. In a large bowl, mix the sugar, banana puree, milk, and oil. Add the wet ingredients to the dry ingredients, and gently mix to form a smooth batter. Add 5 pecans and 5 walnuts to the batter, and gently fold them in. Grease a springform pan that fits in the Instant Pot with some oil. Pour in the batter and tap the pan twice on the counter to break any air pockets. Tightly cover the pan with foil. Pour the water into the Instant Pot and place the trivet inside. Place the cake on the trivet and lock the lid into place. Select Manual and cook at high pressure for 30 minutes. When the cook time is complete, naturally release the pressure. Remove the lid. Remove the cake pan and slowly remove the foil. Let the cake cool for at least 30 minutes. Release the cake from the springform pan. Frost the cake and sprinkle the remaining pecans and walnuts on top. Slice and serve.

Carrot and Date Cake

SERVES 6 | PREP TIME: 10 minutes, plus 1 hour to cool | MANUAL: 45 minutes high pressure | RELEASE: Natural for 10 minutes, then Quick | TOTAL TIME: 2 hours 10 minutes

Nonstick cooking spray
1 cup almond flour
2 teaspoons ground
  cinnamon
1 teaspoon baking soda
¼ teaspoon
  ground nutmeg
¼ teaspoon kosher salt

2 eggs, beaten
¼ cup pure maple syrup
½ teaspoon vanilla extract
1 cup (about 2 medium)
  shredded carrots
¼ cup (about 5) pitted and
  chopped dates
1 cup water

Grease a 6-inch cake pan with nonstick cooking spray. Set aside. In a medium bowl, combine the almond flour, cinnamon, baking soda, nutmeg, and salt. In a separate bowl, whisk together the eggs, maple syrup, and vanilla. Pour the egg mixture into the flour mixture and combine to form a batter. Fold in the carrots and dates. Pour the batter into the prepared cake pan. Cover the pan with a paper towel (without letting it touch the surface of the batter) and then cover the top of the pan with foil. Pour the water into the Instant Pot and insert the trivet. Place the cake pan on top of the trivet. Lock the lid. Select Manual and cook at high pressure for 45 minutes. When the cook time is complete, let the pressure release naturally for 10 minutes, then quick-release any remaining pressure. Remove the lid and lift out the cake pan. Remove the foil and paper towel and let the cake cool on the trivet for 1 hour. Cut the cake into six slices and serve.

Berry-Almond Bundt Cake

SERVES 6 | PREP TIME: 10 minutes, plus 1 hour to cool | MANUAL: 45 minutes high pressure | RELEASE: Natural for 10 minutes, then Quick | TOTAL TIME: 2 hours 10 minutes

Nonstick cooking spray
1½ cups almond flour, plus
  1 tablespoon
1 teaspoon baking soda
¼ teaspoon kosher salt
2 eggs, beaten

½ cup buttermilk
¼ cup pure maple syrup
½ teaspoon pure
  almond extract
1 cup fresh berries
1 cup water

Grease a 7-inch Bundt pan with nonstick cooking spray. In a medium bowl, combine 1½ cups of almond flour, the baking soda, and salt. In a medium bowl, whisk together the eggs, buttermilk, maple syrup, and almond extract. Pour the egg mixture into the flour mixture and combine to form a batter. In a small bowl, mix the berries with the remaining 1 tablespoon of almond flour until thoroughly coated. Fold the berry mixture into the batter. Pour the batter into the prepared Bundt pan and cover the top with foil. Pour the water into the Instant Pot and insert the trivet. Place the Bundt pan on top of the trivet. Lock the lid. Select Manual and cook at high pressure for 45 minutes. When the cook time is complete, let the pressure release naturally for 10 minutes, then quick-release any remaining pressure. Remove the lid and lift out the Bundt pan. Remove the foil and let the cake cool on the trivet for 1 hour. Cut the cake into six slices and serve.

Lemon-Lime Bundt Cake

SERVES 6 | PREP TIME: 5 minutes | MANUAL: 45 minutes high pressure | RELEASE: Quick | TOTAL TIME: 55 minutes

Nonstick cooking spray
1 (15¼-ounce) box yellow
  cake mix
¾ cup lemon-lime soda

¾ cup vegetable oil
4 large eggs
1 cup water

Spray a 7-inch Bundt pan with cooking spray. In a medium bowl, mix the cake mix, soda, oil, and eggs. Pour the mixture into the prepared Bundt pan. Set the trivet in the Instant Pot and pour in the water. Place the Bundt pan on the trivet. Lock the lid. Select Manual and cook at high pressure for 45 minutes. When the cook time is complete, quick-release the pressure. Let the cake cool slightly before serving.

Strawberry-Chocolate Cake

SERVES 8 | PREP AND FINISHING: 15 minutes, plus at least 30 minutes to cool | MANUAL: 30 minutes high pressure | RELEASE: Natural | TOTAL TIME: 1 hour 25 minutes

10 fresh strawberries,
hulled, plus 10 fresh
strawberries, hulled
and halved
2 cups plus 1 tablespoon
water, divided
1 cup sugar
½ cup plain Greek yogurt
1½ teaspoons
baking powder
½ teaspoon baking soda
⅛ teaspoon kosher salt
1¼ cups all-purpose flour
2 tablespoons
cocoa powder
½ cup corn oil
Nonstick cooking spray
1 cup vanilla cream cheese
frosting

In a blender, combine the whole strawberries and
1 tablespoon of water. Puree until smooth. This should
make about ½ cup of puree. In a large bowl, whisk
together the sugar and yogurt until the sugar is dissolved.
Stir in the baking powder, baking soda, and salt. Let sit
for about 5 minutes or until the mixture begins to bubble.
Meanwhile, in a medium bowl, sift the flour and cocoa
powder together. Whisk the yogurt mixture again, then
slowly whisk in the oil. Keep whisking until the oil is
fully incorporated. Add the strawberry puree and mix
again. Add the flour mixture, and gently mix to form a
smooth batter. Grease a springform pan that fits in the
Instant Pot with the cooking spray. Pour the batter into
the pan, then tap the pan twice on the counter to break
any air pockets. Tightly cover with aluminum foil. Pour
the remaining 2 cups of water into the Instant Pot and
place the trivet inside. Place the pan on the trivet and
lock the lid into place. Select Manual and cook at high
pressure for 30 minutes. When the cook time is complete, naturally release the pressure. Remove the lid.
Remove the pan, and carefully remove the foil. Let cool
for at least 30 minutes before removing the cake from
the pan. Evenly spread the frosting over the cake. Place
the fresh strawberry halves on top and serve.

Flourless Chocolate-Espresso Cake

MAKES 6 slices | PREP TIME: 15 minutes | MANUAL:
35 minutes high pressure | RELEASE: Quick | TOTAL
TIME: 1 hour

1 cup (2 sticks) unsalted
butter, cubed, plus more
for greasing
1 pound bittersweet chocolate, finely chopped
8 large eggs, whites and
yolks separated
2 tablespoons
espresso powder
Pinch salt
1 cup water
Powdered sugar,
for serving

Place a round of parchment paper on the bottom of a
7-inch cake pan. Grease the pan and paper with butter.
Set aside. In a microwave-safe medium bowl, combine
the chocolate and butter and microwave in 30-second
bursts, stirring with a rubber spatula at the end of each
cycle, until melted and smooth. (Alternatively, set the
bowl over a double boiler until the chocolate has fully
melted.) Once the chocolate is melted, add the egg

yolks, espresso powder, and salt to the bowl and stir to
combine. In another medium bowl, using an electric
hand mixer, beat the egg whites on high speed until soft
peaks form. Gently fold the egg whites into the chocolate mixture until fully combined. Pour the batter into
the prepared pan, then cover it with aluminum foil. Put
the water in the pressure cooker pot and place the trivet
in the bottom. Prepare a foil sling, center the pan on
it, and lower it onto the trivet. Arrange the sling ends
across the cake pan. Lock the lid. Select Manual and
cook at high-pressure for 35 minutes. After cooking,
quick-release the pressure. Remove the lid. Remove the
cake from the cooker using the foil sling, transferring to
a rack to cool completely. When ready to serve, dust the
cake with powdered sugar (if using), then cut into slices.

Sweet Potato Spice Cake

SERVES 4 to 6 | PREP TIME: 15 minutes | MANUAL:
50 minutes high pressure | RELEASE: Natural
TOTAL TIME: 1 hour 30 minutes

2 tablespoons ground
flaxseed
1¾ cups water, divided
1½ cups white whole
wheat flour
¾ teaspoon baking soda
¾ teaspoon baking powder
2½ teaspoons pumpkin
pie spice
¼ teaspoon salt
1 cup orange juice
6 whole pitted dates
¼ cup no-sugar-added
applesauce
1 cup peeled, grated
sweet potatoes (about
1 medium)
Nonstick spray

In a small bowl, stir together the flaxseed and ¼ cup of
the water. Set aside. In a medium bowl, whisk together
the flour, baking soda, baking powder, pumpkin pie spice,
and salt. In a blender, puree the orange juice and dates.
Pour the mixture over the dry ingredients. Add the applesauce and flaxseed mixture and mix until just moistened.
Stir in the sweet potatoes. Spray a 6-inch cake pan with
nonstick spray and pour and spread the batter evenly.
Cover tightly with aluminum foil. Pour the remaining
1½ cups of water into the Instant Pot and insert the
trivet. Place the cake pan on the trivet. Lock the lid.
Select Manual and cook at high pressure for 50 minutes.
When the cook time is complete, let the pressure release
naturally. Remove the lid. Remove the cake pan, remove
the foil, and let cool for 5 minutes before turning out the
cake on a cooling rack to cool completely.

Browned-Butter Apple Spice Cake

SERVES 6 | PREP AND FINISHING: 25 minutes | MANUAL:
18 minutes high pressure | RELEASE: Natural for
10 minutes, then Quick | TOTAL TIME: 1 hour

6 tablespoons unsalted
butter, plus more to
grease the pan
1 large egg
1 cup Greek yogurt
⅓ cup sugar

1 teaspoon vanilla extract
1 cup all-purpose flour
2 teaspoons
 baking powder
¼ teaspoon ground
 cinnamon
⅛ teaspoon ground
 cardamom
1 medium apple, peeled,
 cored, and diced
1 cup water
¼ cup confectioners' sugar

In a small saucepan over medium heat, cook the butter until the milk solids begin to brown, 3 to 5 minutes. Measure out 3 tablespoons of butter into a medium bowl and set the rest of the butter in the pan aside. Lightly grease a 6- or 7-inch springform pan (or cake pan with a removable bottom) with butter. In the bowl with the 3 tablespoons of browned butter, stir in the egg, yogurt, sugar, and vanilla. In a small bowl, sift together the flour, baking powder, cinnamon, and cardamom. Add the dry ingredients to the wet ingredients. Stir until just combined. Stir in the apple. Pour the batter into the prepared pan. Pour the water into the Instant Pot. Place a trivet with handles in the pot and place the pan on top. If your trivet doesn't have handles, use a foil sling to make removing the pan easier. Lock the lid. Select Manual and cook at high pressure for 18 minutes. When the cook time is complete, let the pressure release naturally for 10 minutes, then quick-release any remaining pressure. Remove the lid. Remove the pan from the pot. Let the cake cool for 5 to 10 minutes, then remove the sides of the pan. Let the cake cool for another 10 minutes. Reheat the remaining browned butter if it's solidified, and drizzle it over the cake. Dust with the confectioners' sugar and serve.

Decadent Chocolate Cake

SERVES 4 to 6 | PREP TIME: 10 minutes | MANUAL: Slow Cook 1 hour 30 minutes high | RELEASE: Natural | TOTAL TIME: 1 hour 50 minutes

1 cup unsweetened
 plant-based milk
2 teaspoons pure
 vanilla extract
1½ teaspoons ground
 flaxseed
1½ teaspoons apple
 cider vinegar
¾ cup gluten-free
 flour blend
⅔ cup pure cane sugar
⅔ cup cocoa powder
¼ cup almond flour
½ teaspoon baking powder
¼ teaspoon baking soda
Pinch of salt
Nonstick cooking spray
1½ cups water

In a medium bowl, stir together the milk, vanilla, flaxseed, and vinegar. Set aside. In a large bowl, whisk together the flour blend, sugar, cocoa powder, almond flour, baking powder, baking soda, and salt. Add the wet ingredients to the dry ingredients, stirring until just combined. Spray a 6-inch cake pan with nonstick spray. Spread the batter evenly into the pan. Cover the pan tightly with foil. Pour the water into the Instant Pot and insert the trivet. Place the cake pan on the trivet. Lock

the lid. Select Manual and slow cook on high for 1 hour 30 minutes. When the cook time is complete, remove the lid. After the steam subsides, remove the cake pan and set it on a cooling rack for 10 minutes before turning it out. Let cool completely on the rack before serving.

Lemon Bars

SERVES 6 | PREP TIME: 15 minutes, plus 2 hours to chill | MANUAL: 12 minutes high pressure | RELEASE: Natural for 15 minutes, then Quick | TOTAL TIME: 2 hours 50 minutes

¾ cup gluten-free
 rolled oats
¾ cup almond flour
¼ cup melted coconut oil
⅓ cup plus
 2 tablespoons honey
1 teaspoon vanilla extract
¼ teaspoon kosher
 salt, divided
2 large eggs, beaten
Zest and juice of 2 lemons
1 teaspoon arrowroot
 powder or cornstarch
1 cup water

Line a 6-inch square cake pan with foil. In a medium bowl, combine the oats, almond flour, coconut oil, 2 tablespoons of honey, the vanilla, and ⅛ teaspoon of salt to form a stiff dough. Press the dough into the bottom of the prepared pan. In a separate bowl, whisk together the eggs, lemon zest, lemon juice, arrowroot powder, remaining ⅓ cup of honey, and remaining ⅛ teaspoon of salt. Pour the mixture over the crust. Cover the pan with foil. Pour the water into the Instant Pot and insert the trivet. Place the pan on top of the trivet. Lock the lid. Select Manual and cook at high pressure for 12 minutes. When the cook time is complete, let the pressure release naturally for 15 minutes, then quick-release any remaining pressure. Remove the lid and lift out the pan. Chill the lemon bars in the refrigerator for at least 2 hours before slicing them into six portions and serving.

Mexican-Style Bread Pudding

SERVES 6 to 8 | PREP TIME: 10 minutes | SAUTÉ: 8 minutes | MANUAL: 10 minutes high pressure | RELEASE: Quick | TOTAL TIME: 30 minutes

2 piloncillo cones
2 (3-inch) cinnamon sticks
4 whole cloves
2 cups water
4 tablespoons vegetable
 oil, divided
4 day-old bolillo rolls, cut
 into 1-inch slices
1 cup peanuts, divided
½ cup raisins, divided
1½ cups crumbled queso
 fresco, divided

In a medium saucepan, combine the piloncillo cones, cinnamon sticks, cloves, and the water. Bring to a boil over high heat, then cover and reduce the heat to low. Simmer, stirring occasionally, until the piloncillo cones dissolve completely. Remove from the heat. Select Sauté and adjust to More for high. Heat 2 tablespoons of vegetable oil in the pot. Working in two or three batches, fry the bolillo roll slices for 2 to 3 minutes, flipping once, until light golden brown on both sides. Repeat until all the bread slices are evenly golden, adding the remaining 2 tablespoons of vegetable oil as needed. Select Cancel. In the Instant Pot, layer half of the toasted bolillo slices. Top with half each of the piloncillo syrup, peanuts, raisins, and queso fresco. Repeat the layering one more time. Lock the lid. Select Manual and cook at high pressure for 10 minutes. When the cook time is complete, quick-release the pressure. Remove the lid. Serve immediately.

Brownies

SERVES 6 | PREP AND FINISHING: 10 minutes, plus at least 30 minutes to cool | MANUAL: 35 minutes high pressure | RELEASE: Natural | TOTAL TIME: 1 hour 25 minutes

1 cup all-purpose flour	¼ cup plain Greek yogurt
¾ cup confectioners' sugar	3 tablespoons plus
¼ cup cocoa powder	1 teaspoon corn
1 teaspoon baking powder	oil, divided
½ teaspoon baking soda	2 cups water
½ cup milk	2 teaspoons sea salt

In a large bowl, sift together the flour, sugar, and cocoa powder. Add the baking powder and baking soda and mix to combine. In a medium bowl, whisk together the milk, yogurt, and 3 tablespoons of oil. Little by little, add the wet ingredients to the dry ingredients, gently folding them together with each addition to form a smooth batter. Grease a springform pan that fits the Instant Pot with the remaining 1 teaspoon of oil. Pour the batter into the pan, and tightly cover with foil. Pour the water into the Instant Pot and place the trivet inside. Place the pan on the trivet. Lock the lid. Select Manual and cook at high pressure for 35 minutes. When the cook time is complete, naturally release the pressure. Remove the lid. Remove the pan and remove the foil. Sprinkle the brownies with the sea salt and let cool for at least 30 minutes. Gently remove from the pan, slice, and serve.

Fudgy Brownie Bites

MAKES 7 bites | PREP TIME: 5 minutes | MANUAL: 22 minutes high pressure | RELEASE: Natural for 25 minutes | TOTAL TIME: 57 minutes

Nonstick cooking spray	1 egg
¼ cup diced walnuts	⅓ cup vegetable oil
¼ cup hot fudge sauce	1 cup plus 2 tablespoons
1 (10¼-ounce) package	water, divided
brownie mix	

Spray a 7-cup silicone egg bite mold with cooking spray. Evenly divide and sprinkle the walnuts in the cups of the egg mold and then drizzle each with the hot fudge. In a mixing bowl, combine the brownie mix, egg, oil, and 2 tablespoons of water as instructed on the package. Spoon the prepared batter into the egg bite mold until

each cup is about three-fourths full, then cover the mold with foil. Set the trivet in the Instant Pot and pour in the water. Place the egg bite mold on the trivet. Lock the lid. Select Manual and cook at high pressure for 22 minutes. When the cook time is complete, let the pressure release naturally for 25 minutes. Remove the lid. Take the mold out and then remove the foil. Allow the brownies to cool completely before popping them out.

Mini Crustless Pumpkin Pies

SERVES 2 | PREP TIME: 5 minutes, plus 10 minutes to cool | MANUAL: 10 minutes high pressure | RELEASE: Natural for 10 minutes, then Quick | TOTAL TIME: 45 minutes

1 cup water	½ teaspoon pumpkin
Butter, at room tempera-	pie spice
ture, for greasing the	1 large egg, lightly beaten
ramekins	¼ cup plus 2 tablespoons
½ cup pumpkin puree	heavy (whipping) cream
3 tablespoons packed light	Whipped cream,
brown sugar	for serving
1 teaspoon cornstarch	Crumbled gingersnap
Pinch salt	cookies, for serving

Pour the water into the Instant Pot and place a trivet with handles in the bottom. Grease two 1-cup ramekins with butter. In a medium bowl, whisk together the pumpkin puree, brown sugar, cornstarch, salt, pumpkin pie spice, and egg. Add the cream and stir to combine. Divide the pumpkin mixture between the prepared ramekins. Set the ramekins on the trivet, placing a third empty ramekin next to them to ensure that they don't jostle during cooking. Lock the lid. Select Manual and cook at high-pressure for 10 minutes; then allow the pressure to naturally release for 10 minutes. Using tongs, remove the ramekins from the pot and transfer them to a heatproof surface. Let cool for 5 to 10 minutes before serving with a dollop of whipped cream and crumbled gingersnap cookies, if desired.

Key Lime Pie

SERVES 6 | PREP TIME: 20 minutes | MANUAL: 15 minutes high pressure | RELEASE: Natural for 10 minutes, then Quick | TOTAL TIME: 50 minutes, plus 4 hours to chill

Nonstick cooking spray	1 (14-ounce) can sweet-
1 cup graham cracker	ened condensed milk
crumbs (about	½ cup key lime juice
5 crackers)	⅓ cup sour cream
3 tablespoons unsalted	2 tablespoons grated key
butter, melted	lime zest
1 tablespoon sugar	Whipped cream,
4 large egg yolks	for topping
	1 cup water

Spray a 7-inch springform pan with cooking spray. In a small bowl, mix the graham cracker crumbs, melted butter, and sugar. Using the bottom of a measuring cup, evenly press the mixture into the bottom of the prepared pan and up the sides. Place in the freezer for 10 to 15 minutes. In a large bowl, beat the egg yolks until they are light yellow. Slowly add the condensed milk and continue to stir until thickened. Add the lime juice, sour cream, and lime zest and stir until smooth. Pour the mixture into the springform pan, smooth the top, and cover the pan with foil. Set the trivet in the Instant Pot and pour in the water. Carefully place the pan on the trivet. Lock the lid. Select Manual and cook at high pressure for 15 minutes. When the cook time is complete, let the pressure release naturally for 10 minutes, then quick-release any remaining pressure. Remove the lid. Remove the pie and check to see if the middle is set (or slightly firm). If not, cover it back up and cook for an additional 5 minutes. Set the pie on a rack to cool and remove the foil. When the pie is cooled, refrigerate it for at least 4 hours or overnight. Top with whipped cream and enjoy.

S'mores Pie

SERVES 6 | PREP TIME: 10 minutes | MANUAL: 45 minutes high pressure | BROIL: 5 minutes | RELEASE: Natural for 10 minutes, then Quick | TOTAL TIME: 1 hour 10 minutes, plus 30 minutes to cool

Nonstick cooking spray	1 egg
1 cup graham cracker crumbs (about 5 crackers)	½ cup vegetable oil
	1⅓ cups water, divided
¼ cup (½ stick) unsalted butter, melted	4 whole graham crackers
	⅔ cup marshmallow fluff
1 (18-ounce) box brownie mix	1 cup mini marshmallows

Spray a 7-inch springform pan with cooking spray. In a small bowl, combine the graham cracker crumbs and melted butter. Scrape the mixture into the prepared pan and use the bottom of a measuring cup to evenly press the mixture on the bottom of the pan and about 1 inch up the sides. In a medium bowl, combine the brownie mix, egg, oil, and ⅓ cup of water as instructed on the box. Pour half of the prepared brownie batter into the bottom of the pan, then place the whole graham crackers on top. You can break them up to fit if necessary. Spread the marshmallow fluff gently over the graham crackers and then carefully top with the remaining brownie batter. Cover the pan tightly with foil. Set the trivet in the Instant Pot and pour in the remaining 1 cup of water. Place the covered pan on the trivet. Lock the lid. Select Manual and cook at high pressure for 45 minutes. When the cook time is complete, let the pressure release naturally for 10 minutes, then quick-release any remaining pressure. Heat the broiler. Uncover the cake and place the mini marshmallows in an even layer on top. Broil for 3 to 5 minutes, until golden

brown. Alternatively, use a kitchen torch and skip the broiling. Allow the pie to cool for 20 to 30 minutes before serving.

Frozen Orange-and-Cream Pie

SERVES 8 | PREP AND FINISHING: 25 minutes | MANUAL: 10 minutes high pressure | RELEASE: Natural for 10 minutes, then Quick | TOTAL TIME: 1 hour, plus 8 hours to chill

6 ounces vanilla wafer cookies	2 teaspoons grated orange zest
7 tablespoons unsalted butter, 3 melted and 4 at room temperature, divided	Pinch salt
	1 cup water
	½ cup chilled heavy (whipping) cream
1 cup freshly squeezed orange juice	1 teaspoon orange juice concentrate
½ cup sugar	½ teaspoon vanilla extract
4 large egg yolks	

FOR THE TOPPING

½ cup heavy (whipping) cream, cold	1 teaspoon orange juice concentrate
	½ teaspoon vanilla extract

Preheat the oven to 350°F. In a small food processor or in a zip-top bag using a rolling pin, crush the cookies into fine crumbs. Transfer to a small bowl and stir in the 3 tablespoons of melted butter. Press the crumbs into the bottom and up the sides of a 9-inch pie plate. Bake until fragrant and set, 6 to 8 minutes. Let cool. (The cooled crust can be stored in the freezer until the filling is ready. Alternatively, you can make the crust while the curd chills; just be sure it's completely cool before the filling goes in.) In a small saucepan, simmer the orange juice over medium heat until reduced to ⅓ cup. In a heatproof bowl that will fit in the Instant Pot, beat the sugar and the ¼ cup of room-temperature butter with a hand mixer until the sugar has mostly dissolved and the mixture is light colored and fluffy. Add the egg yolks and beat until just combined. Add the reduced orange juice, the orange zest, and salt and beat to combine. The mixture will probably appear grainy, but that's okay. Cover the bowl with foil. Pour the water into the Instant Pot. Place a trivet with handles in the pot and place the bowl on top. If your trivet doesn't have handles, use a foil sling to make removing the bowl easier. Lock the lid. Select Manual and cook at high pressure for 10 minutes. When the cook time is complete, let the pressure release naturally for 10 minutes, then quick-release any remaining pressure. Remove the lid. Carefully remove the bowl from the pot and remove the foil. The mixture will appear clumpy and curdled. Whisk the curd mixture until smooth. Place a fine-mesh strainer over a medium bowl and pour the curd through it, pressing down with a flexible spatula to pass the curd through, leaving the zest and any curdled egg bits behind. Be sure to scrape any curd on the outside bottom of the strainer into the bowl. Cover the bowl with plastic wrap, pushing the wrap down on top of the curd to keep a skin from forming. Refrigerate until set, 2 to 4 hours. Pour the very cold cream into a medium bowl and add the orange juice concentrate and vanilla. Using a hand mixer, whip the cream until soft peaks form. Spoon about two-thirds of the whipped cream onto the chilled curd in the bowl. Beat on medium-high speed until thoroughly combined. Gently fold in the remaining whipped cream by hand. Pour the orange cream into the crumb crust and place in the freezer until frozen, 4 to 6 hours. Beat the cold cream, orange juice concentrate, and vanilla to moderately stiff peaks. Spoon over the pie just before serving.

Margarita Pie

SERVES 8 | **PREP AND FINISHING:** 25 minutes | **BAKE:** 6 to 8 minutes | **MANUAL:** 10 minutes high pressure | **RELEASE:** Natural for 10 minutes, then Quick | **TOTAL TIME:** 50 minutes, plus 8 hours to chill

6 ounces salted pretzels	2 teaspoons grated lime zest
7 tablespoons unsalted butter, 3 melted and 4 at room temperature, divided	1 teaspoon orange juice concentrate
¾ cup sugar	Pinch salt
4 large egg yolks	1 cup water
6 tablespoons freshly squeezed lime juice	½ cup heavy (whipping) cream, very cold
	2 tablespoons tequila

FOR THE TOPPING

½ cup heavy (whipping) cream, cold	1 teaspoon orange juice concentrate
1 tablespoon tequila	

Preheat the oven to 350°F. In a small food processor or in a zip-top bag using a rolling pin, crush the pretzels into fine crumbs. Transfer the crumbs to a small bowl and stir in the 3 tablespoons of melted butter. Press the crumbs into the bottom and up the sides of a 9-inch pie plate. Bake until fragrant, 6 to 8 minutes. Let cool. (The cooled crust can be stored in the freezer until the filling is ready. Alternatively, you can make the crust while the curd chills; just be sure it's completely cool before the filling goes in.) In a heatproof bowl that will fit in the Instant Pot, beat the sugar and the 4 tablespoons of room-temperature butter with a hand mixer until the sugar has mostly dissolved and the mixture is light colored and fluffy. Add the egg yolks and beat until combined. Add the lime juice, lime, orange juice concentrate, and salt and beat to combine. The mixture will probably appear grainy, but that's okay. Cover the bowl with foil. Pour the water into the Instant Pot. Place a trivet with handles in the pot and place the bowl on top. If your trivet doesn't have handles, use a foil sling to make removing the bowl easier. Lock the lid. Select Manual

and cook at high pressure for 10 minutes. When the cook time is complete, let the pressure release naturally for 10 minutes, then quick-release any remaining pressure. Remove the lid. Carefully remove the bowl from the pot and remove the foil. The mixture will appear clumpy and curdled. Whisk the curd mixture until smooth. Place a fine-mesh strainer over a medium bowl and pour the curd through it, pressing down with a flexible spatula to pass the curd through, leaving the zest and any curdled egg bits behind. Be sure to scrape any curd on the outside bottom of the strainer into the bowl. Cover the bowl with plastic wrap, pushing the wrap down on top of the curd to keep a skin from forming. Refrigerate until set, 2 to 4 hours. Pour the very cold cream into a medium bowl and add the tequila. Using a hand mixer, whip the cream and tequila until soft peaks form. Spoon about two-thirds of the whipped cream onto the chilled curd in the bowl. Beat on medium-high speed until thoroughly combined. Gently fold in the remaining whipped cream by hand. Pour the lime cream into the crumb crust and place in the freezer until frozen, 4 to 6 hours. Beat the cold cream, tequila, and orange juice concentrate to moderately stiff peaks. Spoon over the pie just before serving.

STAPLES AND SAUCES

"Roasted" Garlic

SERVES 4 | **PREP TIME:** 3 minutes | **MANUAL:** 6 minutes high pressure | **RELEASE:** Natural for 10 minutes | **TOTAL TIME:** 30 minutes

1 cup water	Extra-virgin olive oil (I recommend butter-infused)
4 large heads garlic, tops cut off to expose just the top of each clove	Crusty bread, for serving

Pour the water into the Instant Pot and put a trivet in it. Place the garlic on the trivet, cut-side up. Lock the lid. Select Manual and cook at high pressure for 6 minutes. When the cook time is complete, let the pressure naturally release for 10 minutes. Remove the lid. Using tongs, transfer the garlic to a baking sheet or other heatproof dish. Generously drizzle with olive oil, making sure all the garlic gets oiled. Broil on low until golden and caramelized, about 5 minutes. Remove from the oven and let cool for at least 10 minutes. Serve immediately, plated in the skins as is.

Ghee

MAKES 1½ cups | **PREP TIME:** 1 minute | **SAUTÉ:** 14 minutes | **TOTAL TIME:** 15 minutes

1 pound (4 sticks) unsalted (preferably cultured) butter, chopped

Select Sauté. Place the butter in the Instant Pot and cook for 10 to 12 minutes, until the milk solids (which look like little specks) start to settle at the bottom of the pot and turn a rich golden-brown color. Once the ghee (the liquid portion) turns clear with a golden hue, select Cancel and use oven mitts to carefully remove the pot and place it on a trivet to cool. Once cool enough to handle, carefully pour the ghee through a fine-mesh strainer lined with cheesecloth into a clean, dry, 2-cup mason jar. Discard the milk solids and allow to cool completely before covering the jar with a lid.

Cashew Sour Cream

SERVES 4 to 6 | PREP TIME: 10 minutes

1 cup raw cashews, soaked in water overnight, drained, and rinsed well	¼ cup nondairy milk, plus more as needed
Juice of 1 lemon, plus more as needed	1½ teaspoons apple cider vinegar
	½ teaspoon salt, plus more as needed

In a blender, combine the cashews, lemon juice, milk, vinegar, and salt. Blend until completely smooth. Taste and add more salt or lemon juice as desired. If you want a thinner cream, add a little more milk.

Paneer

MAKES 2 cups | PREP TIME: 2 minutes | PRESSURE BUILD: 15 minutes | MANUAL: Low for 5 minutes | RELEASE: Natural for 10 minutes, then Quick | TOTAL TIME: 1 hours 32 minutes, plus 2 hours to set

4 cups whole milk	¼ cup distilled white vinegar
2 cups half-and-half	

In the Instant Pot, combine the milk, half-and-half, and vinegar. Lock the lid and close the steam valve. Cook for 5 minutes on low pressure. When the cook time is complete, release the pressure naturally for 10 minutes, then quick-release any remaining pressure. Remove the lid and stir the curds and watery whey gently. Line a colander with cheesecloth, making sure that it hangs over the sides, and set it in the sink. Pour the curds and whey into the colander. Let it drain as it cools. After about 5 minutes, gather the edges of the cheesecloth, fold them over to cover the curds, and squeeze as much whey out as possible. Transfer the cheesecloth-wrapped curds to a plate and place a large, heavy can of tomatoes or beans on it. Set it aside at room temperature for 2 hours to firm up and form a cohesive block of firm cheese. Remove the weight and unwrap the paneer; it is now ready to be used.

Chicken Broth

MAKES 1 quart | PREP AND FINISHING: 20 minutes | MANUAL: 90 minutes high pressure | RELEASE: Natural for 15 minutes, then Quick | TOTAL TIME: 2 hours 10 minutes, plus overnight to chill

2 pounds meaty chicken bones (backs, wing tips, leg quarters)	¼ to ¾ teaspoon kosher salt
	1 quart water, or more as needed

Pile the chicken bones in the Instant Pot and sprinkle with the ¼ teaspoon of salt. Add the water, adding more to cover the bones but not filling the pot more than half full of water. Select Manual and cook at high pressure for 90 minutes. After the cook time is complete, let the pressure release naturally for 15 minutes, then quick-release any remaining pressure. Remove the lid. Line a colander with cheesecloth or a clean cotton towel and place it over a large bowl. Pour the chicken parts and broth into the colander to strain out the meat and bones. Discard the solids. Let the broth cool and then refrigerate for several hours or overnight so that the fat hardens on the top of the broth. Peel the layer of fat off the broth. Measure the amount of broth. If you have more than 1 quart, pour the broth into a pot and bring it to a boil over medium-high heat. Reduce the heat to low and simmer until the broth is reduced to 1 quart. If you like, add the ½ teaspoon of salt to estimate the salt level of commercial low-sodium broths.

Vegetable Broth

MAKES 1 quart | PREP AND FINISHING: 20 minutes | MANUAL: 60 minutes high pressure | RELEASE: Natural for 15 minutes, then Quick | TOTAL TIME: 1 hour 40 minutes

1 tablespoon vegetable oil	2 large carrots, peeled and cut into 1-inch pieces
1 onion, sliced	
12 ounces mushrooms, washed and sliced	¼ to ¾ teaspoon kosher salt
	1 quart water

Select Sauté and adjust to More for high heat. Heat the oil until it shimmers. Add the onion and stir to coat with the oil. Cook the onion, stirring occasionally, until browned but not charred, 4 to 5 minutes. Select Cancel. Add the mushrooms and carrots to the Instant Pot and sprinkle with the ¼ teaspoon of salt. Add the water. Select Manual and cook at high pressure for 60 minutes. When the cook time is complete, let the pressure release naturally for 15 minutes, then quick-release any remaining pressure. Remove the lid. Line a colander with cheesecloth or a clean cotton towel and place it over a large bowl. Pour the vegetables and broth into the colander. Discard the solids. Measure the amount of broth. If you have more than 1 quart, pour the broth into a pot and bring it to a boil over medium-high heat. Reduce the heat to low and simmer until the broth is reduced to 1 quart. If you like, add the ½ teaspoon salt to estimate the salt level of commercial low-sodium broths.

Mushroom Gravy

SERVES 4 to 6 | PREP TIME: 5 minutes | SAUTÉ LOW: 6 minutes, divided | MANUAL: 20 minutes high pressure | RELEASE: Natural for 10 minutes, then Quick | TOTAL TIME: 45 minutes

1 tablespoon extra-virgin olive oil
8 ounces portobello mushrooms, diced
½ small sweet onion, diced
2 garlic cloves, minced
2 tablespoons vegan Worcestershire sauce
1 teaspoon Dijon mustard
1 teaspoon rubbed sage
1 teaspoon Montreal chicken seasoning
1¼ cups vegetable broth, divided
¼ cup red wine
1 tablespoon cornstarch

Select Sauté Low. When the display reads HOT, pour in the oil and heat until it shimmers. Add the mushrooms and onion. Sauté for 2 to 3 minutes, stirring frequently. Turn off the Instant Pot and add the garlic. Cook, stirring so it doesn't burn, for 30 seconds more. Select Cancel. Add the Worcestershire sauce, mustard, sage, Montreal chicken seasoning, ¾ cup of broth, and the red wine. Lock the lid. Select Manual, cook at high pressure for 20 minutes. When the cook time is complete, let the pressure release naturally for 10 minutes, then quick-release any remaining pressure. In a small bowl, whisk the remaining ½ cup of broth and the cornstarch. Remove the lid and stir this slurry into the gravy. Select Sauté Low again and simmer the gravy for 2 to 3 minutes until thickened.

Sugar-Free Ketchup

SERVES 12 | PREP TIME: 5 minutes | MANUAL: 5 minutes high pressure | SAUTÉ: 15 minutes | RELEASE: Quick | TOTAL TIME: 30 minutes

1 (28-ounce) can crushed tomatoes
1 yellow onion, quartered
4 pitted dates
¼ cup apple cider vinegar
¼ teaspoon paprika
¼ teaspoon garlic powder
¼ teaspoon kosher salt

In the Instant Pot, combine the tomatoes, onion, dates, vinegar, paprika, garlic powder, and salt. Lock the lid. Select Manual and cook at high pressure for 5 minutes. When the cook time is complete, quick-release the pressure. Remove the lid and discard the onion. Select Sauté and simmer for 15 minutes, stirring occasionally, until thickened. Transfer the ketchup to an airtight container.

Smoky Barbecue Sauce

SERVES 12 | PREP TIME: 5 minutes | SAUTÉ: 4 minutes | MANUAL: 10 minutes high pressure | RELEASE: Quick | TOTAL TIME: 25 minutes

1 tablespoon extra-virgin olive oil
½ red onion, finely chopped
2 garlic cloves, minced
1 cup no-sugar-added ketchup
⅓ cup water
⅓ cup pure maple syrup
¼ cup apple cider vinegar
2 teaspoons Dijon mustard
¼ teaspoon liquid smoke

Select Sauté on the Instant Pot and pour in the olive oil. When the oil is hot, add the onion and garlic. Cook for 3 to 4 minutes, stirring frequently, until softened. Select Cancel. Add the ketchup, water, maple syrup, vinegar, mustard, and liquid smoke and stir to combine. Lock the lid. Select Manual and cook at high pressure for 10 minutes. When the cook time is complete, quick-release the pressure. Remove the lid and serve.

Sweet and Tangy Maple Barbecue Sauce

MAKES 3 cups | PREP TIME: 5 minutes | SAUTÉ: 2 minutes | MANUAL: 4 minutes high pressure | RELEASE: Quick | TOTAL TIME: 30 minutes

2 tablespoons minced onion
2 garlic cloves, minced
1 teaspoon smoked paprika
1 teaspoon ground allspice
1 cup water
1 (15-ounce) can no-salt-added tomato sauce
¼ cup maple syrup
2 tablespoons stone-ground mustard
2 tablespoons apple cider vinegar
½ teaspoon salt (optional)

Select Sauté and cook the onion, adding water as needed to prevent sticking, until slightly browned, about 2 minutes. Add the garlic, paprika, and allspice and stir until fragrant, about 30 seconds. Stir in the water, scraping up any browned bits from the bottom of the pot. Add the tomato sauce, maple syrup, mustard, vinegar, and salt (if using). Whisk to combine. Lock the lid with the steam release knob in the sealing position. Select Manual and cook at high pressure for 4 minutes. When the cook time is complete, quick-release the pressure. Remove the lid. If the sauce is not thick enough for your taste, select Sauté and allow the sauce to reduce, stirring frequently, until it reaches your desired consistency.

Mexican Tomato Salsa

MAKES 8 cups | PREP TIME: 5 minutes | SAUTÉ: 8 minutes | MANUAL: 30 minutes high pressure | RELEASE: Quick | TOTAL TIME: 45 minutes

2 tablespoons vegetable oil
1 medium white onion, diced
3 garlic cloves, minced
3 pounds Roma tomatoes, quartered
1 teaspoon coarse salt, plus more for seasoning (optional)
½ cup water
2 bay leaves
1 teaspoon dried Mexican oregano, crushed

Select Sauté and adjust to More for high. Heat the vegetable oil in the Instant Pot, then add the onion and sauté for 3 to 5 minutes, or until translucent. Add the garlic and sauté for an additional 30 to 60 seconds. Add the tomatoes, season with the salt, and sauté for about 2 minutes. Add the water, bay leaves, and oregano. Lock the lid. Select Manual and cook at high pressure for 30 minutes. When the cook time is complete, quick-release the pressure. Remove the lid. Remove the bay leaves. Using an immersion blender, puree the salsa. Season with more salt, if necessary.

Classic Tomatillo and Árbol Chile Salsa

MAKES 2½ to 3 cups | PREP TIME: 5 minutes | SAUTÉ: 3 minutes | MANUAL: 12 minutes high pressure | RELEASE: Quick | TOTAL TIME: 20 minutes

1 tablespoon vegetable oil	2¼ pounds tomatillos, husks removed
40 dried árbol chiles, stemmed	2 cups water
3 garlic cloves, peeled	Coarse salt

Select Sauté and adjust to More for high. Heat the vegetable oil in the pot, add the chiles and garlic, and sauté for 2 to 3 minutes, or until lightly toasted. Add the tomatillos and water. Lock the lid. Select Manual and cook at high pressure for 12 minutes. When the cook time is complete, quick-release the pressure. Remove the lid. Using a slotted spoon, transfer the tomatillos, chiles, and garlic to a blender. Add 1 cup of the cooking liquid and process until smooth. Pour into a heatproof bowl; season with coarse salt to taste.

Red Chile Salsa

MAKES 5 to 6 cups | PREP TIME: 10 minutes | SAUTÉ: 3 minutes | MANUAL: 10 minutes high pressure | RELEASE: Quick | TOTAL TIME: 25 minutes

2 tablespoons vegetable oil	8 garlic cloves, peeled
8 ounces dried ancho chiles, stemmed and seeded	4 cups water
	2 teaspoons coarse salt
1 large white onion, coarsely chopped	1 teaspoon ground cumin
	1 teaspoon dried Mexican oregano, crushed

Select Sauté and adjust to More for high. Heat the vegetable oil in the pot, add the chiles, and sauté for 2 to 3 minutes, or until lightly toasted. Add the onion, garlic, and water. Lock the lid. Select Manual and cook at high pressure for 10 minutes. When the cook time is complete, quick-release the pressure. Remove the lid. Using an immersion blender, puree the chiles, onion, garlic, and cooking liquid until smooth. Season with the salt, cumin, and oregano.

Gemma-Style Salsa

MAKES 4 cups | PREP TIME: 5 minutes | SAUTÉ: 2 minutes | MANUAL: 12 minutes high pressure | RELEASE: Quick | TOTAL TIME: 20 minutes

1 tablespoon vegetable oil	4 to 6 canned chipotle chiles in adobo sauce
4 dried ancho chiles, stemmed and seeded	1½ cups water
2 dried guajillo chiles, stemmed and seeded	1 teaspoon coarse salt, plus more for seasoning (optional)
12 Roma tomatoes, quartered	½ teaspoon freshly ground black pepper

Select Sauté and adjust to More for high. Heat the vegetable oil in the pot, add the ancho and guajillo chiles, and sauté for 30 to 45 seconds per side. Add the tomatoes, chipotle chiles, and water. Season with the salt and pepper. Lock the lid. Select Manual and cook at high pressure for 12 minutes. When the cook time is complete, quick-release the pressure. Remove the lid. Using an immersion blender, blender, or food processor, process all the ingredients together until smooth. Season with additional salt, if necessary.

Salsa Ranchera

MAKES 3½ to 4 cups | PREP TIME: 5 minutes | MANUAL: 12 minutes high pressure | RELEASE: Quick | TOTAL TIME: 20 minutes

12 Roma tomatoes, quartered	1 cup water
6 serrano chiles or jalapeño peppers, stemmed	1½ teaspoons coarse salt, plus more for seasoning (optional)
4 garlic cloves, peeled	⅓ cup fresh cilantro leaves
1 medium white onion, cut into large chunks	

In the Instant Pot, combine the tomatoes, chiles, garlic, and onion. Pour in the water and season with the salt. Lock the lid. Select Manual and cook at high pressure for 12 minutes. When the cook time is complete, quick-release the pressure. Remove the lid. Using a slotted spoon, transfer the ingredients to a blender, along with about 1 cup of the cooking liquid and the cilantro. Puree until smooth. Season with more salt, if necessary.

Spicy Salsa Verde

MAKES 3 to 4 cups | PREP TIME: 5 minutes | MANUAL: 10 minutes high pressure | RELEASE: Quick | TOTAL TIME: 15 minutes

2½ pounds tomatillos, husks removed	1 medium onion, roughly chopped
	3 garlic cloves, peeled

1 handful cilantro sprigs

4 jalapeño peppers, stemmed

1½ cups water

Coarse salt

In the Instant Pot, combine the tomatillos, onion, garlic, cilantro, and jalapeños. Pour in the water and season with salt. Lock the lid. Select Manual and cook at high pressure for 10 minutes. When the cook time is complete, quick-release the pressure. Remove the lid. Remove the cilantro sprigs, and transfer the remaining ingredients to a blender, along with about 1 cup of the cooking liquid. Puree until smooth. Season with more salt, if necessary.

Tomato Chutney

SERVES 6 | PREP TIME: 5 minutes | SAUTÉ: 30 minutes, divided | MANUAL: 5 minutes high pressure | RELEASE: Natural for 5 minutes, then Quick | TOTAL TIME: 53 minutes

¼ cup canola or vegetable oil

1½ teaspoons mustard seeds

4 large garlic cloves, coarsely chopped

2 pounds tomatoes (about 6 medium-size tomatoes), chopped

2 teaspoons salt

2 teaspoons cayenne pepper

1 tablespoon tamarind paste

Select Sauté, and once the pot is hot, pour in the oil. Add the mustard seeds and cook until they start to sputter, about 30 seconds. Add the garlic and tomatoes and cook for 2 minutes. Stir in the salt, cayenne pepper, and tamarind paste and mix well. Select Cancel. Lock the lid. Select Manual and cook at high pressure for 5 minutes. When the cook time is complete, let the pressure release naturally for 20 minutes, then quick-release any remaining pressure. Remove the lid and stir well. Select Sauté on high and cook until the chutney is thick, 20 to 25 minutes total, stirring once every 5 minutes. Make sure to scrape the bottom so that the chutney does not stick to the bottom and burn. Transfer to a clean mason jar.

Mango Chutney

SERVES 6 to 8 | PREP TIME: 15 minutes | MANUAL: 5 minutes high pressure | RELEASE: Natural for 15 minutes, then Quick | TOTAL TIME: 35 minutes

4 mangos, peeled and diced

2 apples, peeled and diced

2 red chiles, cored and minced

1 cup sugar

¼ cup lime juice

1 tablespoon minced ginger

2 cinnamon sticks

1 teaspoon minced garlic

½ teaspoon ground coriander

¼ teaspoon salt

In the Instant Pot, combine the mangos, apples, chiles, sugar, lime juice, ginger, cinnamon sticks, garlic, coriander, and salt. Lock the lid. Select Manual and cook at high-pressure for 5 minutes. Allow the pressure to release naturally for 15 minutes, then quick-release the remaining pressure. Remove the lid. Transfer the chutney to a heatproof container, and refrigerate uncovered until cool, about 1 hour.

Marinara Sauce

MAKES 4 cups | PREP TIME: 5 minutes | SAUTÉ: 4 minutes | MANUAL: 20 minutes high pressure | RELEASE: Quick | TOTAL TIME: 40 minutes

1 tablespoon extra-virgin olive oil

1 yellow onion, finely chopped

5 garlic cloves, minced

3 pounds plum tomatoes, quartered

½ cup vegetable broth

2 tablespoons double concentrated tomato paste

Select Sauté and pour in the olive oil. When the oil is hot, add the onion and garlic. Cook for 3 to 4 minutes, stirring occasionally, until softened. Select Cancel. Add the tomatoes, broth, and tomato paste. Lock the lid. Select Manual and cook at high pressure for 20 minutes. When the cook time is complete, quick-release the pressure. Remove the lid and stir, pressing down on any large pieces of tomato to break them down. For a smoother sauce, use an immersion blender to blend to your desired consistency.

All the Garlic Red Sauce

MAKES 2½ to 2¾ cups | MANUAL: High for 20 minutes | RELEASE: Natural for 15 minutes, then Quick | TOTAL TIME: 40 minutes

4 medium tomatoes (about 1 pound), quartered

1 small sweet onion, peeled and quartered

⅓ cup strong hearty red wine, plus more as needed

½ cup water, plus more as needed

4 ounces tomato paste

4 or 5 garlic cloves (or as needed), peeled

½ teaspoon dried oregano

1 teaspoon dried basil

1 teaspoon salt

¼ teaspoon baking soda

Pinch red pepper flakes

In the Instant Pot, combine the tomatoes and onion. Add the wine, water, and tomato paste. Cover the veggies with the garlic, oregano, basil, salt, baking soda, and red pepper flakes; do not stir. Lock the lid with the steam release knob in the sealing position. Select Manual and cook at high pressure for 20 minutes. When the cook time is complete, let the pressure release naturally for 15 minutes, then quick-release any remaining pressure. Remove the lid. Use an immersion blender to blend the sauce, adding a bit more water or wine to thin it if desired.

Arrabbiata Sauce

MAKES 4 cups | PREP AND FINISHING: 20 minutes | MANUAL: 12 minutes high pressure | RELEASE: Natural for 10 minutes, then Quick | TOTAL TIME: 40 minutes

3 tablespoons extra-virgin olive oil

1 small onion, minced

4 garlic cloves, minced

2 tablespoons minced or pureed sun-dried tomatoes

1 (28-ounce) can crushed tomatoes

½ teaspoon kosher salt, plus more as needed

1 teaspoon red pepper flakes, divided

¼ cup chopped fresh parsley

Select Sauté and adjust to More for high heat. Heat the oil until it shimmers. Add the onion and garlic and cook, stirring frequently, until the vegetables have started to soften, 2 to 3 minutes. Stir in the sun-dried tomatoes and cook until fragrant, about 1 minute. Pour in the crushed tomatoes with their juices and stir to combine, scraping the bottom of the pot to loosen any browned bits that may have stuck. Stir in the salt and ½ teaspoon of red pepper flakes. Select Cancel. Lock the lid. Select Manual and cook at high pressure for 12 minutes. When the cook time is complete, let the pressure release naturally for 10 minutes, then quick-release any remaining pressure. Remove the lid. Let the sauce cool for about 10 minutes, then stir in the remaining ½ teaspoon of red pepper flakes and the parsley. Taste and adjust the seasoning, adding more salt if necessary.

Ancho Chile Sauce

MAKES 2 cups | PREP AND FINISHING: 10 minutes | MANUAL: 8 minutes high pressure | RELEASE: Natural for 5 minutes, then Quick | TOTAL TIME: 30 minutes

2 ounces dried ancho chiles (3 to 5 chiles)

2 garlic cloves, lightly smashed

1½ cups water

2 teaspoons kosher salt

1½ teaspoons sugar

½ teaspoon dried oregano

½ teaspoon ground cumin

2 tablespoons apple cider vinegar

Pull or cut off the stems from the chiles and remove as many seeds as possible. Put the chiles in the Instant Pot. Be sure to thoroughly wash your hands after handling the chiles. Add the garlic, water, salt, sugar, oregano, and cumin. Lock the lid. Select Manual and cook at high pressure for 8 minutes. When the cook time is complete, let the pressure release naturally for 5 minutes, then quick-release any remaining pressure. Remove the lid. Pour the sauce into a blender. Add the vinegar and blend until smooth, being careful to hold the lid on.

Cranberry Sauce

MAKES 2 cups | PREP TIME: 5 minutes | MANUAL: 15 minutes high pressure | RELEASE: Natural for 10 minutes, then Quick | TOTAL TIME: 40 minutes

4 cups cranberries, fresh or frozen

1 cup sugar

1 (1-inch) piece ginger, peeled and cut into ⅛-inch slices

½ cup freshly squeezed orange juice

Zest of ½ orange

Juice and zest of ½ lemon

In the Instant Pot, combine the cranberries, sugar, ginger, orange juice, orange zest, lemon juice, and lemon zest. Lock the lid. Select Manual and cook at high pressure for 15 minutes. After cooking, let the pressure naturally release for 10 minutes, then quick-release any remaining pressure. Transfer the cranberry sauce to a heatproof container, remove the ginger, and refrigerate uncovered until cool, about 1 hour.

Unsweetened Applesauce

SERVES 6 | PREP TIME: 5 minutes | MANUAL: 8 minutes high pressure | RELEASE: Natural for 10 minutes, then Quick | TOTAL TIME: 30 minutes

6 apples (about 1½ pounds)

¼ cup water

¼ teaspoon ground cinnamon

Peel and core the apples. Cut each apple into roughly eight large chunks. In the Instant Pot, combine the apples, water, and cinnamon. Lock the lid. Select Manual and cook at high pressure for 8 minutes. When the cook time is complete, let the pressure release naturally for 10 minutes, then quick-release any remaining pressure. Remove the lid and use a potato masher or heavy wooden spoon to gently mash the apples into applesauce.

Strawberry Compote

MAKES 2 cups | PREP TIME: 3 minutes | MANUAL: 4 minutes high pressure | RELEASE: Natural for 10 minutes, then Quick | TOTAL TIME: 30 minutes

4 cups frozen strawberries (28 ounces)

¼ cup sugar

1 tablespoon freshly squeezed lemon juice

In the Instant Pot, combine the strawberries, sugar, and lemon juice. Stir to coat the berries. Lock the lid. Select Manual and cook at high pressure for 4 minutes. When the cook time is complete, let the pressure release naturally for 10 minutes, then quick-release any remaining pressure. Remove the lid. Using a potato masher, mash the berries until they are broken down completely. Pour into a container and chill. The compote will thicken as it cools.

Lemon Curd

MAKES 1½ cups | PREP AND FINISHING: 15 minutes | MANUAL: 10 minutes high pressure | RELEASE: Natural for 10 minutes, then Quick | TOTAL TIME: 40 minutes, plus 2 hours to chill

¾ cup sugar
¼ cup unsalted butter, at room temperature
4 large egg yolks

Grated zest and juice of 2 lemons (about 6 tablespoons juice)
Pinch salt
1 cup water

In a heatproof bowl that will fit in the Instant Pot, beat the sugar and butter with a hand mixer until the sugar has mostly dissolved and the mixture is light colored and fluffy. Add the egg yolks and beat until combined. Add the lemon zest, lemon juice, and salt and beat to combine. The mixture will probably appear grainy, but that's okay. Cover the bowl with foil. Pour the water into the Instant Pot. Place a trivet with handles in the pot and place the bowl on top. If your trivet doesn't have handles, use a foil sling to make removing the bowl easier. Lock the lid. Select Manual and cook at high pressure for 10 minutes. When the cook time is complete, let the pressure release naturally for 10 minutes, then quick-release any remaining pressure. Remove the lid. Carefully remove the bowl from the pot and remove the foil. The mixture will appear clumpy and curdled. Whisk the curd mixture until it is smooth. Place a fine-mesh strainer over a medium bowl and pour the curd through it, pressing it down with a flexible spatula to pass the curd through, leaving the zest and any curdled egg bits behind. Be sure to scrape any curd on the outside bottom of the strainer into the bowl. Cover with plastic wrap, pushing the wrap down on top of the curd to keep a skin from forming. Refrigerate until set, 2 to 4 hours.

Chocolate-Caramel Sauce

MAKES 2 cups | PREP AND FINISHING: 20 minutes | MANUAL: 50 minutes high pressure | RELEASE: Natural for 30 minutes, then Quick | TOTAL TIME: 1 hour 45 minutes

1 (14-ounce) can sweet-ened condensed milk
¼ cup heavy (whip-ping) cream
1 tablespoon unsalted butter, at room temperature

½ teaspoon vanilla extract
¼ teaspoon kosher salt
3 ounces bittersweet chocolate, chopped

Pour the condensed milk into a heatproof 2 cup measuring cup or small bowl that is large enough to fit all the ingredients. Cover the cup with foil and crimp the edges over the top. Place the cup in the Instant Pot and add enough water to reach the level of the milk in the cup. Lock the lid. Select Manual and cook at high pressure for 50 minutes. When the cook time is complete, let the pressure release naturally for 20 minutes, then quick-release any remaining pressure. Remove the lid. Lift the cup out of the pot and remove the foil. Add the cream, butter, vanilla, and salt. Use an immersion blender to blend the sauce until it's smooth. While the sauce is still hot, add the chocolate and whisk to melt it into the caramel.

INSTANT POT PRESSURE-COOKING TIMETABLES

The following charts provide estimated times for a variety of foods. To begin, you may want to cook for a minute or two less than the times listed; if necessary, you can always simmer foods for a few minutes to finish cooking.

Keep in mind that these times are for foods partially submerged in water (or broth) or steamed and are for the foods cooked alone. The cooking times for the same foods may vary if additional ingredients or cooking liquids are added or a different release method than the one listed here is used.

For any foods labeled with "natural" release, allow at least 15 minutes natural pressure release before quick releasing any remaining pressure.

BEANS AND LEGUMES

When cooking 1 pound or more of dried beans, it's best to use low pressure and increase the cooking time by a minute or two. You can add a little oil to the cooking liquid to help reduce foaming. Unless a shorter release time is indicated, let the beans release naturally for at least 15 minutes, after which any remaining pressure can be quick-released. Beans should be soaked in salted water for 8 to 24 hours.

	Liquid per 1 cup of beans	Minutes under pressure	Pressure	Release
Black beans	2 cups	8 9	High Low	Natural
Black-eyed peas	2 cups	5	High	Natural for 8 minutes, then Quick
Brown lentils (unsoaked)	2¼ cups	20	High	Natural for 10 minutes, then Quick
Cannellini beans	2 cups	5 7	High Low	Natural
Chickpeas	2 cups	4	High	Natural for 3 minutes, then Quick
Kidney beans	2 cups	5 7	High Low	Natural
Lima beans	2 cups	4 5	High Low	Natural for 5 minutes, then Quick
Pinto beans	2 cups	8 10	High Low	Natural
Red lentils (unsoaked)	3 cups	10	High	Natural for 5 minutes, then Quick
Soybeans, dried	2 cups	12 14	High Low	Natural
Soybeans, fresh (edamame, unsoaked)	1 cup	1	High	Quick
Split peas (unsoaked)	3 cups	5 (firm peas) to 8 (soft peas)	High	Natural

GRAINS

Thoroughly rinse grains before cooking or add a small amount of butter or oil to the cooking liquid to prevent foaming. Unless a shorter release time is indicated, let the grains release naturally for at least 15 minutes, after which any remaining pressure can be quick-released.

	Liquid per 1 cup of grain	Minutes under pressure	Pressure	Release
Arborio rice (for risotto)	3–4 cups	6–8	High	Quick
Barley, pearled	2½ cups	20	High	Natural for 10 minutes, then Quick
Brown rice, long-grain	1 cup	22	High	Natural for 10 minutes, then Quick
Brown rice, medium-grain	1 cup	12	High	Natural
Buckwheat	1¾ cups	2–4	High	Natural
Farro, pearled	2 cups	6–8	High	Natural
Farro, whole-grain	3 cups	22–24	High	Natural
Oats, rolled	3 cups	3–4	High	Quick
Oats, steel-cut	3 cups	10	High	Natural for 10 minutes, then Quick
Quinoa	1 cup	2	High	Natural for 12 minutes, then Quick
Wheat berries	2 cups	30	High	Natural for 10 minutes, then Quick
White rice, long-grain	1 cup	3	High	Natural
Wild rice	1¼ cups	22–24	High	Natural

MEAT

Except as noted, these times are for braised meats—that is, meats that are seared and then pressure-cooked while partially submerged in liquid. Unless a shorter release time is indicated, let the meat release naturally for at least 15 minutes, after which any remaining pressure can be quick-released.

	Minutes under pressure	Pressure	Release
Beef, bone-in short ribs	40	High	Natural
Beef, flatiron steak, cut into ½-inch strips	6	Low	Quick
Beef, shoulder (chuck), 2-inch chunks	20	High	Natural for 10 minutes
Beef, shoulder (chuck) roast (2 pounds)	35–45	High	Natural
Beef, sirloin steak, cut into ½-inch strips	3	Low	Quick
Lamb, shanks	40	High	Natural
Lamb, shoulder, 2-inch chunks	35	High	Natural
Pork, back ribs (steamed)	25	High	Quick
Pork, shoulder, 2-inch chunks	20	High	Quick
Pork, shoulder roast (2 pounds)	25	High	Natural
Pork, smoked sausage, ½-inch slices	5–10	High	Quick
Pork, spare ribs (steamed)	20	High	Quick
Pork, tenderloin	4	Low	Quick

POULTRY

Except as noted, these times are for braised poultry—that is, partially submerged in liquid. Unless a shorter release time is indicated, let the poultry release naturally for at least 15 minutes, after which any remaining pressure can be quick-released.

	Minutes under pressure	Pressure	Release
Chicken breast, bone-in (steamed)	8	Low	Natural for 5 minutes
Chicken breast, boneless (steamed)	5	Low	Natural for 8 minutes
Chicken thigh, bone-in	10–14	High	Natural for 10 minutes
Chicken thigh, boneless	6–8	High	Natural for 10 minutes
Chicken thigh, boneless, 1- to 2-inch pieces	5–6	High	Quick
Chicken, whole (seared on all sides)	12–14	Low	Natural for 8 minutes
Duck quarters, bone-in	35	High	Quick
Turkey breast, tenderloin (12 ounces) (steamed)	5	Low	Natural for 8 minutes
Turkey thigh, bone-in	30	High	Natural

MEASUREMENT CONVERSIONS

Volume Equivalents	U.S. Standard	U.S. Standard (ounces)	Metric (approximate)
Liquid	2 tablespoons	1 fl. oz.	30 mL
	¼ cup	2 fl. oz.	60 mL
	½ cup	4 fl. oz.	120 mL
	1 cup	8 fl. oz.	240 mL
	1½ cups	12 fl. oz.	355 mL
	2 cups or 1 pint	16 fl. oz.	475 mL
	4 cups or 1 quart	32 fl. oz.	1 L
	1 gallon	128 fl. oz.	4 L
Dry	⅛ teaspoon		0.5 mL
	¼ teaspoon		1 mL
	½ teaspoon		2 mL
	¾ teaspoon		4 mL
	1 teaspoon		5 mL
	1 tablespoon		15 mL
	¼ cup		59 mL
	⅓ cup		79 mL
	½ cup		118 mL
	⅔ cup		156 mL
	¾ cup		177 mL
	1 cup		235 mL
	2 cups or 1 pint		475 mL
	3 cups		700 mL
	4 cups or 1 quart		1 L
	½ gallon		2 L
	1 gallon		4 L

Oven Temperatures

Fahrenheit	Celsius (approximate)
250°F	120°C
300°F	150°C
325°F	165°C
350°F	180°C
375°F	190°C
400°F	200°C
425°F	220°C
450°F	230°C

Weight Equivalents

U.S. Standard	Metric (approximate)
½ ounce	15 g
1 ounce	30 g
2 ounces	60 g
4 ounces	115 g
8 ounces	225 g
12 ounces	340 g
16 ounces or 1 pound	455 g

INDEX